DISPATCHES FROM THE FRONT

DISPATCHES

FROM THE

FRONT

MATTHEW HALTON, CANADA'S VOICE AT WAR

DAVID HALTON

McClelland & Stewart

Library and Archives of Canada Cataloguing in Publication

Halton, David (News correspondent), author
     Dispatches from the front : the life of Matthew Halton,
Canada's voice at war / David Halton.

Includes bibliographical references and index.
Issued in print and electronic formats.
ISBN 978-0-7710-3813-6 (bound).–ISBN 978-0-7710-3821-1 (html)

     1. Halton, M. H. (Matthew Henry), 1904-1956. 2. Journalists–
Canada–Biography. 3. War correspondents–Canada–Biography.
4. World War, 1939-1945–Journalists–Biography. 5. World War,
1939-1945–Press coverage–Canada. I. Title.

PN4913.H348H34 2014   070.4'333092   C2014-904636-7
                                                    C2014-904637-5

Published simultaneously in the United States of America by
McClelland & Stewart, a division of Random House of Canada Limited

Library of Congress Control Number: 2013938806

Jacket front photograph:
© Matthew Halton, CBC Senior War Correspondent, records his impressions. He is standing on a hill overlooking Ortona...the scene of a great Canadian exploit in this war (WWII). An artillery barrage was in progress when this picture was taken. CBC Photo, A037546.

Jacket back photographs:
© Canada. Dept. of National Defence / Library and Archives Canada / PA-204812.
© Matthew Halton, CBC senior war correspondent, describing artillery barrage being laid down in the vicinity of Ortona, Italy. CBC photograph, A037544.

Typeset by Erin Cooper
Designed by Leah Springate
Printed and bound in the USA

McClelland & Stewart,
a division of Random House of Canada Limited,
a Penguin Random House Company

www.randomhouse.ca

1   2   3   4   5   18   17   16   15   14

For Matt and Jean

CONTENTS

PREFACE

ON AN EARLY SPRING DAY IN 1987, Zilla Soriano, a student of journalism at Ryerson Polytechnic Institute in Toronto, made her way into the archives of CBC Radio in an old mansion on Jarvis Street. Her professor had assigned her to a research project on Matthew Halton, a World War Two broadcaster whose name until then was as unknown to her as it was to most of her classmates. Closeting herself in a tiny audio booth in the archives, she began listening to dozens of his tapes piled in front of her. The first was an eyewitness account of entering Berlin on VE Day, May 8, 1945. *"Four out of five buildings . . . had been destroyed – that is, completely leveled or completely gutted. This did look like the end of the world. . . . Through the rubble and ashes of Berlin I didn't recognize famous streets I had known well. . . . We were lost for a few minutes in that utter ruin and silence. . . . I was afraid."*

Soriano later wrote that it was the voice that got to her first. It was clear, unhurried, conveying a sense of both urgency and authority. "Suddenly I am no longer sitting in that safe little cubicle at the CBC listening to old tapes. Instead I am moving with Matthew Halton into the 'still-smoking and burning' city of five million people. His fear becomes my fear, his pain mine. The voice hypnotizes and the script – it is more like an essay – mesmerizes."[1]

It was the same voice, as she would discover, that had a riveting impact on a generation of Canadians. For me, it was simply my father's voice – not much more than a passing curiosity for a five-year-old boy at war's end. For millions of people, though, it was the voice of Canada at war – more familiar on the home front than that of any of the country's politicians or generals. Halton's broadcasts, chronicling the victories and losses of Canadian soldiers along the Maple Leaf Route from Sicily to Nazi Germany, were part of the country's wartime experience. They were the link to relatives and loved ones on distant battlefields. When he returned home on the occasional speaking tour, "Matt," as he was widely known, was welcomed as a national hero. "He was bigger box office than Billy Bishop," said a colleague – referring to Canada's legendary flying ace from World War One.[2]

The Ryerson student soon made other discoveries about Matthew Halton. Her initial fears that she had been assigned to study an obscure figure from the past quickly disappeared as she learned that she was dealing with a celebrity in his time. Seven years after his death in 1956, at the age of fifty-two, Matt was still being hailed as "without question Canada's greatest foreign correspondent, both as a writer for the *Toronto Star* and, after 1943, as a reporter for the Canadian Broadcasting Corporation."[3] The son of struggling English homesteaders in rural Alberta, he was to embark on a remarkable journalistic odyssey through the turbulent first half of the twentieth century. It was a journey that put him on the front lines of many of the major political and military events of the era. He was in Berlin on the day Hitler took full power in Germany and – long before most other correspondents – began a prophetic series of reports warning that the Third Reich was "becoming a vast laboratory and breeding ground for war." For the rest of the decade he chronicled Europe's drift to disaster, covering the breakdown of the League of Nations, the Spanish Civil War, the sellout to Fascism at Munich, and the Nazi takeover of Austria and Czechoslovakia. Along the way he interviewed Franklin Delano Roosevelt, Hermann Göring, Neville Chamberlain, Charles de Gaulle, Mahatma Gandhi, and dozens of others who shaped the history of the century.

It was a career that brought him international acclaim of which few journalists can even dream. Matt's wartime broadcasts for the CBC were regularly used on the BBC; his dispatches from the front were widely published by British newspapers as well as by the *Toronto Daily Star* and *Maclean's*. In 1944 the Association of British Publishers named him one of the five best war correspondents of World War Two. He won one of the most prestigious broadcasting prizes in the United States and was admitted to the Canadian News Hall of Fame. King George VI awarded him the Order of the British Empire.

Today though, more than five decades after his death, Matthew Henry Halton is a more or less forgotten name for all but survivors of the wartime generation. Apart from an admirable History Channel documentary about him and a small exhibit in the Canadian War Museum, there are few reminders of an epic journalistic career. Ask students in journalism classes across the country about Matthew Halton and the response will almost inevitably elicit the same blank stares as those of the Ryerson student and her classmates when they first heard his name. Unlike the famous American broadcaster Edward R. Murrow, to whom Matt was often compared, there are no journalism foundations named after him, no plaques, no awards and scholarships in his name, and barely more than a footnote about him in journalism textbooks.

This biography hopes to re-awaken interest in a Canadian legend. For more than four years, I have tracked down and interviewed my father's few surviving colleagues. I have prodded aging relatives for memories and insights. I have followed his path from the birthplace he cherished in rural Alberta to the universities he attended in Edmonton and London, and then to many of the memorable places and battlefields that marked his career. I have spent eighteen months in the national archives reading virtually all of the estimated four million words he wrote for newspapers and radio. I have sifted through his diaries and the large collection of letters he wrote to his friends and family. The sources, many and rich, have drawn me into an absorbing and at times obsessive search for the details of one man's life.

My admiration for my father will be evident at times in this biography. He was, after all, the inspiration for my own decision to become a journalist. But the reader should be assured that this is not a hagiography. I have made a determined effort to assess Matt's flaws both as a reporter and as a human being. I have tried to unravel the many paradoxes and contradictions of his life: the writer who could summon searing, majestic language yet lapse on occasion into purple prose; the fervent Anglophile who detested the British class system; the socialist who befriended millionaires; the war correspondent who loathed bloodshed yet became addicted to the thrill of battle; the loner who thrived in good company; the aspiring but failed poet; and, in some ways most puzzling of all, the womanizer with a deep and abiding love for his wife. This book, I hope, will throw light on some of those contradictions and on one of the most accomplished journalists of his time.

I

SHITHOUSE HALTON'S SON

"We were poor, poor, poor! The homestead just about broke us."

— JIM HALTON, Matt's brother

IN THE EARLY 1900S THE VILLAGE OF PINCHER CREEK, in south-west Alberta, seemed like a faint imprint on a vast and awe-inspiring land-scape. The several dozen wood frame homes and stores in the ranching community were strung out along a creek that meandered through a narrow valley. On the escarpments that flanked the village, settlers could look northwest to the Livingstone Range of the Rocky Mountains; south-west toward the Flathead Range on the U.S. border; and east to where the foothills country slopes into the Prairies. In summer, a blue heat haze often rests over the mountains, giving them a soft and inviting look. In winter, sharper contrasts of dark and white cast the high peaks in a more forbidding but always majestic light. In 1882 the then governor general of Canada, the Marquis of Lorne, visited Pincher Creek and was entranced by its vistas of foothills and mountains. "This is rightly called God's Country," he said. "If I were not Governor General, I would be a cattle rancher in Alberta."[1]

For Matthew Henry Halton, born there on September 7, 1904, Pincher Creek would later evoke the same fervent enthusiasm. Yet nothing about his exact birthplace matched the grandeur of the countryside around it. He was born in what neighbours somewhat condescendingly called "the red shack." Intended as a temporary residence while the Haltons built their homestead, the two-room tin-roofed dwelling stood on Main Street – an unpaved road swept by dust storms in spring and summer that turned into a mud hole after rain or snow. The red shack stood out as primitive even in a village where none of the homes had running water or electricity, and where one hotel boasted of having the only flush toilet in southwest Alberta.

Matt was the third son of Mary Alice Thornley and Henry (Harry) Halton, who had emigrated two years earlier from Euxton, a cotton-mill town in Lancashire, England. His parents had seen the enticing advertise- ments put out by the Dominion government and the Canadian Pacific Railway (CPR) in the popular English press. The ads promised cheap land and a prosperous future in Canada's West. English families were invited to come to "The New Eldorado" and move westward to what the ads called "the Star of Empire."² Pictures of golden wheat fields and spacious farm- steads seemed to offer a bright contrast to working-class life in England, where children were still routinely "put out to service" as domestic and farm labourers or – as in Henry Halton's case – sent to work in a coal mine at the age of twelve.³ In later years, Matt would often say that his parents were both victims of a rigid British class system and rebels against it – fed up, as he put it, with "having to doff their hats to the squire."

The couple made the journey to Canada with ten members of their family: their two oldest sons, Sam and Jim; Mary Alice's parents, Seth and Mary Thornley; and her sister and five brothers. The Thornleys were less concerned about socio-economic conditions in Lancashire than the fact that several of their children were in poor health, one suffering from tuberculosis. They were advised by a doctor that the children would ben- efit from the drier climate in Canada.

The journey was an ordeal. It began with several weeks of discomfort in an overcrowded immigrant ship that docked in Halifax in early June 1902. It continued aboard a "Colonist" – one of the wooden, slat-seated CPR rail cars that carried new settlers to the West.⁴ The family reached Cardston and later set out for Pincher Creek in a small convoy of covered wagons. They passed the teepees of Blood Indians and struggled over the Belly and Waterton rivers and up the first slopes of the foothills to their new home. Weighing down the Halton wagon was a bulky Victorian grandfather clock that Henry and Mary Alice had stubbornly insisted was too precious an heirloom to be left behind.

The Pincher Creek area was where the Department of the Interior had granted free land to both the Haltons and Thornleys. Under the Homestead Act of 1872, heads of immigrant families were allotted quarter-sections of 160 acres (65 hectares) in exchange for a ten-dollar application fee. The fee would be returned if the settlers "proved up" – that is, if they stayed on the site for at least three years, built on the property, and showed some evidence that they were actually farming it.

At the "Halton quarter," nineteen kilometres south of Pincher Creek, the last of the foothills roll up to Victoria Peak, one of the highest in the great wall of the Rockies. It was wilderness terrain of extraordinary beauty. A lake that bordered the east side of the property echoed to the cry of the loon, the cackle of wood duck, and the eerie call of red-necked grebe. Elk cows calved on its banks, and herds of mule and white-tail deer cut through the high native grasses. Wolves, coyotes, black bears, and even grizzlies were occasionally seen on the property.

Settling on the quarter-section was a jarring change of life for a family raised amid the hedged fields, narrow lanes, and factories of semi-industrial Lancashire. It would also prove to be a near disaster. In the early fall of 1902, the Haltons began the exhausting work of clearing the bush and building a cabin whose logs were sealed together with sod ploughed up by their horses. They brought in several hogs and two cows – farming long enough to "prove up" and keep the property but never to make any money. They also had some alarming encounters. A bear broke into the cabin and returned to the homestead the next evening. Mary Alice had to hide the children in a dugout under the floor and send her husband out with a shotgun to chase the bear away.

Within weeks, the Haltons decided they could never survive a winter at the homestead and would have to move back to Pincher Creek. For four years they wintered in the red shack, returning each spring to the homestead to continue their doomed efforts to succeed as pioneer farmers. The class system they had come so far to escape was much less rigid than in England but still bothersome. Better-established families such as the

Milvains and the Lynch-Stauntons tended to look down on the Haltons.[5] It was noted that Mary Alice would sometimes carry paper bags to community social events in order to scrounge leftovers for her family. "We were poor, poor, poor!" Matt's older brother Jim recalled many years later. "The homestead just about broke us."[6]

Mishaps and misfortunes continued to shadow the family. In 1906, two years after Matt was born, the Haltons moved to Fernie, a booming mining and lumber town just across the border in British Columbia. Henry had found a job there in a hardware store and Mary Alice worked as a chamber maid in a local hotel until the birth of their only daughter, Annie Jane. On August 1, 1908, gale-force winds carried a raging forest fire into the town. The Haltons and many other residents were forced to flee with their terrified children to an island sanctuary in the Elk River. They lost their homes and personal possessions when the entire centre of Fernie was reduced to ashes.[7]

The Haltons had no choice but to start over in Pincher Creek. For Henry, that meant becoming what was politely described as the "honey-wagon" or "honey-dip man" – a municipal job that required him to take his horse-drawn wagon from house to house to sanitize the privies. Wearing an old suit and a top hat on his rounds, he was a slightly comic figure who was given the vulgar if not entirely inaccurate nickname of "Shithouse Halton." As Matt grew up, he sometimes helped his father on the wagon and was stung when classmates would call him "Shithouse Halton's son."

By 1911, the population of Pincher Creek had quadrupled to twelve hundred people. Ranchers, traders, cowboys, miners, and others had created a lively community. "The uncultured and illiterate brushed shoulders with men of letters and sons of aristocracy," wrote a local historian.[8] There were now five churches, three hotels, three banks, a self-styled opera house, and more than a dozen stores. There was an annual fair and rodeo, parades and exhibitions, and much excitement when Chautauqua came to town – the itinerant theatre groups that performed popular musical comedy and dance routines. There was even a small brothel. It was on Kettles Street, known then as Goose Alley because of the squawking fowl that residents kept there.

The weekly *Pincher Creek Echo* complained that "the house of ill-fame" was threatening the town with "moral gangrene."[9]

As Pincher Creek grew and prospered, the prospects for the Halton family improved. Matt's father was able to exchange his outhouse job for the better-paying work of hauling coal from the nearby Christie mine and delivering groceries from local stores. The family moved to a four-room cottage with a gabled roof on Charlotte Street just south of the creek. A garden that Mary Alice had planted with rhubarb, sweet peas, potatoes, and carrots was bright from April to September with hollyhock, honeysuckle, and other flowers. At the back of the garden was a barn for their two horses and two cows, and a shack where lodgers were sometimes taken in.

Mary Alice was very much the family matriarch. Exuberantly talkative and friendly, she overshadowed her rather docile husband and became a dominant influence over Matt and his siblings. She was generous beyond her means. Needy residents and homesteaders from out of town knew there would always be a free meal or a helping hand in the little house on Charlotte Street. Mary Alice was also intensely ambitious for her six children (two more sons were born during World War One) and determined that they should have more opportunities than had their parents. She relied on her prodigious energy to organize and cook for the family, make clothes for the children (sometimes out of flour sacks), act as the town midwife, and be a zealous member of many of Pincher Creek's social and church organizations. More significantly for Matt's future, she also wrote for the *Pincher Creek Echo* and served as district correspondent for both the *Lethbridge Herald* and the *Calgary Herald*. In her third son she would develop a gift for words and a passion for journalism.

Ambition to report was already stirring in Matt. As a reporter for the *Echo,* Mary Alice sometimes sent her son to find out who had spoken at community events that she was unable to attend or to run her handwritten reports up to the *Echo*'s office a block and a half away from their home. There Matt watched as type was laboriously set by hand and printed on a clanking old Victorian press. At the age of twelve, he walked shyly into the newspaper office one day and asked if there was any reporting he could do. Amused but not wanting to disappoint him, assistant editor Anna Edwards assigned him to write a few lines about the inauguration of a campsite that evening. She later recounted being taken aback by Matt's description. The ceremony took place, he wrote, "beside the restful brook along the shimmering aspens." "Matthew," she told him, "you have found your vocation. Keep on with your writing."[10]

Matt needed no prompting. He had already begun reading the dispatches of Sir Philip Gibbs, the British war correspondent who had won a knighthood for his colourful reports about the fighting in World War One. Both his mother and older brother, Jim, remembered Matt lying on the carpet of their front room one day and suddenly looking up and saying, "Mum, I'm going to be a great famous war correspondent like Philip Gibbs."[11] Later, Matt was captivated by Gibbs's explanation of why he couldn't abandon journalism: "The lure of the adventure was too strong. The thrill of chasing the new 'story,' the interest of getting into the middle of life, sometimes behind the scenes of history . . . the meetings with heroes, rogues, and oddities, the front seats at the peep show of life . . . the comradeship, the rivalry, the test of one's own quality of character and vision."[12]

Matt was fifteen when he got his first big break as an aspiring reporter. He was recommended as an occasional correspondent for the *Lethbridge Herald*. His first assignment – an interview with a local MLA about crop prospects—was published next day under the byline "Our Own Correspondent." He later wrote that it was an intoxicating moment. "I went to bed saying to myself, I am a writer. . . . And for the next year or so, no cow calved within fifty miles without me trying to get the spectacular news into print."[13] *Herald* editors spared readers such trivia although they did publish a long article Matt wrote about a speech he himself had delivered to a young people's church meeting. A first cheque from the paper for $16 left him "giddy with delight."[14]

The *Herald* connection proved of great value to Matt. Its editor and publisher was W.A. Buchanan, an Ontario newspaperman who had moved west and become a Liberal senator. Combining a sharp interest in local news with an internationalist outlook, Buchanan turned the paper into one of the best small-city dailies in Canada.[15] He was known as the "Senator from Waterton" because of the summers he spent at his cottage in the mountain setting of Waterton Lakes National Park. It was also where the Haltons would occasionally camp on summer weekends. A chance meeting there with Matt led to the first of several invitations to Buchanan's cottage. The sessions turned into informal seminars on journalism that Matt said taught him the basics of reporting and editing.[16] Later it was Buchanan's patronage and his connections in the newspaper world that gave him new opportunities.

It was his own talents, though, that pushed Matt forward. He was precociously well read. He was also endowed with an unusually retentive memory that enabled him to recite page after page of poetry to anyone who would listen. English and history were his favourite subjects but he excelled in other courses as well. The *Echo* published the school test scores every month, and with monotonous regularity during their high school years Matt or his best friend, Willis Ambrose, would come in first. Classmates later recalled that when a teacher asked for someone to read their compositions or a passage from a textbook, it was usually Matt who raised his hand first and would read with an often theatrical flourish.[17]

Outside the classroom a serious incident pointed to a future problem for Matt. In his late teens he began drinking with some of his friends. To get around Alberta's strict Prohibition Law, their practice was to mix a jug of "Concord wine," as they jokingly called grape juice, with pure alcohol obtained through a prescription at the local drugstore. The first time Matt got drunk touched off one of those minor scandals that fed Pincher Creek's gossip mill for weeks. It happened when a school friend, Hugh Taylor, rented a hotel room for a party to celebrate his sixteenth birthday. For Matt, a lasting memory of the party was "tasting for the first time the sweet fire of alcohol."[18] Enough hooch was available to make the five boys in the room not only drunk but extremely rowdy. They learned the next morning that the hotel keeper had laid a charge with the police. The charge was later withdrawn but that didn't prevent a policeman turning up at school, calling the boys out of class, and delivering a stern lecture. The school board in turn sent a letter of reprimand to the boys' parents – one that was especially damaging for Matt's teetotalling mother and father and their quest for respectability. Almost ten years later, Matt wrote, "The wound inflicted at home by that has never left me."[19]

Most of Matt's earlier pursuits were far more innocent. The creek that gave the town its name was the source of many of his pleasures. With his friend, Willis Ambrose, he skated on it in winter, fished in it in spring and summer, and swam where the stream deepened in a nearby canyon. He would also water his father's horses in the creek in the early morning, sometimes chided by his mother for spending too much time there "just dreaming."

In many ways the most marked characteristic of early life in Pincher Creek was its resolutely British character. The pioneer community was a mere sixty-five kilometres from the Montana border and the emerging American colossus to the south. Yet its social, cultural, and emotional links lay ten thousand kilometres away with an imperial Britain that still held sway over a quarter of the world's population. London newspapers, often months old, were eagerly handed from family to family. At Victoria Day parades and other patriotic occasions, the Union Jack was given prominence over the Canadian flag, the Red Ensign. The local chapter of the IODE (the Imperial Order of the Daughters of the Empire) was one of the most active organizations in the community, promoting the Crown and its civilizing mission. So-called remittance men – young British immigrants often subsidized by their wealthy families – kept alive the mores of upper-middle-class England. One of the first polo games in North America was played eight kilometres from the Halton homestead on the ranch owned by a monocled English aristocrat who insisted that his guests dress for dinner.

Even in its much more modest circumstances, Matt's childhood was largely moulded by British values and British culture. His parents may have resented the inequalities of English life but they brought up their family to love English literature and to be staunch empire loyalists. Largely self-educated, Mary Alice read Dickens and Thackeray to her children, introduced them to Shakespeare and the English Romantic poets, and borrowed English books for them from friends and acquaintances. Matt was virtually weaned on Rudyard Kipling and Sir Henry Newbolt, the poets of Empire, and was an avid reader of G.A. Henty, who celebrated colonial heroes in historical novels such as *With Clive in India, With Kitchener in the Sudan,* and *With Wolfe in Canada.*

In a town where thirty young men had volunteered to fight for the British in the Boer War, it was hardly surprising that Haltons and Thornleys were ready to join the much greater number who answered the call of king and country in World War One. Matt was ten years old when the war broke out and probably thought his uncle Seth and his revered older brother, Sam, were off on a glorious adventure when they volunteered for the Canadian Expeditionary Force. For some time Sam's letters from the front remained optimistic. On January 25, 1917, he wrote home that "out here, we look for peace soon – a victorious peace – and keep going on."[20] But already there were hints in the letter that the mud and horror of trench warfare were getting to him. He mentioned walking from a Princess Patricia's Canadian Light Infantry position along a communications trench to talk with Seth: "I can manage easily the few miles back and forth to the trenches resignedly and fatalistically, which is the only way one could stand it."[21]

In late April, Mary Alice received one of those dreaded envelopes from the Department of Militia and Defence. Samuel Thornley Halton was still alive but a bullet had wounded his left leg and shrapnel had ripped apart his right thigh. It had happened at Vimy Ridge, where Sam may also have suffered from shell shock. "My Dearest Mother," he later wrote from the Canadian Convalescent Hospital in Wokingham, England, "My mind is about normal now."[22]

Far worse news reached the little cottage on Charlotte Street in November. Matt's uncle Seth had been killed in the inferno of gas and shelling at Passchendaele. Years later, Matt recounted how enthusiastic he and his mother had been in the first years of the war. The house was often crowded with IODE ladies cheerfully knitting socks and scarves for the troops. They wrapped them up along with jellied chicken and tobacco in parcels that Matt and his brother Jim would rush off to the post office. "When the ladies had gone home," he wrote, "my mother would get out the war map, and together the two of us would take Bapaume in five minutes, and St. Quentin, and the whole Hindenburg line, and sweep the Germans right back to the marshes from which they came. Then a Vimy Ridge would occur, and then a Passchendaele, and in a week or so the cablegrams would come, 'deeply regretting to inform us,' and I can still see mother cooking the meal over the kitchen stove with tears running down her cheek and saying no word, and I can still hear the dogs howling to the moon on a far-off Halloween night which was one of the nights of Passchendaele."[23]

A few years later, Matt's decision to leave Pincher Creek took him on a journey that would lead him eventually into the fury of another war in Europe. But for the rest of his life, wherever he was, he would romanticize the foothills country of Alberta. Pincher Creek long remained his compass.

2

STARTING OUT

"It was obvious to everyone that he was a man who really knew how to write."
– MAX WERSHOFF, Matt's University of Alberta classmate

AFTER GRADUATING FROM HIGH SCHOOL IN 1922, Matt's tall ambitions were quickly brought to earth by his family's poverty. His plan was to attend the University of Alberta and from there to fulfil his romantic hopes of travelling the world as a foreign correspondent for a big-city newspaper. In reality, he could barely afford the train trip to Edmonton let alone the annual four hundred or so dollars he would need for tuition and university residence fees. So Matt worked as a cowboy on a nearby ranch – he was an accomplished horseman from an early age – and later as a construction worker on the new road between Pincher Creek and Waterton Lakes. Still unable to save enough, he turned to the generous loans the Alberta government offered to attend the provincial teacher-training institute in Calgary – Normal School, as it was then called. Teaching would be his path to college.

Matt was soon struggling with a problem that troubled him through much of his life. Even with the government loan, he was constantly in debt. Perhaps as a reaction to the penury of his childhood, he quickly developed a taste for expensive nights out and the latest fashions in men's clothes. In a letter home from Calgary, he thanked his father for a rare gift of fifteen dollars. "Immediately," he confessed, "I sent to Simpson's for a $14 suit."[1] Worries about his ability to afford university, and eventually to help out his parents, added a forlorn note to some of his letters. "My chances of university for a few years seem remote," he wrote. "Again I want to tell you now that you, mother and dad, must not worry on this. When I am earning money, *you* will come first. . . . You can always rely on me."[2] Nothing at the time suggested that the promise would ever be fulfilled. After his eight months at Normal School, he had to ask his parents for a small loan to pay off his debts and allow him to buy a train ticket home to Pincher Creek.[3]

Matt's teaching career began in September 1923, in a one-room schoolhouse in Alberta's Porcupine Hills. It was close enough to Pincher Creek to allow him to join his close-knit family on weekends. Ranchers in the area long recalled a familiar sight – a young man on horseback riding up the slopes from Monday to Friday during the school year.[4] The new teacher was making the five-kilometre journey from the farmstead north of Cowley where he lodged to the tiny rural school at Heath Creek, midway up the escarpment. He was well liked by both parents and students and impressed school inspectors on their occasional surprise visits. The first report about him to the Department of Education described Matt as "skillful and effective" and predicted that he would "prove very successful as a teacher."[5] Skill and a great deal of patience were much in demand at the time in Alberta's rural schools where as many as five grades were crammed into one class. In English and history, Matt's habit was to supplement the official curriculum with his own favourite texts, often those that extolled the glories of the British Empire. Typically, he would have his class recite "Vitae Lampada," the famous poem of Sir Henry Newbolt that promoted the view that battles should be fought and won in the same spirit as a cricket match at Eton or Harrow.[6] Echoing from the log-cabin school in the Porcupine Hills, the classic words of British *noblesse oblige* were oddly out of place:

> *The sand of the desert is sodden red,*
> *Red with the wreck of a square that broke;*
> *The Gatling's jammed and the colonel dead,*
> *And the regiment blind with dust and smoke.*

The River of death has brimmed his banks,
And England's far, and Honour a name,
But the voice of a schoolboy rallies the ranks
"Play up! Play up! And play the game!"

By September 1925, Matt had finally saved enough from teaching for a first year in college. He arrived at the University of Alberta to find a collection of plain brick buildings that stood on the windswept heights overlooking the North Saskatchewan River. The university had been founded only seventeen years earlier in an Edmonton regarded as something of an intellectual backwater. It might well have become just another small, provincial college, uncelebrated outside Alberta. Instead, a visionary president, Henry Marshall Tory, helped turn the U of A into what its historian described as "one of the finest universities in Canada."[7] Tory's special talent was recruitment. Scouring the best of academe in Europe and North America, he attracted a group of brilliant young professors from universities such as Leipzig, Harvard, Queen's, and Columbia.

Several of those professors had an enduring impact on Matt and many of his classmates. Among them was the legendary Edward Kemper Broadus, who had come from Harvard to head the English department. Broadus was an unforgiving teacher who would spit out irony at students who failed to read the required texts or meet his exacting standards of writing.[8] But favoured students – and Matt was one of them – would be invited to his house for tea and scones to discuss the great novelists and poets and to revel in the beauty of the English language. Rache Lovat Dickson, a friend of Matt's who became a distinguished author and publisher in London, later wrote that "the Professor, as much as my father, made me what I am."[9]

Another teacher with an unusual ability to make his subject come alive was Dr. George Hardy, a Classics professor specializing in Hellenic studies. Matt later said that Hardy taught him how the best in modern civilization "had its origin in that heyday of the Greek genius, in that serene Athens where measured reason went hand in hand with the most searching love of beauty."[10] Then there was Professor Édouard Sonet's infectious enthusiasm for the language and culture of France that put Matt on the path to becoming an ardent Francophile.

What made the University of Alberta so valuable for Matt was not only its gifted professors but the small circle of ambitious students around him. Friends and classmates would often crowd into his basement room in the men's residence at Athabaska Hall. There, late into the night, they would debate, play poker, drink cheap whisky, and be entertained or bored by Matt's habit of spouting poetry. He once recited from memory almost all of the hundred and one verses of Edward FitzGerald's *The Rubaiyat of Omar Khayyam*.[11] Among his classmates were Lovat Dickson; Max Wershoff, a future Canadian ambassador; Ronald Martland, a future justice of the Supreme Court; Peter Kilburn, future president of one of the biggest investment companies in Canada; Hugh Whitney Morrison, future Rhodes Scholar, journalist, and public relations executive; and Eric Gibbs, who would become European bureau chief for *Time-Life*. They all became lifelong friends. For the boy from Pincher Creek there could only have been a strong sense of moving up in life.

Matt dove quickly into the swirl of university activities. He was elected secretary-treasurer of the freshman class, took part in a student theatre production, and began writing for the *Gateway*, the student newspaper. Its editor, Walter Herbert, recalled giving him his first assignment – to write a feature on a hermit living in a cave close to campus. Under the headline "Varsity's Most Unusual Character," Matt wrote a colourful and sympathetic report about the hermit.[12] Herbert thought it was good enough to recommend sending it to the *Toronto Daily Star*. "The writing just flowed from him," he remembered.[13]

Social life at the university largely revolved around the weekly Saturday night dances and a dozen or so formals during the year. By 1926 undergrads were dancing the Charleston. A few of the bolder women students dared to wear the "flapper" fashion that shortened skirts and flattened curves. But there were few if any signs of the more liberal sexual mores of the Jazz Age. At Pembina, the women's residence, a ten p.m. curfew was strictly enforced by Dean Florence Dodd. She was known as "the warden" and was fond of using a rhyme to warn girls to

Maintain your virtue
By thinking of Jesus,
Venereal diseases,
And the horrors of having a child.[14]

It was at an off-campus party in his first semester that Matt met Jean Campbell, a first-year Arts student like himself. Dark-haired and demure, Jean had the kind of intelligence and classic good looks that captivated Matt immediately. She in turn was intrigued by the blond-haired, earnest young man who recited snippets of poetry as he walked her home. Jean later recalled that they seemed to agree on everything they talked about that night. They were already holding hands as they crossed the High Level Bridge to the university in sub-zero weather.[15]

On the surface, it appeared to be an unlikely courtship. Jean's background was in almost every respect the opposite of the working-class milieu that Matt grew up in. Her parents, Alexander ("Sandy") Munro Campbell and his wife Laura Joslin, had moved from Woodstock, Ontario, at the turn of the century. Benefiting from a large inheritance, they settled in Lacombe, a small Alberta town halfway between Calgary and Edmonton. Sandy Campbell soon owned the only department store there as well as several other businesses and three farms in the area. They lived in a fifteen-room Edwardian mansion with elegant pillars setting off the front porch. At dinner, Jean's mother would ring a silver bell to summon the maid to bring in the next course. In summer, local workmen were hired to carry out the Campbells' grand piano to their family cottage at nearby Gull Lake. And in winter, no invitation was more sought after by the upper crust of Lacombe than to the Campbells' annual dinner-dance. When Sandy Campbell died, the mayor of Lacombe proclaimed a period of mourning, ordering all stores and businesses to shut their doors for two and a half hours. "The Campbells were royalty," observed one former resident.[16]

The sharp contrast between the family backgrounds of the Haltons and Campbells cast no shadow over Matt and Jean. Their relationship was developing slowly but happily. A much greater threat loomed in the spring semester when Matt realized that, once again, his debts would prevent him from returning to college for the next year. "I don't have a cent," he confided to his parents in a refrain they were all too used to hearing.[17] Matt's fear was less about losing an academic year than the prospect that Jean's affections might turn elsewhere. His concern was magnified when he learned that the only teaching job available to him was near Berwyn, in a remote area of the Peace River country 480 kilometres northwest of Edmonton.

So in April 1926, Matt found himself once again in a place he didn't want to be, in a job he didn't want to have. By now it was a familiar routine: boarding with a local family, riding to work every day to a one-room school-house, and struggling to teach about thirty students in Grades 1 to 8. He had arrived in a suit and tie but was soon wearing jeans, a ten-gallon hat, and even leather chaps.[18] He rarely used the strap, a fixture of Alberta schools at the time, but was credited with keeping order effectively. "Nobody got away with anything in Matt's classes," said one of his former pupils.[19]

The disciplined approach he encouraged at school was noticeably absent in his private feelings. His letters to Jean were sometimes marked by the ramblings of a fevered, romantic imagination. He complained that the gods had dealt him the worst of hands. "I can't find any purpose in it all," he wrote, "and my inward queries of 'What for?' and 'Why?' and 'To what effect?' have absolutely worn my nerves ragged in the last few months."[20] Jean responded with calming words. She urged him to cheer up and realize that a year away from college was nothing more than a temporary setback. There was also a gentle hint that he could save more for college if he cut down on his smoking and tendency to heavy drink-ing.[21] Jean had begun to adopt the role she would always play for him: the practical down-to-earth advisor, the rock on which he could lay his head.

Some of Matt's anxiety eased in the fall when the Department of Education found him another school that was conveniently close to Pincher Creek. On the way home he spent a week with Jean at her parents' summer cottage, passing the first test of acceptance by her father and rather stern mother. The reserved tone of the couple's early correspon-dence changed. Matt no longer signed off his letters with the words "Devotedly" nor did Jean finish with the words "Your friend." Rarely given to understatement, Matt finally declared his love in unequivocal terms: "If there is really purpose in the universe . . . then I know that a million years ago, a thousand eons removed, it was decreed that I love you. If, on the other hand, there is no purpose, and we are just creatures of chance, I still know this – that chance has defeated its own ends, and made a purpose for me. That purpose is to love you."[22] There is no record of Jean's response. But not long after Matt's letter she invited him to take a break from teaching and be her guest at the university's annual mid-winter dance. On her dance card, Jean scrawled Matt's name and the words *"Je t'aime."* She kept the card for the rest of her life.

Returning to university in September 1927, for his remaining two years, Matt managed to get good marks without too much effort. His professors were impressed with him but also quick to chide him for any signs of intellectual pretentiousness. When Matt began a philosophy exam by writing, "In one short hour one can hardly solve the riddle of the universe," his philosophy professor, Dr. John MacEachren, returned the paper with a sardonic message: "Had I known that you could solve the riddle of the universe, I should gladly have allotted more time."[23]

Matt was increasingly preoccupied with trying to establish his credentials as a journalist. He became the Varsity correspondent for the *Edmonton Journal* and later for the *Edmonton Bulletin*. As a sophomore, his writing was judged good enough to make him associate editor of the *Gateway*, the student newspaper, and in his final year he was appointed its editor-in-chief. His editorials on student affairs, education, and other subjects are erudite and elegant. One of his professors later described his student writings as "mature and provocative, and in them you can feel the fire and the vigor and the convictions which he put into everything he undertook."[24] Matt himself described his mission as "holding a bouquet to throw at the meritorious, and a brickbat to hurl at the smug, the self-complacent."[25]

One editorial he wrote was considered so incendiary that it touched off a campus controversy that lasted for months. It was prompted by a visiting Australian debater who argued that science was gradually destroying religion. Matt examined the argument a few days later, agreeing that "if by religion Mr. Sheldon meant the creeds, dogmas, denominations and terrible superstitions which, even today, take to themselves the name of religion, our answer to the charge that science is destroying them is, absolutely and equivocally – 'Thank god.'"[26] The established churches, he argued, deserve contempt. They retard human progress by exploiting people's fears and desires. But despite the sharp attack on orthodox religions, Matt was careful not to deny the possibility of a God who is unknowable. "If . . . a genuine, honest search for the Truth is the hall-mark of religion, we claim to be as religious as any man we know."[27]

It was the belief of an agnostic rather than an atheist. But in the Alberta of the 1920s, even in the relatively freethinking atmosphere of the university, the editorial was seen by many as atheistic and heretical. Protest letters from prominent students were quick to arrive. Matt was denounced as a "pseudo-philosopher, with the obviously infantile intellect."[28] What right did he have, the paper was asked, to criticize established Christian churches for whom millions have died and which have been "the greatest civilizing influence that the world has known?"[29] Other protestors used ridicule. A fellow *Gateway* writer, Felp Priestley, scorned the pretentiousness of "the Prophet . . . Matta All Tin, the Lone Searcher After Truth."[30]

For a while Matt seemed to revel in the controversy he had touched off. Spurred on by his supporters, he wrote a second editorial excoriating those who "talk confidently of trinities, and immaculate conceptions, and profess to know the ultimate." One by one he picked apart the arguments against him. Yes, millions may have died in Christianity's wars, but "was that the ideal of Jesus of Nazareth?" And didn't the persecution of Leonardo da Vinci and Galileo and Voltaire suggest that civilization progressed in spite of Christianity, not because of it? The final outrage for his critics was Matt's rebuttal of their claim that he was cramming his beliefs down the throats of a Christian university. With brazen arrogance, he suggested that Christ would be on his side, fostering freedom of thought and the search for truth, "were he here today."[31]

The uproar over the editorials soon became more serious for the *Gateway* and its editor. Two prominent Roman Catholic students began collecting signatures on a petition intended to cripple the weekly newspaper. The petition demanded an end to the system under which subscription fees for the paper were automatically deducted from Student Union dues. Instead, university president Robert Wallace was asked to declare the editorials offensive and to order that *Gateway* dues be made voluntary. What the two student leaders didn't count on was that Wallace privately sympathized with Matt's views. Proud of the university's secular and non-denominational character, he refused to change the paper's financing. All he promised was "to have a word with Mr. Halton."[32] Nothing is known about that meeting but Matt's next editorial was self-contradictory. He agreed that the religious debate should cool off for a while. But, unrepentant, he wrote, "We have nothing but contempt for those who, rather than answer argument by argument, resort to attempts to discredit the editor and the paper by an appeal to authority. We cannot foster fraternity at the expense of thought and freedom of expression."[33]

Exams were approaching; the U of A's religious debate faded away. Ultimately, it had defined character traits in Matt that would endure: a crusading zeal and impatience, even intolerance, toward those he disagreed with.

Another of Matt's editorial decisions proved costly, if less controversial. After a long stretch of poor results, the University of Alberta football team was poised in 1928 to win the western intercollegiate championship. Fred Hess, its captain, was close to breaking all individual scoring records and was certainly the best player the university had ever produced. Those facts prompted Matt and his sports editor, Hugh Morrison, to conceive of a plan to make money for the *Gateway* and to scoop the two Edmonton newspapers. Morrison would be sent to Winnipeg to cover the final match against the University of Manitoba. A telegraph operator would be hired to sit beside him and file his play-by-play report back to the *Gateway* office. "Extra" editions would then be printed, and a team of students would fan out over the city to sell them before the next editions of the city papers.[34]

On the day of the match, Matt and dozens of volunteers crowded into the *Gateway*'s office in the basement of the Arts building. Morrison's copy began arriving bit by bit and was handed to printers in an adjoining office. All that was needed for the extra edition was for the U of A's Golden Bears to win, and for Morrison to send his opening paragraphs to top off his earlier play-by-plays. The match was close but Alberta finally won 15–8.

Minutes later the *Gateway* was printing Morrison's exuberant description of the winning goal: "Taking the ball behind his own line, with five minutes to go and but two points separating the teams, Captain Freddie Hess made history when he sped through the entire Manitoba team, gained the open field and madly raced 115 yards for a touch-down."[35] It was the perfect ending for the extra edition – or so Matt thought.

His volunteers – with bundles of the paper under their arms – soon began deploying along Jasper Avenue and other key locations in downtown Edmonton. They were the first to get a hint of the *Gateway*'s looming debacle. Paper boys from the *Journal* and *Bulletin* were already out on the streets shouting "Extra, extra. *Vestris* sunk!" Both newspapers had put out special editions about the sinking a few hours earlier of the U.S. steamship *Vestris* off the coast of Virginia. More than 110 passengers drowned. At the time it was the second-deadliest maritime disaster of the century in peacetime. The shocking news and lurid headlines of its competitors cut deeply into sales of the *Gateway*'s extra edition. As a result, the costs of the venture were never recovered. "We lost our shirts," Morrison later admitted.[36]

Matt's final year in Edmonton was preceded and followed by more school teaching. In 1929 he was assigned to Moose Lodge, a remote northern hamlet that made the Peace River village where he'd taught earlier seem like a metropolis. To get there Matt took the once-a-week train from Edmonton to the town of Smith, rode on horseback to the Athabaska River, crossed it by ferry, and was picked up by a buckboard wagon for the final twenty-four kilometres over a muddy trail to the hamlet.[37] He was disturbed to find that none of the fifteen or so families in the district were aware that a new teacher was coming. No chairs or desks or blackboard, let alone textbooks, were in the log cabin that served as both school and community centre. It took a week of carpentry before he was able to welcome a grand total of six children whose swearing, he wrote, "would amaze the most calloused mule-driver."[38]

There were hardships to endure and a number of misadventures in the long summer that followed. The cabin where Matt lodged swarmed with mosquitoes. The half-wild horse he was lent would occasionally take off for days in the surrounding forest. He complained of being severely beaten up in a fight with drunken Métis (he called them "half-breeds" before the era of political correctness). He confessed that when traders sold him a bottle of Haig & Haig, he would occasionally break his promise to Jean to give up whisky.[39] He wrote of "an aching loneliness" and confided to his parents that, without the girl he loved, "it would be too dark a world to contemplate." There were consolations though. Matt described the deep primeval forest, fast-flowing rivers, emerald lakes, and sunsets around Moose Lodge as "Elysian fantasies."[40] In his spare time he enjoyed hunting for moose and deer, shooting wild duck, and fishing for perch and pickerel. He had no idea that, within fourteen months, he would be living a continent away from the pioneer north.

Three months into his final university year, the Imperial Order of the Daughters of the Empire awarded Matt one of its coveted scholarships for post-graduate study in Britain. The scholarship was generous and could be used at the university of his choice. At the time many Canadians considered the IODE award to be second in prestige only to a Rhodes Scholarship. No longer were the Haltons in Pincher Creek the target of condescension.

Matt had an even greater reason to celebrate. He had taken Jean home to meet his family, followed by a three-day camping trip on horseback in nearby Waterton Lakes National Park. At the summit of the Carthew Trail, high above the treeline, the couple marvelled at one of the most spectacular views in the Rockies. They also spent a night together in Edmonton's posh Macdonald Hotel. Not long before Matt left for London, rings were exchanged and, without announcing it publicly, Matt and Jean became engaged.

3

TO EUROPE

"I was at the centre of the Empire which is my religion."
– MATTHEW HALTON in the *Lethbridge Herald*, October 31, 1929

ON THE LAST DAY OF SEPTEMBER 1929, the Canadian Pacific steamship *Melita* sailed into the Irish Sea on the final stretch of its passage to Liverpool. Matt, now twenty-five years old, strained for his first sight of the English coast. It was a time of confused emotions for him: hope and anticipation mingling with apprehension. "I was asking myself a few questions," he later wrote. "Would I find the England of my dreams? I wondered. Would I thrill standing before the shrines of England's history as I had thrilled in anticipation for years? . . . Would I be as ardent an Imperialist when I came to know the English at first hand instead of from a distance?"[1]

Matt had never previously travelled more than twenty kilometres outside Alberta. Now he was landing in the heart of the British Empire, in the port from which his parents had departed for Canada and to which his brother and uncle had come to fight for king and country.

It is tempting to project onto Matt the archetypal literary image of the youth from the provinces seeking his fortune in the imperial capital. A Julien Sorel, for example, the romantic dreamer of Stendhal's *Le Rouge et le Noir*, whose quest for power and status leads him to the sophisticated salons of Paris. Matt's ambitions for the future seemed equally boundless. While still aboard the *Melita*, he wrote to Jean, "I hope that future brings education, enlightenment, pleasure, money and honor – if I can couple the last two in the same phrase."[2] Yet Matt hardly fit the mould of a callow, unproven youth. He was already articulate, extraordinarily well read, and better versed in British culture than most Britons. And with some measurable achievements to his credit, he had few of the rough edges of Stendhal's hero.

Matt's first months in England were intoxicating. He registered at King's College, University of London, because it was one of the few institutions at the time that offered a journalism course. The main college building lay between the Thames Embankment and an arched gateway that led to London's venerable thoroughfare, the Strand. On his first day, Matt walked out of the gate and turned right. Suddenly he heard the chimes of St. Clement Danes, the Wren church a block away down the Strand. The bells were playing "Oranges and Lemons Say the Bells of St. Clement's," the nursery tune he remembered so well from his childhood. He walked further east, past the newspaper offices and crowded pubs of Fleet Street where his hero, Sir Philip Gibbs, worked. Turning back in the other direction, he saw men in top hats and women in expensive furs stepping out of their chauffeured Rolls-Royces in front of the Savoy hotel. At the other end of the Strand was Trafalgar Square, where he gazed for the first time at the statue of Nelson and the imposing vista from Whitehall to Westminster. As he described the moment later, it seemed almost an epiphany. "I was at the centre of the Empire which is my religion."[3]

There were no signs of imperial grandeur where Matt lodged, a fifth-floor garret in a poorly kept student boarding house north of Hyde Park. It held one pleasant surprise: two English students, both girls, who shared a room on the same floor and became his good friends. Kathleen Gordon and Helen Burgess were intrigued that anyone could come from a place called Pincher Creek. At first they were mildly condescending toward the young colonial. They found his fervour for Empire *passé*, his unrestrained enthusiasm for things British rather gauche.[4] Nor could they understand why he felt his soul-searching about religion to be so daring when atheism was no longer controversial in their circles. Despite those concerns, a long and affectionate relationship developed. Matt would drop by their room for tea to unburden himself of ideas and experiences and to talk (sometimes tediously, they felt) about his love for Jean.[5]

The two young women became Matt's companions on excursions in and around London and on frequent visits to the theatre. From cheap seats in the upper gallery, they were lucky enough to see John Gielgud's *Hamlet* and *Richard II* during his brilliant debut season at the Old Vic. Matt was struck by Gielgud's virtuosity and mellifluous voice. He also attended other productions starring such leading British actors as Cedric Hardwicke, Fay Compton, and Sybil Thorndike. "For the lover of the theatre," he wrote, "the first few weeks in London are days of almost pure rapture."[6] He also discovered ballet. Kathleen Gordon, who later would become a director of the Royal Academy of Dance, said that she had to drag him to Diaghilev's Ballets Russes, considered the most exciting dance company of the era. She said Matt ended up loving the performance and became a classical ballet enthusiast.[7] Afterwards, thanks to Gordon's connections, the two were able to go backstage to meet two of the company's greatest ballerinas, Tamara Karsavina and Anna Pavlova.

Another new interest was equally surprising. At school and at the University of Alberta, Matt had shown no interest in team sports of any kind. But within a few weeks of his arrival in London he tried out for the King's College rowing eight and soon was involved in competitive racing. Rowing for Matt became a fusion of poetry and sport. He loved being in a racing shell and hearing the plash of blades on water as eight men strained in perfect rhythm for speed and power.[8] He was judged good enough to win a place in the college first eight that competed in the university championships.

Matt's romanticism about rowing on the Thames was reflected in a fanciful description of one of his crew's practice runs from Hammersmith to Tower Bridge. "Then we passed the Parliament Buildings, and I wondered suddenly if it wasn't a strange dream I was having, instead of actually rowing down the Thames. . . . Surely this was the Athabaska River and I was alone in a canoe, and these other figures with me were but shadows, and that thin mist was Alberta haze. . . . Then the idea reversed itself, and it seemed then that the other part was a dream, that I had never lived in Alberta or paddled down the Athabaska, that those places didn't exist at all. . . . Then a voice boomed: 'Wake up there, five!' and I started in surprise, and Tower Bridge passed over my head, and I caught the odor of fish from Billingsgate fish market, and I knew this was really London River."[9] There was no romanticism, however, during another practice row. The college shell capsized one day in a heavy mist after the cox swung the rudder to avoid colliding with a large boat. Matt and the rest of the crew had to swim to shore in cold, dirty water.[10]

Long and breathless letters to Jean chronicled Matt's infatuation with imperial London. In November, he went early to Whitehall to get a good position to watch the Armistice Day ceremony at the Cenotaph. He was thrilled to see royalty: Queen Mary with her head bowed and the Prince of Wales in his Guards uniform. Near them stood Prime Minister Ramsay MacDonald, Opposition leader Stanley Baldwin, and David Lloyd George, Britain's World War One leader and a heroic figure for Matt. Opposite the politicians, a line of Victoria Cross winners were "staring ahead with hard, unseeing, remembering eyes."[11] The two-minute silence played on Matt's imagination. Despite the huge crowd, "I heard not the slightest sound except the sad, measured tolling of the bells. . . . I know that I heard the beating of wings, and that in the light mist I could see the marching silhouettes of the Legion of the Dead."[12] Later, he wrote: "Lord, Jean, patriotism may not be fashionable, but when you stand here in Whitehall, and realize what a mighty undertaking this little island has set on foot, you cannot help being patriotic."[13]

What helped Matt develop a more nuanced view of Britain and its people was a rare experience of the two Englands – the England of the landed gentry and the England of the working class from which his own parents came. He had left Canada with letters of introduction from Senator W.A. Buchanan, the publisher of the *Lethbridge Herald* who had mentored his early reporting efforts. One of the letters was to Nancy Astor, the first woman to sit in the House of Commons and a controversial figure in British politics. American by birth but married into the British aristocracy, Lady Astor was glamorous, forceful, idealistic, and a fervent advocate of Empire.[14] Her interest in Canada began in World War One when she and her husband allowed a hospital to be built for wounded Canadian soldiers at Cliveden, their country estate. The hospital became a passionate involvement for her, and she later turned over another part of the grounds for a cemetery for the forty Canadians and two nursing sisters who died there.

Matt first met Lady Astor in the House of Commons after she got him into the Strangers Gallery to watch a debate. The earnest young man from Alberta was soon invited to tea at the Astors' London house in St. James Square, then to a weekend at Cliveden, where the Astors would assemble leading politicians, diplomats, and writers to party, hunt, and stroll in their magnificent gardens. The Cliveden mansion was one of England's great country homes. Overlooking the River Thames in Buckinghamshire, it was built in the style of a seventeenth-century Italian palace; copies of Renaissance sculptures lined the approaches and rose from an artificial lake. A female statue representing Canada, said to resemble Lady Astor herself, watched over the war cemetery.

Matt, like other guests, would have been welcomed by the butler and escorted to his room by one or more of the dozens of service staff. In a letter to Jean, Matt seemed awestruck by his surroundings and self-conscious about the impression he would make. "For the first time in my life, I realize that there were heights of culture which are forever unattainable to me. Thanks to mother's far-sighted training, and to my own self-training, I have had a poise that has carried me through all ranks of society . . . without embarrassment. But I must admit that I felt a bit rough before the positively exquisite grace with which Lord Astor and his sons know how to live."[15] Matt was equally fawning toward Lady Astor: "A most remarkable woman. She wants to take all the world to her breast and make it better and happier."[16] In an article for the *Lethbridge Herald* about her care for Canadian soldiers, he described her as "The Angel of Cliveden."[17] She would prove to be a useful friend and patron over the next decade.

Another invitation brought Matt into an entirely different world – the England of grimy industrial towns, of Bovril and fish and chips and betting on the football pools. He was invited to stay with Uncle Billy Halton and his wife, Ann, in Eccleston, close to the Lancashire town where his parents grew up. First the train took him to Wigan, the mill and coal-mining town whose poverty was later made infamous in George Orwell's *The Road to Wigan Pier*. The town was so dirty and smoky, Matt said, that a heavy rain left blobs of wet soot on his face.[18] While waiting two hours for the bus to Eccleston, he wandered through rows of slum housing and concluded that the town was an "industrial hell where great wealth is produced at the cost of the stultification of the human soul."[19] When he got to Eccleston, he was happy to find that his relatives were better off than his parents were when they left England. He got on well with the family and felt comfortable in the cheerful working-class atmosphere that mirrored his own background. There was a sentimental excursion to his parents' old house in Euxton, a visit to the Preston motorbike races, and walks down winding country lanes. The one irritant was that his strict Methodist family insisted he join them at church. On one occasion, he complained that he had to suffer through the "worst sermon I ever heard in my life, smashing all records for sanctimonious self-satisfaction, querulous smugness and platitudinous nothing."[20] After ten days in Eccleston, he was ready to return to his friends in London and the city's wealth of sights and experiences. In an optimistic mood, he wrote to his parents: "I have no quarrel with life. It promises to be a very entertaining affair."[21]

Matt's one major disappointment in London was the King's College journalism course. He found it had little to add to what he had already learned at the *Gateway* and freelancing for Alberta dailies. He boldly decided he was ready to become an instant foreign correspondent and once again Senator Buchanan gave him a break. Matt was told he could write a weekly column for the *Lethbridge Herald* under the rubric "Southern Alberta Student's Impressions in England." His early reports, largely about explorations in and around London, revealed his liking for poetic description. Walking in the forest around the old village of Burnham Beeches, for example, he described it as "almost the England of the Eighteenth Century, and earlier, where the immemorial winds whisper through dark and quiet woods."[22] His first reports enthusiastically portrayed the British Empire as a civilizing and beneficial influence on its peoples. If Matt was aware that British rule could also exploit and discriminate against its subjects, it was not evident in his writing at the time. He was even mildly critical of Britons who failed to appreciate "the creative genius and the constructive courage that made the Empire possible."[23]

After his first six months in England, Matt began to write more about politics and social trends. He sent articles to the *Winnipeg Free Press* and the *Calgary Albertan* as well as the *Lethbridge Herald*. A greater polish and maturity in his writing was rewarded with more frequent bylines. He managed to get accredited to the House of Commons where listening to David Lloyd George and Winston Churchill for the first time "sends thrills up and down the spine."[24]

A column about prominent younger MPs hinted at his approach to journalism in later years. It was elegantly written but highly opinionated. James Maxton, the leader of a small group of radical socialists, was described as "too whimsical and careless and good-natured to make full use of the vast political opportunities which lie to his hand." The Conservative Edward Marjoribanks is "tall and commanding in appearance [as] he sweeps through the House of Commons as though it were created expressly to do him homage." Another Conservative, Major Walter Elliott, fought in World War One: "And now he seems to sleep as he lounges in the gloomy atmosphere of the House to hear the age-old soporific shibboleths being bandied to and fro by the men who muddled the war and wasted the peace." And on Megan Lloyd George: "We watch Miss Lloyd George carefully, not because she is the daughter of her father, but because she is almost the only young Liberal with any claim to intelligence and modernity."[25]

Matt also wrote a dozen articles about European politics. Several included judgments he would later regret, such as his backing for an economic union between Germany and Austria that Adolph Hitler would achieve eight years later. There were also farsighted glimpses of the future, such as support for the idea of a United States of Europe, "the union that must come if Europe is to be saved from herself."[26]

However, it was in social comment that Matt's weekly columns were at their best. By his second year in London, he was less in awe of the British way of life and more inclined to criticize the country's rigid class system. One article confessed that he had fallen into the British habit of judging people on the social scale as soon as they opened their mouths. "From the cockney of Bethnal Green to the titillating sounds of the Mayfair plutocracy . . . accent is the difference in England."[27] Unlike Canadians, he noted, the British feel quite comfortable pigeonholing people by accent. "Even for my ear, there are at least a dozen inflections of the London voice alone. You get so you can tell, for example, whether a voice is lower middle, a little better than lower middle, middle, or upper class with two or three degrees of the latter."[28]

A *Herald* essay entitled "Peculiarly Un-British" was prompted by a report that a magistrate, condemning a foreign resident for robbery with assault, had opined: "This is a peculiarly un-British crime." Matt noted four other occasions when magistrates, judges, or the press had used the words "peculiarly un-British" to describe a crime or misdemeanour. With mock amazement, he took aim at British hypocrisy:

> *Since crimes are occasionally committed, faults occasionally indulged in by the English, I must take it for granted, apparently, that all such unworthy proclivities are borrowed from less fortunate and less enlightened peoples.*
>
> *The fact is, of course, that anything this people dislikes it calls "peculiarly un-British." It is a label applied by the great and powerful middle class bourgeoisie to everything, in crime, in conduct, in ethics or in social convention that does not emanate from British conservation of action and tradition. . . .*
>
> *No one loves and admires the British more than I do. And perhaps you may say that for me thus to belabor them even as I partake of their hospitality is peculiarly un-British! They are a people, to borrow a phrase applied to the French by a German writer . . . a people* "magnifique et insupportable."[29]

Matt was also exasperated by British ignorance about Canada and condescension toward its people. He resented being called a colonial, even when the term was used by those who meant no disrespect. On several occasions, asked if Canada would like to move toward self-government, he would politely explain that the BNA Act had largely achieved that. His time in Britain confirmed his pride in being Canadian but prompted some critical thoughts about Canada's identity. Canadians were described as energetic and enterprising – qualities, Matt said, that "will take us far in the world's race for wealth but will never build us the laborious edifice of a soul – and we still have our soul to build."[30] A touch of snobbery, of the kind that surfaced later in his life, crept into some of his writing. One article deplored the "low-brow" interests of the younger generation in North America: "Talk about sports models and jazz tunes, but don't, for your life, mention Ibsen or Strindberg or Bergson."[31]

In the summer of 1930, after winning a one-year extension of his IODE scholarship, Matt decided to abandon his journalism course at King's and enrol in the London School of Economics (LSE). It was already the Age of Laski at the LSE, when the school's reputation was increasingly tied to a small, bespectacled, and brilliant professor named Harold Laski. For more than twenty years, Laski championed a form of libertarian socialism that combined public ownership with maximum individual freedoms. Seemingly contradictory at times, Laski argued that state power should be limited but sufficient to guarantee equality of opportunity and everyone's right to work, education, leisure, and health – none of which, he claimed, could be secured in a capitalist system. Laski's lectures on the history of political ideas were the hottest ticket at the school. His wit and passion made even the driest subjects vivid and relevant. As the sociologist Ralph Miliband wrote, "His lectures taught much more than political science. They taught a faith that ideas mattered, that knowledge was important and its pursuit exciting."[32]

Matt was as spellbound by Laski as any of the thousands of students (including future presidents and prime ministers such as Pierre Trudeau) who later attended the LSE. At twenty-six, Matt was already leaning toward socialism, motivated in part by his childhood poverty and bitterness over his father's experience as a child labourer in Lancashire. Laski's teachings gave his emotional leanings a reasoned framework. Laski believed that only systemic reform could level inequality, not revolutionary violence or Soviet-style communism.[33] Matt came to share Laski's skepticism about free enterprise and its potential to spread wealth beyond the privileged classes. For him, Laski became something of an idol and socialism an unshakable lifelong commitment. As Jean said much later, "Laski simply changed Matt's thinking."[34]

Despite being separated by an ocean, Jean remained central to Matt's life. Every week throughout his two years in London, he would write at least three long letters to her. He said he thought of her constantly as if she was the music in the background of all his activities. There were outpourings of love, many of them cloying or insipid to an outside reader but no doubt deeply meaningful to the couple involved. Matt revelled in memories of their sexual encounters but was rarely more explicit than to say, "I can remember you gently, ever so gently, suddenly yielding. . ."[35] As she had in Alberta, Jean continued to be the mother confessor for Matt's anxieties and shortcomings. He told her of his occasional bouts of heavy drinking and his frustration at being unable to fulfil an ambition to write good poetry. The verses he sent her often lurched into clumsy lines that rarely scanned.

Matt's desire to write poetry remained a curious obsession throughout his life. In one of his bleaker moods in London, he wrote that "mostly likely I shall go my way to the grave with my songs unsung, and I shall have written only vain nothings and journalese, pandering soullessly to the gods of the market-place."[36]

His letters to Jean also provided clues to his relations with other women. He wrote that he was frequently torn between hedonism (*"le vin est versé; il faut le boire!"*)[37] and a sterner philosophy of striving to improve himself and society. Before his departure for England, Matt and Jean had agreed that they should both be free to date others during their long separation.[38] Occasionally wearing plus fours, and with his blond hair fashionably parted in the middle, Matt appears to have been an attractive figure to his women classmates. He was remarkably frank in telling Jean about his feelings toward many of them. Among his girlfriends was Mara, an aspiring novelist who "has the most colossal bosom I ever saw, and a perpetual grin";[39] Diana Marsden, "a refined and charming girl" from a wealthy family "who introduces me to many interesting people";[40] and Margaret, an actress with whom he "drank a little and danced a little" and felt "the first sharp stirring of longings which my peculiar morality bids me suppress."[41] There are suggestions that his relations may have gone beyond friendship with Louise "Lulu" Samuel, an attractive student with big sparkling eyes and a husky Tallulah Bankhead voice. There was also an evening "carousing, drinking and dancing" with Simone St. Cyr, after which Matt wrote cryptically: "Life became irresistible, and I prefer to leave the subject there."[42]

In August 1930, Matt crossed the Channel to Zeebrugge in Belgium to begin a poor man's version of the Grand Tour of Europe. Despite being in his habitual state of near bankruptcy, he figured he wouldn't need more than five pounds for two weeks if he stayed in youth hostels and travelled third class. Accompanied by John Corner, a rowing friend from King's, Matt went first to the battlefields of Flanders. He arrived at Ypres in time for the nightly memorial ceremony. Buglers emerged at eight p.m. to sound the Last Post at the Menin Gate, the huge monument looking down the blood-washed Menin Road. Along that road tens of thousands of Canadians lost their lives in battles that Matt had followed avidly as a boy: Hooge, Sanctuary Wood, St. Julien, Hill 61, Hellfire Corner. It was here in the Ypres Salient that Canadians held the line after French troops retreated.

A letter home to Pincher Creek reflected both revulsion against the scale of the sacrifice and a fierce pride in Canadian achievement. "After the last war," he wrote, "one should probably be ashamed of patriotism, but these Belgians still speak of the Canadians with reverence."[43] A day later, in driving rain, Matt sloshed through the mud along the ridge at Passchendaele, where his uncle Seth had been killed. He then went to the Commonwealth war cemetery, where "the white marble headstones stretch away and away it seems, forever."[44] He found what he was looking for – Row A, Plot 11, Grave 20. He scattered poppies there beside Seth's grave.[45]

From Flanders Matt backpacked to the Rhine Valley – to the country that would puzzle and obsess him for more than two decades. Germany was then at a turning point. The liberal Weimar Republic was beginning to founder, its legitimacy challenged by both the Nazis and the Communists. Millions were unemployed. In elections less than three weeks after Matt's arrival, the Nazis surprised the world by becoming the second-largest party in the Reichstag.

At first, Matt and his friend John Corner were largely oblivious to the tensions. They stayed in a youth hostel beside the ruins of Schloss Reinfels, the second-oldest castle on the Rhine. The hostel was crowded with Wandervogel, members of the popular German youth movement that the Hitler Youth absorbed three years later. For four days, Matt ate, drank beer, and hiked with the young Germans in the valleys above the Rhine. As they marched they sang folk and patriotic songs such as "Die Wacht am Rhein" ("The Watch on the Rhine") with its haunting refrain "The Rhine, the Rhine, the German Rhine," and its call to avenge Germany's enemies.[46] Matt saw little that was alarming in the Wandervogel. He found them idealistic, tinged with melancholy, and "resolved to create a new Heaven and a new Earth" from the humiliating aftermath of World War One.[47] He understood their anger over the 1919 Versailles Treaty that had stripped Germany of territory and imposed crippling reparations. "Who can blame the German people," he wrote, "for hating a 'peace' treaty which viciously saddled one people with the disgrace and punishment for a war which was the fault of all people?"[48] He had no idea where that hatred might lead until a few weeks later when the Nazi party made dramatic gains in the Reichstag election in September. Back in London, he wrote that "a fateful sense of brooding, like the sultry stillness before a storm, hangs over Germany . . . and I think it is fraught with significance for the nation's future and for Europe's."[49]

Matt's acute sense of history shadowed him as he travelled on to Alsace-Lorraine, the border region fought over by France and Germany for centuries. The French press at the time gave lurid headlines to a rally of twenty thousand German war veterans in Munich. Addressing the rally, Crown Prince Rupprecht pointed his sword toward France and declared,

"Our enemy lies there." Matt noted that there was a *café de la revanche* in some French towns after Alsace-Lorraine was occupied by the Germans in 1871. Now, he predicted, it would be Germany's turn to try to recover the two provinces. "Anyone who thinks that Germany does not want revenge is sadly mistaken. Poor France, poor Germany!"[50] However, European politics faded from his mind when he began a walking tour in the Swiss Alps. He revelled in being in the mountains again and climbed part way up the Jungfrau.

The tour ended in Paris, where Matt's love affair with France began. A visit to Notre Dame made his childhood reading of Victor Hugo come alive. A visit to Versailles and a stroll through the Place de la Concorde brought back the excitement of reading about the Scarlet Pimpernel and, later, Carlyle's epic *The French Revolution*. He found the Winged Victory in the Louvre to be "splendid and irresistible" and gazed in wonder at "the world-weary eyes of the Mona Lisa."[51] He found the outdoor cafés so much pleasanter than grimy London pubs and spent hours watching smart and pretty women pass by – more of them, he wrote Jean, than he'd ever seen before. He was pleased that his French was good enough to allow him to have real conversations and marvelled at the charm of the French language. What other language, he asked himself, would call a brassiere a *"soutien-gorge,"* literally a bosom-support? After only a few days in Paris, Matt embraced some of the clichés about the French: their "extraordinary Gallic vitality," their frankness about sex, and their civilized appreciation of good food.[52] He returned to London, broke, but full of ideas for his newspaper columns.

His last months in London were consumed by LSE studies, freelancing, and a busy social life. He was beginning to find the long separation from Jean unbearable and, despite the sophisticated pleasures of Europe, to feel nostalgic for Pincher Creek. Ever the sentimentalist, he wrote his younger brother, Seth, about childhood pursuits that they shared. "I'd like to go sleigh-riding on Kettle's Hill, or skating at the Beaver Dam; or I'd like to be sitting with my feet dangling out of the back of Dad's rig as it rattled up Main Street with only a few more parcels to deliver before going home to supper and Mother, and the good fire, and books, and dreams."[53]

Again, it was his mentor, Senator Buchanan, who helped propel Matt's career forward. Buchanan sent a sheaf of Matt's best columns to his old friend Harry Hindmarsh, managing editor of the *Toronto Daily Star.* Hindmarsh was impressed; a job would be waiting for Matt upon his return to Canada.

4

A STAR RISING

"The Star *promoted Halton like mad."*

            – GERALD ANGLIN, *Star* reporter

THE TORONTO WHERE MATT BEGAN WORK IN SEPTEMBER 1931 was uninspiring in contrast to cosmopolitan London. The city, overwhelmingly white and Protestant, was smug, self-righteous, and puritanical. Its biggest public event was the annual parade of the Orange Lodge, when as many as 150,000 people would line University Avenue to watch a costumed King Billy celebrate William of Orange's defeat of the Catholics in 1690. Many jobs at City Hall were reserved for members of the Orange Lodge. Toronto was a city in which men could still be arrested and charged with indecent exposure if they removed the tops of their bathing suits on city beaches. In some respects, "Toronto the Good" was also Toronto the Bigoted. Dance halls and many social clubs were closed to Jews, and hotels unashamedly advertised for "gentiles only." Signs were posted at several popular beaches saying "No Jews, Niggers, or Dogs." All this was set against a backdrop of deepening economic and social crisis. In 1931 30 per cent of Toronto's workforce was on the dole. Soup kitchens and breadlines were proliferating. The Great Depression was getting worse.[1]

Matt faced an unnerving set of personal challenges when he first entered the *Toronto Daily Star*'s newsroom at 80 King Street West. At that time the *Star* published seven or eight editions of the paper each day,[2] putting the newsroom under almost constant deadline pressure from noon to six p.m. "It was bedlam," said Gwyn "Jocko" Thomas, a copy boy who often handled Matt's reports and later became a legendary *Star* police reporter.[3] Desk editors shouted at reporters, competing with reporters yelling "Boy!" to summon one of twenty or so copy boys to deliver the newest paragraphs of their stories to the desk. It all seemed like a parody of a Hollywood B-movie about the news business. Many reporters kept their fedoras on as they typed; almost everyone smoked cheap cigars, and some hid a mickey of rye in their jackets.

The paper's owners were teetotalers and drinking on the premises was a firing offence. But even some desk editors kept bottles of whisky in their corridor lockers, and one was often seen taking a surreptitious swig from a metal cigar tube tucked into his inside pocket. Wilf Sanders, a fellow reporter of Matt's, said he could not remember a period when there was so much heavy drinking. "We used to have to prop up some of the guys when they came in drunk for work. We'd sit on either side of the drunk reporter and prop him up so he wouldn't fall forward and hit his face on the desk."[4] Women reporters, usually relegated to weddings and social events, worked in a separate room to protect them from blue language and other improprieties in the newsroom.

At first Matt seemed out of place. He never wore a fedora and was often dressed in a tweed suit that made him look like an Oxford undergrad. He was too reserved to shout "Boy!" to the copy handlers, preferring instead to carry his stories to the editors' desk himself.[5] The new man aroused some suspicion among other reporters, few of whom had been to university, and some who had not even finished high school. Gordon Sinclair, already emerging as a star at the newspaper, recalled that Matt was a curiosity for a while. "He seemed to be a little effeminate, a little gentle. He wasn't like the other guys at the time."[6] Sinclair said he led the ribbing of Matt for being so proud of coming from a place called Pincher Creek. The newcomer was also quickly tagged as "parlour pink" – someone flirting with socialism. Not that Matt was an outcast. He joined his colleagues after work at the Piccadilly or Prince George, nearby beer parlours, or at drunken poker games on weekends.

Matt's debut as a *Star* journalist was notable for its lack of promise. As a cub reporter with no contacts or knowledge of the city, he was given the most tedious assignments: taking down obituaries and doing the "scalps" – rewriting stories from rival newspapers that the *Star* had missed. On the few events he covered at the courthouse and City Hall, his reporting was described by Sinclair as slow and "quite inept."[7]

It was particularly galling for Matt – still aggressively opposed to organized religion – to also be assigned Sunday sermons and church meetings that were extensively covered by the *Star* in the thirties. Obviously dejected, Matt wrote to Jean, who was now teaching in Alberta: "I am just learning how little I know about the newspaper game. I thought because I could write a little I could step into a paper like the *Star* and get a highly paid writing job right away. . . . I was foolish. One has to go through the mill first, learn the ins and outs and tricks of the trade. I am sure I am not exaggerating a single little bit when I say I can write better than the highly paid *Star* men. But they know the business and I'm only learning it – as I now realize. So I'll have to resign myself to being content on the salary at which I am being started, which is, I regret to say, only thirty dollars a week. . . . I simply couldn't bear to say that I won't be able to marry you next summer, my dear one. But I can't marry you on less than fifty a week – and I just may not be getting that much by summer."[8]

Yet Matt soon discovered the advantages of working for the largest and most profitable newspaper in Canada. The two men most responsible for the *Star*'s success were the publisher, Joseph E. Atkinson, and managing editor, Harry C. Hindmarsh. First-rate reporters in their younger days, they were now dictatorial and at times eccentric managers. Both changed the face of the newspaper business in Canada, mostly for the better. And both were of immeasurable help in pushing Matt forward.

Joe Atkinson had taken over the *Star* in 1899 when it was a failing enterprise with fewer readers than any of its five Toronto competitors. He was known to the staff as "The Chief," although some preferred to call him "Holy Joe" because of his zealous Methodism. His formula for success seemed contradictory: to practise high-minded journalism while pandering to popular demand for crime and human-interest stories. On the one hand, the *Star* provided the most serious newspaper coverage of social issues in Canada and sent more correspondents abroad and carried more foreign news than any of its competitors. On the other side of the ledger, it gave prominence to tabloid-style stories about cannibals and man-eating tigers. A typical headline read: "Ghoulish Unprintable Practices Witnessed by Wandering Reporter."[9]

Atkinson himself was a bundle of contradictions. As the *Star*'s profits and his own fortune soared, he would prowl the corridors switching off lights to save electricity. He notoriously demanded that newsmen turn in the stubs of their used pencils before they could get new ones. He ordered his editorial writers to champion labour rights but successfully fought to keep unions out of his own paper.

In one important respect the *Star* was the perfect fit for Matt. It was by far the most left-leaning major newspaper in the country. Atkinson's social and political views may not have affected his business practices but they had a profound and lasting impact on the paper's editorial policy. The so-called Atkinson Principles became (and remain) the *Star*'s guiding philosophy. They stressed the need for economic and social justice, community engagement, protection of civil liberties, and a strong role for government. From the 1920s on, the *Star* was a crusading voice for social reform. Atkinson pushed his writers to promote old-age pensions, unemployment insurance, and a national health care plan. New social programs would be paid for by higher taxes on the wealthy. Public ownership of power, phone, and other utilities would be encouraged. Revolutions in Latin America would be supported. The Chief even confided once to a friend, "I'm a bit of a socialist, you know."[10] He was already regarded as a dangerous leftist by many in the business community. On Bay Street and among rival Tory newspapers, the *Star* was labelled "The King Street Pravda" and "The Red Star."[11] In fact, while comparatively open-minded about the Soviet Union, Atkinson was never to the left of the CCF (Co-operative Commonwealth Federation), the fledgling socialist party whose reform proposals he often supported. But as an advisor at various times to both prime ministers Laurier and Mackenzie King, he always fell into line behind the Liberals at election time.

If Atkinson was the inspiration for the *Star*'s success, Harry Comfort Hindmarsh was his indispensable lieutenant. A burly six-footer with close-cropped hair, Hindmarsh combined a ruthless managerial style with shrewd instincts for pulling in readers. Nothing in the newsroom was more feared than a summons to his office, where he would usually be chomping on a cigar or brandishing, almost like a weapon, a twelve-inch-long pen. As managing editor from 1928 on, Hindmarsh authorized reporters to spend freely to get a good story but was quick to fire those who failed to deliver. With dozens sacked in an average year, the standing joke in the newsroom was that "the *Star* always has three staffs: one arriving, one working, and one being let out."[12] Many who weren't fired simply left of their own accord, unwilling to face Hindmarsh's austere and bullying presence. Such was the case with Ernest Hemingway, who worked for the *Star* in the early twenties. He memorably compared life with Hindmarsh to "working in the Prussian army under a bad general."[13]

For all his faults "HCH," as he was known, was widely respected. Pierre Berton wrote that Hindmarsh "was considered the greatest newspaper-man in Canada by almost everybody who worked for him, and hosts of other journalist who didn't."[14] His many innovations at the *Star* helped it overtake the Tory, Empire-boosting *Toronto Evening Telegram* and to leave the circulation of the *Globe* and the *Mail and Empire* far behind. Among other innovations, Hindmarsh pioneered the use of large photos on the front page, imported American comic strips for the first time in Canada, and brightened and revamped the *Star Weekly*, a syndicated weekend supplement that was read at its peak by almost a million Canadians.

But it was Hindmarsh's fiercely competitive quest for "scoops" that gave the *Star* its edge in the newspaper wars of the period. Joe Atkinson had given Hindmarsh and the newsroom four golden rules for news-gathering: "Get it first; sew it up so the opposition cannot get it; leave no crumbs uncollected; play it big."[15] The rules were implemented by Hindmarsh with near-manic intensity. Reporters were turned loose in large numbers on big stories and given lavish resources and expense accounts to beat the competition. Planes, trains, boats were chartered to track down a big crime or disaster story and publish it first. All angles were covered, and all means – fair or foul – were used to prevent the opposition from matching the *Star*.

The Atkinson-Hindmarsh tactics were dramatically displayed in one of the greatest scoops in North American newspaper history. In April 1928, the German airplane *Bremen* crash-landed on Greenly Island between Quebec and Labrador. It was the first east-west flight over the Atlantic since Lindbergh's historic flight in the other direction. With North American newspapers vying to provide blanket coverage of the event, the Hearst chain and the *New York Times* had purchased rights to the first photographs and the pilots' story. Or so they thought. Shortly after the crash was announced, the *Star* arranged to pay $7,000 to Duke Schiller, a top bush pilot, to fly to the crash site to get photos and an exclusive report on the survivors. When Schiller flew back to Murray Bay on the north shore of the St. Lawrence with one of the surviving pilots, the *Star's* Fred Griffin and his team were able to secure the first interview about the crash. They also paid the local telegraph operator to tie up the wire by filing an entire issue of the *New Republic* magazine to the *Star*. Dozens of furious competitors were thus prevented for hours from filing any remaining crumbs of the story. Meanwhile, the *Star* chartered an aircraft to fly the photographs of the downed *Bremen* to Montreal. When bad weather forced it to land in Quebec City, the *Star* promptly chartered a special train to rush the photos to Montreal where the paper had a taxi ready to bring them to Toronto. Thus did the *Star* trounce all North American newspapers on a story of compelling interest.[16]

The late twenties and the thirties were the razzle-dazzle era of *Toronto Star* journalism. Jocko Thomas, moving from copy boy to esteemed reporter, was in the thick of it. He recalled that, despite the frequent scoops, despite the upward spiralling circulation and ad revenue, there was a darker side to the paper's success. "If you had to lie, cheat, or steal to get the story," he said only half-jokingly, "you lied, cheated, and stole."[17]

Matt learned all aspects of the craft, the good and bad, by watching and sometimes working with the paper's top reporters. His apprenticeship included an assignment to help Gordon Sinclair cover a prison riot that rocked Kingston Penitentiary in October 1932. The circumstances surrounding the riot were uncertain. More than a year earlier, Prime Minister R.B. Bennett had ordered the arrest of Tim Buck, the leader of the

Canadian Communist Party, and seven others. They were imprisoned in Kingston under the controversial Section 98 of the Criminal Code, which allowed police to jail any Canadian merely for attending a rally or reading a pamphlet of an organization considered subversive. It was widely suspected that the riot was deliberately provoked by the authorities to stage what followed: the shooting and wounding by guards of an apparently defenceless Tim Buck in his cell.[18]

Four *Star* men were already staking out the prison when Sinclair and Matt arrived. Sinclair confided that he had a forged prison pass and would try to use it on the pretence of needing to see the warden. If successful, he said, Matt should ensure huge play for the story by sending three messages to the desk in Toronto at intervals of about twenty minutes: "Think Sinclair got behind lines," "Sinclair definitely behind lines!" and finally "Sinclair inside!" Sinclair chose a moment when the guards were changing to show his pass and brazenly succeeded in getting escorted to the warden's office. Matt's alerts reached the desk, "and, oh boy," said Sinclair years later, "did it [the story] ever get a helluva play when I sent it in."[19]

Matt's breakthrough at the *Star* was not the result of sensational reporting but because of his love of language and vivid imagination. Six months after he joined the paper, the desk assigned him to a series promoting the spring fashion show at the city's Sunnyside boardwalk. The *Star* had no ethical qualms about such promotions, which usually turned into a few forgettable paragraphs. Instead, Matt wrote a series of light, whimsical essays punctuated with both real interviews and imaginary conversations. Hindmarsh was impressed and assigned him to several feature interviews with Toronto bachelors. Roy Greenaway had tried writing the first one – an interview with Tommy Church, an MP and former mayor of Toronto. Greenaway's article was rejected and, in the harsh editorial habit of the *Star*, turned over to another writer – in this case, Matt.[20] His version was superficial but amusing, and the bosses liked it. The next day, Hindmarsh told him his salary had been raised by ten dollars a week.[21]

Almost as important was his first byline in a paper notoriously stingy about giving credit to any but its big-name performers. Matt was assigned to interview the Viscountess Violette de Sibour, daughter of Gordon

Selfridge, the millionaire London store owner. De Sibour was a glamorous aviator who had flown around the world with her husband in a tiny Gipsy Moth plane and was nearly shot down in China. After the interview, Matt returned to the *Star* with only a half-hour to write the story and the additional pressure of having Hindmarsh peer over his shoulder to read the first page.[22] The article was framed in the fanciful and personalized style that was a hallmark of his early writing. Questions, sometimes self-deprecatory and often tongue in cheek, were included: "'It must be pretty horrible to be interviewed everywhere you go, and asked foolish questions, isn't it, m'lady?' And then came the supreme moment of a lifetime. . . . 'Oh, I don't know,' said Violette, Lady de Sibour, 'right now I think it is lovely.'"[23] A week later, Hindmarsh summoned Matt to his office to say the *Star* wanted more of his humorous interviews. He told Matt to spend a week or two in New York digging for feature stories and gave him a list of possible ideas and a generous advance for his expenses.[24]

"So here I am, and I can't believe it yet!" Matt wrote breathlessly to Jean after settling into the then-luxurious Hotel Astor near Times Square. From his window he gazed out at this "mad and amazing colossus of serried and castellated buildings hurling themselves at the sky."[25] His nine days in New York were a time of prodigious work and prodigious drinking. The International News Service (INS), a wire agency to which the *Star* belonged, provided Matt with a temporary office and secretary. At lunch he would join other INS reporters at one of the hundreds of speakeasies that illegally sold alcohol in defiance of Prohibition. "We drink two or three strong cocktails . . . starting with a Scotch and soda. With lunch we drink a bottle of wine. After we sit for an hour drinking more Scotch and cognacs, and a *demi-tasse* . . . and that is their regular schedule!"[26] In the evening there would be more drinking and several parties and visits to cabarets.

Drinking and socializing did not prevent Matt from sending a story to the *Star* nearly every day he was in New York. Several required extensive research. The paper, prompted by Ottawa's decision to consider establishing a state-subsidized broadcasting system, wanted an analysis of American radio. Matt interviewed William Paley and Milton Aylesworth, presidents respectively of CBS and NBC, who were predictably in favour of commercial radio and opposed to a government-financed broadcasting network. Others were quoted as favouring a commercial-free channel that would offer more than *Amos 'n' Andy*–style entertainment. Matt wrote that he had no brief for either option but correctly predicted that "Canada is determined to seize some measure of control over the infant colossus of radio."[27]

Two other stories won him the kind of compliments that most reporters crave. Matt decided to write a feature on New York harbour, then bustling with ocean liners in the era before airline flight. The passenger list of one incoming ship included the name Carla Jenssen, a baroness and former spy whom he remembered reading about in London as a "British Mata Hari." Matt talked to her as she emerged from customs, and the two apparently established an immediate rapport. The baroness agreed to give him a long interview in which she undoubtedly inflated the importance of her achievements as a spy. "Here is a woman," Matt wrote, "only 28 years old now, remarkably beautiful, cultured, intelligent to a degree that is said to have fooled some of Britain's cleverest enemies, who says that in ten years she has uncovered, single-handed, a sensational plot to foment a native uprising in Africa; rouged her lips with dope for the undoing of men who made the fatal blunder of being enemies of England and lovers of Carla Jenssen at one and the same time; . . . run the gauntlet of life and death in the heart of Russia; danced her way into the hearts – and secret papers – of men in high places. . . ."[28] It was a perfect story for the *Star* – and it was Matt's first scoop. The New York newspapers picked up the story twenty-four hours later and splashed it on their front pages. Matt wrote to Jean that he was captivated by the baroness, who later invited him to dine and dance with her at the fashionable Roosevelt Grill.[29]

Another interview from New York was less noticed but appreciated for its fine writing. Hindmarsh had suggested that Matt interview Alice Liddell Hargreaves who, as a ten-year-old girl, was the inspiration for Lewis Carroll's brilliant fantasy *Alice in Wonderland*. Hargreaves was visiting New York to mark the centenary of the birth of Charles Dodgson, who wrote *Alice* under the pseudonym Lewis Carroll. Dodgson had been rowing the real Alice and her two sisters on the Thames one languorous summer day when Alice asked him to tell "a story with nonsense in it."[30] That was when he told the girls about Alice falling down a well and about the white rabbit with the magic golden key – the outline of the story that would captivate generations. For Matt, interviewing Alice Hargreaves was a dream assignment. As a child, he had delighted in the fantastic world of Carroll's weird creatures and their absurd conversations, and as an adult he continued to reread both *Alice* and its sequel, *Through the Looking-Glass*. By coincidence, it was Hargreaves's eightieth birthday when Matt visited her in her Manhattan hotel. His poignant account of the meeting mixed her quotes with lines from Lewis Carroll and some of his own invention.

New York, May 4 – "Do they build their buildings here from the inside or from the outside?" asked Alice in Wonderland of the Star, as we stood at a window in the tower of the Waldorf-Astoria gazing across the night at the magnificent tumult which is New York. . . .

This Alice wasn't the wide-eyed youngster, dressed in short frock and pinafore, with straight hair hanging over her shoulder and pink flamingo in her arms. It was Alice grown up – old but undaunted as she gazed out across this newer wonderland of New York. . . .

Alice was a little weary. "Do you know," she said, "this is the 39th floor of the hotel. I have never been this high before. It reminds me of when I fell down a rabbit hole under the hedge 70 years ago."

The excitement of the mad hatters' world of New York had been a little too much for this old lady with the dark eyes and soft skin and polka-dotted dress, and with her two canes. All day she had been too tired to see us and only in the cool of the evening were we invited to come up. . . .

"Such tall buildings!" exclaimed Alice in Wonderland. "Do they grow overnight?" "No, not these days," said the dodo.

"Then what's the point in building them?" demanded Alice. "That's just the point," burst in the mad hatter. . . .

The old lady continued to recall passages from the most delightful of all mad books. Sometimes she actually spoke as if she believed she were Alice.

"What is your favorite passage in the book?" the Star asked. And she answered: "'Will you walk a little faster, said a whiting to a snail, there's a porpoise close behind me and he's treading on my tail.' What was it the Cheshire cat said? – 'What's the porpoise of all this?' 'Don't you mean purpose?' asked Alice. 'No,' said the mock turtle crossly. 'If I had meant purpose I would have said purpose.'"

And the Star went on with: "'But the snail replied, "too far, too far," and gave a look askance, said he thanked the whiting kindly, but he would not join the dance.'"

The old lady smiled, and sat down. "Yes," she said, "the dance is nearly over."[31]

What Matt didn't know at the time was that within three and a half months his affection for *Alice in Wonderland* would help catapult him into the top ranks of Canadian journalists.

The summer of 1932 was a time of anticipation and excitement: the Empire was coming to Ottawa. In London the new Conservative-dominated coalition government had accepted Prime Minister R.B. Bennett's invitation to host an Imperial Economic Conference. It would be the greatest imperial assembly Canada had ever seen – the leaders of the mother country and her dominions and colonies meeting for a month in the capital. Their purpose was to pull the Empire out of the Great Depression. Economic turmoil had resulted from a free fall in global trade, partly caused by a worldwide rush to erect tariff walls. A financial meltdown had forced Britain and other countries to abandon the gold standard that linked currencies to gold supplies. Unemployment was rampant. The Imperial Conference would be aptly described as "a gathering of anxious and suffering nations, desperately intent upon a task of economic salvage."[32]

The "salvage" variously proposed by Bennett and the new British government was called "Imperial Preference" and would mean reversing the long-standing policy of international free trade. Under the new plan, tariffs would rise on imports from the rest of the world and fall on imports from within the Empire. The *Star,* then strongly in favour of free trade, waged a vigorous editorial campaign against Imperial Preference, which it said would put Canada's trade relationship with the United States at risk. The paper's stand created a quandary for Matt, who was still inclined to cheer any move strengthening imperial ties. Hindmarsh asked him to join the *Star's* six-person team assigned to cover the economic summit. But there was one condition. The paper expected him to reflect its hope that Imperial Preference could be quashed. "This bothers me," he wrote to a friend. "I am having a terrible struggle whether I'll take that assignment."[33] He did take it – with unforeseen consequences.

The Imperial Economic Conference opened in mid-July with more than a thousand officials in town. They were soon joined by British Conservative leader Stanley Baldwin, Chancellor of the Exchequer Neville Chamberlain, and a 130-strong delegation from London. Ottawa swarmed with lobbyists from all parts of the Empire. Indian women in saris sipped tea alongside wing-collared statesmen on the terrace of the Chateau Laurier. Angry delegations of farmers and the unemployed arrived by train and bus. The governor general, Lord Bessborough, presided over inaugural ceremonies on Parliament Hill that began with a blare of trumpets and a hearty singing of "God Save the King." For the next month there were state dinners at Rideau Hall, garden parties, and informal dances at the Royal Ottawa Golf Club.[34] There was enough pageantry around the event, and enough public interest, to sustain front-page coverage in dominion newspapers for a few days.

Within forty-eight hours, however, a news drought set in. The negotiating sessions were held in secrecy. Leaders were unavailable for comment. Briefing sessions were bland and boring. Everyone knew the broad lines of the debate at the conference: Canada and other dominions wanted to have free access to the British market for their food and resource exports but insisted on maintaining limited tariffs on British manufactured imports to protect their own industries. The few details that did surface – about tariff schedules, commodity prices, and bimetallism (the use of a monetary standard consisting of both gold and silver) – tended to lull reporters, let alone their readers, into a deep sleep.

Matt was no exception. On the fourth day of the conference, increasingly frustrated, he sat down at his typewriter and wrote two parodies casting the sessions as *Alice in Wonderland* stories. He described leading figures at the meeting engaged in absurd conversations with the Mad Hatter, the White Queen, the Dodo, and others in Lewis Carroll's famous cast of characters. Occasionally, R.B. Bennett appeared as the Mock Turtle, hopelessly unable to explain conference topics like the re-monetization of silver or the need to raise commodity prices. Bennett's embrace of high tariff barriers against foreign imports was scorned: "'The Mock Turtle thinks he owns this country, and can shut the gates at will.'" So too was Bennett's haggling with the British over the size of tariffs within the Empire:

> *"Friends, Romans, countrymen and Dodos," translated the White Queen, "we have made a very generous offer today. First we raised the tariff on lollypops 20 per cent. We now offer to lower the tariff ten per cent, providing they will give us 20 per cent more for our sugar plums."*
>
> *"Yes," cried all the Dodos. "It is a very generous offer. Three cheers for the Mock Turtle."*
>
> *"I don't think it's a generous offer at all," said Alice, indignantly running over to the Mad Hatter. "Do you think it's a generous offer?"*
>
> *"Hush," said the Mad Hatter. "They are now discussing Humbugs. Let's go closer."*[35]

Matt's first story was telegraphed to the *Star*'s editorial desk on the same day he wrote it. There are many accounts of what happened next. The most common version is that the text was picked up by Bill Drylie, the news editor, who dismissed it as pretentious fluff. Drylie then "spiked" the story, which, in newspaper parlance, meant that it would probably be published only if last-minute filler was required. The next morning, Hindmarsh dropped by the news desk, as he often did, and asked if there was anything new from Ottawa. "No," Drylie was quoted as replying, "just this tripe from one of our boys."[36]

Hindmarsh then lifted Matt's copy off the spike and began reading it. According to several accounts, he chuckled as he read it, before turning to

Drylie and saying, "Print it. Front page. Byline."[37] A few hours later, the Chief himself, Joe Atkinson, read the story in the first edition. He pronounced it "delightful" and ordered an *Alice* parody from Matt on every *Star* front page for the remainder of the conference. Furthermore, that young man Halton was to be given a large pay increase.[38]

Matt was delighted by the recognition but worried by the challenge: how to sustain an *Alice* series over three weeks. Along with his liking for the nonsense literary genre and his ability to see the absurd side of life, he had one invaluable asset. His extraordinarily retentive memory enabled him to quote verbatim almost all the key passages of *Alice in Wonderland* and *Through the Looking-Glass*. Colleagues marvelled that he wrote the series without reference to the two books, "pulling it out of thin air."[39] He could also count on readers relating easily to the *Alice* stories in an era when Lewis Carroll was almost a staple of growing up. What remained to be done was to make the Empire statesmen seem as nonsensical as *Alice's* characters, and to weave in the conference issues. One favourite target for ridicule was the debate over replacing the gold standard:

> *We must re-monetize not only silver, but also copper, and zinc and tin, and – "And frankfurters, and baled hay, and pigs' eyes," squealed the white rabbit from nowhere in particular. Everyone glared in anger; and then the ancient one clenched his argument with the words: "Quadro-metallism! What this empire needs is quadro-metallism – or something." And at the "something" his voice died away and he began to cry.*
>
> *"Quadro-metallism!" exclaimed Alice, "What a strange name! It sounds like a disease."*
>
> *"It is," said the Mad Hatter sardonically. "At least it would be if we were unfortunate enough to catch it. What this empire needs is no metallism at all."*[40]

By week's end, five *Alice* parodies had been published and had stirred up much positive comment. Matt received congratulations from many other reporters, and Hindmarsh wired Matt that his lampooning of the conference was "going over in a big way."[41] The Bennett government, a constant target of the *Star*, could hardly have been pleased. In a letter to Jean, Matt said that one Tory newspaper had accused him of "'making a monkey of the conference,' which is not true, though I have certainly tried to show up its absurdities, especially those of Mr. Bennett . . . and the world economic situation in general." With an eye on marriage – his biggest priority of all – Matt added, "Thank God, I have gone over large with the paper on this conference job, and so I can dare to ask for yet another salary increase to get married on."[42]

The *Alice* series seemed to crystallize his status as the golden boy of the *Star*. Within a month, while on assignment near Montreal, Matt received a telegram from Hindmarsh ordering him back to Toronto. On September 3, when Matt showed up in Hindmarsh's office, the managing editor congratulated him on the *Alice* series and mentioned that he had heard about his planned marriage. Hindmarsh then said that the newspaper was displeased with the work of Henry Somerville, its London correspondent. Atkinson and Hindmarsh had agreed that a more talented writer was needed in London and that Halton would be an ideal choice.[43] In addition to hard news reporting and analysis, they wanted more of Matt's style of colourful and amusing features. He would have carte blanche to travel throughout Europe and supplement the work of Pierre van Paassen, the paper's Paris-based correspondent, who was not on staff.

The offer was wholly unexpected. Not only had Matt won one of the most coveted jobs in the Canadian newspaper business but now, at last, he could afford to marry his fiancée.

Matt's appointment as London correspondent at the age of twenty-eight fed the legend about him that developed at the *Star* in later years. Part of the legend was true. Barely nine months after struggling with obituaries and "scalps," the young man from Pincher Creek had apparently achieved the fastest-ever ascent in Canadian journalism. But the legend was embellished with the invention that Matt was still an undistinguished cub reporter sent to the Imperial Conference to do little more than fetch coffee and deliver copy to the telegraph office – until the *Alice* series rocketed him to fame. In fact, he had already impressed the *Star*'s management with his interviews and New York stories and was assigned to Ottawa in the hope that he could brighten coverage with humorous features. When his London appointment was announced, some colleagues were amazed, others impressed, and still others resentful. "It was the depth of the Depression," said a fellow reporter, "it was a dog-eat-dog time, and you have to realize that only a few got to the top . . . and I think a lot of journalists would have been really jealous of Matt."[44]

The marriage of Jean Campbell and Matthew Halton took place in mid-September 1932. Obsessive as ever about his distaste for organized religion, Matt wrote Jean a few weeks earlier to express his preference for a civil marriage. "I have a terrible fear," he wrote, "that we're going to be married by some priest . . . God of all gods, how it will make me boil over with rage to think of people having to be married whether they want it or not by a ritualistic hocus-pocus." Jean, already adept at soothing Matt's more intemperate feelings, gently persuaded him to accept a simple wedding at Bloor Street United Church. He conceded that this would be "our bow to legality and society."[45]

Matt's parents could not afford the trip from Alberta but Jean's parents attended the service. The *Star*'s social reporter commented on the bride's "frock of peach-colored silk net, over taffeta, frilled gracefully with narrow ruching from neckline to hem."[46] The couple's honeymoon began with a minor disaster in Quebec City's Château Frontenac hotel. A complimentary bottle of gin waiting for them in their room turned out to be bootleg gin of inferior quality that made them very sick. Any inclination to romance vanished. No such problems bothered them in New York, though, where they spent the second week of their honeymoon installed in the luxurious Waldorf-Astoria.[47]

Matt returned to work to another prestige assignment – reporting on the final stretch of the U.S. presidential campaign. There was no suspense about the election. It seemed certain that the Democratic nominee Franklin Delano Roosevelt would win in a landslide with his message of hope and promise of a New Deal to rescue Americans from the Great Depression. FDR's victory over Republican president Herbert Hoover was a historic milestone realigning American politics and setting a new economic and social course for the country. Yet Matt's campaign articles failed to convey the election's huge significance. His lack of knowledge about American politics and failure to venture beyond Boston and New York were probably why the stories he filed never rose above journeyman reporting. Nonetheless, he did manage to get a few minutes in private with both Roosevelt and Hoover in an era when access to presidential candidates was relatively easy. Republican aides would allow only a few minutes with Hoover, who charged that Roosevelt's proposed New Deal reforms would undermine the U.S. Constitution.[48]

Matt met FDR in his townhouse off New York's Park Avenue just before a press briefing. He later regretted what he wrote his parents about his first impression of the Democratic candidate. Roosevelt, he judged, had "none of the depths of character that really make great men, but . . . will get a lot of useful things done because of his personal charm, his undoubted administrative ability, and his power of getting people to work with him."[49] Matt did get FDR to comment on the record on one issue of great importance to Canada – the damagingly high tariffs imposed under Washington's Smoot-Hawley Act. Roosevelt said the act had contributed to "a genuine international calamity."[50]

The U.S. election was his last major assignment before leaving North America. In mid-December, Matt and Jean boarded the *Duchess of York* in Quebec City and set sail for England. Now self-confident and proven, Matt was no longer the insecure and fretful young man who had made the same journey almost three years earlier. The *Star* had given him a large cheque for expenses and a big farewell party, sending him off "feeling I had the world in my pocket."[51] Aboard ship, as it churned away from the snow-draped city, he wrote his parents in Pincher Creek. "Jean and I," he told them, "feel half like lovers on a honeymoon, half like conquerors going out to subdue new realms."[52] It was the last letter he ever wrote as a permanent Canadian resident.

5

RETURN TO EUROPE

"This is the finest country in the world. I say also that it is the most
snobbish, smug and exasperating country in the world."
— MATTHEW HALTON, *Toronto Star*, March 29, 1935

SEVEN YEARS REMAINED OF THE 1930S when Matt returned to
London. He would sometimes call them the Locust Years, using the bibli-
cal story of the plague that ravaged the earth as a metaphor for Europe's
drift into the Second World War. They were years in which Matt defined
himself as a journalist with a mission: to sound the alarm about the rise
of Fascism and the craven response to it by the Western democracies. His
output was prodigious. Almost every weekday for the rest of the decade
he would send the *Star* an article – more than two thousand in all. His
dispatches showed a remarkable versatility. Weighty analysis of political
trends in Europe and investigative reports might be followed the next day
by one of his signature interviews or light-hearted features. He was given
remarkable freedom to write what he wanted and go where he wished.
His stories were almost always bylined, usually on the front page. Editors
in Toronto were ordered not to touch his copy. A university friend who
became one of those editors said that "it's hard to believe now the kind of
special treatment he got from the *Star*. . . . At that paper in those halcyon
years, he could do no wrong."[1]

Returning to London was an easy transition for Matt. From his student
days he was familiar with the city he now described as "still the most

charming in the world." He knew where to go in Whitehall and how to find useful contacts in parliament and government. He renewed relations with his old circle of friends and acquaintances and was happy that they took quickly to Jean. Kathleen Gordon, the friend who lived in his old student residence, said she was "bowled over" by Jean's attractiveness and intelligence.[2] Lady Astor, whom Matt continued to admire with gushing enthusiasm, invited the couple to a party at Cliveden, her country estate. Matt commented that there were many people there, "all famous, some beautiful, many pompous."[3] Soon the Haltons were able to entertain their friends in an apartment they rented in a handsome Victorian building just two blocks from Marble Arch. The rental included a maid who could cook as well as clean.

Within three weeks of his arrival in London, Matt was given a totally unexpected assignment in Moscow. Joseph Atkinson, the *Star*'s publisher, had begun a somewhat quixotic crusade to promote a barter deal pro-posed by the Soviet Union to exchange Canadian cattle for Russian oil. A new Five Year Plan had opened up Russia to foreign trade, and Western countries were moving to exploit a potentially huge market. But not Canada. Prime Minister Bennett was opposed to dealing with "godless Communism" and argued that, in any case, Russia would default on repaying the trade credits required for the proposed deal. Matt's mission in Moscow was to try to prove him wrong. A barrage of dispatches quoted Soviet and Western trade officials saying that Russia had never defaulted on a commercial deal. In a series of interviews, Matt was told that Russia would absolutely guarantee the repayment of Canadian credits. Moreover, Soviet officials promised that the cattle-for-oil deal would pave the way for a much more lucrative trade agreement between the two countries.[4] Reporters in Ottawa asked Bennett about Matt's dispatches. No friend of the *Star* nor of the man who had lampooned him in the *Alice* series, Bennett said he wouldn't comment on Halton's reports other than to say they were "without foundation."[5]

Matt's first impressions of the Soviet Union were tinged with less naïveté and wishful thinking than many other leftists in the West. The misery of the Great Depression inclined some to see communism – with its record of rapid industrialization and apparent full employment in the Soviet Union – as the antidote for an ailing capitalism. At the outset of his two weeks in Moscow, Matt said he had some sympathy for a system that had given Russians a better life than under the tsars. But he also stated that he wasn't there "with the eyes bandaged and the ears stopped up."[6] He quickly noted that some Muscovites were too frightened to talk to him – too frightened of the all-pervasive OGPU, the secret police and forerunner of the KGB. He recognized that Comrade Maria, his interpreter, could be an OGPU agent and that the "typical" family she took him to visit may have been specially chosen to give a bright picture of Soviet life.[7] Matt managed to escape Maria on a number of occasions and visit the so-called communal apartments where as many as six people were jammed into a single room. He commented on the drabness of Soviet life and the often empty shelves in Moscow stores. Later he would cite reports of mass starvation in the Ukraine.[8]

Yet Matt could still describe Russia as "that strange, admirable, baffling country," doomed to fail perhaps but one of the greatest social experiments in history.[9] He squeezed what humour he could from the many inefficiencies and oddities of Soviet life. After checking in at the Novo Moscovskaya hotel, he went to his assigned room only to discover there was someone in bed there. He was bemused by the long list of dishes on the menu of the hotel restaurant when there was invariably no choice but pork and rabbit. It took days for him to understand the dual currency system under which it was far more costly to pay in roubles at the official exchange rate than to pay in U.S. dollars, or some other form of *valuta* (foreign currency). After Matt had paid the equivalent of five dollars in roubles for an unappetizing lunch, a helpful Russian waitress told him, "You should have paid in *valuta*. Then it would cost only sixty cents."[10] He was constantly asked, "Roubles or *valuta?*" in stores, taxis, and restaurants. "As I walked across the moonlit Red Square," he wrote, "I came to the conclusion that even if I walked into the mausoleum to see the corpse of Lenin, he would raise himself on one elbow in his cold glass case and say: 'Roubles or *valuta?*'"[11]

Matt was in Red Square again to watch a parade celebrating the launch of the new Five Year Plan. He had never seen a spectacle like it: fifty thousand soldiers and hundreds of thousands of men, women, and children marching past the Kremlin for four hours in the biting cold. "It was my first glimpse," he wrote, "of the tremendous exultation which is Russia as she begins her next historic step." A resident correspondent standing beside him muttered, "It's a beautiful dream but it will never come true."[12]

An admission of the difficulties of building communism came from an unlikely source. In his second week in Moscow, Matt interviewed Nadezhda Constantinova Krupskaya, the widow of Lenin. His ability to draw readers into his account of the interview is evident in an intriguing lead paragraph: "She is an old woman now, this Nadezhda Constantinova Krupskaya, an old woman with gray hair and a rich voice that begins to falter; but once, and not so long ago, she was the comfort and inspiration in dark hours of a man who spent his whole life building the Russian revolution, the man who translated the theology of Karl Marx into action, thereby transforming a medieval society of 170,000,000 people into a society which is feared by half the world, admired by the other half, and closely watched by the whole."[13] What was surprising to Matt was Krupskaya's candour in admitting the failures of Soviet society and the difficulties it faced. "Complete Socialism is not in sight in this generation," she told him. Krupskaya was unstinting, though, in her praise for the achievements of the Revolution. She talked of a day in 1923, the last year of Lenin's life, when the first Soviet-built farm tractor was brought for his inspection. "The tractor went a few feet, then its engine sputtered and died, and we all nearly died of disappointment." Now, she claimed, there were one hundred thousand Soviet tractors in use on the country's collective farms.[14]

On his return to London, Matt devoted much of his time to satisfying the *Star's* insatiable taste for his feature interviews. Over the next six years he sent the paper several hundred of them. The men and women he met and profiled made up a Who's Who of significant achievers in politics, science, the arts, and entertainment. Persuading public figures and celebrities to be interviewed was more difficult then than it is now. Letters would have to be written, sometimes with recommendations from other prominent figures. Matt would usually be well prepared for his interviews, with solid research behind him. Because of his retentive memory, he often didn't take notes, a habit that tended to put interviewees more at ease and encouraged them to open up more fully.

Among the scientists he profiled, none was more famous than Albert Einstein. In September 1933, he met the physicist at a secret location near the English Channel as an armed guard stood nearby. Einstein had taken temporary refuge in England after the Nazis had put a five thousand dollar bounty on his head. He talked of the bestiality and hysteria of Hitler's Germany but, Matt noted, "his statements about the Nazi regime are made as dispassionately as he would frame a new hypothesis, at least in tone."[15] His only moment of passion came when asked if he would ever go back to Germany if his property was restored and his freedom guaranteed. "Never!" he replied. Matt then asked him, "What will be the end of Hitler?" "War," he said. Then, impatiently: "Can't the whole world see that Hitler will almost certainly drag it into war. . . . The whole civilized world should unite to stamp out Hitlerism."[16] It would take more than a decade for that to happen.

Matt's interviews would often yield startlingly accurate glimpses of the future. Guglielmo Marconi, the Italian pioneer of wireless radio, talked about "the vast and almost fantastic possibilities" of technology. He told Matt that physicians in New York would one day be able to use television to diagnose the ills of patients in London. He also foresaw the use of pilotless aircraft being used in war.[17] The Cambridge scientist J.B.S. Haldane predicted space travel that would include a lunar voyage.[18] The great Swiss psychologist Carl Jung sketched a grim future for mankind in a two-hour interview with Matt. "One day we will pass away," he said, "perhaps through changes in the earth's climate. Perhaps through killing ourselves off."[19] Matt couldn't resist telling Jung about a dream he had that week. "I was talking to my wife. For some reason she looked like a different person, yet I knew it was my wife." Jung said no one should be psychoanalyzed unless they were in real need. But after a few more exchanges with Matt, he ventured the tantalizing comment that "the person you saw in your dream was not your wife, it was yourself."[20]

Matt also tracked down film stars and other celebrities. The interviews were often amusing but sometimes disappointingly thin on content. He was allowed a few minutes with Marlene Dietrich on the set of her first British film, *Knight Without Armor*. "Dietrich entered the room, more arrogant and lovely than any queen. She looked languorously around her, and her eyes were smoldering even though the eyelids were a little weary. 'Miss Dietrich,' said my voice, 'do you die in this picture?' 'Yes,' she sighed, 'I die. You see, this is a ve-eery sad picture. But I like to die.'" She told Matt she had few recreations and that her greatest pleasure was her work.[21] Other interviews were with Douglas Fairbanks; Merle Oberon; the newly discovered Canadian star, Victoria Hopper; and Leni Riefenstahl, the German director whose films glorified Nazi Germany. Matt also spent time with John Gielgud, whom he judged to be the finest English-speaking actor and who, "onstage, quietly and without tearing passion to tatters, holds men spellbound."[22] Gielgud revealed some of the quirks of his acting technique. He said he ate well before playing a comic role but tried to fast before acting in a tragedy. "You can't play tragedy after a heavy meal. To get that lean and hungry look, you should be hungry."[23] He also confided that in moments of high tragedy, he so identified with his role that sometimes tears would flow, as they did in the farewell scene with the queen in Shakespeare's *Richard II*.

Matt's long tally of interviews included authors and playwrights such as George Bernard Shaw, G.K. Chesterton, and H.G. Wells. Only one star of the sports world was interviewed, a reflection of Matt's disinterest in team sports. The exception was George Herman "Babe" Ruth, one of baseball's greatest hitters. Babe Ruth, then close to retirement, was visiting London when Matt went to see him in his room in the Savoy Hotel. He was in his pyjamas and smoking a cigar. He laughed scornfully when Matt mentioned the English claim that cricket takes much more skill than baseball. "Skill!" said the Babe. "Cricket's not a game at all, it's a tea party. It seems to me all they do is hold the bat and enjoy it or they wouldn't do it so much."[24] On occasion, Matt would pander to the taste of his managing editor, Harry Hindmarsh, who had a special interest in stories about lions. When the Bertram Mills circus was in London, Matt interviewed its famous French lion tamer, Violette D'Argens. She invited him to come into a cage to visit her favourite lions, Sevila and Ramona. "Ramona was looking me over," Matt wrote, "and with only half an eye, I could see I was nothing to her but a potential steak. 'No,' I said, 'I didn't think I'd go in.'" But, terrified, he did go in. "Do you t'ink yu want to stroke Ramona?" said the French lion tamer. "'I t'ink ay go home,' I said, and together we left the cage. I didn't want to see Ramona again, let alone stroke her."[25]

Persistence on Matt's part and good contacts would usually help him secure the interviews he sought. But there were notable failures. He was never able to interview Winston Churchill, whom he hero-worshipped, and whose early and fierce opposition to Nazi Germany mirrored his own concern. Churchill regularly turned down interview requests, preferring to save his insights for his own newspaper articles, which paid him well. Lady Astor, Matt's patron and now friend, promised to introduce him to the notoriously secretive T.E. Lawrence (Lawrence of Arabia) in the hope that it might lead to an interview later. Astor, who shared with Lawrence a passion for motorcycle riding, arranged to take Matt to a meeting with him in Plymouth. Lawrence, used to shunning the press, showed up on his motorbike, politely but briefly acknowledged Matt's presence, then asked Astor to climb on behind him. He then took off, "with the lady in question hanging on with one hand and waving goodbye with the other."[26] There would be no interview. Equally frustrating was Matt's failure to get Canada's new governor general-designate, John Buchan (Lord Tweedsmuir), to utter more than a few banalities. "I have had some practice in getting great men to talk," he wrote, "but I couldn't wear Mr. Buchan down. A Trappist initiate vowed to silence is loquacious in comparison."[27]

Matt was more successful in persuading some prominent international figures to be interviewed for the *Star*. In August 1936, Stalin launched the first of the Moscow show trials that signalled a tightening of Soviet repression. Seventeen old Bolsheviks were accused of plotting with Leon Trotsky to kill Stalin. Trotsky was in exile in Norway as the trial began. After persuading Trotsky's entourage that he wasn't a spy, Matt was able to get a phone call through to the founder of the Red Army and the man who was once second only to Lenin in the Soviet hierarchy. Trotsky was scathing about the charge that he had conspired to assassinate Stalin. "Any fool knows," he claimed, "that all real Marxists renounced terror as a weapon thirty years ago." The Stalinist regime, he added, had betrayed Marxism. It "calls every criticism against it a conspiracy."[28] Matt agreed with him that the Moscow trial was a sinister farce that signalled a turn for the worse in Russia. Four years later, Trotsky was murdered by a Soviet agent posing as a Canadian admirer.

A longer and more glorious career awaited another of Matt's foreign interviewees. Jawaharlal Nehru was also a rebel and a Marxist, albeit of a moderate Cambridge-educated sort. A decade later he became the first, and eventually longest-serving, prime minister of an independent India. When Matt interviewed him in London, Nehru had served five years in a British jail in India for preaching non-violent resistance to the Raj's imperial rule. Already seen at home as the political heir of Gandhi, Nehru had just learned that he had been elected president of the Congress Party. He quickly disabused Matt of his Kiplingesque image of India and his belief in the Empire's benign role there. Britain was blamed for India's shockingly high unemployment and illiteracy and for stifling local industries that might compete with British ones. Nehru said advocates of independence like himself were frequently jailed, and some were brutally beaten. At one point he asked Matt how he would like to work in India where he said journalists have to make a cash deposit to the authorities that could be confiscated if their articles were judged seditious. Nehru did not exclude the possibility of an independent India remaining in the British Commonwealth but only if it was on the basis of equality and freedom. "Think," he concluded, "if I said in my own country what I am saying to you, the British would put me in jail."[29] Nehru was indeed jailed for another three years before leading India to independence.

Matt tended to be excessively enthusiastic about the politicians he admired. Twice during the thirties he had long interviews with David Lloyd George, Britain's great social reformer and World War One leader. The fact that the "Welsh wizard" was on the margins of British politics for most of the thirties didn't discourage Matt from suggesting that Lloyd George "may again become the man of the hour."[30] After a ninety-minute session with the aging statesman, Matt wrote that "no one else in British political life has his fire and strength."[31] Four years later, in 1939, Lloyd

George invited him to his farm in Surrey, where he showed off his apple orchard and mused about the mediocrity and weakness of successive British governments over the decade. "The famous statesman's eyes flashed as he recalled the days when he held the burden of the world on his shoulders. His arms swept through the air in great arcs as he flayed mistakes that have brought the world to today's bitter pass."[32]

Matt's commitment to socialism was reinforced in the 1930s and it seeped into much of his reporting. He even casually acknowledged it in one of the weekly newsletters he sent the *Star* in which, speaking of himself, he used the phrase "Even though you are a Socialist."[33] Left-leaning as it was at the time, the *Star* allowed no other reporter to editorialize to the extent that Matt did. On his return to London, he renewed contact with his old LSE professor, Harold Laski, an ever more radical critic of capitalism's failures. A disproportionate number of Matt's political interviews were with leading socialists such as Clement Attlee, Stafford Cripps, and Herbert Morrison. He found the Labour Party demoralized and in disarray. Its former leader, Ramsay MacDonald, was expelled from the party in 1931 after agreeing to lead a Conservative-dominated National government. Conservatives would govern Britain for the rest of the decade with disastrous consequences, in Matt's view, for the country's domestic and foreign policy.

Matt's politics were shaped as much by personal experience as by any theoretical attraction to socialism. As a London-based correspondent, he reported regularly on Britain's more than two million unemployed, travelling to blighted areas of Scotland, Northern England, and South Wales. In Glasgow he visited districts where thousands of residents were crammed into unheated and dilapidated tenements and where one toilet on a spiral stair served thirty or forty people.[34] He joined one stage of a five-hundred-mile hunger march to London where protesters provided evidence of malnutrition among many of the poor.[35] He trekked through the slums of London's East End, describing them as "a festering canker in the heart of a great civilization."[36] Twice he spent time in the severely depressed coal-mining valleys of Wales. Perhaps because of memories of his father's grim past as a teenage miner, he wrote movingly of what he saw in the Rhondda Valley – "the terrible sight of men with no hope and no place in the world." Seventy-five per cent of the adult population there were on the dole, living in a landscape of cramped row houses and huge piles of slag. "Unused cranes and rusting pit gear stand like gloomy ghosts over the once thriving valleys. Men wearing cast-off clothing stand on corners bravely trying to conquer the apathy that is eating into their souls. As they grow old and die, their wistful ranks are reinforced by boys from school, who have left school to find themselves unwanted in the scheme of things. They read rose-colored stories in the daily press about returning prosperity in other parts of the island and wonder why even the shadow of it passes them by."[37]

Matt blamed rapacious industry, and its supporters in government, for putting profits ahead of people. He favoured public ownership of key industries as proposed by the Labour Party in Britain and by the CCF in Canada. He was convinced that only socialism could bring about a fairer distribution of the country's wealth and he predicted, correctly, that a Labour government would deliver it. He also deplored the absence of equality of opportunity. The rigid British class system, he wrote, made success dependent on having the right accent and going to the right "public" school, which in the peculiar British definition meant a private school. In one article, Matt singled out a statement by Prime Minister Baldwin about his first cabinet. "I have decided to have six old Harrovians in it," Baldwin said in reference to the exclusive Harrow school that six of his ministers had attended. It was one more indication, Matt concluded, that "the government of this country is still partly a closed corporation for chaps who went to 'good' schools."[38] In another article, he regretted the fact that the school leaving age for the great mass of British children was only fourteen, compared with sixteen in many other European countries.

Visiting Canadian friends were struck by Matt's ambivalence about Britain. For all his exasperation with the snobbishness and inequality of British life, Matt still felt that "this is the finest country in the world." He was inspired by its history and traditions and wrote affectionately about its eccentricities. For one feature article, he put on a red coat and top hat and rode with a fox hunt. Even as an accomplished horseman, he confessed to shrinking at the sight of some of the ditches and eight-foot hedges that English men and women breezed over fearlessly. Other features celebrated the charm of the English countryside. A whimsical essay on the odd names of many villages focused on Helion Bumpstead in Essex:

> Now for all my life I have wanted to go to Helion Bumpstead just as I have always wanted to go to Tring and Lillyhoo, Chalfont St. Giles and Bishop's Stortford and Chipping Norton. When in the dead dear days beyond recall, as a student making the best of two years in England, I used to tramp down the winding lanes with a pack on my back and the wind in my face, I did manage to see these last five English villages, places that should exist only in dreams, but are actually real. . . .
>
> But I never got to the one with the most delightful name of them all, Helion Bumpstead. And now I have been to Helion Bumpstead – may God preserve it forever![39]

His return to Europe also enabled Matt to renew his infatuation with France. As a self-assigning correspondent, he used the freedom the *Star* gave him to visit the country three or four times a year, sometimes for the flimsy reason of interviewing an obscure cabinet minister. He wrote of stimulating discussions with French friends, of Paris's chic women and marvellous restaurants, and of memorable drives through the countryside along roads lined with Lombardy poplars. "Of all the countries I have ever seen," he noted, "France is most favored of the gods for smiling scenery and fertility of soil and pleasantness of life."[40] He identified with Thomas Jefferson's famous line "Every man has two countries, his own and France," and he loved to quote an Oxford professor who once jokingly said that if ever Western civilization disappeared, "an astral observer will still be able to distinguish a faint light over France."[41]

Matt plunged into a darker side of France when he rushed to Paris in February 1934. The country had been shaken by *l'affaire Stavisky*, a scandal involving a crooked financier, Serge Stavisky, who had issued huge amounts of fraudulent bonds. When Stavisky was found dead early in the year, it was widely assumed he had been murdered by the police to cover up his ties to cabinet ministers and senior government officials. The scandal partly motivated ultra-right and Fascist groups – some of them paramilitaries bent on overthrowing France's Third Republic – to stage a violent riot on February 6. Sixteen people were killed and more than six hundred wounded.[42] Matt flew in the next day and was in the thick of four more nights of pitched battles between police and rioters, many of whom were now Communists. Walking into the Place de l'Opéra one evening, he couldn't quite believe that so many of the demonstrators were armed. "Men were kneeling behind barricades, sniping at the mounted police who advanced at the trot, firing as they came. . . . Just as I saw a policeman fall from his horse, a bullet flattened itself on a stone wall behind me, and I ducked faster than anyone ever ducked before."[43] Later, the rioters broke and ran and Matt found himself facing an onrush of policemen. He managed to dodge a gendarme whom he said swung his club viciously at him. Finally, he was dragged to a police van before being able to show his passport and told to scram. It made for the kind of "our-man-on-the-spot" story that the *Star* relished.

Geneva was another familiar stopover in Matt's itinerary in the 1930s. He described the huge marble Palais des Nations, the Geneva headquarters of the League of Nations, as "a monument to What Might Have Been, a mausoleum for the noble dream."[44] The "noble dream" was the hope that the League, founded in the embers of World War One, would maintain world peace through collective security. Matt was one of its most ardent supporters and one of the first to be disillusioned. The League's solidarity began to crack when Japanese troops invaded and occupied Chinese Manchuria. Matt interviewed Yosuke Matsuoka, the Japanese delegate to the League and a future foreign minister, who blithely told him that his country wanted peace but needed Manchuria to expand its empire.[45] The League agreed that Japan was the aggressor but then had neither the will to impose sanctions nor to gather an army as it was supposed to do under the League's covenant. As early as December 1934, Matt wrote prophetically that "it is now clear that the high hopes we held after 1918 were a great folly and delusion."[46]

He was much more closely involved when the Italian invasion of Abyssinia (Ethiopia) in 1935 sent the League to its deathbed. As the first troops were shipping out, the *Star* rushed Matt to Italy for a series of articles on Benito Mussolini's plan to recreate the Roman empire in Africa. At dockside in Naples, he described a wild scene as thousands of young soldiers embarked to the cheers of a large crowd and the singing of "Giovinezza," the Fascist anthem. "Glory and romance and music, sweat and dirt and the shadow of death – all joined hands in a *danse macabre* here on this quay under the hot sun."[47] In Rome, Matt wrote more reflectively about what he judged to be Italians' overwhelming support for the war and the economic benefits colonization might bring. He warned that Abyssinia was just a first step in Mussolini's plan to take over Egypt and the Suez Canal.

Even before the Italian conquest of Abyssinia, Matt was pessimistic about the League of Nations being able to prevent it happening. He had good contacts with young members of the Canadian delegation in Geneva, notably Albert Rive, Louis Rasminsky, and Mary Craig McGeachy. They were all disappointed by Ottawa's refusal to accept effective sanctions against Italy and willing to feed Matt inside information about Canada's faint-hearted response. Editorializing in the *Star*'s news pages, as he often did, Matt wrote, "On some dark future day, Canada's niggardly stand may be remembered against her."[48] He didn't have long to wait. In October 1935, Walter Riddell, Canada's representative to the League, was widely applauded for proposing to toughen sanctions against Italy by adding a crippling oil embargo. Within a short time his proposal was scrapped by Prime Minister Mackenzie King, who opposed any kind of coercion by the League. It was a huge embarrassment for Canada. King was even quoted as telling the governor general, "I wish the League of Nations could be gotten out of the way altogether."[49]

Seven months later, Matt touched off a minor storm over the League with one of his dispatches. As an Imperial Conference opened in London in May 1937, he learned from a high-level source that British anti-League forces planned to use Mackenzie King to lead an effort to drop all the sanctions clauses from the League Covenant. "Powerful forces are at work here," he wrote, "to make the Imperial Conference an instrument for emasculation of the Covenant of the League of Nations and Premier King has been chosen to wield the knife."[50] Matt attributed the move to the increasingly strong group of British Conservative leaders trying to appease Fascism in Italy and Germany. His report was picked up by the correspondent of the London *Times* in Ottawa, prompting an embarrassed King to put out a statement denying Halton's allegation.[51] By this time though, with Italy occupying Abyssinia (Ethiopia) and Nazi Germany resurgent, the League was irrelevant, and everyone knew it.

At the end of 1937, Matt travelled to Somerset to interview the most prominent victim of the Abyssinian crisis. Ousted by the Italians, Haile Selassie still called himself Emperor of Ethiopia, Lion of Judah, and King of Kings. Matt described him as frail and impoverished, a figure of pathos now living in a plain building with a "House for Sale" sign displayed outside it. The exiled emperor needed to move to a more affordable home. Selassie showed no signs of bitterness but insisted that Abyssinia's cause should be seen not just as an African issue but as a test of justice and decency in world affairs. Despite the League's betrayal of his country, he predicted that Abyssinian sovereignty would be restored.[52] Three and a half years later he returned to his capital, Addis Ababa, in triumph after Allied forces had driven the Italians out.

In London Matt was increasingly comfortable in both his professional and social life. He faced no serious competition from the five other Canadian correspondents in London with the exception of the extremely able Grant Dexter of the *Winnipeg Free Press*. After working out of his apartment for several years, Matt prevailed on the *Star* to set up an office for him on Fleet Street and to hire a secretary/researcher. He would often take Jean to the theatre and sometimes to dine at the fashionable Café Royal. They were invited to the annual garden party at Buckingham Palace – Matt wearing rented pinstripes and top hat, Jean elegant in a long dress with a fox fur over her shoulders and a wide-brimmed hat worn at a jaunty angle. Friends from London and visitors from Canada would often drop by their London apartment. *Star* colleague Gordon Sinclair – in transit from India – recalled their generosity in putting him up as he recovered from a bout of malaria.[53]

In the summer of 1935, Matt took Jean back to Canada for their first home vacation. They spent a few days in Montreal and Toronto, then flew to

Alberta to see their parents and to camp in the Rockies. In Pincher Creek, there was a sentimental ritual to follow. Matt would climb the rickety steps to his old room in his parents' home on Charlotte Street where as a boy he had stared out at the foothills and listened for the wail of the CPR train as it passed nearby. He would also walk along the creek to the canyon where he and his friends used to swim on hot summer days. This time, his visit also included a week-long camping trip on horseback into the high Rockies. Accompanied by friends, he rode along the Continental Divide separating Alberta and British Columbia. "No words of mine," he wrote, "will ever describe the scenery. I slept for seven nights under the stars; war and crisis seemed utterly futile and millions of miles away."[54]

There were also the first signs that Matt's loyalty might be drifting away from Canada. At the end of his vacation he wrote an impressionistic account of what it was like coming home after five years as a student and correspondent in London. He was enthusiastic about North American food and the well-dressed women he saw and the fact Canadians aren't judged immediately by their accent. But he also wrote about the ugliness of Yonge Street in Toronto and much of urban Canada; about the lack of theatres and bookshops; and about men and women whose "only sign of life is the movement of two jaws on chewing gum."[55] If England had corn on the cob and barbecued chicken and the Rockies, he mused half-seriously, he would stay there for the rest of his life.

Matt's loyalties remained divided, and some of his friends later said that he had been infected by a touch of Anglophile snobbery. But his pride in Canada and his roots there were undiminished. "Canada, my Canada," he wrote. "The safest place in the world to live in the dark hours coming on."[56]

6

"THE GERMAN SERIES": SOUNDING THE ALARM

"Germany enters a nightmare. I feel it in my bones."
— MATTHEW HALTON, *Toronto Star*, March 1933

THREE MONTHS AFTER ARRIVING IN LONDON, Matt found himself at the epicentre of what became the biggest story of the twentieth century. At dusk on March 4, 1933, he checked into Berlin's luxurious Adlon Hotel situated across from the Brandenburg Gate and overlooking the city's famous avenue, the Unter den Linden. It was the eve of the Reichstag election that would seal the Nazis' fatal grip on Germany. Adolph Hitler had become chancellor five weeks earlier. Civil rights had already been suspended. A reign of terror had begun that quickly got worse after the burning of the Reichstag, almost certainly by the Nazis as the pretext for consolidating their power. The *Star* had neglected the story initially but decided to make up for the lapse by assigning Matt to cover the election and its aftermath.

As night set in, Matt heard the distant skirl of pipes and the rolling of drums coming closer. He went to a hotel balcony, as he later recounted, and saw that thousands of Berliners were lining the avenue as a torchlight parade approached. First came the Stahlhelmer, steel-helmeted veterans of the First World War. They were followed by the Sturmabteilung, goose-stepping storm troopers in their brown shirts. Then, in the rear of the parade, came the Schutzstaffel, the black-uniformed SS who were already becoming the terrifying vanguard of Hitler's regime. As each detachment passed there were frenzied shouts of "Heil! Heil! Heil" from the crowd, and a forest of arms were thrust up in the Fascist salute. Fascinated and repelled by what he was watching, Matt decided to go down to the avenue and squeeze into the crowd. At one point, he saw SS troops slow down as they passed the French embassy. They began singing a favourite Nazi song, "Siegreich Wollen Wir Frankreich Schlagen" – "Victoriously We Must Smash France." The crowd erupted in a huge cheer. Matt wandered further down the Unter den Linden and came across a group of the so-called Potsdamer women who had lost sons, husbands, or fathers in the First World War. They were dressed in black and calling for revenge. At the end of the parade route, hundreds of storm troopers threw their torches into a giant bonfire. A Nazi with a megaphone shouted: "Thus does Germany in her resurgence kindle an undying flame."[1]

For Matt, it was a chilling occasion, one that framed a lasting impression of Nazi Germany. The parade, the first of scores he witnessed in coming years, seemed to be much more than just an exuberant display of nationalism. It was something more sinister – a people seemingly carried away in a collective delirium. Back in his hotel room he sat down at his typewriter and wrote some remarkably prophetic words. "I saw a microcosm of the new Germany which is . . . putting the fateful hour-glass of Europe back to 1914."[2] The next day, he described the swastikas and flags flying everywhere in Berlin, noting that the black and yellow flag of the dying, liberal Weimar Republic was nowhere to be seen. The Nazis had won the election and now, Matt wrote, "the nation is being urged to prepare for a war of revenge. France again is trembling in her shoes."[3] His reaction was immediate: "Germany enters a nightmare. I feel it in my bones. She has heard the call of the wild. Pan-Germanism, six centuries old, is on the march again, but in a new and demoniac form."[4] In a later dispatch, Matt described incidents of Nazi thuggery and anti-Semitism. He saw four people dragged away from a crowd and shoved into a police wagon and watched a parade of children carrying swastikas and shouting, "The Jews must be destroyed."[5] The transformation of Germany was taking place with shocking speed.

Matt's views on the Nazi threat weren't shaped overnight. He had read similar reports from Pierre van Paassen, a Paris-based colleague at the *Star,* and Edgar Ansel Mowrer, the Berlin correspondent of the *Chicago Daily News* who was expelled from Germany. But in March 1933, Matt was bolder and more outspoken about the threat of German Fascism than almost any other journalist. Instinctively, he sensed that an extraordinarily destructive power had been unleashed by the Nazis. He conveyed that message in his typically dramatic style. It was the beginning of a long and frustrating crusade in which he practised the journalism of righteous advocacy, was pilloried for his views, and ultimately was vindicated.

Matt's coverage of the German election drew both praise and denunciations. Walter Winchell, the most popular columnist in the United States, read Matt's dispatches in an American newspaper in which *Star* articles were syndicated. Winchell complimented "Halton, that very expert *Toronto Star* correspondent in Berlin" for laying bare the plans of Hitler and his "gangsters."[6] On the other hand, an editorial in the Toronto *Globe* condemned the *Star* for its sensationalist reports from Germany. The *Globe*, which would soon publish articles sympathetic to the Third Reich, said: "It will be a sorry day if this sort of thing becomes mistaken for Canadian newspaper accuracy."[7] There was similar criticism from the Toronto *Evening Telegram*.

Because of the high expense of telegraphed news at the time, Matt sent most of his Berlin dispatches by mail. That meant they didn't reach Toronto until at least ten days later – an advantage because the regime was not immediately alerted to his outspoken hostility to it. Before leaving Germany, Matt was able to have a curious session with Hermann Göring, the former fighter pilot who was already emerging as Hitler's most powerful lieutenant. The meeting was short and strictly off the record, as was the case with most interviews given by top Nazis at the time. In his later memoir *Ten Years to Alamein*, Matt recalled how he asked about the foreign policy of the new Germany. "Simple," Göring barked, "'*Frieden und Freiheit*'" ("Peace and Freedom," an early Nazi slogan). "Peace and freedom, and how many aircraft?" was Matt's skeptical response. At that point, according to his account, Göring laughed and said, "As many as we need for peace and freedom." Then, as if thinking aloud, the future chief of the Luftwaffe said: "He who has 20,000 aircraft is master of the world." Göring also said that Germany would move to liquidate the Treaty of Versailles, and he predicted (correctly, as it turned out) that there would be no interference from Britain or France.[8]

Back in London, Matt's interest in Hitler's Germany became almost obsessive. He worked hard to brush up his knowledge of the German language; he read German newspapers; he established a network of contacts with German refugees. One of them, Hans Wolfsohn, was an anti-Nazi journalist who escaped Germany shortly after Matt met him in Berlin. Hans and his wife, Elsa, became close friends with Matt and an invaluable source of information about the persecution of German socialists, Communists, and Jews. Matt would interview refugees arriving in the London docks or meet them in dingy residences in the city's east end. They gave him first-hand evidence of the humiliation and violence inflicted by Hitler's Reich. One Jewish refugee showed him the scars on his chest from a beating. Another showed a photo of an elderly Jew paraded through the streets in a scavenger's cart.[9] Numerous accounts of torture and even murder appeared in several dozen of Matt's dispatches. He concluded one report with a line likely to have startled many of his readers: "For what is happening in Germany today, all of us are partly to blame. Gentiles of our own nations as well as Prussian bullies."[10] Matt's view of Nazism was reinforced by Maurice Eisendrath, a young liberal rabbi at Toronto's Holy Blossom Temple. They met in Paris after Eisendrath had finished a fact-finding mission in Germany's already shattered Jewish communities. "Over all of them," he told Matt, "hung utter despair and hopelessness for they knew that for them the future held absolutely nothing."[11]

In early September 1933, Matt returned to Germany for an extended two-month assignment. It produced what became known as "the German Series," thirty reports that chronicled almost every defining aspect of Nazi Germany. Apart from Berlin, Matt travelled to tiny villages in Thuringia and the Rhineland, as well as to a dozen major cities, including Hamburg, Heidelberg, Bonn, Leipzig, Munich, and Nuremberg. He visited factories, schools, universities, Storm Troop centres, and a concentration camp. He interviewed dozens of Nazi officials from senior party functionaries to Brown Shirts staffing local party headquarters. And he made surreptitious contact with victims of Nazi tyranny – the few, that is, willing to risk speaking to a foreign reporter. In terms of investigative reporting, the "German Series" was Matt's greatest accomplishment.

"Parachute" correspondents – those who drop into a foreign country for short assignments – are rarely able to match the knowledge of a resident correspondent. In Matt's case, though, it was a distinct advantage. The 110 foreign correspondents based in Berlin faced a stark choice. If they wrote too aggressively about the excesses of Hitler's regime, they would be expelled, as nineteen were between 1933 and 1937.[12] Most of the resident correspondents self-censored their reports to avoid jeopardizing their prestigious posting or risk displeasing their employers back home. Louis Lochner, bureau chief of the Associated Press in Berlin during the 1930s, later summarized the message Berlin correspondents were getting from home management: "To tell no untruth, but to report only as much of the truth without distorting the picture, as would enable us to remain at our posts."[13] As a consequence, the correspondents tended to rely heavily on statements by Nazi leaders and press releases from the government. There was a reluctance to report on the dark side of the regime, and a general avoidance of critical analysis. Even as accomplished an American correspondent as William Shirer (later author of the bestselling *The Rise and Fall of the Third Reich*) wrote guiltily in his diary that he softened up a story to avoid angering the Nazis: "If I had any guts, or American journalism had any, I would have said so in my dispatch tonight. But I am not supposed to be 'editorial.'"[14]

Another factor helping to create a generally tame foreign press in Germany was the extent to which it was courted, as well as threatened, by the Nazi regime. Hitler himself occasionally invited pliant correspondents for off-the-record sessions at his mountain retreat in Berchtesgaden. Josef Goebbels's Orwellian-named Ministry of Public Enlightenment and Propaganda would do much of the legwork for correspondents in providing sources and interviews – all, of course, with Nazi sympathizers. The ministry supplied other favours: help in leasing apartments and arranging travel, special passes to big events, and tickets at reduced rates for concerts and operas. It built a lavish club for foreign journalists with a well-equipped press room that served as an office for some correspondents. It also organized regular *bierabend*, beer-and-sausage evenings where correspondents would be briefed by Nazi insiders. Few correspondents objected to the rather cosy relationship with their hosts. The annual Foreign Press Association ball in the Adlon Hotel was the social event of the Berlin season, attended on occasion by Goebbels himself and leading members of the party hierarchy.

The Nazis also used more sinister tactics to encourage a docile foreign press. Correspondents were allowed to exchange their salaries into German currency at a rate two or three times better than the official exchange rate. For some correspondents that meant tripling their income – a not-so-subtle form of bribery.[15] One Nazi party document even stated explicitly that "the friendship of newspaper people is to be secured, if possible, by bribery."[16] Another German practice was to plant fabricated anti-Nazi stories which, if published, would then be revealed as false and used to discredit the correspondent. In London, in 1935, Matt was himself targeted. A German claiming to be a refugee gave him a story about an alleged Nazi atrocity. Fortunately, Matt checked out the informant's identity and was told the "refugee" was a suspected German agent.[17]

As a temporary correspondent, Matt was free of most of the constraints faced by resident foreign correspondents in Germany. He had also decided to hold back most of the "German Series" from publication until he left the country to avoid harassment by the authorities. Once again, he settled into the opulent Adlon Hotel whose frescoed salons and chandeliered rooms were frequented by celebrities, visiting foreign statesmen, and top Nazi leaders. Jean accompanied him for almost a month, as she sometimes did on his foreign trips. They would take walks along the Unter den Linden and among the trees and flowers of the lovely Tiergarten. A photograph at the time shows the couple arm in arm in front of the Brandenburg Gate, Jean elegant in a long fox-trimmed overcoat. They would often dine at the Taverne, the favourite meeting place for foreign correspondents, where one of the occasional guests was Martha Dodd, the bright, promiscuous daughter of the American ambassador.* Gestapo spies were conspicuous, watching and trying to listen from nearby tables.

---

* Dodd managed the extraordinary feat of being the lover of the Gestapo chief and then of a Soviet embassy spy before becoming a Soviet agent herself. Her story is told in *In the Garden of Beasts* by Erik Larson.

Matt got his accreditation from the propaganda ministry where he met Ernst "Putzi" Hanfstaengl, the eccentric Harvard-educated foreign press chief. Hanfstaengl ingratiated himself with Hitler by regularly playing piano excerpts for him from Wagner and Beethoven. Four years later he fell out of favour, defected, and ended up first as a prisoner in Canada then as a consultant in Washington D.C., building a psychological profile of Hitler for the Roosevelt administration.[18] In 1933, though, he was still the faithful Nazi. His message to Matt was the same as he gave other foreign correspondents: report the news but don't interpret it. Matt did precisely the opposite.

The changes since his last visit to Berlin were immediately noticeable. The security was tighter, the mood grimmer. Books by Proust, Gide, Hemingway, H.G. Wells, and Thomas Mann had long since disappeared from bookstores, many to be destroyed in public book-burnings. Gestapo agents could be seen checking documents at rail stations. Everywhere there were signs of the rapid militarization of the Third Reich. The streets were full of uniformed men. Teenage boys and girls paraded in columns in the streets. Swastikas hung out permanently on many buildings. Lurid posters in shop windows denounced the Treaty of Versailles and called for "Death rather than slavery." At a restaurant in the busy Potsdamer Platz, a uniformed Hitler Jugend boy, not even in his teens, went around collecting money for Nazi projects. At each table he would raise his arm in the Fascist salute and click his boots together. In the street and in government offices, Matt's refusal to return the salute often attracted scowls and occasional threats even when he said, *"Auslander"* (foreigner).

The *Star* published the first of the "German Series" under a headline bannered across its front page: "GERMAN CITIZENRY WAR MAD, SAYS HALTON." The lead paragraph was characteristically portentous. "During the last month in Germany," Matt wrote, "I have seen and studied the most fanatical, thorough-going and savage philosophy of war ever imposed on any nation. . . . Germany is literally becoming a laboratory and breeding ground for war, unless I am deaf, dumb and blind."[19] At this stage, in the autumn of 1933, almost no politicians and very few commentators were making that kind of sweeping judgment. Even the great

American journalist Walter Lippmann praised Hitler at the time as "the authentic voice of a genuinely civilized people."[20] Matt conceded that "in the German towns and cities through which I am wandering, everything on the surface is sunshine, energy, resurgence."[21] But it wouldn't take more than twenty-four hours, he added, for anyone who could read or hear in Germany to see beyond the façade.

It was at a theatrically staged rally in Berlin that Matt had his first opportunity to listen to and evaluate Hitler in person. A large band thumped out triumphalist marches until the Führer walked onto the platform in the glare of a searchlight. Matt described him as "unprepossessing, even absurd" with mannered gestures and a ridiculous Charlie Chaplin moustache. But his severest scorn was levelled at the content of the speech and its harping on Germany's treatment after World War One.

> Using all the tricks of oratory with the most patent disingenuousness, the little Austrian house-painter in his ugly brown uniform described the "degradation" of Germany in searing phrases and a thundering voice that turned his hearers into maddened, moaning fanatics.
>
> And what did he say?
>
> He says what he always says . . . the words that have forged the revolution which is the most amazing phenomenon of our times. He told of Germany's "wrongs." His voice alternating between the zenith of high-pitched hysteria and the nadir of whispering solemnity, he told how Germany, surrounded by an iron ring of foes and fighting against an embattled world, had won tremendous victories in every sphere of war. And then been stabbed in the back. "Who stabbed us in the back?" he shrieked. The waiting multitude, every member of which knew well what he would say, sat breathless, absolutely silent except for an occasional sound that can only be likened to a moan. The little man clenched both fists and held them before him. He contorted his face. . . . He repeated, his voice now a roar: "Who stabbed us in the back? The Jews!"
>
> The crowds went berserk with fury and applause, and I know that my feeling was suddenly horror, for I was hearing a mob clamoring for "revenge."

*Der Führer (the Leader) spoke again, his voice low and passion-
ate . . . "Why was the face of the Fatherland scarred with the iron fist of
France? Why, why, why? Because of the Jews."*

"Warum? Die Juden!" *I can hear those words today.*[22]

Matt later went to Berchtesgaden in the hope of seeing Hitler at his
weekend retreat. Hitler didn't show up, leaving Matt to settle in with Jean
at a small country inn, talk to the villagers, and write, "I think I know that
Hitler will destroy Germany."[23]

Matt admitted to being perplexed by the astonishing speed with which
the liberal Weimar Republic had been replaced by a totalitarian dictatorship. How could the country of Goethe and Heine and Schiller descend so
quickly into barbarism? he asked. What had happened to the nineteen
million Germans who had voted for parties other than the Nazis only
seven months earlier? His fifth dispatch in the German Series went beyond
some of the obvious explanations – the harsh punishment for dissenters
and the resurgence of national pride. Matt focused on the concept of
Gleichschaltung, literally meaning "bringing into line," which he said was
the most important word in Germany's new political vocabulary. It was a
concept the Nazis enshrined to describe both the forced and willing con-
formity of the Germans to the principle that they exist to serve the state
rather than the state existing to serve the people. *Gleichschaltung*, Matt
wrote, was "bringing into line" every aspect of German thought and
activity. It was the rationale for the state to suppress political parties, trade
unions, independent churches, even the long-standing provincial governments whose powers were stripped away. In Berlin Matt sat down with
the Canadian representative of a big U.S. bank and asked him whether
there were any independent thinkers left in Germany. "They have all con-
formed," the banker replied. "Give them a job and a uniform and a band,
and they will play follow the leader." "Even into another war?" Matt
asked. "Watch them," replied the banker.[24]

The militarization of Germany was a constant theme in the series.
Matt visited schools where children six and older were first exposed to the
need for war, and where children twelve and above were trained in war

games and the use of small arms. In a Berlin suburb he saw older school-boys throwing disarmed grenades at cardboard dummies. In the old university town of Heidelberg, he got off the train with Jean to encounter familiar sights: "flags and uniforms and bugles and the constant tramp of marching feet." He talked to university students who told him that Hitler had restored the practice of student duelling, which had been banned for years. A Nazi edict stated that duelling, causing the mutilation of men's faces with sword cuts, "is a symbol of German courage and German honor."[25] A student explained to Matt that there was a standard insult to bring about a duel. "It is enough," he said, "to suggest that a man has Jewish blood."[26] In Nuremberg, already a shrine to Nazism, he watched several hundred children put on a bizarre display. First they formed themselves into a map of the pre-war Germany, then other children, obviously representing something evil, crept forward and formed a map of the smaller Germany of the Versailles settlement. Finally there were songs and orations about the sacred task of recovering lost lands and freeing German minorities in Austria, Czechoslovakia, Poland, and elsewhere.[27]

A minor controversy was stirred up when Matt wrote a column about a high school textbook preparing German children for war. The manual, *Wehrwissenschaft* (Military Science), was written by Ewald Banse, a professor at the Technical School in Brunswick. Matt quoted extensively from the book, which called on teachers "to create an unshakable belief in the high ethical values and deeper meaning of war." Banse's aim was to develop the psychological readiness of Germans for sacrifice in the cause of the nation.[28]

One particularly chilling paragraph said children should be taught techniques such as infecting the enemy's drinking water with typhus germs. After Matt's report was published, Ludwig Kempff, the German consul-general in Montreal, wrote the *Globe* (presumably because of its sympathetic view of Hitler) asking it to correct the *Star* report. Kempff said Banse's book did not represent the views of the German government and had been prohibited.[29] The *Globe* commented that the *Star* was again biased against Nazi Germany. What it didn't say was that *Wehrwissenschaft* had been widely used in schools and universities and had been disavowed by Berlin only three weeks earlier because of adverse foreign comment. Banse continued to hold his teaching position and continued to be a leading teacher of military science.

Matt's extensive contacts with Jewish exiles in London gave him a special interest in investigating the Nazi campaign against the Jews. It wasn't easy. Most Jews he contacted were simply too scared to talk to a foreigner, especially a foreign journalist. He dropped into a number of Jewish shops in Berlin where the store owners refused to say much about their situation. Typically he would say, "Well, your shop hasn't been closed by the Nazis," and get the response, "It might as well have been; nobody buys here anymore."[30] Not all his information was first-hand. He quoted a resident American businessman who told him about a Jewish clothes manufacturer who was beaten up by two of his Nazi employees and was too afraid to protest. He quoted an American correspondent who had seen a German girl paraded through the streets with her head shaved and forced to carry a placard with the words "I wanted to give myself to a Jew." In Leipzig, however, Matt was able to gather more of his own information. He interviewed a number of Jews in the ghetto and in the Brühl district, a centre of the world fur trade where Jewish merchants controlled much of the business until forced out by the Nazis. "I met some who still seem fairly prosperous," he wrote, " but most of them are on the edge of poverty, and many are over the edge. The better off ones have made their escape to Czechoslovakia, France or Britain; some are in concentration camps; some are doing forced labor; the rest sit behind their counters or in their homes waiting for they know not what, sure only that it will be degradation and misery. I never before met such unhappy people."[31] In a previous article, Matt had already come to a conclusion that would prove devastatingly accurate: "The terror goes on unremittingly in the form of a deliberate and implacable intention to wipe the Jews out of the economic and social life of Germany."[32]

Unlike many of his journalistic colleagues, Matt saw German anti-Semitism not as a marginal phenomenon but as part of the central core of Nazi ideology. He had read the German version of Hitler's *Mein Kampf*, much longer and more explicit than its English translation and more fanatical in its hatred of Jewry. He understood that Hitler's concept of a master race depended on contrasting the Aryan ideal with lower levels of humanity, primarily the Jews, who must be purged if the Aryan nation was to be racially pure.

Matt rarely missed a chance to ridicule Nazi race theories, which he described in one article as "tribal mumbo-jumbo." He commented on the absurdity of German women being ordered to avoid French fashions because they were "non-Aryan"[33] and flocking to beauty parlours to have their hair dyed blond – "some because it is fashionable, some because blonde hair is a protective coloration."[34] With an eye for telling detail, he quoted a pathetic ad in a Munich newspaper from a doctor seeking employment. The ad explained that the doctor had been discharged because his mother was not considered an Aryan.[35] Matt ended one article in the series with a warning: "The things I saw being taught and believed everywhere in that nation – the superiority of one race and its destiny to rule – will one day become the intimate concern of all of us."[36]

In the first week of October, Matt boarded a suburban train in Munich for the sixteen-kilometre ride to Dachau. After laborious negotiations for a permit, he was about to become one of the first correspondents to visit a Nazi concentration camp. At the entrance, under the infamous *Arbeit Macht Frei* sign, SS guards swung open a heavy gate and carefully examined Matt's credentials. "I heard the shouting of staccato commands through the crisp autumn air and saw men being drilled at the double. . . . Suddenly, we came upon a group of about fifty prisoners lounging in the sun, dressed in grey smocks and trousers. 'Achtung!' cried a voice, and they jumped pitifully to attention."[37] The camp governor, SS Gruppenführer Theodor Eicke, and several guards were always at Matt's side as he was shown barracks and workshops. Matt described his visit as "a pre-arranged farce." He was not allowed to visit certain areas of the camp and was never allowed to speak to the prisoners privately except for one brief moment when the governor was distracted. "Are you treated well?" he asked a middle-aged prisoner. *"Ach, wunderbar"* was the deeply ironic reply.[38]

There were three thousand prisoners in Dachau. About two-thirds of them were former communists, socialists, social democrats, union leaders, and clergymen. About a third were Jews. Asked about reports that prisoners had been flogged, tortured, even in some cases murdered, the governor insisted that the camp did not sanction corporal punishment. But he did admit that Dachau was a model for other Nazi camps, and that its large numbers of SS guards – four hundred in all – were there partly "to harden our potential young leaders and teach them reality."[39] On instinct rather than hard evidence, Matt concluded that the regime "was deliberately inuring its young men to torture" or worse.[40] His judgment was confirmed by camp regulations found by Allied troops after the war. They required guards at Dachau to impose "merciless punishment" – such as twenty-five strokes for minor offences and hanging for disobeying orders or political agitation.[41] One of the young trainees at the camp was Rudolf Höss, who later became the notorious commandant of Auschwitz, responsible for the murder of more than a million people. Matt wrote that he left the camp with the unnerving conviction that, if he were a German, he too would be in Dachau.

There were few major aspects of Nazi policy that were not examined in the German Series. Matt wrote about the country's barely concealed rearmament program and the fact that more than a million men could be quickly mobilized – far more than the 100,000 army sanctioned by the Versailles treaty. He examined the Nazi takeover of religious institutions noting, with irony, that even God had been *gleichschaltet* (brought into line) in Hitler's Reich. He wrote about the role of German women and the dictum that "the duty of German women is to provide children for the battlefield and recreation for tired heroes."[42] He visited the labour service camps for young German men and women and praised their role in breaking down class barriers and reducing unemployment. He wrote about German industry, arguably overestimating its influence on Hitler. He travelled briefly to Austria and Danzig, predicting correctly that Hitler's territorial ambitions included Austria, Poland, and parts of Russia.

On one of his last nights in Berlin, Matt sat in the Adlon leafing through his notes. He decided that a German friend had a near-perfect answer when he asked him what was the essence of the Hitler revolution. "It is the triumph of faith and the debacle of reason," his friend replied.[43]

Matt's German assignment was about to end abruptly. In the last days of October, while he was still in Berlin, the *Star* decided to begin publishing the first of the series. The articles were immediately read by German diplomats in Canada. In the first week of November, a Nazi official warned Matt that he should leave the country. At first he ignored the warning until he was advised that he was being followed and would be foolish to stay. "That night," he wrote in his final dispatch from Berlin, "I hardly slept. I learned that feeling of hearing steps come down the corridor, wondering if they would stop at my door. . . . Morning came with leaden wings. I had travelled determinedly from one end of Germany to the other for two months, and now suddenly I was nervous. I couldn't wait to get out. I drove down to Tempelhof aerodrome. Two policemen were standing at the door but they weren't for me. I climbed into a great airplane and swept into the morning, toward England and freedom and home."[44] Was Matt over-dramatizing? Possibly. But he was also aware that Noel Panter, a correspondent for the London *Daily Telegraph,* had recently been arrested and jailed by the Nazis before being expelled.

The German Series brought Matt both glory and opprobrium. No other major newspaper in North America had published as comprehensive and as prophetic a picture of Hitler's Germany, not even the *Winnipeg Free Press*, one of the few other Canadian newspapers that was strongly critical of the Nazis. No other reporter had laid out Hitler's road map to war with such accuracy. The *St. Thomas Times-Journal* hailed the series of articles as "the most informative, most damning, most crushing exposure of what Hitlerism means that have been penned by any foreign correspondent. Mr. Halton has performed an international service."[45]

In the context of 1933, however, the German Series was deeply controversial, even offensive to many Canadians. Isolationism was firmly entrenched. The Bennett government was obsessed with communism and saw it as the sinister shadow behind labour unrest during the Depression. Many Canadians and Americans regarded Hitler as a bulwark against the Red menace. As the historian John Herd Thompson notes, "Fascism . . . was excused as an over-zealous form of anti-Communism."[46] The Toronto *Mail and Empire* even stated that it "might prefer Fascism to the Moscow-bred program of the CCF," Canada's newly established socialist party.[47] The Montreal *Gazette* wrote admiringly of the discipline and patriotic spirit of Nazi youth, which it suggested was a model for other countries.[48]

Less than two months before Matt's series was published, there was a startling example of the contrast between his reporting and what most Canadians were reading about the Third Reich. In late July, the Toronto *Globe* and Montreal *Gazette* began publishing a thirteen-part series that lavished praise on the Nazi regime. The series was written by Erland Echlin, a Canadian freelance journalist who was later interned by the British during the Second World War as a suspected German agent. Echlin depicted a near-idyllic Reich where "order, peace and hope have been restored,"[49] where throngs of proud Aryans attended concerts and operas,[50] and where Catholic and Protestant churches thanked Hitler for saving religion from Bolshevism.[51] Reports of outrages against Jews were dismissed as "imaginative lies."[52] So pleased was Goebbels's Propaganda Ministry by the series that it provided 500 Reichsmarks to Echlin so that he could extend his stay in Germany.[53] An interview with Hitler was arranged in which Echlin was not allowed to quote the Führer but could write about his impressions. At his sycophantic worst, Echlin described Hitler as "strong and fearless . . . without vanity. . . . He stands for peace. . . . Germany has only one desire – to preserve her independence."[54]

Almost as soon as Matt's first dispatches from Germany were published, he was accused of being a "sensationalist" and "a warmonger." Some of the more virulent attacks on his credibility came from Roman Catholics, many of whom applauded Hitler for holding back the red tide. There were reports that the Roman Catholic Archbishop of Toronto advised his congregation to stop buying the *Star*.[55] An angry letter to the *Lethbridge Herald*, which ran Matt's series, was typical of the hostile reaction. The Reverend C.H. Phillips wrote: "The scare headlines . . . savored so much of pure (or impure) jingoism that many beside myself must have been sickened. . . . As if that were not bad enough, you . . . commenced a series of articles from the pen of an itinerating [sic] journalist whose irresponsibility and all too evident love of cheap sensationalism leads him to speak without due regard to the consequences on matters of the gravest international import." The letter added that Matthew Halton had no busi-ness "expressing his thoughts on such grave matters as his host's internal policies" and engendering "a war-mindedness in your reading public which all right-thinking people deplore."[56]

Later in his life, Matt complained about being a prophet scorned in his own country. His widely syndicated German Series did alert hundreds of thousands of Canadians to the Nazi threat. But the series had no discernible effect on government policy and little success in changing public attitudes. Isolationism had taken hold. Memories of the slaughter of World War One were still vivid. From the political left to the right, most Canadians felt that there was no reason to take sides in Europe's distant problems.

Matt, though, was undeterred by his critics and by what he felt was a craven leadership and complacent public in the Western democracies. His crusade against Fascism continued with vigour for the rest of the decade.

ROYAL INTERLUDES

"Scarlet, silver and gold were there and Britain's chivalry and beauty."
— Matthew Halton, *Toronto Star*, May 7, 1935

Matt's persistent and ominous warnings about Fascism in the 1930s were often interspersed with lighter stories. Royal events were a staple: visits, weddings, funerals, coronations. While some socialists were inclined to be critical of royalty, Matt was a cheerleader. His enthusiasm may have originated as a child when Victoria Day in Pincher Creek was the biggest celebration of the year and when he lapped up stories in *Boy's Own* about a beneficent British Crown leading the Empire forward. Now he saw a different role for the monarchy: to rally the Empire in defence of freedom and democracy.

He was by no means an uncritical supporter of royalty. "The existence of the monarchy," he wrote, "helps to perpetuate the English caste system, which is by far the most rigid in the western world."[1] He complained that royal weddings and coronations at Westminster Abbey were "full of social 'nobodies' who owe their position to privilege rather than great men who have served their country."[2] But, in Matt's view, the disadvantages of the monarchy were more than offset by its value as a pillar of freedom and – after the Statute of Westminster in 1931 – as the crowning link between the independent countries of the Commonwealth. Even royalty's escapist appeal to the public was seen as a force for good, its rituals and ceremonies providing "a romantic interlude in a prosaic age."[3]

The young Matthew Halton.

Pincher Creek, Alberta, early 1900s.

Halton siblings: (from left) Jim, Annie, Matt, and baby David.

Charlotte Street –
a step up from the
Red Shack.

Matt, shortly after graduation.

Jean Campbell, Matt's girlfriend and
classmate at the University of Alberta.

Matt and Jean, a romantic ride on the Carthew Trail.

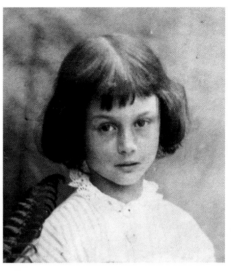

Lady Nancy Astor,
one of Matt's patrons.

Alice Liddell Hargreaves, the inspiration
for *Alice in Wonderland*, a connection
that would help catapult Matt into the
top ranks of Canadian journalists.

The *Toronto Daily Star* at
80 King Street West where
Matt began work in September 1931.

Matt and Jean attending
the annual garden party at
Buckingham Palace.

Matt and Jean at Berlin's Brandenburg Gate in September 1933.
Matt's "German Series" for the *Toronto Star* was described as "the most
informative, most damning, most crushing exposé of what Hitlerism
means that has been penned by any foreign correspondent."

At Windsor Castle for a photo shoot. Matt with King George VI, the Queen, and daughters Elizabeth and Margaret. The two extended photo sessions offered the *Star* team were unprecedented.

At the birth of celebrity journalism, Matt's name was often blazoned on the front page.

Matthew Halton interviewing Canadian general Andrew McNaughton during the Phoney War.

Matt, wearing the winter camouflage of Finnish troops, during Finland's war with Russia.

Throughout the war, Matt wrote frequently to Jean,
sending three or four letters a week.

Sean Fielding (far left) and Matt (second from left) after leaving Sidi Omar in 1941.

After a swim, near El Alamein. Matt, far left.

From far right: Sean Fielding, Matt's conducting officer and former newspaperman. Middle: Ronnie Noble, a news-film cameraman. Matt (far left).

Matt was twice assigned to report from India. Here, armed in what are now the tribal areas of Pakistan.

Matt would sometimes criticize other reporters for being "obsequious, in some cases, to the point of fawning and bootlicking" in their coverage of the royal family.[4] He was not immune from the same criticism. George V, whom historians have described as stodgy, tradition-bound, and anti-intellectual, was not the type of person who would normally be idolized by Matt. Yet the King's fervour for Empire, and his early dislike of the Nazis, won him high praise. Matt was thrilled by the accounts that as the King was dying, he cried out, "How is the Empire?"[5] There was unstinting praise for his reign: "His honesty and sincerity, even his shyness and humility, helped make him the perfect exemplar of a constitutional monarch, and his plain, straightforward family life set a model for untold thousands of English homes that worship the monarchy."[6]

Matt also praised George V for inaugurating the tradition of a Christmas Day address to the Empire – an opening on one occasion for Matt to poke fun at the English obsession with accents. It happened when London's popular press started a controversy over whether the King had dropped two "aitches" while pronouncing the words "hope" and "home" during his 1935 Christmas broadcast. The claim was apparently without foundation and Matt was quick to ridicule it:

> *This controversy rages hot but we in London deny the allegation. It can't be true! His majesty, tired, dropped one aitch and that only by inadvertence. . . . If he dropped more than one, it must have been in a special broadcast arranged separately to please his humble subjects. . . .*
>
> *Yes, said one cockney, "The King's speech is wonderful English. He makes us all feel at 'ome." And it is much better than that of radio announcers who say "quate" for "quite." Quite . . . Better drop an aitch than a brick.*
>
> *There are few aitches in the 'omes of 'alf the King's people and if he had dropped one, it would have been a very kindly gesture. But the British Broadcasting Corporation's language expert denied that any letters were dropped. "Why," he said, "our announcers model their English on the King's."[7]*

Unwilling to let the story rest there, Matt sought the opinion of Harold Nicolson, the brilliant young MP, diplomat, and acknowledged expert on British accents. Inadvertently adding another layer of absurdity to the story, Nicolson said George V spoke the very best King's English: "It is rich and strong and completely unaffected. . . . It is the accent of a wholesome, human country gentleman of the best type. . . . And there is a slight touch of the sea about it."[8]

An incurable romantic, Matt was inspired by the drama and majesty of royal events to some of his most colourful and eloquent writing. In January 1936, his description of George V's funeral, attended by the King's grieving wife, Queen Mary, and successor, Edward VIII, was grandiose and rich in detail:

> Within Windsor Castle's towering gray walls stands a beautiful little chapel, so old that England's history is written in its exquisitely carved stone; and here today, with an empire's lamentations, George V came home. Nothing is here for tears, nothing to wail, yet men and women cried. But not the Queen Mother, borne along on her courage and will power.
>
> The great Sebastopol bell in Windsor's ancient round tower rings only for the death of kings. Today it tolled one hundred and one times, but more poignant, far, was the sad wailing of "Flowers of the Forest," played by the king's pipers as the long funeral procession of kings, princes, soldiers and sailors moved slowly up Windsor's steep hill overlooking Eton college and that fair English view of river, forest and valley which King George loved so well. Only that bell and those wailing bagpipes cut like swords through a silence that was almost palpable, and Queen Mary's people saw her sighing but unbowed. . . .
>
> It was an unforgettable scene of high and moving splendor and dignity as the procession came through the Henry VIII Gate, under the Round Tower, and swept in a circle to the great west door. The cavalry were there, brilliantly caparisoned Horse Guards in front and rear, their long scarlet robes and white plumes moving slowly in the wind. Three thousand pairs of feet moved in slow rhythm to the melancholy music of the

Scots Guards band and the measured boom of minute guns and the toll-
ing of the Sebastopol bell. . . .

As they entered the church, the choir chanted "I Am the Resurrection
and the Life." King Edward and his mother, he in admiral's uniform and
haggard, she all in black and erect, walked at the head of the coffin. . . .
Almost throughout the fifteen minute service, Mary stood straight, almost
unmoving. The new King, white-faced, for once didn't make his character-
istic nervous gestures and quick movements but stood wide-eyed and lost.
The bishop of Winchester read the lesson from Revelation. Then the black-
robed choir sang the dead king's favorite hymn, "Abide With Me". When it
was over, Mary seemed suddenly to realize that her husband's body would
soon disappear from sight, and she wept a little and her shoulders trembled.
King Edward then touched her hand and she bravely raised her head.

At that moment the gray old chapel was momentarily lit by dancing
sunbeams through colored glass, and ghosts of English history seemed to
pass over our heads. Complete silence fell, and the end was near. The
crown, sceptre and orb, which are the king's insignia of office, were
removed from the coffin and placed on a crimson cushion.

Taking up his book, the Archbishop of Canterbury began the slow,
sad words of the burial service, which commits men's bodies to the dust.

And then, before tortured eyes, the coffin began to sink slowly
through the floor into the vault below. Edward VIII stepped forward. In
his hand he held a silver urn containing earth, which he sprinkled on the
coffin as his father disappeared from sight of men. The Archbishop of
Canterbury pronounced the last word of committal in his rich, sonorous
voice. The Queen Mother's eyes were glued to the floor. In this chapel,
where Cromwell's men once stabled their horse in contempt for the head-
less body of Charles I lying below, silence now passed into a faint rustling
like the beating of wings. The coffin had disappeared from sight. . . .

The Georgian era which saw the world transformed is over; the
Edwardian era begins today.[9]

Strong in his praise for George v, Matt was even more admiring of
the ill-fated Edward VIII. He had met the heir to the throne by chance at

a London nightclub while he was still Prince of Wales. They talked briefly about the lure of the Alberta foothills where the Prince owned a ranch not far from Pincher Creek. "He offers you a drink and you talk then for a few minutes about riding through the valleys of the foothills on a late summer afternoon with the saddle leather creaking and about fishing in a mountain stream, and how wonderful it would be to be there, and a few things like that; and after a while when you begin to feel your welcome has run its course, you shake hands and sidle back to your own table, thinking what a fine person the Prince of Wales really is."[10] Later, Matt was attracted by Edward's informality and desire to shed the stuffier traditions of monarchy. He was also impressed by his decision to visit depressed areas of the country and to incur the wrath of Conservative diehards with his comment that "England was once a land for the few; now it's a land for the many, but we must make it a land for all."[11] Matt correctly predicted that Edward would continue to push for better conditions for the working class.

As he began his reign, Edward was already immensely popular in English Canada. Matt's glowing profiles of the new King would not have been considered sycophantic by most *Star* readers but, in retrospect, they were certainly exaggerated. Edward was described as "the most intensely dynamic monarch who ever sat on the throne of Britain,"[12] with a personality that was "magnetic, dominating."[13] Matt did mention two faults: impatience and a sharp temper. But there was no hint that the Prince was also spoiled and self-indulgent – the verdict of both his private secretary at the time and later biographers.[14] Matt's greatest misjudgment was one made by other journalists as well. On several occasions he predicted that the King would never marry.

The abdication crisis burst like a giant bombshell over the Empire. For six weeks, U.S. and European newspapers had trumpeted stories that Edward planned to marry Wallis Simpson, a divorced and twice-married American socialite. The King had secretly informed Prime Minister Baldwin that he intended to marry Mrs. Simpson. Baldwin's view was that "Wally" could be tolerated as "a respectable whore" behind the throne,[15] but it was made clear to Edward that a royal marriage was unacceptable. Rumours flew about the love affair, which was widely reported in the

United States but went discreetly unmentioned by a deferential press (including the *Star*) in Britain and Canada. Then, on December 1, Alfred Blunt, an obscure Anglican bishop in England, gave a speech saying that Edward was in need of more divine grace than he was demonstrating.[16] That cryptic comment unleashed a flood of headlines, at last making the story public in the Commonwealth. There was shock, anxiety, even near-hysteria. Newspapers warned that the foundations of the Empire were in danger of crumbling. From Rideau Hall, the governor general, Lord Tweedsmuir, informed London that Canadian puritanism would be outraged if Edward married a divorcée and a commoner.[17]

For a few days, Matt's byline was conspicuously absent from the Empire's biggest story of the decade. He had been in Barcelona covering the Spanish Civil War (see next chapter) when frantic cables from Toronto ordered him to return to London immediately. For his editors, the fact that tens of thousands were being killed in a war that presaged World War Two was far less important than the royal drama shaking the Empire. Back in London on a dismally dark and foggy evening, Matt rushed to make the final editions of the *Star*. He described the thousands of people anxiously waiting outside 10 Downing Street and the mood of high suspense gripping the public. He quoted extensively from the British press, most of which demanded that Edward choose either marriage to Mrs. Simpson or his throne. Then he carried out his own straw poll of several dozen Londoners, reporting considerable support for allowing the King to marry without stepping down.[18] Other papers reported majorities in favour of abdication.

Matt carefully avoided taking sides in the crisis but hinted at his sympathy for the King's position. Doubtless he was influenced by two of his political heroes – Churchill and Lloyd George – who both favoured some solution that would allow Edward to stay on the throne.[19] Rumors began flying that the King's supporters led by Churchill would form a "King's Party," an incendiary development that would have dragged the monarch into the thick of party politics. Matt wisely ignored the rumours, which appeared to have little substance. But he did give some weight to speculation that the government was using the marriage issue to force Edward out because of his political views. In November, the King had visited impoverished coal mining villages in South Wales. His comment that something must be done for the unemployed miners was seen by some as critical of the government and a breach of the role of a constitutional monarch. "It is known now," Matt wrote, "that Baldwin and the Tory ruling class have always feared trouble from eager, independent and stubborn King Edward. And the Foreign Office is most reliably reported to have been highly incensed at the very fact that Edward intended to be more than a figurehead and was attempting to take a hand in formulating foreign policy."[20] While Matt accurately reflected Establishment feelings, there was no evidence that Tory concern about the King's political views were determining factors in the abdication.

Two days after Matt's return to London, Baldwin announced in the House of Commons that the King had agreed to renounce the throne. "The common people of Britain are shocked and subdued, incredulous and deeply perplexed," Matt wrote, "but cognizant of the great democratic fact that parliament and the constitution are, as our ancestors fought that they should be, more powerful and important than the throne."[21] Millions across the Empire listened to Edward's farewell speech, his voice close to breaking when he mentioned "the woman I love" and ending with the words "God save the King." Matt described it as drama on the scale of a Shakespearean tragedy, and he witnessed its final scene in darkness at the gates of Windsor Lodge. After a farewell visit with his mother and brother, the soon-to-be-proclaimed King George VI, Edward began his journey into exile. As his car drove slowly off, the flash of camera bulbs gave Matt a momentary glimpse of a man stripped of his crown and now to be known as the Duke of Windsor. "What I will remember," Matt wrote, "is his haggard face and startled eyes."[22]

Far from sating readers' appetite for stories about royalty, the abdication crisis increased the demand for them. The *Star* wanted profiles of the new King and every member of his family as well as detailed previews of the coming coronation. Over the next four months Matt found himself writing about the obscure rituals and protocols of crowning George VI; about such details as the underwear and brassieres sewn with Union Jacks that were selling in London shops; about the new lion cubs christened

George and Elizabeth in the London zoo; about the extra ration of grog for the Royal Navy in coronation week; and about the fact that the Nawab of Bhopal had arrived from India for the coronation with twenty-five polo ponies. He confessed to having to write "coronation froth."[23]

Another frustration was the difficulty of prying information from snooty Palace officials for whom "Colonial newspapermen – don't think for a moment that the English don't call us colonials ! – are just a little lower than sea level."[24] But he also skewered some of the hoary traditions of the monarchy. In an article on the Court of Claims, which judges competing claims to perform honorary services at coronations, Matt reverted to the absurdist genre of writing that he so enjoyed:

> I walked trembling into the office of Bernard Marmaduke Fitzalan-Howard, 16th Duke of Norfolk, Earl of Arundel, Baron Maltravers, Clun and Oswaldestre, Earl Marshal, Hereditary Marshal and High Chief Butler of England, and when a man has got as many titles as that you have to be careful not to speak out of turn. . . . It's practically like approaching divinity, but the thing had to be done. As Earl Marshal of England, young Bernard Marmaduke Fitzalan-Howard is running the coronation, and there were things I wanted to know.
>
> Three of the duke's minions, themselves so noble they could hardly bear it, transfixed me with their eyes. "Where's Marmaduke?" I asked – I mean, that's what I wanted to ask, in bold irreverent tones; but instead I practically apologized for being alive. "I just wanted to ask some questions about the court of claims," I whispered hoarsely. The noble minions hemmed and hawed and were more embarrassed than I. "The court of claims," said the first minion. "The court of claims," said the second minion. "Ah, the court of claims," echoed the third minion. "Yes, the court of claims," I gasped. " I wanted to ask the Earl Marshal about the court of claims."
>
> Now a camel has a far fatter chance of getting through the eye of a needle than any reporter has of getting into the presence of the Duke of Norfolk and the minions were so aghast they were almost polite, which is a notoriously unusual thing for court officials to be to newspapermen

in this country. *The Earl Chamberlain's office and the Earl Marshal's office both have a press officer, though I don't know why, because they always refuse to tell you anything; but this time they were so startled by my presumption that in practically no time I was talking to Major William le Hardy, and he told me about the court of claims, the most picturesque court in the world.*

The court of claims (it really ought to be written in capital letters because it's a pretty holy thing) was founded in 1377 to decide which nobles should have certain honors at coronations. For example, there was a dispute between the Earl of Ancaster and the Earl of Oxford as to which of the two had the right "to draw on the king's shirt, stockings and drawers" on coronation morning and the court of claims settled it. The same claim has to be settled in 1937. There is the question of who shall have the honor of drawing a velvet glove onto the King's right hand just after he is crowned. There is the matter of who shall lead him to the throne of Scone. There is the matter of who shall hand him his golden spurs. Who shall be the keeper of the King's Conscience? Who shall present him with two falcons? Who shall have the linen from the bed in which he sleeps on coronation eve? The court of claims decides.

"It looks like baloney to me," I said – I mean, that's what I hoped I would say as I walked in to see Major le Hardy, one of the doughtiest constitutional lawyers of the realm, but actually I merely asked who was going to be the Lord Great Chamberlain for 1937. "Probably Ancaster," he said and he told me about that.

The Lord Great Chamberlain is the man who has the right to hand the King his shirt, stockings and drawers on coronation morn. "Until a couple of centuries ago," said Major le Hardy, "the man who fulfilled this office had the right to take everything in the King's bedroom – the bed, the linen, the furniture, everything." "Do they still do that?" I asked. "Oh, no," said Major le Hardy. "They couldn't very well do that any more, so now the Lord Great Chamberlain receives 40 yards of coronation velvet free." "That's not very much for pulling on the King's pants," I said. "Oh, it's quite a bit," said Major le Hardy; "coronation velvet costs about ten pounds a yard."[25]

Matt's profiles of the new King were considerably more restrained than those he wrote about Edward. George VI was described as "a typical and unassuming Englishman of the privileged class. Say that and you have an adequate description of the looks, personality and character of our King."[26] Matt wrote that, unlike Edward, George disliked society life, nightclubs, and modern dancing, preferring instead quiet evenings with radio, books, and family. There was no mention of his famous stammer until much later but his heavy smoking and liking for Scotch were noted. His wife, Queen Elizabeth, was "sweet and charming,"[27] and Matt seemed entranced by the eleven-year-old Princess Elizabeth, heir to the throne. He caught a brief glimpse of her at 145 Piccadilly where the family lived before moving to Buckingham Palace. "Destiny is calling her like a far-off bugle to one of the three or four highest positions under the sun. Yet today I heard her laughing and saw her dance down a stairway like a sunbeam."[28]

Matt was now well known enough to the Palace to be given one of the sixty coveted press seats in Westminster Abbey to witness the coronation. At six a.m. on the day of the ceremony, he walked along the parade route where tens of thousands of people had waited all night in heavy rain. He chatted briefly with a policeman about the extraordinary appeal of the monarchy and was given an unexpected explanation. "Don't you see," the bobby said, "our people are crowning themselves."[29] Matt thought the comment was unusually shrewd and quoted it several times.

Inside the Abbey, Matt wrote one of his flamboyant descriptions of a ceremony that had not changed much in a thousand years. Seated high in the triforium, he would write several pages then hand them to a royal usher to be run to a telegraph operator in time for the early editions of the *Star*. "As I sat in the Abbey, I heard history whispering down its Gothic aisles and felt that here, as in no other country, yesterday, today and tomorrow are all of a piece."[30] Matt described a tableau of crimson and ermine robes and flashing gems, of blaring trumpets and elaborate rituals leading to the climactic moment when George was anointed with oil and crowned King. "A flash of brilliant color across the back-drop of English time has passed into history," he concluded.[31]

Of the many stories about royalty that Matt reported, none generated more copy than the preparations for the Royal Tour of Canada in the spring of 1939. It was the first visit of a reigning monarch, an event of great excitement in a devotedly monarchist English Canada. For Prime Minister Mackenzie King it was an opportunity to demonstrate the changed constitutional reality: George VI was now King of an independent Canada, not just the British King of a British Empire. For the now post-appeasement British government, there was an entirely different objective – to rally support for Britain in the coming war in Europe.

Matt filed more than fifty stories about the visit in the four months before the King and Queen departed for Canada. The *Star*'s appetite for royal news was again insatiable. He was asked for profiles of senior palace officials accompanying the royal couple. The paper even wanted interviews with the two ladies-in-waiting travelling with the Queen, an unexpectedly pleasant task for Matt since he found one of them, Lady Nunburnholme, to be exceptionally attractive.[32] Nothing was too trivial for Matt to write about, not even the fact that the King's fourteen-year-old bellboy was instructed to have dry biscuits ready if the monarch got seasick.[33] At times he sounded almost apologetic about writing such stories as the world approached a cataclysm.

Matt's frequent visits to Buckingham Palace, where he was a familiar if not always welcome figure to press secretaries, helped him get one of the biggest and most unexpected scoops of his career. Three months before the Royal Tour, he spent several frustrating days seeking permission for the *Star* to photograph the King and Queen. The pictures, he said, would be used to promote the Royal Tour in the highest-circulation newspaper in Canada. A condescending press officer refused the request with a "such-things-aren't done-here, old boy" kind of response. Matt recounted the incident to his parents with the bitter comment that "if Canadians and Americans really knew how . . . [the] ruling caste here despise us rude colonials, we wouldn't be half so enthusiastic about their visit to the New World."[34]

That perception changed instantly in April when a letter sealed with the royal coat of arms was delivered to Matt at the *Star*'s London office: "Their Majesties wish that your photographer should come to Buckingham

Palace at half-past two tomorrow to take photographs in color and black-and-white." There would be a second "sitting" at Windsor Castle later. Matt would be allowed to supervise both sessions. The one condition was that the photos would have to be made available later to other Canadian and American newspapers.[35]

Matt arrived at the Palace well in advance with two Canadian photographers, the *Star's* Lawrie Audrain and Gerald Richardson. They drove in a humble London black cab, which looked out of place as it dropped them off at the Privy Purse entrance at the Palace. A scarlet-clad footman opened the door, then various major-domos escorted them down a long corridor to the imposing Bow Room. Uncertain whether photographs would be taken inside or outside, the cameramen prepared to do both. It was an intimidating moment for the three Canadians when the King and Queen approached, with Princesses Elizabeth and Margaret in tow. Matt later said he forgot to make the proper bow when the Queen offered her hand and he addressed her (in fact, correctly) as "Your Majesty" instead of what he thought was the required "Ma'am." But he was soon put at ease as the royal family led the Canadian trio outside to the Palace gardens. There the King's private secretary, Alan Lascelles, spread out a map of Canada on a table and the royal family pored over it in front of the cameras. The King traced on the map the route he would take across Canada for the benefit of the curious princesses who would be staying at home.[36] Perhaps spoofing the reverential tone of royal press coverage, Matt described the King as "regal" and, yes, the Queen as "radiant."

There were comic moments when King, Queen, and princesses returned to the Bow Room to be photographed sitting informally on a settee. As Matt recounted later, there was a problem:

> *Their Welsh corgi was moving at their feet and wouldn't keep still. Lawrie left his camera and approached the settee, fixed the queen with his eye and stammered words: "Your Majesty, much though I love –"*
>
> *There was a second of silence. Now what's he trying to say, I wondered. But Queen Elizabeth was quicker on the uptake. She smiled and said coaxingly the word, "dogs."*

"Dogs," confirmed Lawrie. "Much though I love dogs, this photograph must have a half-second exposure and I'm afraid the dog might move."

So someone called the dog, but he wouldn't budge. "He wants to be in your pictures," said Princess Elizabeth. "Madam," I ventured, "shall I pick him up?" "I'm afraid he would bite you," replied the Queen. "Shall I take him out?" said Princess Elizabeth, indicating another great room. "Goodness, no," said the Queen, "he might bite someone else." But at this moment Dookie realized that he was de trop and crept grumbling away.[37]

The second photo shoot at Windsor Castle allowed Matt more time to chat with the King and Queen. Matt would laughingly recall that when they were standing in a semicircle on the Castle terrace and he was addressed by the Queen, he had his back to George VI for long moments. They discussed the almost daily speculation that the visit to Canada might be postponed because of the looming war with Germany. "Three to one you go," Matt said, and the Queen nodded and said, "I think so, too."[38] He also asked whether the visit, with stopovers in scores of places in every province in Canada, would be an ordeal for them. "Of course, it won't be," the King replied and the Queen added that it would be one of the biggest events of their life. They talked about their itinerary, a chance for Matt to venture how much they would enjoy the Rockies and "the flawless jewel of Lake Louise."[39] Thirteen-year-old Princess Elizabeth said she would like to canoe on Canadian rivers one day.[40] There was even a brief discussion of George's interest in photography, a hobby he said he no longer had time for.

Matt had not expected to be able to write about the two photo sessions, observing strict protocol at the time that the monarch never gave interviews to the press and allowed no exchange with journalists to be quoted. But shortly after the Windsor session, Matt received a telephone call from Captain Michael Adeane, who had worked for two governors general at Rideau Hall and was now assistant private secretary to the King. Adeane said the royal family were pleased with the "sittings," and he gave Matt permission to describe them as well as his conversations with the King and Queen. According to former Palace press secretaries, that concession was unprecedented, as were the two extended photo sessions offered the

Star team.[41] After the photos were published in the *Star*, they were splashed over the pages of newspapers and magazines across North America. Some included Matt's account of the sessions. It was an enormous coup for the paper. Joe Atkinson, the *Star's* publisher, cabled Matt that the sessions were "unique in the annals of journalism."[42]

Matt continued to feed Canadian excitement over the Royal Tour until the final moments of the King and Queen's departure. He was in Portsmouth as the royal couple boarded the CPR's *Empress of Australia*. As the ship eased away from the dock, the King and Queen waved goodbye, the band played *Farewell to Thee*, seagulls screamed, guns boomed out a parting salute, and George threw a few flowers down to his mother, Queen Mary. Wonder and tears, Matt said, were in the eyes of the princesses as they waved from dockside. For the sentimental monarchist from Pincher Creek, these were inspirational moments. "This was majesty at its best," he wrote. "One forgot that storms and barbarism were hammering at the gates of civilization. One forgot the poor, rickety children, cheering below. . . . One thought only of these colorful, gorgeous scenes that stir the blood."[43]

The Royal Tour proved to be a "public relations masterpiece,"[44] touching off a wave of Canadian pride over a King who was now Canada's King. There was a renewed sense of national and empire unity that would make it easier for most Canadians to say "Ready, Aye, Ready," when the nation was called to arms. Many historians would later agree with the judgment that "it was for imperial solidarity that they (Canadians) went to war, not to fight fascism."[45]

8

TWILIGHT OF PEACE

*"It is now clear that the high hopes we held after 1918 were a great folly
and delusion."*

— MATTHEW HALTON, *Toronto Star*, December 6, 1934

IN MYTH IF NOT REALITY, the 1930s were the best of years to be a
foreign correspondent. Clad in trench coat and fedora, foreign correspondents were cast in Hollywood movies and pulp fiction as glamorous
and sometimes heroic figures. Their world was one of intrigue, war, and
romantic entanglements. In Alfred Hitchcock's 1940 movie *Foreign
Correspondent*, the New York newspaperman Huntley Haverstock tracks
down Nazi spies and, of course, ends up with both the big scoop and the
gorgeous girl. But Hitchcock wanted to add a serious message. As the film
opens, a dedication to foreign correspondents is scrolled down the screen:
"To those forthright ones who early saw the clouds of war while many of
us at home were seeing rainbows. . . To those clear-headed ones who now
stand like recording angels among the dead and dying."[1]

Matt would certainly have considered himself one of those "clear-
headed ones." He was part of a small fraternity of mainly British and
American journalists who shared the same left-wing views and a rage
against Fascism. Some of them became lifelong friends. In Paris, Matt met
James M. (Don) Minifie, a *New York Herald Tribune* reporter who, like him,
had grown up in a poor, homesteading family in the Canadian West and
would end up as a correspondent for the CBC. In Berlin and Vienna, he

became friendly with William Shirer, a scholarly American who worked for the Hearst wire service before becoming one of Edward R. Murrow's legendary group of CBS correspondents. In Geneva and Paris, he lunched with Geneviève Tabouis, a French correspondent so well informed about Nazi intentions that Hitler once sneered at her in public for "knowing yesterday what I am going to say today."[2] Like Matt, she was accused of being a warmonger for arguing that only a credible threat of force could check German aggression. Among other colleagues, Leland Stowe, a Pulitzer Prize–winning American journalist, would tease Matt about his hometown boosterism. Stowe later said that "the kid from Pincher Creek could keep pace with the best among us."[3]

Events brought Matt and his colleagues together more frequently as Hitler's new order in Europe took hold. In January 1935, Matt and other correspondents gathered in the Saar, the small industrial region bordering France, to witness the first major expansion of the Reich's frontiers. The Saar had been shorn from Germany under the Treaty of Versailles and placed under League of Nations control. Now, fifteen years later, a plebiscite was required to determine whether the Saarlanders wished to return to Germany, continue under League government, or join France.

When Matt arrived, it was already clear that the Saar's half a million largely German voters would choose to rejoin the Fatherland. The For Sale signs on stores with Jewish names were one indication of what was to come. Although the Nazis were banned from campaigning openly, their undercover agents swarmed over the territory. Walking through Saarbrücken, the capital, Matt was puzzled by the evergreens displayed on most homes. He was told they were put out on orders from a Nazi front organization to indicate support for the pro-German option. The message was unmistakable: after the plebiscite the Gestapo would know who opposed joining Hitler's Reich and action would be taken against them.[4]

When the plebiscite results were announced, an unexpectedly high 90 per cent of Saarlanders had chosen to cast their lot with Germany. Matt concluded that Nazi intimidation was less important than the ties of *"Blut und Boden"* (blood and soil) – the slogan used so effectively by the Nazis to foster German nationalism. Matt's morning cable to the *Star* described a tumultuous scene: church bells ringing as people surged into the streets to celebrate; young hotheads rushing to the frontier to dig up boundary posts between the Saar and the Reich; schoolchildren chanting the popular slogan *Deutsch ist die Saar, Deutsch Immerdar* (The Saar is German, German forever).[5]

There were other demonstrations, bigger in size and far more frenzied in tone, when the Saar was officially turned over to Germany in the first week of March. Returning to Saarbrücken, Matt watched goose-stepping Storm Troopers arrive for thirty-six hours of parades by day and torch-light processions by night. When word spread that Hitler would make a surprise visit, two hundred thousand people poured into the streets. Matt described a near-hysterical roar from the crowd as the Führer arrived. Bare-headed in drenching rain and wearing his brown Nazi uniform, Hitler stood in his open car, thrusting his arm out in the Nazi salute. His clothes were soaking wet when he appeared a few minutes later on his hotel balcony, shouting, "This day should be a lesson. . . . Blood is stronger than paper." Matt cabled the *Star* that "it was his old, terrible cry of unreason. Pacts don't count, only blood."[6]

Darker consequences of the Saar plebiscite were already being felt. The territory had been a sanctuary for German Jews, Communists, and socialists escaping persecution in the Reich. Now they were fleeing again. For weeks, hundreds of men and women seeking visas lined up outside the French consulate. Matt witnessed hundreds of others dragging their possessions to the station for trains to France. "It is a spectacle," he wrote, "of people in torment, lost, desolate and despairing."[7] The situation quickly got worse after the handover. Political dissidents were rounded up. New anti-Semitic laws were imposed that made it harder for Jews to leave. Nor was there any help from the stricter immigration policies being adopted in the democracies, most severely by Canada. "The 20th Century is no century for refugees," said Matt in his last dispatch from the Saar. "In this respect the world is now more callous than it has been for two centuries."[8]

Matt's vivid, judgmental style of journalism also coloured his reporting of the Nazi Olympics in 1936. He correctly predicted that the games would be a colossal propaganda operation. "Foreign visitors," he wrote, "will be met with nothing but kindness, mass enthusiasm and sweetness and light, and most of them will go away without seeing anything of the ugly background behind the façade."[9] Joseph Goebbels's Propaganda Ministry spent freely to project an image of Germany as friendly, orderly, and safe. Extraordinary efforts were made to cater to the needs of athletes and the large foreign press contingent. Translators and guides were provided free of charge, and food and drink were lavished on the visitors. Willing German girls were even made available to white athletes in the Olympic village in Berlin.[10]

The winter games were held in the twin Bavarian villages of Garmisch-Partenkirchen in February. Almost as soon as he arrived, Matt began writing about what became known as the "Olympic pause" – the suspending of anti-Jewish repression while the games were on. He noted the removal of the ubiquitous anti-Semitic signs such as "Jews Not Wanted Here" from the Olympic areas, and the orders to Nazi organizations to suspend attacks on Jews. Visitors saw no evidence of the vicious Nuremberg laws passed only six months earlier that stripped German Jews of their citizenship and many other rights. Many visitors were convinced that foreign correspondents were to blame for creating a distorted picture of Nazi rule. A young figure skater on the Canadian team provoked an angry response from Matt when he told him he had read his articles on Germany but no longer believed them. "Did you expect to see blood running down the gutters at the Olympic games?" Matt asked. "No," said the skater, "but no people as courteous as these could persecute Jews or militarize their whole country."[11] It was an opinion widely shared among foreign visitors enjoying the *gemütlichkeit* atmosphere of the games.

Matt had been personally in favour of boycotting the Olympics. He told Elmer Dulmage of the Canadian Press, the only other Canadian correspondent covering the games, that taking part in the Olympics would help to legitimize Hitler's regime. At dinner one night, Dulmage recalled Matt saying, "These Olympics depress me terribly. I see the razzle-dazzle but I think of the thousands of Jews in this country who, as soon as the games are over, will again be tormented and many of them killed. . . . By coming here, we are encouraging Hitler."[12] In fact, the boycott movement lost much of its momentum when the Nazis agreed to allow two token half-Jews to compete on the German team. One of them was Rudi Ball, who was allowed back from exile to play for the German hockey team. Ball knew it was a cynical ploy by a country that had systematically excluded Jews from sports clubs and competition. But he told Matt that "it may help us for the nation to think that a Jew and German played side by side" – a statement Matt described as "a thin, pathetic hope."[13] Sammy Luftspring, a Canadian Jewish boxer, was more realistic. He refused to compete in a country that he said "would exterminate them [the Jews] if they had the opportunity."[14]

The Nazis went to unusual lengths to prevent critical coverage of the Olympics. In Matt's case, there was a behind-the-scenes effort to exclude him from the summer games. In June, a German representative in Toronto tried to persuade the *Star* to replace Matt with a more sympathetic reporter. In a letter to Berlin, the official described Matt as *"ausserordentlich deutschfeindlich"* (extraordinarily hostile to Germans).[15] The *Star* ignored the German's request.

The summer Olympics were the biggest event ever staged in Berlin. Rapturous crowds – more than a million on some days – lined the route from Hitler's chancellery to the Reichssportsfeld where the games were held. On opening day, Matt was both excited and repelled by a scene he said could only be reproduced by "the stark reality of the Roman coliseum or the illusory gaudiness of Hollywood."[16] As the giant airship *Hindenburg* drifted overhead, Hitler entered the stadium through a forbidding cordon of Storm Troopers and his elite Black Guard. Trumpets blared and an artillery salute thundered over the arena. Then "a hundred thousand zealots with rapt religious eyes stretch out their arms and sing"[17] "Deutschland über Alles" and the Horst Wessel Song, the belligerent anthem of the Brown Shirts. Marching past Hitler's reviewing stand, Canada's athletes received a roaring ovation when they raised their arms in what appeared to be the Nazi salute. Embarrassed Canadian officials later explained that the team was using the slightly different Olympic salute. The distinction wasn't mentioned in Matt's story that day, perhaps because of deadline pressures. Nor was the fact that the American, British, and many other teams carefully avoided any similar gesture. The salute by the Canadian athletes was later given a prominent place in Leni Riefenstahl's *Olympia*, the documentary film exalting Nazi values.[18]

Hitler and his deputies attended the games almost every day. Sitting in the press box just above the reviewing stand, Matt was intrigued to be so close to the Nazi hierarchy. In later years, he would often fantasize how – with a bullet or a grenade – he might have saved the world from vast agony. At the time though, he was fascinated to watch the men who were about to reshape Europe:

> *Caesar, dressed in his brown uniform sits down to watch the gladiators. His face is whiter but plumper than I have seen it before. When he is not talking to someone, his eyes have an unseeing look – as of a man hearing voices, or at least thinking of something not in that stadium. . . . Hitler's left-hand man Goebbels sits between Hitler and Göring. . . . Anti-Nazi Germans hate him [Goebbels] far more than they hate Hitler. They call him "The Fox". He it is who has killed thought in Germany and welded most of those 65,000,000 people into one vast, sentient mass whose emotions, feelings, loves and hates he controls with diabolical skill. Every single instrument of publicity in Germany . . . is part of his great pipe-organ that has one, and only one tune, played with variations: the preparation of Germany for the domination of Europe."*[19]

Matt was far more interested in the politics and spectacle of the Olympics than its sporting events. Dulmage, his Canadian Press colleague, joked that "Halton didn't know a javelin from a boxing glove and didn't care."[20] His assessment was not entirely off the mark. Apart from hockey, rowing, and long-distance running, Matt was bored by most Olympic sports. A week into the games he wrote that he "had had his fill of running, jumping and hopping."[21] His description of some events was sometimes quaint. "Loaring ran and jumped like a hare," he said in reference to Johnny Loaring, the Canadian silver medallist in the 400-metre hurdles.[22] He also provided a textbook example of what newspaper reporters call the "buried lead." When Frank Amyot won Canada's only gold medal in the 1,000-metre canoe singles, Matt did not mention it until the fourth paragraph of a roundup of the day's events.

On several occasions, Matt gave his readers glimpses of the Germany beyond the Olympic façade. During the winter games, he went to Munich for a day to check out reports that heavy spending on armaments was causing food shortages. In Berlin, he was taken by a German-Canadian acquaintance to meet a young Jewish pianist who had spent a year in a concentration camp. They met in a bar on the east side of the city, far from the bright lights of the Kurfürstendamm and tourist Berlin. The pianist was one of the extremely few German Jews who dared to speak frankly to a foreigner. He had been beaten and imprisoned for refusing the demands of Nazi Jew-baiters to humiliate himself in public. Matt asked him why he wasn't afraid of being sent back to a concentration camp for speaking so openly. "I know I'll go back," he replied, before suggesting fatalistically that he might be dead before long: "That's why I speak my mind."[23]

Most foreign visitors never saw through the fog of Nazi propaganda. Typical of the generally positive press reaction was the comment by Frederick Birchall of the *New York Times* that he found "not the slightest evidence of religious, political or racial prejudice" at the Olympics.[24] As the games began, the visiting Canadian trade minister, W.D. Euler, met Hitler and was impressed by what he said was his "active mind" and strong desire for peace.[25] As Matt predicted, the world had been largely hoodwinked. It was a victory not only for the Nazis but for the growing forces of appeasement in the democracies.

Forty-four years after the games, the former CP reporter Elmer Dulmage was inspired to write an article about the young *Star* correspondent he met at the Olympics. "Should we have been in Berlin in 1936?" he asked. "I think Matt Halton was right. A boycott would have been better."[26]

At home in London, Matt was anchored happily by his marriage. Jean was ever the practical, grounded force in his life, curbing his extravagances and managing the family finances. Their social life was lively: dinners with friends, theatre-going, drinking and dining at the fashionable Café Royal. The couple, and their housekeeper, moved from their apartment to an attractive Georgian house across the road from Regent's Park. Their daughter, Kathleen Jeanette Halton, was born in January 1937. Matt became the doting father, taking her for walks in the park, helping her feed the ducks in the Serpentine, and gaze at the animals in the nearby London zoo. "Jean and I are having a grand time," he wrote his parents. "I have Europe for my stamping ground and love my work and the paper treats me most handsomely."[27]

A good salary and a fat expense account were some of the advantages of working for the most profitable and most read newspaper in Canada. So too was the generous travel budget the *Star* gave Matt, often permitting him to be the only Canadian correspondent covering a story on the continent. The favour of publisher Joe Atkinson and managing editor Harry Hindmarsh was important for other reasons. It gave him wide freedom to choose his own stories and the continuing privilege of keeping his copy largely free from editing by deskmen in Toronto.

Matt repaid the *Star* by giving the paper what it wanted: sharp-edged political and social reporting leavened by interviews, features, travelogues, "Canadian-angle" stories, and a weekly notebook of gossip and personal impressions.

His interviews, especially those with celebrities, continued to be appreciated in a paper bent on entertaining as well as informing. Among scores of his subjects in the late thirties were screen heart-throb Gary Cooper, actor-singer Paul Robeson, Canadian news magnate Lord Beaverbrook, sculptor Jacob Epstein, and aviator Louis Blériot. When Matt interviewed Gracie Fields, he established an instant rapport with the actress and comedienne who had become the most famous woman in Britain outside royalty. He began by telling her that his parents came from near Wigan, the drab Lancashire town where Fields grew up and worked in a cotton mill. Fields laughingly responded by breaking into a thick Lancashire accent: "Ee my lad, dost tha come from Wiggia too?"[28] Matt's account of the interview played up her pride in her working-class roots. "I feel like a bloody toff," she told him, "when I ride in a limousine."[29] He wrote that it was her ability to be clownish at times and transparently emotional on other occasions that explained her huge success on stage and screen.

One of his interviews led to a long-lasting friendship with the Canadian multimillionaire Garfield Weston. Already becoming the world's biggest bread and biscuit maker, Weston would soon become a Conservative MP at Westminster and eventually the owner of Loblaw's and a chain of bakeries and grocery stores in seven countries. On the surface, it seemed an unlikely friendship: a socialist like Matt, suspicious of capitalism, and a business magnate like Weston, who personified capitalism's success. But at their first meeting to discuss Weston's reluctance to be interviewed, they took a liking to each other and discovered much in common. Both shared an enthusiasm for the British Empire and hoped it would evolve into a Commonwealth of more equal nations. Both disliked the rampant snobbery in Britain, Weston to the extent of refusing to send his older son to the Establishment school at Harrow, and not allowing his daughters to be presented at court.[30]

Matt's profile of Weston in the *Star* was flattering to an extreme. He described him as having the face of a Nordic film star, as a magnetic speaker, and as the kind of enlightened capitalist who "would create comfort and plenty for all." Even before the interview was published, Matt was invited to Wittington, the lovely estate on the Thames at Marlow where Weston lived at the time with his wife and children. It was the first of many visits there over the years, often with Matt bringing his family or friends. In Canada after the war, Weston sometimes called him to discuss British politics and, on one occasion, Matt showed him around his cherished foothills country near Pincher Creek.[31]

Matt had few opportunities for investigative reporting, but one exception was what the Star labelled "the hoax of the century." In April 1938, the *North Bay Nugget* revealed that Grey Owl, the celebrated Indian conservationist who had just died, was really an Englishman named Archie Belaney. Matt had interviewed him two years earlier on a triumphal lecture tour in England. Introducing himself by his Ojibway name Wa-Sha-Quon-Asin, Belaney riveted audiences, including the royal family, with his tales of the woodlands of Northern Ontario and his emotional appeals to protect the wilderness. Matt met him as he was being sketched in an artist's studio and fell for his romantic story of being the son of an Apache woman who was once an Indian knife-thrower in Buffalo Bill's travelling circus. "Few white Canadians," Matt wrote, "have raised Canada's prestige over here as high as Grey Owl has done."[32] It was probably a complete coincidence that, deep into his story, Matt wrote: "He looks too good to be true to life, with his marvellous sculptured face, his great feather and fringed buckskin costume."[33]

The exposé in the *North Bay Nugget,* based on allegations by the first of Grey Owl's four Indian wives, touched off a press stampede. At the *Star,* Hindmarsh assigned five of his top reporters, including Matt, to track down the full story. There was still uncertainty about whether Grey Owl/Belaney was an impostor. Matt immediately called his old University of Alberta friend, Lovat Dickson, who was Grey Owl's English publisher and tour organizer. Dickson was so confident of his client's identity that he pledged to spend the entire resources of his firm to prove it.[34] He withdrew the pledge quickly after Matt and other reporters sifted through birth certificates at a London record office and discovered that Archibald Belaney was born in Hastings, England. Ottawa had already confirmed that he had been briefly married to an English woman and served with Canadian forces in World War One.

Matt rushed to Hastings to search for relatives and appears to have been the first reporter to knock on the door of Ada and Clara Belaney. In a copyrighted story, he explained that the two maiden sisters were Archie's aunts who had reared him as a boy. They showed pictures of Archie in a sailor suit. Even at an early age, they said, he had begun living in a fantasy world of Red Indians. "He must have had hundreds of books about Indians. We ourselves made him dozens of Indian costumes and head-dresses and at school, when he was only ten years old, he used to tell the other boys he was part Indian. Someday, he said, he would return to America and take over the leadership of his tribe."[35] The Grey Owl myth was dead. But, for Matt, the romance of the actor's story and his achievements as a conservationist would live on.

Matt's ambivalence about Britain was still striking. In some articles, he described the country as one of the most sane and civilized in the world. Other articles prompted accusations in the *Star*'s Letters column that he was anti-British. Matt regularly criticized British society for its class consciousness and for allowing millions to be hungry and unemployed. On assignment in Scotland, he wrote of the vast game preserves still owned by absentee English aristocrats and about complaints that Scotland's economic development was being squeezed by British rule. He devoted an entire article to the secessionist Scottish National Party (by 2012 the largest party in the Scottish parliament) at a time when the two-year-old movement was barely noticed in England or elsewhere.[36]

In April 1936, Matt visited the Irish Free State to write a series on Ireland's bitter brew of politics. He criticized Britain's "blindness and lack of goodwill" in past dealings with Ireland but praised her current efforts to accommodate both Irish independence and Northern Ireland's determination to remain British.[37] He travelled through the southern counties, stopping in Limerick on Easter Sunday to watch the ritual parades and wailing bagpipes stir up memories of the 1916 Easter Rising against the British. He talked to members of the Irish Republican Army, attended political rallies, and interviewed the Free State's former president, William T. Cosgrave, whom he found refreshingly moderate. Matt concluded that the Irish were so "burned by their memories," so obsessed with past conflicts, that they would in the future "spring easily and often unnecessarily to arms."[38] He held out little hope for a settlement between north and south or an early peace between Protestants and Catholics in Ulster.

From midsummer 1936, news stories from Britain began to be rapidly eclipsed on the *Star's* front page by reports about the Spanish Civil War. On July 17, right-wing military units seized control of garrison towns and large parts of Spain in a revolt against the leftist Popular Front government. The rebels, self-described "Nationalists," were led by General Francisco Franco. They represented the military, the Roman Catholic Church, business, landowners and the Fascist Falange movement. Arrayed against them were the Republicans: an uneasy coalition of left-wing parties and groups seeking autonomy for Catalonia and the Basque region. The war lasted almost three years and turned the Iberian peninsula into a vast killing zone. Atrocities were frequent on both sides although

Franco's forces were responsible for most of the half-million or more people killed. German and Italian troops and arms tipped the war's outcome in favour of the Nationalists, outweighing the support that international volunteers and the Soviet Union gave the Republican side.[39]

No other event in the thirties inspired the left as much as the struggle to save socialist Spain from Fascism. For writers, journalists, and politicians of the left, involvement in *La Causa* was almost a rite of passage. Some, like George Orwell, volunteered to fight. Others, like Ernest Hemingway and Willy Brandt (the future German chancellor), reported from Spain with an obvious sympathy for the Republican side. A flock of authors and poets, including André Malraux, John Dos Passos, Sean O'Casey, and W.H. Auden, travelled to Spain and embraced the cause. There was little room for detachment or nuance. The war was seen as a conflict between democracy and dictatorship, between socialism and capitalism, between rich and poor. The French trade unionist Léon Jouhaux spoke memorably of a struggle "of the light against the night."[40] The Irish poet Louis MacNiece wrote, "Our spirit would find its frontier on the Spanish front."[41] Herbert Matthews, the *New York Times* correspondent in Spain, said the war "gave meaning to life . . . it taught us what internationalism means."[42]

Matt too would become a crusader in Spain – hardly surprising given his fervent anti-fascism and support for democratic socialism. His assignment began under strange circumstances and lasted for a disappointingly short time. When the uprising began, the *Star* sent its Paris-based correspondent, Pierre Van Paassen, to cover the war. He filed a series of dramatic and graphically detailed stories, often claiming to have been an eyewitness to savage fighting. Within weeks reports surfaced that Van Paassen was in Paris, not Spain, and was rewriting and embellishing what had been published earlier in French newspapers. The *Star*'s managing editor, Harry Hindmarsh, was sent to Paris to investigate and was shocked to find that Van Paassen had indeed remained at home. The disgraced correspondent was promptly fired,[43] and Matt assigned to go to Spain.

Spanish politics were already familiar to him. On a visit to Spain in June, he had reported melodramatically (but correctly as it turned out) that "the smell of blood was in the air" and that civil war seemed inevitable.[44] Battle lines were being drawn. In Madrid, Matt witnessed angry demonstrations by unions and panic in the streets after Fascist agitators set off bombs near the Pardo palace. He was impressed by Largo Caballero, leader of the Spanish Socialist Party and later prime minister, who told him how the privileges of the Catholic Church were being curbed and land turned over to an impoverished and largely illiterate peasantry. After the war began, Spanish ambassador Juan Araquistàin in London told him that "if we [the Popular Front] lose, Spain's lights will go out for 40 years."[45] (The interview took place almost exactly thirty-nine years before Franco died and Spain began the return to democracy.) Matt was given useful contacts by the CCF's Graham Spry, who was organizing the Canadian Committee to Aid Spanish Democracy. Doctor Norman Bethune phoned to brief him on his plans to take a Canadian mobile blood transfusion unit to Spain to help wounded Republican soldiers.

Arriving in Barcelona in November 1936 Matt was thrust into one of the most remarkable social revolutions in history. Unlike Madrid, where the less radical Popular Front government was in control, Barcelona was governed by a bewildering alliance of Anarcho-Syndicalists, Trotskyites, liberals, socialists, Communists, and Catalan separatists. Overnight, Catalonia became a workers' state. Industries, banks, and public services were taken over by workers' committees. Matt had expected chaotic conditions in a city shaken up by war and revolution. Instead he found public services and newly nationalized industries operating with surprising efficiency. Spain, he wrote, was successfully throwing off the shackles of its past.[46]

It was an exhilarating time for foreign sympathizers in Barcelona. Almost every day, crowds would cheer ragtag groups of volunteers as they marched off to war. In the evenings, Catalans and visitors in the thousands paraded along Las Ramblas, the city's famous boulevard. Revolutionary songs and exhortations blared from loudspeakers. Cafés and nightclubs were crowded. William Krehm, a young Trotskyite from Toronto whom Matt met later, described the mood in the city in the early months of the war: "It was the sort of lyric, spring-like affair, where everything that a youthful, and hence naive radical might have dreamed of came to pass."[47]

If not that naïve, Matt shared the rose-tinted view of Spain of many of his fellow correspondents. For some months he overestimated the unity of the Republican factions, which soon were riven by fierce infighting. After organized religion was banned, he gave undeserved credit to the Barcelona authorities for giving fair trials to priests suspected of helping the Nationalists. In fact, hundreds of priests had been summarily executed in Catalonia and dozens of churches burned down.[48] He did write that "any priest who appeared on the street in ecclesiastical garb would be taking an awful chance."[49]

Toward the end of his Spanish assignment, Matt travelled down the coast to Tarragona to interview Dolores Ibarruri, better known as La Pasionaria (the Passion Flower). His tendency toward hero worship burst out in his portrait of a woman he described as "an oriflamme for the Spanish people . . . a wonderful combination of political sagacity and reforming passion."[50] La Pasionaria's story was bound to appeal to Matt: the miner's daughter who became a crusading journalist, a founder of the Spanish Communist Party, and the brilliant orator whose signature lines – "It is better to die on your feet than to live on your knees" and *"No Pasaran!"* (they shall not pass) – were rallying cries for Republican Spain. Matronly, always dressed in black, she was described by Matt as "strong and sombre."[51] The two of them shared their bitterness that Britain and France had signed the Non-Intervention Treaty, pledging to stay neutral in the Spanish conflict while two other signatories, Germany and Italy, were sending bombers and troops to help the Fascist side. She complained to him that for too long the world had seen Spain as all castanets and bull fights, ignoring the reality of a feudal country where peasants were lucky to earn ninety dollars a year. She admitted Republicans had sometimes foolishly burned churches but said it reflected the deep resentment of a Church that exploited the people.[52]

From his first day in Spain, Matt set about realizing his boyhood ambition to be a war correspondent. It was a frustrating process. He couldn't reach Madrid, which was under siege by the Nationalist rebels and where the heaviest fighting was taking place. So he requested permission to go to the Aragon front where the Barcelona militias were engaged in sporadic combat. Getting there involved tedious dealings with competing political factions: "You get a suitcase full of passes and safe conducts and are never sure which one impresses whom."[53]

After more than a week, he finally had the required documents and a militia guide to accompany him on the three-hour drive to the front. He arrived near Huescas, about 250 kilometres west of Barcelona, in a cold and rainy dawn. Militiamen, some wearing only thin canvas shoes, were preparing to attack Fascist positions. Matt was given coffee by a militia captain then ordered to take shelter behind a stone wall as German bombers dropped their payload nearby. In his account of the battle, Matt said he heard the groan of a wounded man and the sound of another man vomiting. He said his excitement at being in battle disappeared into a fearful desire to be anywhere but where he was. Later he watched from the rear as militiamen advanced toward rebel lines, and he saw his first men die in battle. "It all seemed unreal and a dream. Until a man screamed. Apparently he was hit in the stomach, for he doubled over in agony and fell to the ground and screamed so that the awful sound was heard above the crackling and whining of the guns. Then it all seemed too real and I felt sick."[54] The militia succeeded in driving Franco's men off one strategic ridge but Matt was no longer close. "I stayed where I was behind the barricades."[55]

It was a long time before Matt became the self-confident war correspondent finding inspiration and excitement on the front lines. On his return to Barcelona, urgent phone messages and cables from the *Star* summoned him to fly to London immediately. King Edward was about to abdicate. Matt's assignment in Spain was over less than a month after it began.

Distressed as he was to leave Spain, he remained deeply committed to the Republican cause. He continued to write about the "ghastly farce" of non-intervention by the democracies and to denounce Germany and Italy for using the war to train their troops and test their weapons. "The German and Italian bombers in Spain are trying not only to help Franco win the war but also they are . . . learning an important lesson for the big war when they will drop 3,000 tons of bombs a day on London instead of 30 tons a week on Madrid."[56] As it turned out, the tonnage was exaggerated but not the uncanny accuracy of his prediction. Hugo Sperrle, the German commander of the Condor Legion, which infamously bombed civilian populations in Guernica and Madrid, led the Nazi fire-bombing of London and Coventry during the Blitz.

By the summer of 1937, Matt found himself drawn into a civil war within a civil war. The Communists were becoming increasingly powerful within the Republican government and moving to purge anti-Moscow elements from the Popular Front. The Toronto radical William Krehm was one of scores of supporters of the Trotskyite POUM party who were arrested and jailed in June on the orders of Soviet secret agents.[57] In London, Matt joined a group of British socialists pressuring the Foreign Office to demand the release of Krehm and other foreign prisoners. After nine weeks in a crowded, lice-infested cell, Krehm was deported. On his way back to Canada, he sought out Matt to thank him for his help and to provide a grim picture of how Stalin's secret police operated in Spain. OGPU/NKVD agents, he said, had infiltrated the non-Communist left and were gradually taking control of it.[58] The interview was one of the few examples in which Matt provided evidence of a darker side of the Republican struggle. Rare as it was for him, it set him apart from Hemingway and some other left-wing correspondents who rigorously chose to avoid criticizing the Soviet role in Spain.

Despite those concerns, Matt's support for the Republicans never wavered. For him, nothing symbolized the heroic and ultimately tragic struggle more than the fate of the fifteen hundred Canadian volunteers who went to Spain to fight Fascism. Most of them served in the Mackenzie-Papineau Battalion, proudly named after the leaders of the 1837 rebellion for more freedom in Upper and Lower Canada. The "Mac-Paps," as they were called, came from all across Canada. Most were working-class, unemployed men trying to escape the grim Depression-era relief camps where they were paid twenty cents a day for hard labour. Many were Communist sympathizers and CCFers willing to risk their lives to defend the democratically elected Popular Front. Spain was where they hoped the tentacles of Fascism could be cut off before they choked the rest of Europe. It was a lost cause. More than seven hundred Mac-Paps were killed by the combined forces of Franco, Hitler, and Mussolini. The survivors would face a grim journey home.[59]

On a Sunday night in January 1939, Matt received an urgent phone call. Albert MacLeod, a representative of the Mac-Paps, was on the line from Paris with news that three hundred survivors of the battalion were stranded in Le Havre. The French government had delivered an ultimatum: the Canadians would be sent back to a refugee detention camp at Perpignan unless they left France within four days. The CPR was prepared to transport the Mac-Paps to Canada for a payment of $10,000 (the equivalent of nearly $165,000 in today's dollars). Could Matt help raise the funds before the deadline expired?

"I sat beside the telephone, sick at heart," Matt recalled much later. "Three hundred of my countrymen who had joined a gallant and unselfish crusade; 300 young men who had been ready to die for the democratic cause which was being betrayed by democracy's leaders, were now waiting like a herd of criminals either for someone to find $10,000 or be taken to the ghastly camps at Perpignan."[60]

Matt knew only two wealthy Canadians who might help. The first was former prime minister R.B. Bennett, who had retired to England and would undoubtedly have remembered Matt's scathing portrayal of him in his *Alice* series in the *Star* six years earlier. In a phone conversation, Bennett assured Matt that he had "a good deal of admiration for these young men, whether they were misguided or not." But he was unable to contribute, he claimed, because of "some unusual expenses" that had come up. Disappointed but not surprised, Matt next phoned his millionaire friend, Garfield Weston. He began an eloquent plea, describing some of the surviving Mac-Paps as wounded and starving. Before he could finish, Weston interrupted him: "I'll send you a cheque for $5,000 in the morning."[61]

The remaining five thousand dollars came from other sources in time to meet the French government's deadline. Released on January 17, 1939, the Mac-Paps arrived at the English Channel port of Newhaven. Matt and two other reporters were the only welcoming party, and the *Star* had a memorable story:

No flags waved, no bands played at the little English harbor of Newhaven in the cold darkness of three o'clock this morning as some 300 Canadian members of the famous International Brigade which flocked from 30 nations to the defense of democratic Spain, landed in England on the last stage of their odyssey of courage and ideals. . . . As I write, they are en route to Liverpool in sealed trains like so many lepers. Another hundred, still waiting for visas allowing them to cross France had to be left behind. . . . The other 600 lie forever in the plains of Aragon and Castille. . . . We travelled with them to London, and I had two hours I won't soon forget. . . . A few of them, no doubt, are soldiers of fortune and aliens, but most are intelligent Canadians who saw what everyone is beginning to see now that it is too late, and who had the courage to do something about it.[62]

Before the train pulled into a London siding at daybreak, Matt had interviewed seven of the survivors and chronicled their stories of victories and defeats on battlefields unknown to most Canadians: Teruel, Belchite, Gandesa, Sierra Pandalos, and Fuentes de Ebro. As he was talking to Cecil Smith, the battalion commander, he learned that there was a Lionel Edwards aboard who had been cited for exceptional bravery on the Aragon front. Matt immediately went looking for Edwards, a boyhood friend from the Pincher Creek area whom he remembered as a violin player and avid reader. He found him to be barely recognizable, bearded and hollow-cheeked and "too done-in to be surprised at the encounter."[63] From Smith, he learned that Edwards had held back repeated assaults for two days until forced by Fascist bombing and artillery to retreat. Matt noted bitterly in his memoir that "it was members of the International Brigade such as Lionel Edwards whom the Right Reverend W.R. Inge, formerly Dean of St. Paul's, called 'international gangsters.'"[64] Nor were the Mac-Paps treated much better on their return to Canada. The federal government, which had made their service illegal, now allowed the RCMP to spy on them and blacklist them as subversives. It was not until 2001 that their sacrifice was recognized by a national monument unveiled in Ottawa.

Matt continued to stray across the line between journalism and activism, breaching norms of journalistic convention as he lent his support to the Popular Front government. In London, he helped organize so-called

Food and Freedom for Spain conferences to raise funds for the Republic. He was also able to persuade Garfield Weston to contribute more money to help repatriate another, smaller group of Canadian volunteers.[65]

Although long expected, Franco's final defeat of democracy in Spain was as deeply upsetting for Matt as it was for many of his left-wing colleagues. No one summed up their feelings better than the French writer Albert Camus: "It was in Spain that men learned that one can be right and yet be beaten, that force can vanquish spirit, that there are times when courage is not its own recompense."[66]

There would be other searing disappointments as Europe drifted toward a wider war.

9

TO THE ABYSS

"Star writers did some of the most vigorous and well-informed writing to come out of Europe in those years. The misfortune is that they were too often lonely voices."

– ROSS HARKNESS, *Star* reporter

BY THE LATE 1930S MATT HAD BECOME the Cassandra of Canadian journalism: gifted with a talent for prophecy but fated never to be believed – at least not by anyone in government. From his first dark warnings in the German Series, his predictions about Nazi actions were almost clairvoyant in their accuracy. He foresaw almost every step in the breaching of the Versailles settlement: the huge Nazi rearmament program, the reoccupation of the German Rhineland, the Anschluss – the forced union of Austria and Germany – and then the jackbooted takeover of Czechoslovakia. Eventually, Matt warned, the Nazis would not only march eastward but also put France and Britain in their gunsights. As early as February 1936, he wrote that "within five years . . . enemy bombers will roar across the Channel bent on [England's] swift destruction."[1] Hitler's goal was to dominate Europe and the world – a judgment reasonable, even obvious, in hindsight but dismissed by critics at the time as sensationalist and irresponsible.

What troubled Matt as much as the spread of Nazism was the feeble reaction of the democracies. Nineteen thirty-eight would see the high watermark of appeasement: the policy of giving Fascist dictators most or all of what they wanted in the hope of curbing their aggressive appetites and avoiding war. Unlike many on the left, Matt had shed his pacifism as he watched the League of Nations fail to enforce peace in Manchuria, Ethiopia, and Spain. Force, or the threat of force, was the only solution to Fascist aggression, he wrote – not a democracy "groveling in its neutrality."[2] He was astounded by the respectful treatment Hitler continued to receive from foreign leaders long after the Nazis' murderous record was known. Matt's explanation was coloured by his own political leanings. He argued that the appeasers, notably Britain's ruling class, simply saw Fascism as less of a threat than its alternative. "Their strongest instinct was property; and the mainspring of policy was their quite accurate realization that if Hitler, Mussolini and Franco and what they stood for were suppressed there would be an immediate growth throughout Europe of, at worst, communism, and at best those socialist-democratic ideas which had come over the horizon of history to threaten their best-of-all-possible worlds."[3]

If partly true, Matt's analysis was one-dimensional. It neglected the fact that appeasement found support among many on the left as well as the right who were still mindful of the carnage of World War One. In Canada, pacifism fed the strong isolationism of the 1930s. Many shared the opinion of CCF intellectual Frank Underhill: "We must make it clear to the world, and especially to Great Britain, that poppies blooming in Flanders fields have no further interest for us. . . . European troubles are not worth the bones of a Toronto grenadier."[4] Matt took a contrary view. Nazi aggression that went unchecked would ensure that far more "grenadiers" would end up dead in a later, more terrible war.

Matt soon saw Canadian appeasement at its most abject. In June 1937, he was assigned to cover Mackenzie King's four-day visit to Berlin. King was already an apostle of the British policy of mollifying Hitler. He had taken a leading role in undermining the League of Nations, arguing that collective security should be scrapped in favour of compromise and conciliation. He even warned British prime minister Neville Chamberlain that Canada would not automatically be at Britain's side in the event of a war in Europe.[5] King's underlying motive was honourable – to preserve national unity at home. But Matt would certainly have viewed his approach to the Nazi leaders as at best sycophantic, at worst shameful.

The assignment was an awkward one. While the *Star* was one of the toughest critics of Hitler, its publisher, Joe Atkinson, was a close friend and confidant of Mackenzie King. As a result, Matt knew that the editorial licence he normally enjoyed would have to be reined in. On this occasion there would be no outrage over the prime minister cosying up to a Führer whom Matt often described as a gangster.

The meeting with Hitler took place in the old presidential palace on Wilhelmstrasse, the nerve centre of Nazi power. Matt was outside in a small cluster of reporters and photographers when King arrived in a British embassy car. Drums rolled as the prime minister was saluted by a platoon of the Berlin Guards Regiment. The meeting was scheduled for thirty minutes but lasted for an hour and a quarter. When King emerged, Matt reported that he was "obviously impressed and apparently moved. . . . Over and over he repeated to me that the interview was 'most interesting and most valuable'. No other word would he say."[6] Later, an official statement merely added that King found the meeting with Hitler "reassuring." The lack of information was frustrating but Matt knew enough about King's record on Nazi Germany to capture the tenor of the session. "They say in Berlin," he wrote in his lead paragraph, "that Adolph Hitler never gives more than 15-minute interviews unless he meets 'a sympathetic soul'."[7]

Canadians would have to wait until Mackenzie King's diary was published in the 1970s to find out how extraordinarily "sympathetic" he was toward Hitler. After the meeting, King recounted his impressions: "My sizing up of the man as I sat and talked with him is that he is really one who truly loves his fellow-men. . . . His eyes impressed the most of all. There was a liquid quality about them which indicate keen perception and profound sympathy. . . . He has a very nice, sweet [smile] and one could see how particularly humble folk would come to have a profound love for the man. . . . As I talked to him, I could not but think of Joan of Arc. He is distinctly a mystic."[8] Hitler assured his guest that Germany would never start a war. King, in turn, praised the Nazis' "constructive work" and said nothing should be permitted to destroy it.[9]

Matt stayed as close as he could to King for his other events in Germany: a visit to youth camps and meetings with Luftwaffe commander Hermann Göring and Foreign Minister Konstantin von Neurath. King appears not to have objected when von Neurath talked of the need to clean the Jews out of Berlin.[10] Nor did he question the Nazi leaders' claims of peaceful intentions. He described the visit as "the most informative and inspiring I have ever had."[11] In Brussels two days later, Matt could no longer hide his skepticism. "Have they spoken frankly to you or tried to throw dust in your eyes?" he asked King. "They have really been extraordinarily frank," King replied. "I don't think they have tried to hide their real motives."[12]

If Matt was disgusted by appeasing politicians, he was no less frustrated by their supporters in the press. After 1936, the media on both sides of the Atlantic became increasingly pro-appeasement. The British press, in particular, entered what one prominent journalist called "the most inglorious period in its history."[13] Even the fiercely anti-Nazi *Manchester Guardian* stopped short of advocating the threat of force. Lord Rothermere's *Daily Mail* openly sympathized with Fascism. Lord Beaverbrook's *Daily Express* argued for isolation from Europe and withdrawal from the League of Nations. Lord Kemsley's *Sunday Times* and his chain of provincial newspapers favoured an Anglo–German rapprochement. As for *The Times*, the voice of the Establishment, it flatly declared, "It can be no part of British policy to resist [German] expansion."[14] Its editor, Geoffrey Dawson, proudly declared: "I do my utmost night after night to keep out of the paper anything that might hurt their [Nazi] susceptibilities."[15] Matt wrote in disgust that *The Times* "practically agrees with Dr. Goebbels these days about what British foreign policy should be."[16]

The pro-appeasement line in the British press also resulted from manipulation by the Chamberlain government. At a meeting with Hitler in November 1937, Lord Halifax, the foreign secretary, agreed to put pressure on the British press not to endanger good relations with Germany. On his return to London, he urged editors and publishers to avoid "needless provocation" of the Nazis.[17] "If only we can get the press in both countries tame,"[18] he wrote the British ambassador in Berlin. Mackenzie King appeared to feel the same way. He wrote in his diary:

"The one danger to all countries is the Press; through its misrepresentations and persistent propaganda."[19] King may have been thinking of the strongly anti-Nazi *Star* and *Winnipeg Free Press*, although there is no evidence that he tried to interfere with their editorial freedom. However, in an earlier letter to his parents, Matt mentioned that for the first time he had written six articles that the *Star* "were afraid to print."[20] Their subject matter remains a mystery but it is likely that they were considered too critical of King's German policy.

Appeasement cast a shadow over Matt's personal as well as professional life. For several years, it cost him his long-standing friendship with Lady Nancy Astor, the MP who had been an invaluable friend and contact since his student days in London. In November 1937, an incendiary article entitled "The Cliveden Set" was published in an influential British newsletter. Written by the maverick left-wing journalist Claud Cockburn, it alleged that Lady Astor and her husband regularly hosted pro-Nazi meetings at their country estate at Cliveden or at their London residence. Powerful members of the Establishment attended, including five cabinet ministers, three lords, the governor of the Bank of England, and the editors of two Astor-controlled newspapers: *The Times* and the *Observer*. All were supporters of appeasement. According to Cockburn, they were also plotting to make a deal with Hitler that would allow the Nazis to expand in central and eastern Europe in exchange for an Anglo–German truce. It was alleged that Lord Halifax, soon to be foreign secretary, would secretly present the offer to Hitler on his forthcoming visit to Berlin.

The Cliveden Set quickly became a hot story in the British and foreign press. Nancy Astor was portrayed as part of the conspiracy – the reigning queen at "Schloss Cliveden."[21] In the House of Commons, she was taunted as "the honorable member for Berlin."[22] Matt reported that her upper-crust guests were being compared to the Cagoulards, or hooded ones, the name given a Fascist organization in France.[23] In fact, Cockburn's original story was part myth. Most of the supposed conspirators were in favour of appeasement but so at the time were the Chamberlain government and a majority of the British people. As for Lady Astor, she supported a peace offer to Germany but had no fondness for the Nazis. No evidence was produced of a conspiracy to influence the government. As even Claud Cockburn acknowledged years later, some of those named in his story simply went to Cliveden for a good dinner.[24]

For Matt, though, the involvement of Lady Astor with the group was a shock. Was the woman whom he once called the "angel of Cliveden," who had turned her estate into a hospital for wounded Canadian soldiers in World War One, now in the vanguard of appeasers? He sought the answer over a long lunch with Astor at her London residence and wrote about the interview in the *Star*. "There is no such thing as a Cliveden set," she told him. "Why shouldn't we have friends at Cliveden without people snooping around for such silly, fantastic stories." "Then why is everyone who goes there pro-Fascist?" Matt asked provocatively. "You've been there," she replied, "and are you a pro-Fascist? Am I a pro-Fascist, for heaven's sake? I am a democrat. I used to be called a socialist. You know this is all nonsense. . . . Listen, would Canada fight for Czechoslovakia?" "No," Matt replied, "but that's no reason England shouldn't." "You are talking nonsense again," said Astor. When the conversation turned to the Canadians nursed at Cliveden, she still seemed angry. "I loved those men . . ." she said. "*That* was a 'Cliveden set,' if you like."[25]

After the interview, their relationship appears to have soured. Matt was not invited to a lunch Astor organized for Neville Chamberlain to meet a group of foreign correspondents, including one from the *Montreal Star*.[26] There was no further mention of her in his letters and reports until 1941 when she made Cliveden available again as a hospital for Canadians soldiers. She later admitted that her ardent support for appeasement had been a grave mistake.

In the summer of 1938, Matt and Jean returned to Canada for three weeks of home leave. In Toronto, they were feted by the *Star* management and put up at managing editor Harry Hindmarsh's twenty-two-acre estate near Oakville. In Alberta, there was the usual pilgrimage to Pincher Creek, fishing expeditions with Matt's brothers, and days of riding and hiking in the Rockies. His sentimental attachment to the foothills country was as strong as ever. "I was back in the place I dream of when Europe seems a nightmare," he wrote, ". . . back where my youth was and my dreams."[27]

Midway through the visit, the *Star* asked Matt to stay on to write a series on the phenomenon of Social Credit in his native province. Three years earlier, Albertans had elected the first Social Credit government in the world. Squeezed by the Depression – by crashing grain and cattle prices, drought, and foreclosures – they turned to a party that offered both economic and spiritual salvation. Its leader was William "Bible Bill" Aberhart, a radio evangelist who preached that good Christians would be "raptured" away from earth but not "the Sons of Satan" who were his political opponents.[28] In the meantime, Aberhart promised to implement Social Credit's curious economic theory that poverty could be eliminated if people had enough money to balance their purchasing power with the total cost of goods and services. To make it happen, every adult in Alberta would be given $25 a month (approximately $400 in today's dollars). Voters were soon disappointed. The "social dividend" was never paid. Key parts of Social Credit's program, such as taxing banks and limiting press freedom, were disallowed by Ottawa and the courts as unconstitutional. Yet the party, casting itself as the defender of Alberta against Eastern Canada, held on to power for more than three decades.

Matt already had some knowledge about Social Credit. In London, a year earlier, he had tracked down Major C.H. Douglas, the founder of the movement, and John Hargrave, leader of the British Social Credit party. Douglas explained Social Credit theory and accused Aberhart of failing to practise it. Hargrave was more scathing. He described Aberhart as "a man of rapture rather than a man of reason"[29] whose decision to raise taxes betrayed Social Credit principles. In Alberta, Matt had other useful contacts. Mary Alice, his adored mother, was an organizer for Social Credit in the Pincher Creek area. He was also helped by Solon Low, once a classmate of his at teacher training college and now treasurer in the Alberta cabinet.

Not surprisingly, Matt found Social Credit's mix of fundamentalist religion and right-wing populism to be distasteful. In a letter to his parents, he wrote of "the nauseating features of Aberhartism"[30] – probably referring to the anti-Semitism of some of its supporters and their dismissal of anyone on the left as subversive. In print, he was a little more restrained: "It was strange . . . to find that ideas that are merely mildly Liberal in backward, old-fashioned England are regarded here as 'dirty Red.'"[31]

Matt's left-of-centre views were known in Alberta, where his articles were syndicated in several of the province's newspapers. Nonetheless, Aberhart, who detested the press, was persuaded to give Matt an interview. It was a frosty exchange with the premier stating at the start that interviewers almost always lied about him or distorted what he said. Matt was equally blunt, asking about opposition comments that "Bible Bill" had become enamored of political power. "It's a lie," Aberhart responded. "I stay here for one reason only, which is that I feel it is God's will that I should stay here."[32] Pressed to explain his failure to deliver the $25 social dividend, Aberhart said he was still committed to paying it. Matt gave him some credit for improving Alberta's finances and concluded that the premier was "a curious mixture of idealism and egomania."[33]

The minutiae of Alberta politics, and the peculiarities of its premier, would soon be a distant memory. In the last of his series on Social Credit, he wrote: "I am going back to Europe where the lights are going out."[34]

By the time Matt returned in late August 1938, war fears were rolling over the continent. A partial troop mobilization in Germany was soon followed in France and Czechoslovakia. The Royal Navy took up battle stations in the North Sea. Gas masks sold briskly in London and Paris, and trenches were dug in Hyde Park and alongside the Eiffel Tower. For a few days, stock exchanges were suspended and blackouts tested for the expected bombing of European cities.[35]

It was Czechoslovakia that was now the tinderbox of Europe. Having absorbed Austria earlier in the year, Hitler prepared to swallow the most successful and prosperous democracy in Central Europe. His pretext was the alleged mistreatment by Czechoslovakia of its German-speaking minority, the three million Sudetens. In mid-September, pro-Nazis began staging provocations in the Sudetenland, which was made up of areas along the border with Germany. Paramilitary groups trained by the SS attacked

Czech police stations and army barracks. An ultimatum was issued: unless Czechoslovakia bowed to Nazi demands to cede control of the Sudetenland, the territory would be taken by force.

On September 15, Matt arrived in Prague to begin the most exciting, most exhausting, and most rewarding four weeks of his career until then. He had reported from Czechoslovakia two years earlier, full of admiration for the country that produced Jan Hus, one of the fathers of the Reformation, and that was "the only European nation east of France with enough intellectual and moral fibre to rule herself democratically."[36] In London, he was friendly with Jan Masaryk, minister in the Czech embassy and son of the country's revered first president. In April he quoted Masaryk: "If Czechoslovakia dies, Europe dies."[37] Now that seemed to be happening. As he checked into the Ambassador Hotel, he learned that Neville Chamberlain was travelling that day to Hitler's mountain retreat at Berchtesgaden. The sellout of Czechoslovakia had begun.

From his room overlooking Prague's fabled Wenceslas Square, Matt watched hundreds then thousands of people gather, some despairing, others defiant. Rumours had circulated quickly that Chamberlain would acquiesce to the Sudetenland becoming part of the Third Reich and would return for a second meeting with Hitler later. Matt described the scene outside in his characteristic style: personalized, emotional, didactic – drawing his readers into a conversation: "I wish you could see this beautiful historic city and its people today. The city cradled the Renaissance and Protestantism five centuries ago – as I write I see John Hus's statue – and today it is freedom's central keep. Make no mistake, this is your bulwark and mine and, if it goes under, retribution will follow for you and me. . . . Their suspense today is intolerable, as they crowd the streets, waiting for news . . . believing their chances are about 50–50. They are afraid Britain is going to sell the pass but they keep hoping. . . ."[38]

The day after his arrival, Matt set off with the American correspondent Vincent Sheean for the Sudetenland. They drove to Karlsbad (known in Czech as Karlovy Vary) then toured small towns near the Bavarian border that were centres of Nazi agitation and where Sudeten rebels had attacked Czech police. There were few people in the streets apart from soldiers and an occasional villager giving them the Nazi salute. Swastikas were scrawled on doors and walls. Both Matt and Sheean wrote about the ominous quiet everywhere and the brooding tension, and the Czech army detachments preparing to defend a heavily fortified frontier.[39]

The visit marked a milestone in Matt's career. There was no "hard news" to report that day from the Sudetenland but, on Matt's return to Prague, his CBS friend Bill Shirer asked him to broadcast his impressions on the network's nightly news roundup. Shirer and Ed Murrow had launched the roundup during the Anschluss and it quickly set a new standard for quality in radio journalism. Atkinson and Hindmarsh at the *Star* agreed to Matt's appearance, pleased that the prestige of the paper would be enhanced by having its correspondent heard across the United States. They were even more pleased when a hook-up was arranged with the CBC to make the broadcast available simultaneously in Canada.

The CBS broadcast was Matt's first experience with radio apart from a brief interview on Toronto's CFRB three years earlier. His comments on the Sudetenland echoed his earlier report for the *Star,* describing a region and a country "where men, women and children are leading their lives on top of a volcano."[40] CBS apparently liked what they heard. Matt was invited back on the air three days later.

This time, the negotiations with Chamberlain had shifted to the little town of Bad Godesberg beside the Rhine. Hitler was installed in the charming old Hotel Dreesen where a temporary broadcast booth was set up in the porter's lodge. CBS wanted Halton there to be interviewed by Bill Shirer but ran into a problem. Their guest was in the British press hotel several kilometres away and access to the Dreesen was blocked off. Hitler's press officials had to be persuaded to send an escort to pick him up. Matt would long remember the curious sensation of being driven by an SS officer in a large black Mercedes as crowds, thinking he was a high official, raised their arms toward him in the Nazi salute.

Ever more demanding, Hitler now insisted that Czechoslovakia evacuate the Sudetenland in four days and hand it over to the Reich. As the Führer was delivering his latest ultimatum to Chamberlain, Matt was on the air with Shirer from the porter's lodge. "You have to pinch yourself," he told Shirer, "to realize history is in the making here . . . a few feet away in this very hotel."[41] His assessment of Chamberlain's efforts to accommodate Hitler was sweeping: "Czechoslovakia, it seems, is liquidated."[42] Matt correctly anticipated that once Prague had lost the Sudetenland, it would only be a matter of time before the rest of the country was swallowed up. Hitler, he said, had a genius for seizing opportunities and exploiting the weakness of his adversaries. "Today he comes [here] as the greatest German in history."[43]

Matt soon got an indication of the instant power of radio. Letters to CBS, CBC, and the *Star* complained about his description of Hitler as "the greatest German in history." Had Matthew Halton turned Nazi? Had he heard of Goethe and Einstein? Why was he praising a despot? A Toronto veteran wrote sarcastically: "As the flag of the British Empire flutters to half-mast forever, you seem to be wisely falling in behind our new master."[44] Matt, of course, had meant to describe the German who had made the greatest *impact* on history. He saw no need to apologize for a misleading choice of words. In response to critics, he wrote, "Perhaps the names of Goethe, Einstein and Thomas Mann will live when Hitler is forgotten but I doubt it. The strange little Austrian dreamer, compounded of shrewdness and mysticism . . . whose oratory has changed the world, is certainly in one sense the greatest German in history."[45] There was an ironic postscript to the story. The day after the broadcast, which was monitored by Nazi officials, several German radio stations quoted approvingly his line about the "greatest German in history." And for that, Matt did apologize.[46]

Chamberlain left Bad Godesberg with a lame promise to consult his allies about Hitler's latest ultimatum. The war scare was now at fever pitch. School children were evacuated from London while, in Paris, train stations and roads were clogged with people trying to leave the city. Matt flew to Berlin, noting in a dispatch that anti-aircraft guns and their crews had appeared on rooftops along the Unter den Linden. That night he went to the city's Sports Palace to listen to the Führer at his most bellicose and hysterical. Pledging that German troops were set to attack on October 1, Hitler hurled abuse at Czechoslovakia and its president, Edvard Beneš: "My Germans, come with me! March with me! . . . We are ready. Let Beneš choose."[47] Every time Hitler mentioned Beneš, whom Matt regarded as one of Europe's most impressive statesmen, the huge crowd of Nazis cried, "Hang him! Hang him!"[48]

For almost a month, Matt had shuttled back and forth between Germany, France, and Czechoslovakia, getting little food and less sleep and sometimes filing two or three times a day for different editions of the paper. After Hitler's rally, he caught the night train to Paris, intending to return to Prague. Instead, he rushed to Munich next day when he learned that Hitler and Mussolini would meet there with Chamberlain and the French prime minister Édouard Daladier. A few hours earlier, Chamberlain had broadcast his infamous opinion that it was inconceivable to go to war over "a quarrel in a faraway country between people of whom we know nothing."[49] Daladier had caved in to British pressure to abandon France's military commitment to Czechoslovakia. The final, climactic moment of appeasement was at hand. In Matt's view, the only issue was how and when the Czechoslovak republic would be torn apart.

Shortly after arriving in Munich, Matt was phoned by Max Jordan, the European representative of NBC. The CBS broadcasts had raised his profile. Now it was NBC's turn to bid for his services. The network wanted him to be its analyst that night and provide a fifteen-minute commentary. Matt was glad to accept, and a lucky break ensured he was exceptionally well prepared. He ran into Karl Boehmer, a young spokesman for the propaganda ministry and the only Nazi with whom he had a somewhat friendly relationship. Boehmer was cosmopolitan, fluent in English, and a heavy drinker.* He told Matt that the four leaders had reached an agreement that essentially met all Hitler's demands. A token force of Wehrmacht troops would march into a border area of the Sudetenland the next day and occupy the rest of German-speaking Czechoslovakia in stages over the following ten days.[50] There were guarantees that Britain and France would protect the new boundaries of the country – guarantees that Matt instinctively knew were worthless.

At midnight in Munich, 6 p.m. EDT, Matt was sitting in a makeshift studio in the Führerhaus, the Nazi headquarters where the conference

---

* Boehmer was later killed on the eastern front after being demoted for revealing to Bulgarian journalists, in a drunken moment, that Germany planned to invade Russia.[51]

was held. In New York, a sonorously voiced NBC anchor announced: "The National Broadcasting Company presents Matthew Halton, correspondent of the Toronto *Star*, with the latest first-hand views of the four-power parley."[52] The Munich agreement would not be signed for another hour but, thanks to the tip-off from Boehmer and other sources, Matt was able to reveal the broad lines of the deal. He chose his words carefully. He was aware that this was the first analysis of the Munich agreement to be heard by millions in the United States and Canada (CBC again took the broadcast live). He knew there would be enormous relief that European armies could now stand down, that it would sound churlish to criticize a peace agreement that would be overwhelmingly popular. But while acknowledging that "there is peace now and hope," Matt repeatedly noted that the peace was "precarious" and "temporary" and may merely have postponed a war that would be more disastrous later on. "It seems that mankind has been reprieved but the awful swift march of events may not have stopped tonight." He added that the peace was achieved "at the sacrifice of a nation. . . . Small but remarkable Czechoslovakia has been emasculated."[53]

Then, addressing his listeners directly, Matt wove in the touches of descriptive detail and context that so often coloured his writing. There was a snapshot of a city preparing to celebrate Oktoberfest:

Picture Munich, or München as the Germans say. It is the most beautiful, the most lively, the most gemütlich of all German towns. . . . In Munich, unlike Berlin, women dare to powder their cheeks and use lipstick, for example. In this town, people still laugh and food is still good . . . , and the people are just as relieved as you are that the war has been postponed. . . .

This is Munich, the beloved of Adolph Hitler. This is the city where Hitler and a handful of his lieutenants and followers made their famous but short-lived attempt to seize power on November the ninth, 1923. Hitler was imprisoned after that putsch, and he was laughed at all over Germany. Today he is master of Europe. . . .[54]

A copy of Matt's NBC commentary is preserved in the sound archives of the Library of Congress. The broadcast was delivered with assurance, a mid-Atlantic accent overlaying an unmistakably North American voice. A front-page headline in one of the *Star*'s early editions that day trumpeted "HALTON BROADCASTS OFFICIAL PEACE NEWS AS PACT BEING SIGNED."[55] A cable from publisher Atkinson fed Matt's ego: "I admire your work immensely and consider it of great value to the paper. Your Munich broadcast was really splendid."[56] Adept at self-promotion, Matt described it later as "the biggest scoop of my career."[57] In fact, Shirer of CBS went on the air a half-hour earlier with a report that lacked the punch of Matt's broadcast but did reveal some details of the agreement.

Matt's skepticism about the Munich sellout contrasted sharply with the euphoric reports that quickly surfaced in most of the media. As Chamberlain returned to England with his hollow claim of "peace in our time," British newspapers gave him a hero's welcome. Only three of fifty newspapers studied at the time either opposed or were critical of the agreement.[58] The *Observer* gushed that "Mr. Chamberlain was a thousand times right in saving peace at Munich."[59] *The Times* wrote that "no conqueror returning from the battlefield has come adorned with nobler laurels."[60] The *Sunday Times* even praised Hitler for his "healing statesmanship."[61] Apart from the *Winnipeg Free Press* and the *Star*, most Canadian newspapers joined the chorus of praise. In Ottawa, Mackenzie King said Chamberlain would "go down in history as one of the greatest men who ever lived."[62] Churchill was one of the very few prominent Western politicians to denounce the agreement. "We have suffered a total and unmitigated defeat,"[63] he told the House of Commons.

Before leaving Germany, Matt was given another break by Karl Boehmer, his friend from the propaganda ministry. Boehmer secured a place for him with the small number of foreign newsmen allowed to accompany the German army into the Sudetenland. Depressing as the event was, it gave Matt a vivid sense of being on the cusp of history – to accompany Wehrmacht soldiers as they achieved another stage of Grossdeutschland, Hitler's Greater Germany. For fifty kilometres from Passau to the frontier, Matt was driven through tens of thousands of German troops, tanks, and armoured transports. Ready for battle, they had now been handed a bloodless victory. From his open army car, Matt heard children shrieking *"Heil Hitler"* and noted a wayside shrine where a swastika was attached to the figure of Christ with the words "In *this* sign ye shall conquer."[64] At the frontier village of Sarau, Matt followed five hundred German soldiers as they marched across the disappearing border. Cheering girls garlanded the soldiers with flowers, and the local Sudeten mayor thanked the Nazis for the "liberation." And so, Matt wrote, "the last sad scraps of Versailles were torn to shreds."[65]

Next day he returned to Prague, now a city in despair. On Wenceslas Square, men and women were weeping. Driving to Karlsbad, he ran into "the terrible march of Europe's refugees"[66] – tens of thousands of non-German and anti-Nazi Czechs streaming out of the Sudetenland. Gestapo agents were already moving in. It would be five and a half months before Germany seized the rest of Czechoslovakia. But shorn of its fortified border, major industries, and more than a quarter of its territory, the rump state was no longer independent. President Beneš and his democratically elected government were quickly replaced by a servile pro-German administration. In one report Matt mentioned a popular anecdote among Czechs. Beneš had received a telegram of condolences from Haile Selassie, another leader betrayed by the democracies. "God bless you," it said. "I had the same friends."[67]

Almost overnight Munich injected a new recklessness into Hitler's exercise of power. It had proved, as he put it, that "our enemies are small worms."[68] So now he could act with impunity. Constraints were lifted, freeing Hitler for vaster conquests in Europe and more deadly repression at home. It was no coincidence that on November 9 – barely six weeks after Munich – he unleashed Kristallnacht, the murderous night of attacks against German Jewry that foreshadowed the Holocaust. (The pretext for Kristallnacht was the assassination in Paris of a German diplomat by the Polish Jew, Herschel Grynszpan.) Most accounts estimate that about 100 Jews were murdered during the pogrom, 25,000 arrested, 7,500 Jewish stores damaged, and hundreds of synagogues set on fire.

For Matt, Kristallnacht was no surprise. As early as 1933, he had warned that the Nazis intended to eliminate the Jews from the social and economic life of Germany. In 1936 – long before it was known that Nazis might resort to wholesale genocide – he quoted Julius Streicher, Hitler's friend and the publisher of the Jew-baiting *Der Stürmer*. Streicher declared that "'one must go the bloody way' to achieve a final solution. 'In order to assure the safety of the whole world, the Jews must be extirpated.'"[69] Matt's words "final solution" were not in the direct quote, nor in common usage at the time, suggesting that Matt might have coincidentally chosen the two words that would become a synonym for the Holocaust.

Matt also wrote about the wider phenomenon of anti-Semitism, which was still pervasive in Britain and Canada. He felt that Ottawa's policy of barring Jewish immigrants was not only immoral but short-sighted. In an article entitled "The 20th Century Huguenots," he demonstrated how industry, science, and culture in other countries were enriched by the influx of Jewish refugees.[70] His own explanation of anti-Semitism was hardly original: that the Jews were a convenient scapegoat for people's problems and generated jealousy because of their success in the professions. His views were shaped by friendships with Jews and by his sympathy with Jewish struggle. After interviewing Meir Dizengoff, the founder and mayor of Tel Aviv, Matt was enthusiastic about the vision of Israel as "a haven [for Jews] from the devouring curse of gentile madness."[71] But he also asked probing questions about Arab rights in Palestine. The chief British rabbi, Herman Herz, assured him, "We are not asking for the expulsion of the Arabs. We ask only for the equality of status."[72]

Throughout the year, Matt rarely missed an opportunity to visit Paris, the city that always captivated him. In late November, he checked into his favourite hotel, the Chatham, a block away from the Opéra. He liked to cross the street to drink at Harry's Bar, frequented by foreign correspondents and, on occasion, by Hemingway, Humphrey Bogart, and Rita Hayworth. He was in Paris to cover a meeting between Chamberlain and Daladier but confessed in print that the event left him "paralysed with boredom."[73] He disliked waiting for hours to hear diplomatic banalities spewed from press attachés and knew that, if there was real news, the *Star* would use the wire services. Instead, Matt wrote an impressionistic account of his day. He revisited Napoleon's tomb, which he had first seen as a student when he was so broke he had to borrow money to get back to England. It was St. Catherine's Day when unmarried women in France traditionally pray for a husband. Matt watched the so-called Catherinettes dressed up and partying in the streets, noting the sad shortage of husbands in a country that lost one and a half million men in World War One. He bought a silk dress for his daughter, Kathleen, and ate oysters and *poularde de Bresse* with a friend at a Michelin-starred restaurant. Walking back to his hotel, an old woman offered to pray for anything he wanted in return for a few francs. "What shall I pray for ?" she asked. Sentimental as ever, Matt replied: *"Que la France soit béni"* (that France be blessed).[74]

He had no idea how tragically absent that blessing would be. A mere eighteen months later, France's Third Republic collapsed, overrun by the German blitzkrieg and cursed by its collaboration with the Nazis. Despite the superficial gaiety he found in Paris that week, Matt wrote of a France "defeated and pessimistic after Munich and wondering if perhaps her days as a great power are ended."[75] It was a rare observation for him. His analysis, so accurate on most aspects of European politics, tended to be off the mark on France, blurred by his love of the country. In earlier years, he was over-impressed by French leaders he interviewed. He described Léon Blum, the socialist leader of the Popular Front, as a great man.[76] But it was Blum who accepted non-intervention in Spain and hailed the Munich agreement. He talked to former prime minister Édouard Herriot, "France's most trusted statesman," who assured him that the French would never accept Fascism.[77] As late as 1939, Matt described the French army as "the finest in the world"[78] – a year before it was routed in six weeks by Hitler's Panzers. In the same report, he wrote of a renewed sense of confidence in a country where, in reality, defeatism and war-weariness were deeply ingrained.

Matt's own spirits began to lift within six weeks of Munich. For all its horror, Kristallnacht had one positive effect: it shocked many people out of their apathy toward Nazi Germany. Support for appeasement began to ebb and, in Britain at least, it largely disappeared after the jackboots marched over the rest of Czechoslovakia in March 1939. The policy was officially buried a few days later when Chamberlain guaranteed that, if

Poland was attacked, Britain would be at her side. For Matt, at long last, it was a kind of vindication: "Ever since 1933 I have been describing with an accuracy of which I am proud just what a mess Europe was in, and how disastrous it would be until Britain made a stand and lined up with her friends. Today Britain has made that stand after the most startling *volte-face* in the history of British foreign policy."[79]

Matt predicted that the war would begin before the end of 1939. He wrote that Hitler would probably gamble on a localized war in the hope that Britain and France would again dishonour their commitments. In Canada, there was renewed criticism that he was an alarmist whose pessimistic talk was spoiling the royal visit then underway.[80] But with Britain rearming at full tilt and introducing conscription for the first time in peacetime, he could no longer be credibly accused of being a warmonger.

In that last summer of peace, Matt could not conceal his satisfaction that the "locust years" of British governance were ending. The Great Britain of his youthful reveries was reasserting itself. "Britain has awakened from sleep," he wrote. "She has heard some bugle call. Reluctantly but with courage, determination and remarkable cheerfulness she is polishing her sword."[81]

TO WAR

"This time you have action and heroism to report instead of betrayal and infamy."

— MATTHEW HALTON, *Toronto Star*, February 17, 1940

ON SEPTEMBER 3, 1939, two days after blitzkrieg was unleashed on Poland, the war that Matt had predicted for most of the decade was declared by Britain and France. He had little time to reflect on it. That same evening, the Montreal-bound passenger ship *Athenia* was torpedoed by a German submarine off the northwest coast of Ireland. Of the 1,418 passengers and crew aboard, 117 drowned, including a ten-year-old girl from Hamilton who became the first Canadian to die in World War Two. Banner headlines about the sunken ship vied with others proclaiming EMPIRE AT WAR![1]

Matt rushed to Glasgow, where rescue ships brought back about six hundred survivors, many suffering from hypothermia and shock. Among the hundred or so Canadians who were saved, Matt came across two friends, actress Judith Evelyn and her fiancé, radio announcer Andrew Allan (later head of CBC Drama). Their stories resembled those from the *Titanic*. The couple had begun an elegant dinner when the torpedo struck, forcing the ship to list heavily. They managed to get down a ladder to a lifeboat but were thrown into the sea when the boat hit the propeller of a rescue ship in high waves. They drifted for some time among drowned bodies before being rescued. A Montreal woman recounted how a mother who lost her child started screaming "My baby" and sprang into the sea. An Alberta survivor told Matt her cabin flooded when the torpedo struck, forcing her to swim out through swirling water.[2]

Forty years later, another survivor of the *Athenia* recalled opening her hotel room door in Glasgow to a young man in a tan raincoat with a hat worn at a rakish angle. Mrs. Jess Bigelow was with her husband and two children. She recognized Matt's name from his *Star* articles and agreed to talk to him about their ordeal. "He had that homespun quality that made one comfortable and at ease," she said. When he was told how her husband had rescued the children from rising water in the ship's hold, Bigelow said Matt put his arms around the kids and told them how brave they were. She remembered him as quiet and intense, someone who "spoke feelingly of Canada and the part she would have to play in the war." Matt persuaded the couple to appear on the BBC next morning and tell their story to a wider audience.[3]

The drama of the *Athenia* was the last war action Matt would cover until the new year. The "Phony War" had begun – the nine-month stretch in which there was no major bombing or land battles between Germany and the Western Allies. "We had expected an immediate avalanche of fire and steel from the skies,"[4] Matt wrote. Instead, London was so peaceful that he bought a bicycle to benefit from an unusually warm autumn. At night, the blackouts seemed an unnecessary inconvenience in getting to pubs and nightclubs that were as busy as ever. There were complaints about a much bigger disruption: the evacuation of a million and a half women and children from the cities. In Matt's view, the exodus, and the compulsory billeting of city residents in villages and farms, was breaching the ramparts of the British class system. "Today a kind of social revolution is taking place in the villages of Britain," he wrote. "The dock worker's daughter from Limehouse is now billeted with the vicar in Stow-on-the-Wold, and has to learn not to use her table napkin as a handkerchief. The postman's son from Tooting Broadway now has school lessons with the squire's children in the remote village of Nether Wallop and is learning that 'today' is not pronounced 'todye.'"[5] Matt mentioned that he, too, had sent his wife and daughter to safety away from London, and that his little

Kathleen was playing with city children who had never seen cows before. His article, under the headline "CHILDREN OF THE STORM," was over-drawn. In fact, the evacuation caused considerable friction between city and rural people and many (including Jean and Kathleen) returned to their homes soon after the Phony War began. But Matt was perceptive in developing a theme he would return to often – that the war would usher in a much more egalitarian post-war Britain.

By mid-November, Matt was tired of writing about war preparations. He briefly reverted to the mock-serious style that had first established his reputation. One target was the government's strict ban on any kind of weather forecasts that might facilitate Nazi bombing raids:

If there were no weather there would be no conversation among Anglo-Saxon people. But we can't talk about it in the papers any more . . . the thing has become a secret. So I got on my bicycle and hurtled down Oxford Street today and had tea with a meteorological expert and asked him why.

"Don't the Germans have weather?" I asked. "Don't they have meteorologists? Have they no old men with rheumatism? Why should weather be a secret?" . . .

"Because most of Germany's weather comes from the British Isles," explained the meteorologist. Which explains why the Nazis hate us. . . .

It is a fact that our pre-knowledge of the weather will be an important factor in helping us win the war. I thought about the line from Rule Britannia about "the nations not so blest as thee." I began to see why England always wins her wars. Even the weather is on her side. I suggested that if the Germans worked on the assumption that there would be rain in Britain every day in summer and fog every day in winter, they couldn't go far wrong. My friend passed this off as frivolous and went on with his talk.

"By the way," I said suddenly, "suppose there is an east wind. Suppose it's one of those days when the weather is coming from Germany." There was anxiety in my voice.

My friend calmed me. "We know there is going to be an east wind before it ever arrives," he explained. "You see east winds are merely the

backwaters of west winds. A stiff west wind blowing across France to
Germany almost always means that we will have a fresh east wind." . . .

I felt enormously bucked. The weather being what it is, I don't see
how we can lose the war.[6]

That sally into humour was his last of the war years. Matt's tone was becoming more solemn and more patriotic, yet he was still prepared to take unpopular, contrarian stands. He questioned Neville Chamberlain's qualities as a wartime leader at a time when some Canadians would have regarded it as almost treasonous. Even before Chamberlain became prime minister and the voice of appeasement, Matt was scathing about his record as Chancellor of the Exchequer: "If he becomes Premier, Britain will have the most uninspired leadership she has had since Lord North"[7] – the eighteenth-century prime minister often remembered for losing the American colonies. Now he felt that Chamberlain lacked energy, imagination, and even the will to fight the war. He pointedly wrote, "We shall eventually need a man who has not only cool determination but also some high strategic vision."[8]

In his view, that man was Winston Churchill. "There is little doubt," Matt wrote in December 1939, that "Churchill will be called to the supreme leadership of the British Empire."[9] His prediction was far from obvious at the time. Despite being appointed to the cabinet as First Lord of the Admiralty in September, Churchill had many critics who felt his judgments were impulsive and erratic. Mackenzie King described him as "one of the most dangerous men I have ever known."[10] For Matt, though, Churchill's early denunciation of Hitler and appeasement made him a hero. Now he was destined to become "Britain's man of the hour . . . endowed with supreme strategic genius, courageous as a lion and shrewd as a fox, and with that gift of high eloquence which stirs men's imaginations and inspires them with hope even in the darkest times. . . . His greatest days are still to come."[11]

Matt also predicted great days ahead for the young Canadians in uniform who began arriving in Britain in the last months of 1939. Stories about the Canadians flying Spitfires and preparing to defend the south coast of England became staples of his reporting. He was at dockside in Greenock, Scotland, when units of the 1st Canadian Division disembarked. "Seldom have I been more moved and thrilled than when, in last Sunday's gray mists, I saw the vanguard of the Canadian army – sons and brothers of the men of Vimy Ridge – land on British soil." Censorship was already so tight that he couldn't name the regiments or even say where the event was happening. But he described the flag-waving, emotional response of spectators as the troops marched away and proudly quoted *The Times*: "The first of freedom's fighters from the empire overseas are here."[12]

At year's end, Matt was preparing to go to France to report on the British Expeditionary Force when a cable from Hindmarsh told him to change course. He was to hurry to Finland, where thirty Soviet divisions had stormed across the border. Instead of reporting army exercises along France's Maginot defence line, Matt was drawn into a war that he would find both ghastly and thrilling.

The Winter War, as it was known, is now something of a forgotten side-show. Because it did not directly involve Germany, it has largely disappeared from the narrative of World War Two. Yet at a time when no other major fighting was happening, the David-and-Goliath aspect of the Russo-Finnish war gripped the attention of an admiring world. Here was a tiny country of three and a half million people that for several months not only held the Soviet colossus at bay but inflicted huge losses on it. Here was "Finland, superb – nay sublime – in the jaws of peril"[13] – in Churchill's magic words. And here was a conflict perfectly fitted for Matt's tendency to portray war in epic terms.

The Red Army had expected to crush Finland in two weeks. It invaded with more than three times as many soldiers, thirty times as many aircraft, and a hundred times as many tanks as the Finns. Yet it was ill-prepared for fighting in sub-Arctic forests where there were almost no roads and where harsh temperatures often dropped to 40 below. Its leadership was weakened by Stalin's purges and by inept political commissars who undermined the authority of senior officers. By mid-January, the Soviets were outfought and outmanoeuvred by the skill and courage of a mere 175,000 Finnish soldiers.

Exploiting the terrain and weather, small bands of ski troopers on the central and northern fronts adopted guerilla tactics against the invaders. They staged lightning attacks at night then retreated into the forest before the Russians could counterattack. With few anti-tank weapons, petrol bombs were used with devastating effect. The Finns gave the world the phrase "Molotov cocktail" and lessons in guerilla warfare.[14]

After a tiring journey from Stockholm to the border, Matt slung his rucksack over his shoulder and with typewriter in hand crossed a long, narrow bridge into northern Finland. With Geoffrey Cox, a friend from London's *Daily Express*, he drove through a blizzard to the headquarters of the Finnish North Command in Rovaniemi on the edge of the Arctic Circle. From the start, his reporting was infused with excitement and a rich sense of place. He described his arrival at night when the skies had cleared and the northern lights provided an awe-inspiring spectacle: "great shafts of blue, green, orange and incandescent white light dancing and flashing down the sky."[15] The only hotel in town had been converted into a combined command centre and hospital. A press room had also been set up on an open gallery overlooking the foyer where wounded soldiers were being treated. It was a strange setting – reporters typing their stories as nurses below them ministered to groaning, bloodied victims of the war.[16]

Next day Matt and three other correspondents were driven three hundred kilometres to the village of Suomussalmi. It was a name that was about to become a legend. Shortly after the invasion, the Red Army captured the town and advanced west in the hope of cutting the country in two at its narrow "waist." Fourteen thousand Soviet troops, strung out along a narrow snowbound road, entered a trap. They were repeatedly ambushed by "ghost patrols" – small units of Finnish soldiers so-called because of the white camouflage they wore. The patrols would attack at night, often machine-gunning Russians as they ate or slept, then disappear into the wilderness. Finally, two Finnish regiments ambushed a supply convoy in what became a massacre. At least 6,000 Soviet soldiers were killed or wounded at Suomussalmi compared to fewer than 1,000 Finnish casualties.

The battle was tapering off when Matt arrived and saw "what I think Dante would have hesitated to include in the Inferno."[17] The village seemed to him to resemble a strange necropolis. Only its white porcelain fireplaces and chimneys were left standing while its wooden buildings were burned to the ground. The more appalling sights lay along a four-mile stretch of frozen road outside the village. The ice was strewn with discarded weapons, shattered tanks, dead horses, and hundreds of Russian corpses, their eyelashes white with frost and faces yellowed. "I saw the horses with their feet in the air and the snow-covered mounds of dead Russians. . . . Blissfully they slept in their white winding sheets, the madness and the agony finished with forever. . . . I saw a dead Russian with his knees folded under him and his face in the snow as if he were a Moslem at prayer. When he was lifted up I saw that his face, unlike some others, had a benign waxen dignity like dead men I had seen in Spain. . . ."[18] Adding to the macabre scene, horses with chunks of flesh carved from their rumps by hungry Soviet soldiers wandered along the road.

The prisoners seemed to Matt as pitiable as the dead. "Some had frozen hands or feet, some had wounds roughly bandaged. Almost all had the memory of hell in their eyes."[19] The Finns allowed Matt and several colleagues into a large barn to interview dozens of prisoners. Under the Geneva conventions, there were restrictions on press interviews with POWs but Matt ignored the rules. He gave the prisoners cigarettes and asked them what they had been told about the invasion. Several replied that they thought Finns would welcome them as liberators. Another confirmed that many Russians were shot by NKVD troops if they retreated or hesitated to attack. One prisoner was laughing weirdly and another put his head in his hands and shook uncontrollably.[20] It was Matt's first exposure to a sickness he came to know well in World War Two: chronic battle fatigue or what is now classified as PTSD, post-traumatic stress disorder.

Other visits to the front lines were more uplifting. Matt requested permission to report on the ghost patrols harrying Russian forces on the Salla front north of the Arctic Circle. At a command post, he was fed a reindeer stew, then a guide took him forward on one of the light sleighs used so effectively by the Finnish army. He recounted an exhilarating night journey through pine-clad hills with ski patrols gliding out of the woods and soldiers occasionally galloping by on horseback. At an infantry dugout he was shrouded in *lumipuku*, the white hood, cape, and trousers that made Finnish soldiers almost invisible against the snow. He accompanied a foot patrol that moved to within half a kilometre of a Russian camp and spent the night in a camouflaged tent with twenty Finnish soldiers.[21] All was silent outside apart from the occasional crack of rifle shots and boom of shellfire.

The experience appealed to Matt's boyish sense of adventure. "On this night," he wrote, "I wouldn't have traded my profession for anyone's. I was intoxicated with the stunning beauty, with the thrill of excitement and the spice of danger. . . . I felt immensely alive."[22] It was the first hint of an attraction to being on battle fronts that, in later years, became perilously close to an addiction.

Part of the appeal was the camaraderie with other correspondents. In Rovaniemi, between visits to the front, Matt spent time with old and new friends: Cox of the *Express*, Leland Stowe of the *Chicago Daily News*, Walter Kerr of the *New York Herald Tribune*, and Carl Mydans, the famous *Life* photographer. They went skiing together, basked in the local sauna, and flirted with the Lottas, young women from Lotta Svärd, the paramilitary organization that enlisted women as nurses, couriers, and lookouts. The good times were occasionally broken up by the wail of warning sirens. Correspondents then joined Finns in rushing to primitive shelters before Russian bombers flew over, dropping bombs and machine-gunning indiscriminately. "The sickening evil of war comes home," Matt wrote, "when you see men, women and children huddle in holes in the ground and see their set faces in the lantern light as the first bombs explode, and hear the nervous laughter when they realize they are still alive."[23]

The *Star* exploited Matt's presence to the full. His name would often be splashed over the front page, sometimes in banner headlines: "HALTON WITH FINN TROOPS IN ARCTIC," "HALTON IN FRONT LINE OF FINNS." Sometimes the headline would bear little relation to his report, as in "ENCIRCLED BY RUSSIANS HALTON NEARLY TAKEN."[24] The publicity helped give him a profile that eclipsed that of the paper's other big names, Gordon Sinclair and Greg Clark.

It was the birth of celebrity journalism, and the *Star* was one of its midwives. The trend may have flattered Matt at the time, although later he objected strongly to war correspondents being lionized over the front-line soldiers.

In February, Finland's heroic stand in the Winter War began to collapse. Its troops were exhausted and short of weapons and ammunition. The Red Army, still willing to accept huge losses, poured in more troops. It breached the key Mannerheim Line, a chain of Finnish bunkers and trenches across the Karelian Isthmus between Lake Ladoga and the Gulf of Finland. Promised aid from Britain and France never came, and without that aid, Matt wrote, a Russian victory was inevitable. Surprisingly, the censor allowed that statement to pass, perhaps because Matt also compared the bravery of the Finns to the three hundred Spartans at Thermopylae.[25]

Moving south to cover the battles along the Mannerheim Line, Matt witnessed intense Soviet bombing and shelling. For the first time, he was close enough to see bombs actually dropping from low-flying aircraft. "The bomb falls and explodes 30 or 40 yards away. The world roars in your ears. You see branches and frozen earth cascade into the sky."[26] Wearing the standard snow camouflage, Matt was taken by an army guide to a dugout only a hundred yards behind the front. A badly wounded sergeant was lying on a bed of straw waiting to be evacuated in darkness. From the dugout, Matt and his guide were partly in view of Soviet positions as they crawled from tree to tree to get to the front. He admitted in print that it was silly to risk his life just to say that he had been to the real front line.[27] But if bravado was involved, he was also frank in confessing that at times he shook with fear.

Matt's war reporting was beginning to take on a recognizable style. It was graphic, sentimental, and personalized. If at times he glamorized soldiers, he never glamorized the anguish of war. His description of a train ride from Helsinki to Viipuri (Vyborg) near the front illustrated his ability to turn simple, even banal events into a compelling picture:

> It takes 14 hours to get to Viipuri and we sit like sardines all night in the packed train, with just enough light to see who is sitting across the aisle, and no air except when I go out on the platform, when I freeze.

There is war-time prohibition of liquor all over Finland except in Helsingfors (Helsinki), and the soldiers have brought bottles of cognac and wine to take to the front, but none of those bottles ever get to the front. They are consumed on the Viipuri train. . . .

The Viipuri train, the Viipuri train. The fine soldiers going to hold the Mannerheim line against 20 to one odds or more. The Lotta girl going to the front to nurse and carry supplies and become look-outs for bombers. . . . The singing of Tipperary in Finnish. The wayside stations where more men board the train. The rushing out for fresh air and coffee and a sandwich, and finding the way back in the dark. The Russian bombers coming over in the starlight and scaring us into the trees. . . . The officer who was a schoolteacher and shows me his wife's picture. And the women at the little stations saying good-bye.

Good-bye to the Viipuri train. Good-bye indeed. . . . The tears. . . . the last embrace, "Hyvaesti, hyvaesti" – "good-bye, goodbye" . . . The Russians are thundering at the gates of Viipuri only a few miles away. . . . Good-bye to the Viipuri train, and hope, and summer; for the line must be held.

The train is painfully slow. Less than 200 miles but it takes 14 hours. . . . "Do you hate the Russians?" I ask. "No," comes the familiar reply, "but we hate Russia."

Ten o'clock in the morning and journey's end for the Viipuri train.

Outside the station we see the partly wrecked town, and hear like rolling thunder the distant rumbling of the guns. . . .

The soldiers don their packs and sling their rifles and walk quite gaily away. To the Mannerheim line. We shout good-bye to our friends of the night. Hyvaesti, hyvaesti ! . . .

I meet some of them later in dugouts at the front. In the Mannerheim line I learn what it is to be bombed and shelled all day. But I don't learn what it is to have thousands of men coming at you in wave after wave. That is happening now. The Finns on the Karelian Isthmus are fighting one of the great defensive battles. . . .[28]

But Finland could not hold out much longer. In mid-March, a peace treaty was signed in Moscow that ceded 11 per cent of the country's territory to the Russians. Matt had been disillusioned with Soviet Communism long before the Winter War. Like many on the left, he had been shocked by Stalin's decision to forge a non-aggression pact with the Nazis in August 1939. Now he wrote of the betrayal of Lenin's dream and the transformation of Soviet Russia into yet another expansionist power.[29]

Russia's pyrrhic victory in Finland led many in Europe to conclude that the Red Army's strength was grossly overrated. Hitler was encouraged to think that a German invasion of the Soviet Union would be as easy as cutting through soft cheese. Matt was not convinced, noting that "despite this war, it's just a bit too early to say the Red Army has feet of clay."[30] In fact, the Russians quickly applied some of the lessons of the Finnish war, re-equipping many of their soldiers with winter clothing and reforming their military tactics.[31] The Red Army that the Wehrmacht faced later in Operation Barbarossa would be formidable.

Despite his anger over the Soviet aggression in Finland, Matt still saw Communist Russia as a lesser threat than Nazi Germany. For five years, Matt had argued for a strong defence alliance between Britain, France, and Russia as a sure way to deter Hitler or crush him on the battlefield. Such an alliance seemed a real possibility after Moscow offered the French and British a mutual assistance pact against Germany in the spring of 1939. But Chamberlain and Daladier dithered, no doubt influenced by right wingers for whom a deal with the Communists was unacceptable. Negotiations dragged on until Stalin ran out of patience and sprang his Non-Aggression Pact with Hitler. One of the great "what if's" of history is whether a triple alliance at that time could have prevented the Second World War. Churchill felt that it might have. In his post-war memoirs he wrote: "There can be no doubt even in the afterlight that Britain and France should have accepted the Soviet offer. . . . The alliance of Britain, France and Russia would have struck deep alarm in the heart of Germany in 1939, and no one can prove that war might not even then have been averted."[32] To which Matt would have added, "Amen."

In London, Matt returned to routine coverage of the Phony War: interviewing Canadian generals and covering training exercises with the

23,000 Canadian troops now in Britain. Already he was emerging as a cheerleader for the Allied war effort, a role in which he felt comfortable given his fervent belief in the cause. At times, however, his boosterism was excessive. "For pride, confidence and efficiency I have never seen troops to surpass them, not even the Finns,"[33] he wrote, after watching Canadian soldiers digging trenches and lugging Bren gun carriers over rough countryside. It was unlikely they merited such praise at that point since half the recruits had no military training prior to serving overseas.[34] Matt also wrote glowing profiles of General Andrew McNaughton, commander of the 1st Canadian Division, and other senior officers. Several used the phrase "No more Passchendaeles" to pledge to him there would be no reckless squandering of Canadian lives.[35] The commitment may have haunted them two years later when more than three thousand Canadians were killed or wounded in the disastrous raid on Dieppe.

For Matt, the tedium of the Phony War ended with brutal suddenness on May 10, 1940. At dawn that morning, Hitler's Panzer divisions cascaded over the borders of Holland and Belgium and advanced toward France. The Germans had invaded Denmark and Norway earlier but somehow it seemed that the "real" war began only when the British and French armies were fully engaged on the Western Front. In Germany four years earlier, Matt had written knowledgeably about German blitzkrieg tactics, stressing their emphasis on fast-moving armoured columns backed up by air power. "The core of this policy," he wrote at the time, "is that war must be launched on such a scale and with such speed that the enemy will be crushed in two weeks."[36] As it happened, that was more or less exactly how the catastrophe for the Allies unfolded. Yet, as the German offensive began, Matt echoed the false optimism that prevailed almost uniformly in British and Commonwealth media: "At long last, the cruel bullies of Europe are meeting forces as good as their own."[37] A headline in the *Star* shouted, "Nazis Stopped in Their Tracks" as Wehrmacht columns broke through Allied defences and surged westward.

The same optimism, much more justifiable, surrounded Churchill's appointment as prime minister. In several dispatches, Matt celebrated the replacement of the feckless Chamberlain by a man he described as probably the greatest leader in British history. He was in the House of Commons when Churchill declared that he had "nothing to offer but blood, toil, tears and sweat." Matt wrote that "no more thrilling declaration has ever been made by a leader of a free people. . . . Today there is no thought but of resistance and then victory. And then vengeance."[38] In reality, British opinion could not be so neatly categorized. While the press and the public quickly came to see Churchill as their champion, King George VI, the Whitehall Establishment, and most of the Conservative party were initially unenthusiastic, if not opposed to Churchill's appointment. Even Matt's former hero, Lloyd George, turned down an offer to join the coalition, believing that resistance to the Germans was a lost cause.[39]

British confidence in victory was certainly not as ironclad as Matt suggested. As the British Expeditionary Force fled Belgium and France at the end of May, the spectre of defeatism reappeared. Lord Halifax, the foreign secretary, proposed to Churchill's war cabinet that Italy mediate a peace settlement that would recognize Hitler's domination of Europe while giving autonomy to Britain and its empire. Churchill argued that the deal would make Britain a Nazi satellite and amount to a second Munich.[40] But his view prevailed only after four days of intense cabinet debate. Churchill himself was less sure of victory than in his bold public statements. Serious consideration was given to the possibility of embarking the British army to Canada in the event of a successful German invasion. Secretary of War Anthony Eden was even instructed to sound out how British troops would react to such an order. He was told by senior officers that in the event of imminent defeat, most conscripts and married men would prefer to give in rather than face a long exile in Canada.[41] But few of these facts were known at the time, and Matt's portrayal of a dauntless British people was the norm in the Anglo-Saxon media.

It was an unsettling time for Matt. For the first time in six years, some of his dispatches were relegated to the inside pages of the *Star*. He now had to share coverage of the top stories from Europe with three other *Star* correspondents sent abroad at the outbreak of fighting. His friend and rival, Greg Clark, was assigned to the continent, where he covered the evacuation of Dunkirk and the fall of France. Senior correspondent

Frederick Griffin was sent to British military headquarters, and Claude Pascoe to live with Canadian troops. The closest Matt got to the fighting was Dover, where he interviewed Royal Air Force pilots and stood on the famed white cliffs, watching the distant flames from the French channel ports and listening to the far-off reverberations of bombs and shellfire.[42] It was not his idea of being a war correspondent.

Staying at home had one consolation. Jean and three-year-old Kathleen were now living safely in Beaconsfield in Buckinghamshire, an easy commute for Matt from London. It was one of the loveliest springs in memory. Rhododendrons and roses flowered early, larks and blackbirds were in full throat, and a nightingale could be heard at dusk near their cottage. Matt wrote in his memoir that nature was giving England one last gift before dreadful days ahead.[43] He took his wife and daughter on short walks into the Chiltern Hills – short because Jean was in the last month of pregnancy. I was born on May 28 in a country hospital that would soon be treating wounded evacuees from Dunkirk. On that same day, 17,000 British soldiers made their escape from France, Belgium surrendered to the Nazis, and Churchill secured his crucial cabinet victory over the last supporters of appeasement: Britain would never negotiate with Hitler.

Earlier that month, Matt and Jean were listening to the BBC when a news bulletin announced that "the Germans have broken through at Sedan."[44] Matt knew instantly what that meant. The Germans had breached France's supposedly impregnable Maginot defence line, enabling them to move westward and encircle the Allies' armies in Belgium and northern France. The French troops at Sedan were badly equipped, badly trained reservists who broke and fled under devastating Luftwaffe bombing and Panzer assault. But Matt, the constant Francophile, was angered by subsequent British sneers about the cowardice of the French army. He acknowledged the poor generalship and antiquated tactics of the French military but noted that some units fought with great skill and courage. He singled out the relatively unknown Brigadier Charles de Gaulle, whose armoured division inflicted heavy losses on the Germans and whom he would later compare to Churchill.[45]

Matt soon found himself defending France again. This time he was angered by criticism that France was "rotten to the core" because of its armistice with the Germans and the emergence of Marshal Pétain's Fascist-tinged Vichy regime. Matt argued passionately that France's problem was that it was rotten at the top rather than at the core. He wrote that the country was betrayed by a right-wing oligarchy that preferred collaboration with the Nazis to democracy. "Who were the quislings when France was falling?" he asked. "The Pétains, who had never in their hearts accepted the Revolution, the clerico-authoritarians who still smarted at the disestablishment of the Church."[46] Matt acknowledged that the French public was profoundly averse to another blood-letting so soon after World War One. But he stopped short of recognizing another reality: the lack of will to resist; the popularity of the armistice with the Germans; and, at least initially, the widespread support for Pétain's regime of collaboration. His love of France led him to ask a provocative question: Would there have been a British Vichy-style government if there was no English Channel to deter a Nazi invasion? "What would have happened if she [Britain] had not had that precious little strip of water? The world would probably have been saying today that Britain was 'rotten to the core'."[47]

By mid-June 1940, Nazi soldiers had goose-stepped down the Champs-Elysées and the first bombs had fallen on London. As if Matt's world wasn't already in turmoil, a cable from Toronto sent him into near-despair. The *Star's* management ordered all its correspondents home. With so much fast-breaking news from the war fronts, Atkinson and Hindmarsh decided it was foolish to risk their correspondents' lives to duplicate stories the wire services were providing.[48] Matt was told that he would be sent to Washington to cover the presidential election that year and stay on to set up the *Star's* first bureau in the U.S. capital. Most reporters would have regarded it as a dream assignment, but not Matt. Europe had become the centre of his universe and now he felt he was being dragged away from the biggest story of the war: Britain standing alone against tyranny.

A dozen or so close friends gathered at London's Euston station to say goodbye to Matt, Jean, three-year-old Kathleen, and five-week-old David as they boarded the boat train to Liverpool. On that day, Matt wrote, the grimy old station was the hardest place in the world to leave. He wondered if he would ever return to the London he loved and envied his friends who were staying for its hour of trial.[49]

There was little time for nostalgia after their heavily protected convoy began the Atlantic crossing. Jean was very sick with an abscess of the breast and was told by the ship's doctor to stay in bed. Changing and washing nappies, feeding his children, and getting them to sleep was something Matt could just about manage. His problem was that there were fourteen hundred other women and children aboard seeking sanctuary in Canada. As one of the very few male passengers, he was frequently asked to help out other mums, some of them seasick, and many of them without the nannies they were used to at home. He did bottle feeds and various chores for other children, realizing that an engaging feature story could be salvaged from what he jokingly called the "hell-ship." From 6 a.m. to bedtime, he was on his feet, dealing with challenges that included "finding assuagements for upset little tummies and inspirations for little bowels that won't upset." He claimed that "being a nurse on that ship . . . made me expert in many aspects of motherhood."[50]

At the end of the day, though, he still had a few minutes to reflect that he was journeying away from the place he most wanted to be.

11

A SHORT TIME IN EXILE

"I was never unhappier than my three months in Washington. London was burning and Britain had come alive."

                   − MATTHEW HALTON, *Ten Years to Alamein*

MATT ARRIVED IN WASHINGTON WHEN THE Battle of Britain was reaching its peak. The fate of the free world depended on a few hundred RAF pilots and British courage in the face of savage bombing. In his mind Matt was still living in beleaguered London. That was where *the* story was; that was where his friends were; that was where his heart was. "In Washington," he wrote in his memoir, "I did little but sit in the National Press Club reading each new edition of the papers"[1] – searching for the latest news of the Blitz.

For a reporter sympathetic to President Franklin Delano Roosevelt, covering FDR's America should have been an exciting challenge. Matt admired the liberal Democrat who defined himself as "left of centre" and denounced the excesses of capitalism. Yet rarely in Washington was he inspired to produce the kind of textured reports about politics and society that illuminated his writing from London. Almost nothing was written about the successes and failures of Roosevelt's New Deal, about the creation of a new welfare state, or about FDR's controversial decision to become the first American president to run for a third term. Nor was there any analysis of the Democratic coalition of unions, ethnic voters, African-Americans, and white rural southerners that would shake up U.S. politics for decades.

Gerald "Gerry" Anglin, an editor at the *Star* at the time, noticed that Matt's work had lost its usual glow. "I remember thinking how flat it was for someone who had built up a great journalistic voice."[2]

Matt focused almost obsessively on war-related stories. Debate was raging in the United States between interventionists who wanted to help arm the British and isolationists bent on keeping the country free of foreign commitments. Matt was on Capitol Hill frequently to interview mainly pro-British politicians from both parties. Senator Charles Glass told him America would do everything to help Britain short of declaring war. "Unless Britain wins," the senator said, "the young men of the United States can look forward to a perilous lifetime."[3] In contrast, Matt portrayed the isolationists, represented in the extreme by aviator Charles Lindbergh and the anti-Semitic radio priest Father Charles Coughlin, as "a malignancy in America."[4] He cheered Roosevelt's promise to make the United States the "arsenal of democracy" through agreements such as exchanging fifty American destroyers for British bases in Newfoundland and the Caribbean. But he also expressed impatience with Roosevelt's need to placate the isolationists by pledging that "your boys are not going to be sent into any foreign wars."[5]

In August, Matt travelled to upstate New York to watch Roosevelt and Mackenzie King sign the Ogdensburg Agreement. On the surface, the agreement appeared modest – to set up a permanent joint board to study the defence needs of both countries. In effect, its implications were enormous. For the first time, Canada and the United States entered an alliance that put them on the path to an integrated continental defence. Canada implicitly recognized that it could no longer rely on Britain for her security. Some Canadians accused King of betraying the Empire,[6] but Matt welcomed the agreement with gusto. "It was hearteningly plain," he wrote, "that the great republic and the great Dominion were conscious of their destiny and really getting together, though they had waited until flames were licking the London sky. It seemed clear to me that here was the germ of the union of English-speaking peoples which is the hope of the world. . . ."[7]

Shortly after his return from London, Matt was invited by Canada's director of public information to do an unpaid fifteen-minute broadcast on Britain's struggle for survival. Ottawa wanted to use his stature as Canada's best-known foreign correspondent to rally public support for the war effort. Accepting such an invitation today would be an unacceptable breach of journalistic ethics. It would open a reporter to charges of conflict of interest and of being a propagandist for the government. But for Matt, and most of his fellow journalists in wartime Canada, it simply wasn't an issue. Doing what one could for the Allied cause was considered a matter of duty.

Matt's broadcast, "Britain the Citadel," was one in a government-sponsored series known as *Let's Face the Facts*, which was carried by the CBC. His delivery was quiet but this was Matt at his most emotional. It was the voice of the Anglophile saluting the country he had grown up to love and which he now saw rising again to greatness. The tone was Churchillian:

> *This little misty island on the shoulder of Europe is fighting once more for the world. She stands there, the last old world citadel of civilization now that France is gone, and she stands alone. But to every Briton, there is now magic in that word, "alone." Two weeks ago Britain really awoke and it was worth living to see. In eight years in Europe for the Toronto Star I have seen most of the great sights, from Spain to Finland, from the Reichstag fire in 1933 (which started the whole world burning) to the first bombs on London – sights that were terrible and sights that were splendid – though most of them were terrible – but none so splendid as England awake, determined once more, as in Pitt's day, to "save herself by her exertions and Europe by her example." And I say this, that with each disaster of the last few months the British step becomes a little jauntier. The monstrous German machine stormed west early in May and Britain said, almost with relief, "Now we can get at them." The B.E.F. [British Expeditionary Force] was cut off in what Churchill the Great called "a colossal military disaster" – only to be followed by the glory of Dunkirk when . . . "the rags and blemishes which had hidden the soul of democracy fell away. . . ." France collapsed – and every Englishman squared his shoulders and took himself quietly aside and whispered with a secret exultation: "Now we're alone!" The darker the day, the brighter shone the island's courage. And it will be like that to the end, whatever the end may be.*[8]

The broadcast encapsulated Matt's style: vividly poetic at its best, dramatic at times, but delivered with transparent sincerity. From today's vantage point, its patriotism seems excessive. At the time, though, it was a perfect fit for a still resolutely loyal English Canada in deep alarm about the future of the mother country. Letters to newspapers indicated an overwhelmingly favourable public response. Typically, one reader said, "This was one of the very finest things that has come over the air for a long time, and certainly makes one more than ever proud to belong to the British empire."[9] The Universal Life Assurance Company was so impressed that it printed and distributed thousands of copies of the text across the country.

The broadcast brought a request from the director of public information for Matt to make another contribution to the series. This time, it was late in September, and the Blitz was wreaking havoc in London. Broadcasting from New York, Matt warned that Canada's own future was at stake:

> If decency were to go under in Europe, this continent would have to become an armed camp, prepared to fight for its place in a strident and hostile world. Conscription, crippling taxation and colossal armaments would become as commonplace here as they are in Europe. . . . Canada, the fifth greatest trading nation on earth, would lose her best markets overnight. Who would buy our wheat? Who would buy our motor cars? Not Britain, because she would be impoverished. Not the United States, because she has enough of her own, and would be trying to buy South American goods in an effort to keep the sister continent out of the conqueror's orbit. . . . We would have to arm to the teeth, and we should have less wealth with which to arm. There is no doubt whatever that the issue being fought out by the British people with such glittering splendour is not only for decency and safety but for the daily bread and ordinary happiness of Canadians and Americans in every province and state and class.

The broadcast ended with praise for the young British and Commonwealth pilots fighting the Battle of Britain. It was not just a battle of survival, Matt said, but a battle of ideas:

It is Churchill against Hitler. . . . It is some measure of the truth against the
lie. . . . It is the sane, homely philosophy of the English soil against the wild
polysyllabic bellowing of Hitler and his medicine men. . . . It is the law
against the pogrom. It is the hope of the world against the call of the wild.
The call of the wild must not prevail. Canada is doing her part, but
she must do more. No small nation has ever had a proportionately larger
role to play in the drama of history. . . . There are only 11,000,000 of us
in Canada, but the issue is largely up to us. We must see to it, if we can,
for our own sake and our children's sake and for our glory, that the words
"not enough machines" do not go calling and calling into history.[10]

The broadcast again drew a chorus of praise. The *Ottawa Journal* wrote
about the discovery of "a new radio personality" and described the address
as "the stuff of authentic eloquence."[11] The CBC noticed the response and
commissioned him to do a bi-weekly series called *American Commentary*.
Matt was reminded of the powerful impact of radio that he had felt after
his broadcasts for CBS and NBC during the Munich crisis.

In Washington, the family moved into a spacious rented house in
Spring Valley, one of the capital's upscale residential areas. Matt and Jean
were frequent and popular guests of two Canadian diplomats, Loring
Christie and Escott Reid. But it was not the satisfying time it could have
been for Matt. He still felt he was in a kind of exile, wondering morosely
at times whether he would ever work again in Europe. Beyond Washington,
he simply had no idea of his future.

Not even the presidential election campaign was much of an inspiration. His dispatches tended to state the obvious and contained few original insights into American politics. He wrote admiringly of Roosevelt,
"who represents the cause of labor and liberalism against Wall Street."[12]
But he also sympathized with the Republican challenger, Wendell
Willkie, the last genuinely liberal candidate ever nominated by the
party – an internationalist who reluctantly had to court the isolationist
vote. Matt's liveliest work during the period was a weekly column, "The
War Reviewed," that he was asked to write for several months. On the
familiar ground of European news, Matt wrote knowledgeably about

the Blitz and predicted with uncanny accuracy that Germany and Russia would soon be at war despite their non-aggression pact.[13]

Matt did pull off one journalistic coup – getting a few words with Roosevelt on the night of his re-election. A week earlier he had visited Hyde Park, the Roosevelt family estate in upstate New York, to interview the president's eighty-six-year-old mother, Sara Delano Roosevelt. It was apparently a warm encounter. As he left, Matt asked if she could leave his name with the secret service and state troopers on election night so that he could join FDR's anticipated victory party. She agreed.

On the evening of the vote, Matt broadcast for CBC from nearby Poughkeepsie, then arrived at Hyde Park in time to watch Roosevelt greet jubilant supporters. True to her word, Roosevelt's mother had ensured that Matt's name was on the list for access to the estate, enabling him to join forty or so family, friends, and insiders in the mansion's library. It gave him the opportunity for a brief exchange with Roosevelt in which Matt, with enormous chutzpah, congratulated the president on behalf of Canada. "Mackenzie King will be pleased, won't he?" asked FDR. "He will be pleased," Matt replied, "and so will Churchill."[14] It was thin gruel but enough for a front-page headline in the *Star*.

At the same gathering, Matt met Eleanor Roosevelt, who agreed to give him an interview for a profile he wanted to write about her. A few days later, he was ushered into the Red Room at the White House and sat down for tea with the First Lady. Having described FDR as "the greatest American statesman since Lincoln," Matt was equally in awe of his wife. He admired her independence – astounding even by today's standard – which allowed her to write a newspaper column, deliver lectures, and keep an apartment in New York's bohemian Greenwich Village. But it was her progressive social and political activism that most impressed Matt. In his profile, he described her as "a female Sir Galahad . . . a woman who will break lances with any black knight, whether his name is sweatshop or race prejudice or Hitlerism; a woman who has never said or done anything insincere."[15]

He asked her about criticism that she had strayed from the traditional role of a First Lady whose place was defined as being in the background and in the home. Her reply was feisty: "Of course, women's place is in the home, but the home has to be protected, and to protect it you have to go out and fight the things that threaten it, such as social insecurity, and child labor, and poverty and ignorance."[16] Matt also used the interview to raise an issue that the American press rarely touched. He asked Eleanor Roosevelt about the polio that paralysed FDR for most of his life. "There is no doubt he is a greater man because of it," she replied. "Suffering developed his natural sympathy for the unfortunates of the world, the struggle against suffering developed his perception, his thinking qualities, his courage . . ."[17] After the interview, the First Lady showed Matt some of the rooms in the White House, stopping to point out a portrait of Abraham Lincoln. Matt remarked that Lincoln had been called on to save the union but that her husband had been called on to help save the world.[18]

In November, Matt received news that lifted his spirits. He was in Toronto to address a special Remembrance Day service where he was introduced by Anglican bishop Robert Renison as "a man whose name is known in every household in Canada."[19] During the visit, he met with the *Star*'s Hindmarsh and Atkinson and was told he could return to London and cover the war fronts in Europe and elsewhere. There is little evidence to explain how and why they changed their mind about keeping him in Washington. Was it because of pressure from Matt? Was it because they felt the paper would be better served by a less unhappy correspondent? Or, more probably, had they simply realized they had an asset who was at his best in Europe? Whatever the answer, the decision to reinstate Matt as a war correspondent proved a highly successful one for the paper. Ironically, though, its very success would eventually propel him away from the *Star* in a new direction.

THE DESERT WAR

"And then the battlefield is left behind, with its little crosses in the sand.
The battlefield where the East was held, where so many of us learned in the
drifting smoke-rack what we were."
— MATTHEW HALTON, CBC broadcast, October 4, 1942

IN THE LAST WEEK OF JANUARY 1941, Matt boarded the SS *Nerissa* in Halifax. Saying goodbye to Jean and the children was painful. Matt long remembered four-year-old Kathleen, her arms clinging to his neck, saying "Daddy, just don't talk, don't talk,"[1] and Jean turning away to hide her tears. It was Matt's tenth Atlantic crossing and far more dangerous than his last one. German submarine attacks were becoming more frequent, and the *Nerissa* – carrying two thousand tons of airplane parts and two hundred Commonwealth pilots – was considered fast enough to sail without an escort. There were complaints about rough seas and tense days. Soon though, everyone aboard had reason to be profoundly thankful for the timing of their voyage. Three months later, a U-boat fired two torpedoes into the *Nerissa* off the Irish coast. The ship sank in four and a half minutes, drowning more than seventy of its passengers. If Matt had travelled a few months later, he would have been on the only troopship to lose Canadian soldiers en route to England in World War Two.[2]

Matt's return to London was like a homecoming. He arrived on a typically wet and foggy morning, exhilarated to be back in the city where "history's most decisive battle has been fought."[3] He checked into a suite at the still luxurious Savoy Hotel which he had once walked by every day as an impecunious student. Friends trooped in to see him, and he confessed to Jean that he partied and drank too much for most of the first week. There were reunions with Eric Gibbs, a close friend at the University of Alberta, now deputy chief of public relations at Canadian Military Headquarters; Don Minifie of the *New York Herald Tribune*; Graham Spry, who shared Matt's socialist views; his German refugee friends Hans and Elsa Wolfsohn; Garfield Weston, now a British MP but still running his bread and biscuit empire; and a lively group of Canadian diplomats that included Charles Ritchie and Lester Pearson. Evenings would often begin in the River Bar at the Savoy, a favourite of CBS's "Murrow boys," and end up at nightclubs such as Ciro's and the Coconut Grove. Old friendships were renewed and new ones made. Matt wrote to Jean that "war may be hell, but I am beginning to think I enjoy it."[4]

German bombing was less intense in the first few weeks of Matt's return to London. On the day of his arrival, he was impressed by the outward normalcy of life. Eccentric orators were still haranguing people from their soapboxes at Speakers' Corner in Hyde Park. The old lady selling tulips and gardenias in Piccadilly Circus was still at her post and told him she had stayed there through the worst days of the Blitz. The famous buildings in Trafalgar Square and along Whitehall were largely intact. St. Paul's, seemingly invincible, still loomed over the city. It was only when Matt walked around the cathedral that he discovered the devastation nearby – famous old streets lined by shattered buildings and huge piles of rubble. Visiting his old home on Regent's Park, he found its windows blown out and the building itself tilting toward the street.[5]

Luftwaffe attacks on London and other British cities resumed a deadlier tempo in March. Matt got used to the nightly ritual: the banshee wail of air-raid sirens followed by the drone of aircraft, the flash of explosions, and the boom of anti-aircraft guns. From his hotel room or friends' homes, he would watch pillars of smoke rising under a sky lit by searchlights, flares, and tracer bullets. His dispatches regained the colour and vigour that had largely disappeared from his reports in Washington. Now, in London and other bombed British cities, Matt found the human drama on which his wartime journalism thrived. On Easter Friday, he rushed to Coventry the day after it was attacked by more than two hundred German bombers. Delayed-action bombs were still exploding and civil defence workers were "digging with a sort of cold, desperate frenzy for those who have been buried alive." The raid left twelve hundred people dead and wounded and thousands more homeless. Yet after talking to survivors, Matt found a city that reflected a defiant Britain. At an Easter service, he heard the prayer of a white-haired Anglican vicar: "We thank Thee, O God, for our unconquerable souls."[6]

Even if Matt witnessed instances of panic or hysteria, he would not have been allowed to describe them in any detail. As an accredited war correspondent, he was subject to Britain's stringent wartime censorship. War Office regulations unashamedly ordered correspondents to cooperate "in the great and almost sacred task of leading and steadying public opinion in times of national stress or crisis." On the prohibited list were reports "likely to cause despondency or alarm to troops or civilians."[7]

However, Matt's portrayal of a steadfast people was undeniably accurate. In a *Star* article, he puzzled over the solidarity and courage of the British. He decided that Churchill's inspirational oratory made average people feel like heroes. But projecting his own feelings on the public, Matt surmised that there was another factor. "There was the exhilaration of danger," he wrote. "You were alive. You were playing a part in the greatest drama of history."[8] As the civilian death toll from the Blitz mounted above thirty thousand, he also offered an explanation for the absence of fear among so many people: The "egotism of the human soul . . . the belief that while catastrophe may touch other people, nothing can happen to you yourself. After all, few people really realize inwardly that they themselves are ever going to die, let alone die from being struck by a bomb."[9]

Matt himself was in direct danger on only two occasions. The first happened after he hurried to the scene of a bombing at the Café de Paris, a fashionable dinner-dance club. As he watched first-aid workers treat the wounded outside, he was knocked over by the blast from a second bomb that fell a hundred yards away.[10] He was shaken but unhurt – grist for another "*Star*-man-on-the-spot" story that the paper relished.

There was no such story written about Matt's second encounter with danger. On the night of April 15, he went out for a late dinner with a friend. When he returned to the Savoy at midnight, the worst bombing of the Blitz had begun. It lasted eight hours, four hundred German aircraft turning some London streets into canyons of flame and destruction. Matt was about to go to his room when he ran into his colleague Don Minifie, who was also staying at the hotel. They agreed to go down to the basement bar for a nightcap – quite a few Scotch and sodas as it turned out – before going to bed.[11] Exhausted, probably drunk, and feverish after a series of inoculations that day, Matt went to sleep almost immediately. Minifie was less fortunate. He was still on his feet when a delayed-action bomb exploded in the backyard of the hotel. It blew out his window and shot a shard of glass into his right eye that half-blinded him for the rest of his life. Twelve other hotel guests were injured by the blast. But Matt didn't wake up until the next afternoon. As he wrote to Jean, he slept through one of the heaviest Nazi air raids of the Second World War in a building that had just been bombed.[12]

Matt's drinking was certainly excessive at times. In one letter home, he wrote that "I've been at so many parties and so many bottles [after-hours drinking clubs] that I can hardly see, and haven't done half the work I should, and tonight I am signing off though I may just need an eye-opener tomorrow morning."[13] In another letter, he told Jean about drinking "millions of whiskey sours" and having "awful headaches" and promised to reduce his drinking.[14] If Matt showed some of the symptoms of alcoholism, he was never an alcoholic according to any clinical definition of dependence. Most of his friends and acquaintances would later comment on his ability to moderate his drinking most of the time. It was also an era when heavy drinking (or "getting tight," as mild inebriation was called) was much more socially acceptable than it is today – and almost the norm among many journalists.

Matt lived extravagantly in London, as he tended to do everywhere. The *Star*, the highest-paying Canadian newspaper, had given him a big raise when he left Washington. He was earning an annual salary equivalent to at least $133,000 today, supplemented by a large freelance income and a lavish expense account. That enabled him to frequent expensive restaurants, bars, and nightclubs, keep Jean and the children in comfort, and send monthly cheques to support his family in Pincher Creek.

London was becoming the capital of transients. There was a constant coming-and-going of Commonwealth soldiers and exiles from Nazi Europe. The streets were full of different uniforms by day: army, navy, air force, everyone from Free Poles to Free French. At night, the blacked-out streets in the West End were a ghostly spectacle: people groping their way through the darkness to shelters, pubs, and cinemas. The wartime atmosphere encouraged conviviality. The sense of shared danger brought people together; barriers of class and reserve were relaxed. Howard K. Smith, a young CBS correspondent who became a good friend of Matt, described "a mood that loosens morals and inhibitions like nothing else."[15] With more subtlety, the Canadian diplomat Charles Ritchie wrote that "wartime London was a forcing ground for love and friendship, for experiments and amusements snatched under pressure. . . . People drifted apart and together again as the war pattern dictated."[16]

Matt himself was about to enter the world of casual attachments. He began going out with a librarian at the Ministry of Information. Her name was Maureen Church, a tall and very pretty woman in her mid-twenties who had once been a governess for the Minifies' children. George Weidenfeld,* a wartime friend of Matt, suggests that Maureen was something of a socialist groupie. She enjoyed the company of left-wing intellectuals such as author Arthur Koestler and the future Labour MP Richard Crossman. According to Weidenfeld, Matt, handsome and attractive to women, was "a trophy for her."[17] He described the relationship as "a long love affair"[18] but, for Matt at least, it may have offered little more than companionship and sexual release during his sojourns in London.

Matt was still sending love letters to Jean three or four times a week. In a typical one, he wrote, "There is no one like you and never will be. . . . I would give a little of my soul if I could have you once more,

---

* Weidenfeld, who worked during the war for the BBC Overseas Service, later founded his own publishing firm and was created a life peer as Lord Weidenfeld of Chelsea.

lovingly, sweetly . . . for the infinity of a few seconds, and your eyes looking up and saying the things lips don't dare to say."[19] It is easy to conclude that writing such letters while having an extramarital affair was an example of male hypocrisy. But there were unusual aspects to Matt's relationship with Jean. His letters were often confessional in tone, telling her about his drinking and desires and spendthrift tendencies. Without being more explicit, he would tell her about taking Maureen Church to dinners and outings, sometimes with friends who knew Jean as well. Was this the proverbial "open marriage"? Helen Silverthorne, a friend and bridesmaid at their wedding, said Jean was aware that Matt had some affairs in the four years he was away from her. "Jean knew all about it," she said. "She wasn't jealous. He would tell her about it."[20] More than three decades later, my mother told me that she accepted that her husband had "the occasional one-night stand" during the war.[21] Curiously, his affairs appeared to have had no effect on a marriage that all their closest friends agreed was one of enduring love.

In May 1941, the Luftwaffe attacks on Britain tapered off. Hitler had turned his attention to Operation Barbarossa, which was about to hurl vast Nazi armies against the Soviet Union. The threat of a Fascist invasion of Britain had largely disappeared so the *Star* sent Matt to cover a new war front: the Empire's battle for the Middle East. The conflict had begun as an effort by British troops to prevent Mussolini from fulfilling his dream of building a new Roman empire across North Africa. When the Italian army collapsed, Hitler sent in the Afrika Korps under General Erwin Rommel to reinforce it. Immediately, the geopolitical stakes were raised. If the Germans could drive the British out of Egypt, they would control the Suez Canal and choke off the oil supplies that fed the British war effort. They might also link up with the Nazi troops that had overrun the Balkans.

For most of the next eighteen months, Matt was the only Canadian correspondent covering the Desert War. His dispatches were now syndicated in twenty Canadian newspapers. Other articles by him were carried by the Allied Newspaper chain in Britain, and *PM*, a new left-wing newspaper in New York that published Hemingway, James Thurber, and Erskine

Caldwell. For long stretches, Matt would be embedded with the legendary Eighth Army in the Egyptian and Libyan deserts. It was a time of hardship and self-discovery that he said taught him to control his fear. It also developed what was aptly described as his enthusiasm "for the sheer adventure of living on the edge" and his "keen appetite to savour, close up, the fury of combat."[22] The experience inspired some of his finest war reporting and formed the main part of his bestselling memoir, *Ten Years to Alamein*.

Matt arrived in Cairo after a long sea journey around the Cape – troopship convoys through the Mediterranean were considered too risky. War correspondents were considered part of the military, given the honorary rank of Captain, and required to wear military uniform in combat areas. So Matt's first stop was the Officers Club, where he was outfitted with dress uniform and standard field khakis: knee-length socks, bush jacket, baggy shorts, and steel helmet. He insisted on getting a red tab with "Canadian War Correspondent" inscribed on it rather than the standard British one. He was also issued with a revolver. Under the Geneva Conventions, it was illegal for war correspondents to bear arms but the British said the weapon could be used if necessary against unruly natives.

Matt's first assignment was unexpected. In June, instead of going to the desert, he was told to join British, Australian, and Free French forces advancing into Syria and Lebanon. Their objective was to overthrow the Vichy French army that controlled the region and secure the British flank in the eastern Mediterranean. With a conducting officer and a French correspondent, Matt was driven from Jerusalem, past the Sea of Galilee, to a front line just south of Damascus. Two days later, they were given permission to follow troops leading the attack toward the Syrian capital. For the first time since Finland, Matt found himself in the thick of fighting as British troops were shelled by Vichy forces. He was about to have what he described as "the worst ten minutes of our lives."[23] After deciding to retreat from the action, his group found itself stuck on the road when its car blew a tire. As they were replacing the tire, a Messerschmitt fighter began targeting a gun battery fifteen metres away. Machine-gun bullets spattered the road. There was no cover so all Matt could do was to "push his nose into the ground and contract like a worm."[24] He admitted that he was so terrified his legs were shaking uncontrollably, even after the air-craft had disappeared.

Several days later he followed Allied troops as they captured Damascus. For someone with Matt's romantic sense of history, there was the thrill of watching prayers in the Great Mosque of the Umayyads, the fourth-holiest place in Islam, even as fighting still raged in the city. Later he joined Australian troops as they captured the Crusader fort at Marjayoun and began pushing the Vichy French from Lebanon. He was invited to go in with another attack but found an excuse to avoid having to say he was simply too frightened. In his dispatch that day he admitted that one of the great advantages of war correspondents is that they can usually leave when they have had enough at the front.[25] He was equally candid in recounting how he and his colleagues then drove to Palestine where they stayed in a comfortable hotel in Haifa and drank champagne in a nightclub.

No such comforts were easily available in the desert campaign. For periods up to seven weeks without a break, Matt lived with Eighth Army troops in one of the most desolate landscapes in the world. He described the desert battleground as "a hot white nothingness."[26] It stretched for almost two thousand kilometres from close to Alexandria in Egypt to the western border of Libya. Sand was the soldiers' nightmare. Whipped up by hot winds, it layered everything in its way with dust – matting hair, getting into eyes, mouth, and every pore. At its worst in the sandstorms blown up by the winds of the *khamsin*, it blotted out visibility like a thick fog. Matt wrote about other hardships: "the flies, the mosquitoes at night, the prickly heat rash, the sweat – these sometimes seem worse than the blood and tears. Men who will advance joking through a curtain of enemy fire curse and are nauseated when the flies get in their stew."[27] That stew – sliced and warmed-up bully beef – was his staple diet on the front. It was accompanied by hard biscuits, tinned vegetables, and tea made from usu-ally brackish, chlorinated water. There were complaints too about flea-in-fested sleeping bags and scorpions.

Yet for all its challenges, the desert campaign was one of Matt's most defining and most cherished experiences. It offered adventure and the intense comradeship of shared danger. Enduring friendships were made:

the closest with Matt's conducting officer, Sean Fielding, a captain in the elite Green Howards infantry regiment. Fielding was a former news-paperman, an urbane Anglo-Irishman with a dry, sophisticated sense of humour. He could describe grim situations as "a trifle sticky"[28] without sounding affected. He was in charge of Matt, two other correspondents, and the drivers of their convoy of a station wagon and two supply trucks. Matt wrote that it was Sean's "energy, skill and courage [that] not only saved us from Rommel's tanks but enabled us to do our job through six weeks of steady battle and through difficulties I cannot begin to describe."[29]

Like many other correspondents, Matt saw the Desert War in heroic terms. The Eighth Army was "the Empire on the march."[30] It brought together troops from Britain, Australia, New Zealand, India, and South Africa: the great imperial grouping he had grown up to admire. His one disappointment was the absence of Canadian troops on the ground. He tried to compensate for it by writing about the impressive record of the 130 Canadian pilots in the Western Desert Air Force. He flew on a reconnais-sance mission with one of them and interviewed a wounded pilot from Calgary shot down as he strafed Axis forces.[31]

Warring in a largely empty desert had one advantage: there were no civilians to be terrorized or caught in the crossfire. That made it easier for soldiers and journalists to put a chivalrous gloss on the campaign. Rommel, the "Desert Fox," is said to have described it as a *Krieg ohne Hass* – a war without hate.[32] He insisted that German and Italian troops under his command respect the Geneva Conventions and treat their prisoners humanely. Field hospitals on both sides gave the same treatment to enemy soldiers as they did their own. On the rapidly shifting front, Rommel once visited a casualty clearing station where a British surgeon remained on duty just after it was overrun by the Germans.[33] On another occasion, British and German soldiers played soccer against each other between the lines during a lull in fighting.[34]

Despite the mutual respect, the conflict was as brutally fierce as any other campaign. Matt's accounts were vivid but inevitably sanitized to meet the army's rigorous censorship. Early in the campaign, he wrote to Jean that "war is far uglier than one can dare to tell in articles. The phrase 'wounded soldier' doesn't sound bad but when you hear them screaming, it's different."[35] No young men would ever enlist, he said, if one described the real sights and sounds of battle. In another letter, he told Jean how sickened he was after visiting an artillery position of "the Buffs" (the Royal East Kent Regiment) just after it had been destroyed by the Germans. "I had read about shaking violently all over and now it was happening to me. . . . Vomit, but stagger back to the car and write about what a wonderful adventure it is. 'The Buffs died on their guns.' It sounds fine, doesn't it? But what if one of them wasn't quite dead? His bowels were draped round his gun but he was still crying for his mother."[36]

Even in the desert, Matt's odd obsession with trying to write good poetry never left him. He wrote little rhymes for Kathleen and love poems for Jean. Rarely did they rise above the amateurish. One effort was about the warmth of remembering Jean when his eyes were shut in the desert:

> *. . . I open them, and heaven is gone.*
> *Here's rue for you, and wilderness of sand,*
> *And evil gaudy sunsets, and white light*
> *And the adjutant's crisp voice, "No mail for you,"*
> *And warplanes storming silver down the sky,*
> *And diving into trenches in the ground,*
> *And rising from the ground half sick and dazed,*
> *After the fearful crunching of the bombs.*
> *What price now is gallantry and high emprise*
> *If heaven is lost by opening my eyes?*[37]

As Matt's exposure to war became routine, he became more of a risk-taker. He decided to run the gauntlet into Tobruk, the besieged Libyan port that had become a symbol of British courage. For five months, Australian and British troops had defended the enclave against Rommel's Afrika Korps. Access was only by sea so Matt did what few other correspondents had done before him. He boarded the Royal Navy destroyer *Kandahar* in Alexandria to make the dangerous voyage along the North African coast to Tobruk. The last 244 kilometres was known as "the death ride" because the ships were frequently targeted by German aircraft.[38] Matt's journey was no exception. He was below deck suffering from a parasitic infection (known then as sand-fever) when the ship's alarm bells began ringing. Allowed to go up to the bridge, he watched four Stuka dive-bombers appearing in the sky overhead. One of them swooped down to within two hundred metres of the *Kandahar* to drop a bomb that narrowly missed the ship. Anti-aircraft fire drove the other Stukas away. Four months later, Matt was sitting in the desert reading an old Cairo newspaper. It announced that the *Kandahar* had been sunk by an Italian mine.[39]

In ten days in Tobruk, Matt displayed what he would later refer to as his "gee-whiz" style of reporting – a tendency to unrestrained enthusiasm for people he admired and events that inspired him. He was in awe of the mainly Australian force defending the battered port and the fifty-kilometre perimeter around it. The troops, the original "desert rats," were dive-bombed from three to twenty times a day and shelled frequently. Matt went forward several times to the perimeter:

> You bump across the desert in a car and come to the headquarters of an Australian brigade. How they welcome a visitor with news of the outside world, and how fine it is to be treated as a comrade by men for whom there is only one word and that is "hero." The brigadier puts you into a truck and sends you forward. You set your teeth and hang on and are jolted across the rocky plain in full view of enemy observation post, and under intermittent shell fire. The guns roar and columns of sand and black smoke suddenly rise to left or right behind or in front. You reach battalion headquarters, more dug-outs in the sand, and battalion sends you on in a Bren carrier. You reach a deep ravine with enemy posts on the opposite crest and crawl into the hillside. Australian officers open the only bottle they've had for weeks and drink your health to Canada – and, as the toast goes around, shells from the enemy's 75's break on the rocks immediately above our heads. . . . We try to remain unperturbed – and wonder how even Australians can stand five months of this.[40]

Matt's temporary home was a tiny stone hut in a partially protected *wadi* (gully) near the port. He shared it with the only other correspondent in Tobruk at the time, Willie Forrest of the London *News Chronicle* whom he first met in Finland. The two would occasionally swim in the Mediterranean during lulls in the fighting. If they couldn't sleep because of shelling, they would compete to see who could recite the most verses of Gray's *Elegy* or remember the old Methodist hymns they both grew up with. Matt later recalled the slightly comic scene: "To the rolling of the guns or the hum of enemy planes we would join in singing *Jesus wants me for a sunbeam* or *When the roll is called up yonder I'll be there.*"[41]

Matt probably didn't realize it at the time but he was witnessing a small part of the first significant defeat of Nazi troops in the entire war. Outgunned and outnumbered, the Tobruk garrison successfully held out until it was relieved by British forces three months later. Hitler's elite troops were no longer seen as invincible.

When Matt "had enough" at the war fronts, he took a few days' rest in Cairo. The Egyptian capital was the headquarters of the British military and staging point for an army of half a million men. The presence of thousands of soldiers moving to and from the desert added to the normal noise and chaos of the city. Matt described honking jeeps and armoured cars trying to overtake horse-drawn cabs and camel teams; servicemen jostling hawkers, beggars, and black-veiled women on the street; and Australians on leave, primed with drink, staging "spectacular and perilous chariot races down the narrow streets in horse-drawn gharries."[42] British officers and correspondents often lunched at the Gezira Sporting Club where they could watch cricket and polo while served by waiters in white gowns and red cummerbunds. At night, they could ogle the belly dancers at the Kit-Kat Club, Madame Badia's, or thirty other "respectable" nightclubs. Lesser ranks frequented seedy bars in the brothel district. Alan Moorehead, a friend of Matt's and a celebrated British correspondent, described Cairo as having a "Sodom and Gomorrah atmosphere . . . exactly what we wanted after the austerities of the front."[43]

Matt stayed at Shepheard's, one of the best hotels in the city, or at the apartment of his friends, the Canadian diplomat Arnold Smith and his wife, Eve, both then working for the British. He would luxuriate in white sheets and take his first bath in weeks. There were picnic lunches at the Pyramids, dinner parties at the Smiths and Mooreheads, and much drinking and night-clubbing with Sean Fielding and fellow journalists.

On one visit to Cairo, Matt was introduced to Clare Booth Luce, who was touring the Middle East as a war correspondent for *Life* magazine. Married to the publisher of *Time,* Luce was talented, provocative, and renowned for having a voracious appetite for men. She also had a reputation for using her blond good looks and her celebrity to undercut other correspondents. Worse, for Matt, she represented the "sulking brooding right-wing in America [who] are still worrying more about the menace of socialism than the menace of a German victory."[44] Yet her attractiveness proved irresistible. Matt later confided to friends that he had a brief affair with her and hinted as much in a letter to Jean. Probably drunk, and writing incoherently, he quoted snippets of a Shakespearean sonnet about the pursuit of a siren: "To hell with TimeLife and blonde beasts. The women. 'What potions have I drunk of Siren's tears, distill'd from limbeck's foul as hell itself'. . . . Love is not TimeLife's fool."[45] Luce asked Matt to write an article for *Life* and join her on a reporting trip to Turkey and Palestine. He did neither. Later, though, he met her again in India and described the woman who would soon become a prominent Republican in Congress as "a good friend of mine."[46]

In November 1941, Matt returned to the front in time for Operation Crusader, one of the biggest British offensives of the African campaign. The Eighth Army rolled into Libya from Egypt, aiming to lift the siege of Tobruk and destroy the Axis forces. For six weeks, the opposing armies chased each other back and forth across the desert. It was highly mobile tank warfare fought over hundreds of miles with front lines that were constantly shifting. Matt wrote vividly about the confusion of the battlefield:

> *Smoke plumes and sand clouds drifting across the dreary wasteland; a thousand vehicles dispersed, a hundred others scurrying this way and that; yellow-masked liaison officers asking directions that no one ever seemed to know, and a harassed signals officer telling someone by telephone that he wasn't where he thought he was and didn't really know*

where he was; the ambulance bouncing back with the wounded (that is
what kills the wounded, the jolting over rocks and through sand); two or
three tanks or trucks burning in black smoke; here and there a troop of
gunners, naked to the waist and burnt black, feeding the guns; a few
exhausted prisoners lying in the sand; a camel strutting lugubriously in
front of the guns, lifting its puzzled, petulant face to stare at strange new
creatures on his desert; the dazzling light and the pounding heat; and
then the malign beauty of the sunset seen through veils of smoke and
dust, and the green tinge of the sand.[47]

Matt was again with his intrepid conducting officer, Sean Fielding, as
well as Alaric Jacobs of Reuters and Sam Brewer of the *Chicago Tribune*.
The group had a freedom of action that would never be allowed in any
major army in combat today. Its little convoy of three vehicles would usually move alone by day and shelter (or "leaguer" in army jargon) at night
inside a circle of tanks and armoured cars. The correspondents were
expected to master map and compass readings and take turns logging
their positions to avoid getting lost in the featureless desert. Fielding commented in his diary that they never grumbled about the hardships and
"never buck at going into a good battle."[48] But Matt did complain about the
difficulty of writing when pinned down in slit trenches and the problem
of finding dispatch riders to take his stories back to Cairo.[49]

Soon there were far graver developments to worry about. Five days after
the British attack, Rommel staged a bold counteroffensive, annihilating a
British brigade and chasing other units back over the Egyptian border.
Sean's group joined retreating troops in what was described as a "contagion
of bewilderment and fear and ignorance."[50] Surrounded by the Germans,
their only escape route was through a minefield along the border. Matt later
wrote of an awful night as they threaded their way through the mines. At
one point they were lost and separated from a British column that was also
fleeing. German flares soared into the sky to illuminate potential targets on
the ground. Shells exploded around them, kicking up clouds of sand and
dust. A British armoured car blew up on a mine. Matt scribbled in his diary,
"My breathing becomes very rapid and my belly trembles."[51]

Fielding's group got back over the Egyptian border but it was another twenty-four hours before it was able to contact divisional headquarters. Neither Matt nor his colleagues had been heard from in three days. At the *Star's* news desk in Toronto, a Reuters story clattered over the wire announcing that Matt, Jacobs, and Brewer were believed captured or missing. Managing editor Hindmarsh, fearing the worst, immediately assigned the *Star's* veteran reporter Greg Clark to prepare a detailed account of Matt's life and career. Much of Clark's published story had the reverential tone of an obituary. But several lead paragraphs, apparently added at the last moment, hailed Halton's "thrilling escape from surrounding enemy forces."[52] Matt was lucky. Three other correspondents who were captured at the same time in the same area spent the next three and a half years in POW camps in Italy and Germany.

By the end of November 1941, the Eighth Army was again advancing westward. The siege of Tobruk was lifted. One after another, the coastal outposts of Halfaya, Fort Capuzzo, Sollum, and Bardia were evacuated by Rommel's men. Italian soldiers were surrendering in thousands. A note of exhilaration crept into Matt's dispatches: "You can stand dirt in every pore and cordite fumes and thirst and bursting shells which shake you when you know, as we know, how British soldiers and British commanders, reasonably equipped, can outfight German soldiers and German commanders."[53] Like many others at the time, Matt felt the Afrika Korps was collapsing. Six weeks later they discovered how badly they had underestimated the enemy.

On Christmas Eve, Matt and his group arrived in newly captured Benghazi. An apartment was requisitioned in one of the few undamaged buildings. He had a bath and slept in sheets for the first time in weeks. There was also the opportunity to plunder local stores and homes. Matt confessed to Jean that "looting is a horrible thing when other people do it but great fun when you are doing it yourself. . . . We found a brand new set of dishes for our Xmas dinner and beautiful wine and liqueur glasses and 20 bottles of German beer and whole vats of Chianti."[54] Pre-ordered Christmas parcels brought other luxuries: whisky, ham, plum pudding, and fresh fruit and vegetables not seen in months. Friends joined them for a "great feast." The dinner was followed by singing Christmas carols, army and love songs, and finally, Matt wrote, by "Auld Lang Syne" "as I have never heard it sung before."[55] It took another day to recover from their hangovers.

Twice during periods of stalemate in the desert, Matt reported from a place that had always fascinated him: the Indian subcontinent. At the front he had written admiringly about Indian Army troops – among them the tough, highly professional Sihks, Rajputs, and Gurkas, whose senior officers were British. He was pleased to accept an invitation to tour military installations in India because it included a visit to the Khyber Pass. War games were being held there, and tank traps and gun emplacements hastily built for fear that the Germans would invade India if victorious in their Russian campaign.

At the Khyber Pass on the Afghan border, Matt could see the peaks of the Hindu Kush and the Kabul River in the distance. He described scenes "right out of Kipling," quoting lines from his favourite boyhood poet: "There's the river up and brimmin', and there's 'arf a squadron swimmin' 'Cross the ford o' Kabul river in the dark."[56] Sentries stood outlined against the sky at a fort where successive conquerors had passed for centuries. "Romance couldn't invent a fort like this," he wrote, "men at their embrasures and a Union Jack whipping in the breeze and bugles ringing and calling and reverberating from some picket high above, and the ghosts of Alexander's armies and Akbar's armies and Roberts' armies almost visible in the hot haze."[*] From the Khyber Pass Matt travelled to North Waziristan, a lawless tribal area as violent then as it is today. He spent two days with the Tochi Scouts, a British-led militia trying to suppress a local Pashtun rebellion. The visit produced colourful copy and a photo in the *Star Weekly* of Matt reviewing the militia.

A second assignment in India focused on a landmark event for the Empire. In March 1941, Sir Stafford Cripps, a socialist member of Churchill's war cabinet, was sent to Delhi to offer India its independence in return for

---

[*] The reference is to three empire-building leaders who led successful invasions through the Khyber Pass: the Greek King, Alexander the Great, in 326 BC; Akbar the Great, the Mughal emperor who subdued the Afghan tribes in the late sixteenth century; and Lord Roberts of Kandahar, the British general who captured Afghanistan in the 1879–80 campaign.[57]

supporting the British war effort. Matt was well placed to cover the negotiations. His Canadian socialist friend Graham Spry was Cripps's personal
assistant and an invaluable contact. Spry proudly confided that there was
extensive discussion of Canada's path to self-government as a model for the
subcontinent.[58] Matt was enthusiastic about India becoming a member of a
new Commonwealth of independent nations. But he predicted that the
Cripps mission would probably fail because of disagreements, not just
between London and Delhi but between India's Hindu and Muslim factions.
Nehru and other leaders of the largely Hindu Congress party were opposed
to the British offer because it allowed for the possibility that Pakistan would
break away from India and form an independent Muslim state. Matt quoted
one Hindu delegate asking how Canadians would react if French Canada
tried to secede.[59] Cripps's offer was eventually rejected for other reasons
as well: disputes over the timetable for independence and over who would
control the Indian army in the remaining years of the war.

Looming over the negotiations was the charismatic figure of Mahatma
Gandhi, still the most powerful political figure in India. On one evening,
Matt went to Gandhi's residence to watch him preside over evening
prayers. The poorest of India's poor – the Untouchables – crowded around
as Gandhi, naked apart from his dhoti, knelt and prayed with them. Nine
years earlier, Matt had memorably described the nationalist leader as "that
incalculable little lawyer-mystic who sits on his haunches and makes an
empire scratch its head."[60] The British were still guessing about his next
move when Matt was allowed a brief interview with him. Gandhi wouldn't
talk about the negotiations with Cripps other than to say that, as a preacher
of non-violence, he couldn't accept that India take part in the war. "By
violence you degrade yourself," he said; "by non-violence you conquer
yourself, and in time the enemy."[61] Unconvinced, Matt suggested the
world would be a much more degraded place without the use of force to
stop aggression. Gandhi quietly disagreed. Several months later, he called
for a campaign of civil disobedience against British rule. He was jailed,
like other Indian leaders, for almost the remainder of the war.

After the breakdown of the Cripps mission, Matt hoped to cover the war
in Burma, where British and Indian troops were trying to hold back a

Japanese invasion. In Calcutta, he discovered he was too late: Burma was largely overrun. There was little he could do but interview retreating troops at the border and fly on an RAF bombing raid over Burma. It was now feared that Japan might invade India so the *Star* advised that he stay on in Calcutta. In fact, nothing happened and Matt spent two weeks with little to write about in a city he found dirty and depressing. Part of the time was spent making a final, unsuccessful effort to get a visa for the Soviet Union. Using all his best contacts, Matt had tried for months to cover Operation Barbarossa from the Russian side. Stafford Cripps, a former British ambassador to Moscow, promised that he could get him a visa but was baffled when it wasn't forthcoming. He wired Matt that "they must think you are a liberal reformist."[62] "It was terribly exasperating," Matt wrote, "the most terrific battles in history and I couldn't get near them."[63]

His normal good fortune seemed to have given out. He decided to take ten days' leave in the Himalayas. In Darjeeling, he marvelled at the sight of Kinchenjunga, the second-highest mountain in the world, and planned a trek to see Everest. The excursion never happened. Shortly after his arrival, he learned that Rommel had launched a new offensive. Matt had to rush back to battles that would decide the Desert War.

When Matt returned to Egypt in mid-June 1942, Britain had entered its darkest hour in the Middle East. The Eighth Army was in headlong retreat. Two hundred and thirty of its tanks had been destroyed in a single day. Tobruk was about to be captured, and Empire troops were pushed back to within two hundred kilometres of the Nile. The Nazis were closer than ever to seizing control of the Suez Canal, securing the Arab oil fields, and inflicting a shattering defeat on the Allies.

In Cairo, Matt prepared quickly to return to the front, packing six suitcases that included food and seven bottles of whisky. "Please, don't think I am drinking too much," he assured Jean in a letter. "I'm not, I can't take it anymore, and when I do it ruins my thinking."[64] He set out with an Australian correspondent and the same tank force captain who had been his conducting officer in Syria. They were soon back in the familiar world of swooping Stukas and reverberating shellfire – a world in which Matt was becoming strangely comfortable. "Here one is alive," he wrote Jean. "There's good comradeship . . . and lots of excitement and the heady stimulant of danger."[65] He had partly overcome his fear; combat now seemed to be a magnet. In an earlier letter, he confided to an old friend: "I'm sick for Jean, yet I'd hate to leave the war. Gets in your blood. Something pushes you."[66]

On June 23, something pushed Matt and his group to go forward to an encounter that was insignificant in itself but that haunted his memory. The day before, they had watched thousands of British military vehicles streaming down the coast road during the British retreat from Libya to Egypt. At the same vantage point next day, there was an eerie silence. "The desert was itself again. There was nothing but the white sandhills and the debris and graveyards of old battles and the turquoise sea lapping on the sands."[67] When a South African armoured car drove up, Matt asked an officer if it was all over at Sollum, a much-contested outpost further west. He was told that a few infantry and gunners were still there under orders to fight a delaying action to give the main force more time to retreat. Deciding to take the risk, Matt's group went forward a few kilometres to where a battery of four howitzers was firing at the Germans on the other side of a ridge.

Front-line troops are usually pleased to get a press visit, and this was no exception. The group was welcomed by a tall young English lieutenant. He offered them beer, which he said he wouldn't need by evening. They sat there drinking in a little dugout as shells fell nearby, as the howitzers thundered back, and as fighter aircraft wheeled and dived above them. From time to time, the lieutenant would talk on his radio phone to his commander behind the front. "This is Oxford calling Bristol – I can't hear you, sir – Oh yes, sir, I still have 800 rounds . . . yes sir, we've got our wounded out . . . Yes, sir, we're all prepared if they come."[68] Minutes later, the lieutenant pointed out enemy vehicles that were now edging along the ridge and told his guests they had plenty of time "to do a bunk." He shook their hands and said, "How nice of you to come and see us."[69] For Matt, it became a lustrous memory: the young English lieutenant and his small band of gunners forming a thin sacrificial line against Rommel's advancing army.

Matt wrote about the encounter and mentioned it in a broadcast carried by both CBC and the BBC. He doubted whether "Oxford" would survive the "brown ear-splitting godforsaken hell's kitchen" at Sollum.[70] Two years later, he wrote about it again in an article recalling events that marked him during the war. Shortly after it was published in a British newspaper, he received a letter from the lieutenant's father: "I feel that you might be interested to know that the 'tall grinning young English lieutenant' who commanded the four guns managed to get away all right. . . . He had a very strenuous time because they were completely surrounded and it was little short of a miracle that he 'made it'."[71]

By the end of June, the Eighth Army was dug in for what many feared would be its last stand. Its new defence line began at El Alamein, a sand-blown railway station whose name would soon be among the most famous battlegrounds of World War Two. The line stretched about fifty kilometres south from the Mediterranean to the Qattara Depression, a vast area of salt marshes and sand dunes impassible to armoured vehicles. Alamein itself was just a few hours' drive from the Nile Delta, where insecurity was rife. In Alexandria, the Royal Navy abandoned its base and dispersed its warships. In Cairo, British headquarters staff began evacuating the city; an eight p.m. curfew closed the brothels and nightclubs; and many Egyptians prepared to welcome the Nazis with swastika flags.[72] Morale among Britain's "desert rats" was at an all-time low.

In contrast, Matt found the German prisoners he interviewed to be remarkably confident. He was unstinting in praise of their professionalism and the dynamism of Rommel's leadership. He also greatly admired the courage of the "Tommies," but it was not matched by much respect for their British generals. The censors allowed him to write that "disaster followed disaster"[73] in the retreat but they cut even his muted criticism of the conduct of the war on the grounds that it "encourages the enemy." Matt complained to Jean that the censors' approach was dangerous "because the only way we win our wars is by the public getting to know what's wrong and demanding heads."[74]

Another issue goaded him into greater anger: the fact that most of the forty or so correspondents covering the war would rarely, if ever, visit the front. Some sat in the safety of Cairo but put datelines on their stories indicating they were with the troops in combat. Others would go to divisional headquarters usually five kilometres or more from the action and fake eyewitness stories. "It's maddening to the real war correspondent," he told Jean. "I have really been ashamed of my profession."[75] He was also aggressive in confronting the fakers, insulting them publicly on his visits to Cairo. He would do the same throughout the war with other "magic carpetters," as such war correspondents were labelled. It made him some bitter enemies.

August was the turning point for the Eighth Army. Churchill made two visits to the Alamein front, lifting spirits and restoring a zest for victory. Matt described "old great-heart" as being at his superb best as he gave the V-sign, handed out cigars, and wisecracked with soldiers. When one officer asked Churchill what he thought of the desert, he quipped that "it's much the same" – a reminder that he had led a cavalry charge in the desert at Omdurman forty-four years earlier, before most of his audience was born.[76] While morale-building was important, the real value of his visit was to restructure the desert command. Underperforming generals were fired and the crusty but inspirational Bernard Montgomery was brought in as the new commander of the Eighth Army.

"Monty," soon to become a national hero, issued an immediate order prohibiting further withdrawals: "We will stand and fight here. If we can't stay here alive, then let us stay here dead."[77]

For two months, Matt chronicled the British success in holding the Alamein line against constant German probes. He was at the front most of the time, filing for the *Star* almost every day and broadcasting on weekends from Alexandria or Cairo. His CBC reports were routed via London, many of them rebroadcast by the BBC, which seemed to appreciate their colourful, emotional quality. Richard Dimbleby, BBC's Middle East correspondent (and eventually its iconic commentator), told him that London would welcome a fifteen-minute broadcast every two weeks.[78]

In the first week of September, Rommel threw his forces against the Alamein line one last time. Facing an Eighth Army reinforced in men and weapons, the Axis troops were "mauled and repulsed" in what Matt described as "a splendid victory."[79] It was Rommel's last major offensive of the campaign, and the Nazis' first big defeat. Within three months, the Axis forces were driven back to Tunis and eventually to expulsion from North Africa. Churchill wrote (not quite accurately) in his memoirs that "before Alamein we never had a victory. After Alamein we never had a defeat."[80]

Matt was not there to witness the breakout from Egypt. The hard life in the desert had finally weighed too heavily. He admitted he had "had enough" of the sandstorms and shellfire, the diving Stukas and stuttering machine guns, not to mention the sight of dead and wounded soldiers at the front. For the time being, the adrenalin rush of battle had been sated. His most pressing desire now was to end the eighteen-month separation from his family. In mid-September he cabled Jean: "Sweetheart leaving Cairo on our wedding anniversary . . . Its true I am coming."[81]

Still it was a wrenching departure. In his last letter home, he wrote that it was in the desert that "I have lived the greatest and worst days of my life."[82] He recalled those days in a nostalgic fifteen-minute broadcast for the CBC. At several points in these excerpts, his voice is close to breaking:

> Only a few days ago I was wakened at first light in a British tank leaguer near the Quattara Depression, and there was a knocking in my heart – I was going home. We broke leaguer and dispersed into battle formation. We rolled up our beds and made tea. I bumped once more across and through the yellow sands, and called at Brigade headquarters to say goodbye, and then at Divisional headquarters and then at Corps, and then reached the coast road near the hot white blinding garden of death called Alamein. I had a last swim in the sea, and then drove for the last time down the dark and cruel road along which a great host of British soldiers have gone to war. . . . I was glad to go but sad to leave. Down every foot of that road I had seen something of courage or humour or agony.
>
> Here was the spot where we saw the gunners die on their guns on the day of July the third. Here was the advanced dressing station where we were machine gunned. Here's where our new boys were caught in the minefield. Here's where we went in with the Ghurkas in the night attack. . . .

*And then the battlefield is left behind, with its little crosses in the
sand. The battlefield where the East was held, where so many of us
learned in the drifting smoke-rack what we were. . . .*

*It was our last day in the desert. There was the dreary wasteland
stretching away for a thousand miles. There was the vast plain of hard
gravel and soft sand, the dead land. There was "distance piled upon
distance, farther than human enduring" – except that men endure it.
The desert scene was at its wildest and dreariest. Our guns were shelling
the withdrawing enemy, and enemy shells whistled in and hit among us.
Plumes and clouds of sand mixed with black smoke drifted across the
desolate plains and soldiers were covered thick with yellow dirt. An
enemy petrol truck would explode from time to time in a paroxysm of
flame and the sound of it, a deep vomiting roar, reached us a few seconds
later. The enemy dead and some of our own lay there with their troubles
and suffering over. . . .*

*Night fell at last, and coolness came. Our tank crews sat there,
silent and grim, with victory on their shoulders. . . . My last night in a
tank leaguer! I got into my sleeping bag and looked up at the stars and I
was a man of many memories. Memories of victories and memories of
defeat . . . and the positive certainty that we often withdraw but always
at the last return, whether it be to Dunkirk or Benghazi. . . .*[83]

Matt ended the broadcast by saying that he would never forget the
Eighth Army. But neither, he added, should anyone else.

In his war correspondent's
uniform.

With daughter, Kathleen, aged three.

The author, aged four, as aspiring
war correspondent, during Matt's
visit home in 1944.

Matt with his parents, Mary Alice
and Henry, on a brief visit to
Pincher Creek in August 1940.

(from right) Halton, Peter Stursberg, and Marcel Ouimet in Sicily.

Reporting from Italy.

Jean, with David and Kathleen.

Matt was teamed with Charles Lynch, a twenty-four-year-old Canadian working for the Reuters news agency, to cover the D-Day invasion. It would lead to a lasting friendship. Here, Lynch is interviewing soldiers from the Royal Winnipeg Rifles.

Canadian soldiers patrolling in Caen, July 10, 1945. Matt and Radio-Canada's Ouimet followed Canadian troops into the city, witnessing some of the most stirring scenes of the Normandy campaign.

Matt (bottom right) helping to evacuate equipment from the Canadian Press Centre near Courseulles just after it was bombed by the Germans.

French civilians take cover as the Place de la Concorde is raked with sniper fire, and a Resistance fighter looks on. In the background (right), the Ministère de la Marine, where Matt, Christiane, and Col. Dick Malone took refuge.

A book signing for the bestselling *Ten Years to Alamein*.

From left, Prime Minister Mackenzie King, Marcel Ouimet,
and Matthew Halton, during a post-war visit to Normandy.

Members of the notorious Thursday Club, clowning after a well-lubricated dinner. From right: Matt (standing), Sean Fielding (with glasses), Prince Philip (seated).

14 Oakhill Avenue, the Halton residence in Hampstead.

Interviewing Marshall Tito in Belgrade.

In the late 1940s, broadcasting for the CBC.

Matt, on assignment in Yugoslavia.

More than 4,200 people watched Matt receive his doctoral degree from the
University of Alberta, and deliver the convocation address, in April 1956.

13

THE ROAD TO ORTONA

"His voice during the war was certainly the voice of Canada."
— ELSIE GOWAN, University of Alberta classmate

WHEN MATT BEGAN HIS HOME LEAVE IN CANADA in the fall of 1942, nothing suggested it would lead to a startling break in his career. There was a long-awaited reunion with Jean in New York, their marriage seemingly as strong as ever despite Matt's infidelities abroad. There was the usual pilgrimage to Pincher Creek, fishing trips with his brothers in the foothills, and hikes in the mountains above Waterton Lakes. Matt then settled down with his family at his mother-in-law's home in Vancouver where Jean, Kathleen, and I spent most of the war.

Secluding himself in an attic room, he began writing *Ten Years to Alamein*, a memoir of his turbulent years as a foreign correspondent. The book was largely based on his *Star* reports since the rise of Hitler. Personal anecdotes and colourful descriptions of people and events were woven together in very readable form. The political analysis was typically Matt – passionate, blunt, and without nuance. He framed the book with his favourite theme: "the dark paralysis of democracy" that allowed Nazi power to expand in the locust years of the 1930s.[1] Singled out for the greatest blame were not just the appeasers like Baldwin and Chamberlain but a British ruling class that, " clutching its dividends and a dying order to its frightened bosom, croaked that 'Hitler is a bulwark against Communism.'"[2] Pacifists and isolationists were also blamed. "There are no 'far-away peoples of whom we know nothing.' . . . Trouble in Timbuctoo means trouble in High Street quite as literally as pain in one organ of the body means pain in another unless it is attended to."³

In the last paragraph of *Ten Years to Alamein*, Matt wrote five words that became his credo: "Idealism is the only realism." It was a phrase he had first heard in a slightly different form from U.S. vice-president Henry Wallace. Shortly before beginning *Ten Years*, Matt was sent by the *Star* to Washington to interview Wallace, who was an early champion of the United Nations, a world court, and an international peacekeeping force. Republicans and some Democrats denounced Wallace as a "woolly-minded idealist" and a purveyor of "wild dreams" but, for Matt, he was a hero. "If these wild dreams do not come true," Matt concluded, "this will be only the second world war, not the last, and the world of our children will be 'a darkling plain.'"⁴

Writing in his usual manner, fast and fluently, Matt finished the book in four months. However, the timing of its publication in both Britain and Canada could not have been worse. Because of paper shortages in London and inefficiency in Toronto, the book was not on sale in either country until after D-Day, a full year later. By then, the desert campaign had faded from prominence. Even so, *Ten Years to Alamein* turned into an instant bestseller in Canada: over seven thousand copies sold in five months in only the second of its six printing runs. Libraries across Canada reported that for weeks it was the hottest book on demand.

Its popularity was helped by glowing reviews on both sides of the Atlantic. In London, the prestigious *Times Literary Supplement* wrote that Matthew Halton "is not only a first-class war reporter who supplies some of the most illuminating pictures of desert warfare that have yet appeared. He is also a man of strong political views and a sledge-hammer mode of giving them expression. . . . Judging by the way he writes at times one can tell Mr. Halton is a poet."⁵ The London *Star* said *Ten Years to Alamein* is "rich in new stories of gallantry and self-sacrifice" and "flays in fine anger all those who would not listen to Churchill's warnings."⁶ In Canada, the *Globe and Mail* described the book as "a masterly piece of journalism, made exhilarating by reason of the writer's own emotions, freely revealed. . . .

It is so much more than a piece of reporting. It is a statement of political faith."[7] For the *Montreal Gazette* reviewer, *Ten Years* "has everything that makes a book of this kind great – vast enthusiasm, great indignation, clear judgment, prophecies that come true, ardent patriotism, deep and intimate knowledge of world affairs. . . ."[8] Most gratifying to Matt, though, were not so much the newspaper reviews as a handwritten letter from Field Marshal Montgomery saying how much he appreciated the book and its dedication to the men of the Eighth Army.[9]

During his seven-month stay in Canada, Matt was invited by the National War Finance Committee to help promote the sale of Victory Bonds to support the war effort. He was asked to make broadcast appeals on CBC, some of them recorded at big public rallies. At one event in Vancouver, the audience was warmed up before Matt's speech by a band playing military marches, followed by the future pop star Juliette, only nineteen at the time, singing "As Time Goes By."[10] Then Matt, always in uniform on such occasions, would advance to the microphone, recount battlefield stories, and appeal to Canadians to invest generously in Victory Bonds. He would end on a grim but patriotic note: "Countrymen, a day is coming soon which will be splendid and terrible for Canada. It will be the day when the soldiers of Canada take the road to Berlin. It will be splendid because it will be the beginning of the end of the most evil years in recorded history, and it will be splendid because the ardent greatness of Canada will shine again. It will be terrible because it will cost a dolorous price in blood and tears."[11]

The Victory Bond engagements were a duty Matt was pleased to accept; he wasn't concerned that they blurred the line between reporting and propaganda. For him, the broadcasts were simply an extension of his decade-old crusade against Fascism. They were also self-serving. They enhanced his reputation and gave him a profile he never had before, especially in rural and small-town Canada.

It was Matt's success in radio that propelled him into making the toughest decision of his career. In March 1943, he was approached by Ernest Bushnell, program head of CBC, and invited to become the corporation's senior war correspondent in Europe. The offer was not a surprise: it had been broached more tentatively at the outset of the war when it was of little interest to Matt. After all, why would he want to leave a paper that had nurtured his career, given him extraordinary editorial freedom and a fat salary, and whose left-of-centre politics were close to his own?

This time the situation was different. Radio was involved in war coverage for the first time and beginning to dominate the mass media. It offered a sense of immediacy and a personal connection to soldiers in the war zone that print media couldn't achieve. Tuning in to war news was becoming a habit; American war correspondents like Ed Murrow and Bill Shirer were almost as well-known in Canada as in the United States. In contrast, the CBC had no news service and no reporters for the first year of the war – only announcers such as Charles Jennings and Lorne Greene recycling news bulletins from the Canadian Press (CP) newswire. At the time of Canada's historic declaration of war on Germany, an announcer broke into a pop music show to read a CP bulletin, then promptly returned listeners to a silly, bouncy song: "Inka Dinka Doo."[12] The corporation was shamed in the press for its lack of gravity and the absence of correspondents to examine one of the most important decisions in the country's history. Because of the obvious need to cover Canada's war effort, a CBC news service was finally created in January 1941. Five news bureaus were set up across the country, and an Overseas Unit was based in London. It was hoped that Matt would be the unit's star performer.

"We want you badly. How much do you want?"[13] asked Bushnell, the CBC's blunt-spoken program director. Matt told Jean that he demanded at least $125 a week (equivalent in today's dollars to an annual salary of about $110,000) plus a generous expense account and right to freelance for print media. Bushnell apparently agreed as long as Matt accepted being on contract without staff benefits. Matt agonized over the decision for several weeks, discussing the issue in secret with Atkinson and Hindmarsh, his patrons at the *Star*. All his doubts about the move were eased when they offered to take an article from him every week or two for the *Star Weekly*, enabling him almost to double his CBC salary.[14] Between CBC, the *Star*, and his other print markets, he would be wealthier than ever before.

The announcement in mid-April that the paper's favoured son was leaving touched off a wild flurry of rumours and speculation in the *Star's* newsroom. At first it was widely assumed he had been fired. Bryan Vaughan, assistant city editor, said many believed that Matt was drunk and with a woman when Hindmarsh tried to reach him for an assignment.[15] Others decided that the managing editor felt Matt had become too much of a prima donna, cutting him down to size as he had with Hemingway, Gordon Sinclair, and other big-name reporters. It was true that Matt was unhappy to learn that Hindmarsh had chosen Fred Griffin and Greg Clark to cover the impending invasion of Italy, an assignment he coveted.[16] But according to Ken Edey, an executive who helped negotiate Matt's new relationship with the paper, both sides were pleased with the final deal and parted on the best of terms.[17]

In August 1943, Matt arrived in Sicily, excited to be back at war and impatient to prove himself as a CBC correspondent. British, American, and Canadian forces had invaded Sicily a month earlier. The aim was to drive Italy out of the war and relieve pressure on Russia and a planned second front in France by tying down German divisions in Italy. Politics played a big role in Canada's involvement. A public heavily invested in the war effort clamoured to get Canadian troops out of barracks in Britain and into battle. Its hunger for battle honours would soon be satisfied.

Matt was disappointed to land in Sicily on the same day that the 1st Canadian Division ended combat operations there. Fighting as part of General Montgomery's Eighth Army, the Canadians had successfully fought small-scale but fierce battles against the Germans. The names of dusty mountain villages – Assoro, Leonforte, Agira, and Regalbuto – were now on the honour rolls of their country. "It was thrilling," Matt wrote, "to hear Monty say 'the Eighth Army is proud of its Canadians.'"[18] Later, captured German documents spoke admiringly of the Canadians' *Indianerkrieg* (Indian warfare): "very mobile at night, surprise break-ins, clever infiltrations at night with small groups between our strong points."[19] Neither Matt nor any of the other correspondents mentioned that the Germans were outnumbered by the Allies by as much as eight to one,[20] and that the planned retreat of the Nazis was so skilful that almost their entire army was able to escape to mainland Italy.

Apart from several nights spent with British and American troops still in combat, Matt had an easy time in Sicily. The Canadian correspondents were lodged in a comfortable villa at the foot of Mount Etna. Cheap local wine, sometimes of the gut-wrenching kind, was in ample supply, and eggs and fruit were available to supplement army rations. From his balcony Matt could see the magnificent ruins of the Greek theatre in the old town of Taormina. In a letter to Jean, he quoted Keats and Shelley on the beauty of the Italian landscape and mused about the Phoenicians, Romans, Saracens, and others who conquered Sicily. Then, with brutal honesty about his failed aspirations as a poet, he deplored the fact that "I can only QUOTE poetry and REMEMBER history, not write the one and make the other."[21]

If he couldn't make history, he would soon be broadcasting a reporter's "first draft" of it. He covered the British capture of Taormina and was with U.S. general George Patton's Seventh Army in Messina when it completed the liberation of Sicily. Despite his earlier success in broadcasting, Matt was insecure about his radio voice. He felt he was too much of a tenor in a medium that favoured the basso profundo voices of Lorne Greene and other newscasters. Wallace Reyburn, a correspondent for the *Montreal Standard*, claimed that Matt would get his sound engineers to "twiddle dials" to make his voice deeper: "I overheard one of them saying 'I am sick and tired of putting balls in Matt Halton's voice.'"[22] But the concern about his voice did not appear to have lasted for long. In a letter to Jean (whom he sometimes called his "mother confessor"), he said "I . . . have suddenly realized I should just be myself, do my own stuff in my own way."[23]

A somewhat leisurely pace in Sicily gave Matt the opportunity to learn the then primitive craft of radio reporting from the field. Live broadcasting from the war zones was impossible, tape recorders non-existent. So all recording was done by the old-fashioned method of a cutting needle on a rotating disc similar to a 78 rpm gramophone record. News reports were recorded in a small truck converted into a mobile studio, or on portable equipment – two large boxes weighing eighty pounds each, usually carried on a jeep. Peter Stursberg, the able CBC correspondent whom Matt replaced,

recorded the pipes and drums of the Seaforth Highlanders of Canada playing in newly captured Agira. It was the first actuality sound from conquered
Axis territory and broadcast across the world. Soon Matt, his Radio-Canada
colleague Marcel Ouimet, and their radio engineers would be bringing the
sounds of battle into homes across Canada.

At nightfall on September 2, Matt and several other correspondents waited
tensely on a beach near Messina along with hundreds of young soldiers
from Maritime regiments. They had been chosen to go in with the first
assault wave of Canadian troops invading mainland Italy. While the landing
in Sicily had been easy, few had forgotten the horror of Dieppe – the disastrous Canadian raid across the English Channel that ended in a massacre.
Earlier in the day Matt wrote an "in-case-anything-happens" letter to Jean,
mentioning financial details if he was killed, and telling her, "You are my
life's love and there is nothing more to say."[24] He apologized for sounding so
morbid a few days later. After one of the heaviest Allied bombardments of
the war, the flotilla of assault boats was largely unopposed as it landed on
beaches near Reggio di Calabria. The Germans were gone, and Italian soldiers swarmed up to surrender. Mussolini had already been overthrown,
and the new Italian government would formally capitulate on September 8.

Of many sights that morning, Ross Munro of the Canadian Press
recalled that the most remarkable was Matt Halton and his sound engineer, Paul Johnson, struggling to come ashore. Each of them was lugging
a bulky waterproofed case containing parts of the portable recording unit,
and Matt had the additional weight of his typewriter. They dropped the
equipment beside the water, rested a moment, then carried it to the safety
of a nearby culvert. It was at that moment that a Stuka dived and bombed
close to where the recording unit had been carried ashore.[25]

In a fifteen-minute broadcast from the beach, Matt exulted that
Canadians were among the first to breach Hitler's Fortress Europe. Over
the next two months, he advanced with them from Reggio for more than
five hundred kilometres up the toe and boot of Italy. Apart from a firefight
in Potenza, encounters with the retreating Germans were rare. Matt was
impatient, craving what he sometimes called the "unholy thrill" of battle.

Leaving the Canadians for three weeks, he crossed the peninsula to join the U.S. Fifth Army, which had been badly mauled by the Germans when it landed at Salerno south of Naples. He arrived when the Allies had finally broken out of the beachhead and were fighting in the dramatic setting of Pompeii. His CBC report that day described how unreal it felt to be watching a battle from the walls of a Roman amphitheatre as shells whistled overhead and tanks clanked through nearby streets. He wrote Jean, angered by what he felt was unnecessary American bombing around the Roman ruins. "Jesus Christ," he asked, "is there nothing we don't bomb?"[26] He would often mention subjects in his letters home that the censors would not allow in broadcasts or articles.

Matt entered Naples on the heels of British troops to find it in chaos. The city had been bombed repeatedly by the Allies, its water mains and power plants destroyed by the departing Germans, and bodies of Italian resistance fighters still lying in some streets. Matt reported on the poverty and hunger in Naples, but also on the resilience of citizens who reopened stores and restored services in a few days.[27] There was no discomfort for war correspondents. U.S. Army public relations put them up in a villa overlooking Vesuvius and the Bay of Naples. Matt typed his reports on his balcony, and for the first time in a week had good food and a plentiful supply of rum.

When Matt rejoined the Canadian troops in October, they were out of the line to rest and be re-supplied. The division settled in and around the mountain town of Campobasso, soon to be widely known as Maple Leaf City. Canteens and recreational activities were quickly organized by groups such as the YMCA and the Canadian Legion.[28] But the soldiers' main pursuit, in the words of their commander Chris Vokes, was "to get drunk" and "to get laid."[29] It was not the stuff that would pass the censor or inspire the home front.

By mid-November, 1st Division's relatively easy days in Italy were over. Hitler had decided that the Wehrmacht's tactical retreat had gone far enough. German forces were ordered to dig in along the so-called Winter Line – a series of heavily fortified defensive positions stretching from Gaeta, 177 kilometres south of Rome, across the peninsula to Ortona on the Adriatic side of Italy. The order went out from Hitler: No more withdrawals, "This line will be held."[30] One of his most accomplished generals, Field Marshal Albert Kesselring, was promoted to supreme commander in Italy, and his army was reinforced by elite panzergrenadier and parachute divisions. Two weeks earlier, in curious symmetry, Churchill had advised his generals "to accelerate the build-up in Italy" and "nourish the battle."[31] The Eighth Army was about to face its bloodiest fighting since Alamein, and this time Canadians would be its spearhead.

As encounters with the Germans became tougher, Matt went to the front frequently. He travelled in the CBC's recording van or a jeep, and sometimes on foot or donkey along tracks where vehicles could not pass. He was usually accompanied by a conducting officer, his sound engineer Paul Johnson, and Marcel Ouimet of the CBC's French network – sometimes urging them farther forward than they really wanted to go.[32] Bill Gilchrist, an army public relations officer, saw Matt in action and later recalled that "he seemed to have no fear whatsoever. He was up there where the shells were flying around and bursting around him."[33] Part of it may have been vainglory, and part of it was certainly his need for the adrenalin rush of battle. But he also developed a deep admiration for the young Canadian soldiers at the front and felt that if he was to tell their story, he should be with them, at least some of the time.

There was another compelling reason to go forward. Both Matt and Ouimet had become fascinated with recording the sounds of war. Whenever possible, they included actuality sound in their reports, adding a drama and intensity to their broadcasts that their voices alone could not achieve. For listeners back home, it was a new and sometimes chilling experience. They could hear the clank of advancing tanks, the drone of aircraft, the crash of heavy bombs, the scream of incoming shells, and the rat-tat-tat of machine-gun fire. The recordings were often of poor quality by today's standards but they brought a sense of the horror of war to the home front.

Matt would sometimes record his reports live from the front but usually returned to the CBC van where his voice could be mixed with actuality sound of the fighting. There was a CBC requirement that sound could not be dubbed in with a voice track unless the correspondent had been at its source on the front[34] (making its coverage more authentic in that respect than some radio and television war reporting today). For one fifteen-minute broadcast, Matt was briefed in advance of a planned Canadian attack and crawled forward to an observation post with a microphone and four hundred feet of cable leading back to the portable recorder. Pinned down for the next twenty-four hours, he recorded a series of thunderous barrages as artillery attacked German positions on an opposite ridge. As he ad-libbed, shells suddenly started to crash down on the O.P. One of them knocked down his sound engineer, Paul Johnson, and sent the stylus skidding over the uncut portion of the recording disc. Johnson picked himself up and put on a new disc and a few minutes later recorded the voice of a signals officer using his radio phone to report the grim toll at their position. "Able One to Able Two. Shelling Report. Two killed . . . eight wounded."[35] In his broadcast, Matt gave full credit to Johnson, who wrote his wife afterwards saying they were "almost too damned forward. . . . I guess my number wasn't on that [shell], or on the two that landed right after."[36]

While Matt frequently praised the courage of Canadian troops, he could hardly be accused of sugar-coating their experience. His report on the burial of three of Vancouver's Seaforth Highlanders was grimly appropriate. It included a sound clip from a chaplain reading from the Book of Common Prayer: "Man that is born of a woman hath but a short time to live and is full of misery. He cometh up and is cut down like a flower."[37] Surprisingly, Matt was even able to get the censor's approval in mid-November for a broadcast on battle exhaustion – the nervous breakdown commonly known then as "shell shock." He had seen soldiers who had snapped under the strain of combat, shouting uncontrollably or being led away from the front shaking like a reed in the wind. The 1st Division's chief psychiatrist, Major Arthur Doyle, told him there had been only ninety-three cases, most treated successfully.[38] Within a month, Doyle's optimism faded as battle exhaustion numbers quadrupled. Matt would broadcast again about the ravages of combat neurosis despite its troubling impact on morale at home.

It was the dirty little secret of war correspondents that most never actually witnessed a battle scene. George Powell, an army press officer, noted after the war that only a small minority of the 120 Canadian journalists accredited as war correspondents in World War Two actually got to the front.[39] Matt estimated that, apart from Ouimet and himself, only two other Canadian reporters – Ralph Allen of the *Globe* and CP's Doug Amaron – regularly got close to the fighting in central Italy.[40] He claimed that eight others rarely strayed from the press camp when it was based in Vasto on the Adriatic.

Not surprisingly, given his disdain for the so-called magic carpetters, Matt's relations with his fellow correspondents were often strained. He found most of them parochial, particularly Bert Wemp of the *Toronto Telegram* who was mocked for writing ledes that would often begin "Such-and-such a town was liberated today. Among those present from Toronto were . . ."[41] Matt, in turn, was regarded with mixed feelings. No one seemed neutral about him. His reputation was admired and his company enjoyed by older reporters such as Ralph Allen and CP's Ross Munro (who left Italy earlier). Doug Amaron said he looked up to him as a mentor.[42] Others, though, regarded him as aloof and a bit of an intellectual snob. They found his efforts to write poetry odd, if not pretentious. One of his critics, Wallace Reyburn of the *Montreal Standard*, described him as "very conscious of being the experienced war correspondent and we were the rookies."[43] Like his colleagues, Reyburn would occasionally hear Matt's CBC broadcasts on the BBC and joke about his dramatic style. "Matt's coat-of-arms," he once told the press camp, "should be a typewriter rampant on a field of corn."[44]

Matt was irked that most of his colleagues were exclusively focused on covering Canadian troops and rarely reported on other units in the Eighth Army. Benefiting from his desert war contacts, Matt could fit in easily with British, New Zealand, and Indian troops, as he did occasionally when there was a lull in Canadian operations. He joined British units for the first big offensive against the Germans' Winter Line – an assault over the Sangro River. The pontoon bridge over the river had been swept away by a flood when Matt tried to cross in a convoy of three mule trains carrying ammunition and supplies to forward units. Men and mules waded and swam across the icy water, six feet deep in places, only to face heavy shelling on the other side. Matt's report caught the grimness of the operation as it turned into disaster. Terrified mules hit by shrapnel started stampeding back toward the river, their hoarse screams mixing with the whine of incoming shells in a weird cacophony. Matt said he and others around him threw themselves into the mud churned up by pelting rain that night. Several soldiers were killed and the convoy never made it.[45] It was a night he would never forget.

It was now the Canadians' turn to face the full fury of the Nazis' Winter Line. Montgomery ordered the 1st Division to attack across the Moro River. His plan was to capture the town of Ortona and from there to open up the vital road just north of it that stretched across the mountains to Rome.

On December 8, Matt began recording from behind an old wall in San Vito Chietino.[46] He was on high ground overlooking the Moro Valley and the escarpment on the other side where the Germans were dug into ideal defensive positions. Briefed on the timing of the attack, Matt gave his audience a sense of immediacy about what was to happen: "It's twenty-six minutes past three . . . Four minutes from now there will be a tremendous artillery barrage laid down on the enemy positions across the Moro River from here. The barrage will continue intermittently for an hour or so, and at half-past four our infantry – will move across the valley . . . to attack the enemy positions."[47] In those four minutes before the barrage began, Matt described how unreal it felt to be about to watch a battle on a cloudless day with "the Adriatic dancing in the light" and the valley "an enchanting patchwork of vivid reds, greens and yellows – like daubs of paint – like a painting by Cezanne. . . . But now I'll take the microphone outside because it's almost half past three." Then, after recording thirty seconds of explosions and gunfire, Matt retired behind the wall where he described Allied aircraft chasing a German spotter plane: "Now they are shooting! Perhaps you can hear the bursts." There were more "sound-ups" as the shelling got worse and, later, as the troops stormed across the Moro. Matt used a favoured technique, addressing his audience directly: "No doubt you heard the ghastly whine and explosion of one small shell that fell fifty yards from here, and perhaps the barking of a dog. A little black dog was barking in anger"[48] – a trivial detail but one that helped listeners visualize the battleground.

Another mark of Matt's reporting was its focus on individual soldiers and their stories. Like the celebrated American war correspondent Ernie Pyle, his sympathy was with the gunners and riflemen on the front lines.

On one occasion, he watched as a sapper drove his lumbering bulldozer down to the Moro to level its bank for a pontoon bridge. He interviewed the driver, Milton McNaughton of Manitoba, who later won the Military Medal for his courage that night in working as shells and machine-gun fire raked his position.[49] When the single-lane bridge was built, Matt devoted another report to a Corporal Fred Stichman of Montreal, a military policeman directing traffic under fire.[50] It didn't matter that the recorded interview with Stichman was short and banal. For the home front, just hearing their men's voices was riveting. Others listened in the hope their own relatives might be mentioned.

In San Vito, Matt, Ouimet, and the CBC sound engineers were part of a small group set up in a forward press camp near the fighting. From their village, Ortona was clearly visible across the Moro Valley – a prize that seemed close enough to capture in a few hours. In fact, it took another ten days of what Matt described as "little Paschendaeles of mud and blood"[51] before the Canadians could get a foot in the town. As 1st Division troops advanced up the slopes above the Moro, they ran into a wall of German fire and were battered by counterattacks from enemy tanks. Matt mentioned that there were scores of dead Germans lying in the blasted olive orchards and vineyards. Censorship proscribed any report of heavy Canadian casualties but Matt did mention a platoon "mowed down by flanking machine guns."[52] No one listening to his broadcasts could have had any illusions that Canadians were escaping the carnage.

> *Soaking wet, in a morass of mud, against an enemy fighting harder than he's fought before, the Canadians attack, attack and attack. The enemy is now fighting like the very devil to hold us, but he can't do it. He brings in more and more guns, more and more troops, and the hillsides and farmlands and orchards round San Leonardo, and between that village and the sea, are a ghastly brew of fire, and our roads for four miles behind the forward infantry are under heavy shelling. . . . Sometimes a battlefield looks like a film of a battlefield, but not this. It's too grim. To cross the gorge of the river now and go up the spiralling road into San Leonardo, by day or night, is a fierce thing. You run not only through shell-fire . . . but*

also through machine-gun fire. When you get there the enemy's multiple
fire mortars are pounding the village. They fire six shells at a time and
they come with six loud, evil moans in quick succession. The Canadians
call them Moaning Minnies, or the Wailing Willies, or the sobbing sisters.
You hear such jokes as these as you lie in the deep mud. . . . One soldier
said: "Why worry? If a shell has your name on it, you get it, and if it
hasn't, you don't." Another Canadian replied: "Sure, but what about the
ones that are marked: To whom it may concern."[53]

Day by day, Matt reported on the battles that slowly drove the Germans
off the northern ridge of the Moro. Names like Casa Berardi (where a
Vandoos officer won the first Victoria Cross of the campaign) and
Slaughterhouse Hill and Cider Crossroads became bywords for Canadian
valour. Yet they were about to be overshadowed by another name: Ortona.

On the home front, Matt owed much of his growing popularity to a cap-
tive audience. Canadians were deeply engaged in the war and avid for
information about their soldiers. There were myriad ties to the million
Canadians in uniform. More than a million women worked in the war
industries. Hundreds of thousands of others did volunteer work to support the war effort. Jean drove a truck in Vancouver collecting magazines
for the troops. Others recycled scrap metal and rubber or knitted socks
and scarves for the men overseas. Women cheerfully put up with the
rationing of food and gasoline. Some painted their legs with a make-up
product called Velva to make it appear they were wearing nylon stockings, which were unavailable in stores. Patriotism flourished, whipped up
by extensive propaganda from government agencies but mostly reflecting
a genuine pride in the country's role. But with pride came a deep anxiety
about the men at the front – and an insatiable appetite for news of them.

Audience surveys at this time showed that an astonishing 86 per cent of
adult English-Canadian listeners tuned in nightly to the CBC's war news.[54]
There were few more solemn moments in Canadian homes than when CBC
newscasts and the longer *News Roundup* came on the air every evening. It
was a time, as I remember well, when kids were shushed. Huddled around

their radio sets, families would wait for the latest reports from the front, often straining to listen through the buzz and crackle of poor recordings or faulty transmission. In Sicily, Peter Stursberg's voice became well known. Then, for the first six months of the mainland campaign, the sign-on "This is Matthew Halton speaking from Italy" was heard almost every night. Historian Mark Zuehlke wrote that Halton became the "war's narrator."[55]

No one knew that better than Helen Piddington. Twelve years old at the time, she had already lost two brothers – one of them torpedoed aboard the battleship *Royal Oak*, another shot down over Hamburg. Listening to the news after supper in their home in Esquimault-Saanich, B.C., was a ritual in Piddington's family. She would sit with her parents in front of one of the big RCA Victor radios that resembled a piece of neo-Gothic furniture. Her mother often undid Helen's pigtails and brushed her hair until the newscast ended. To this day, she recalls the urgency and intensity of Matt's voice. "For all of us," she told me, "Matthew Halton was a hero. Somehow your father's reports gave [my parents] the strength to carry on. He seemed almost like part of the family."[56]

For Aileen Oder, Matt's broadcasts were also a daily routine. Oder lived in Lac du Bonnet, a small Manitoba community that reflected the dedication of wartime Canada. To boost the morale of local servicemen abroad, Oder sent them "Hello Soldier" letters with news of Lac du Bonnet. Much of it was trivia: Campbell's store raised $450 for the "Stamp Out the U-boat" campaign; the new hit on the jukebox was "Won't You Tell Me When You'll Come Back Again"; a dance was held to raise money for the soldiers' Cigarette Fund Committee.[57] She wrote in one letter that people hung on every word of the CBC broadcasts and were "dreaming, just as you are, about the time when you'll be home again."[58] In another "Hello Soldier" letter, Oder added that "my favorite war correspondents are Matthew Halton and Ernie Pyle because they helped me to understand what you are enduring and how you are fighting."[59] More and more Canadians would come to share that view.

For a week over Christmas, the home front was fixated on the battle raging in the Adriatic port town of Ortona. At daybreak on December 20, battalions of the Loyal Edmonton Regiment (the Loyal Eddies) and the Seaforth Highlanders of Vancouver, backed up by tanks from the Three Rivers Regiment, slipped into the outskirts of the town. Within hours they discovered that the German defenders, the 1st Paratroop Division and the 90th Panzer Grenadier Division, had turned the Adriatic port into a death trap. Mines and booby traps were everywhere. Narrow side streets were blocked by rubble, channelling the Canadians down the main street and into the crossfire of German machine guns and mortars. Savage fighting at close quarters kept Matt out of Ortona for several days. When he got there, just before Christmas, he described an inferno:

> *If it wasn't hell, it was the courtyard of hell. It was a maelstrom of noise and hot splitting steel. Perhaps thirty or forty Canadian machine guns were brrppping at once. It sounded like hundreds. High explosive shells from our tanks in the square seemed to be ripping the town to pieces. . . . And the enemy's anti-tank shells and mortars were crashing into the buildings everywhere. . . . Their air-bursting shells were splitting themselves apart in black smoke over our heads.*[60]

The intensity of the fighting quickly made Ortona an international story. Matt's broadcasts were picked up by the BBC, and Canadian Press reports were widely read. *The Times* of London sent in Christopher Buckley, one of its top correspondents. The Associated Press wire service labelled the battle a "miniature Stalingrad" and the description caught on immediately.[61] Suddenly, the media focus on Ortona raised the stakes of the battle far beyond the town's limited strategic value. Field Marshal Kesselring griped to one of his commanders that "we do not want to defend Ortona decisively, but the English have made it as important as Rome. . . . It is only too bad that . . . the world press makes so much of it."[62]

Christmas saw no lull in the violence. In one of his most memorable broadcasts, Matt reported that "the more murderous the battle, the harder both sides fought, from window to window, from door to door, in a carnival of fury. There was something different there, something heroic, and almost superhuman and at the same time dark as night."[63] Matt was even more direct in a letter to Jean. The Canadians and Germans "seem beyond exhaustion and beyond fear," he wrote. "They've become bloodthirsty. . . . There is something dark and apocalyptic there, something fearful."[64] His description sounded over-wrought, melodramatic. Yet one veteran told me that my father perfectly captured the horror of the battle. Edmund Griffiths, a tank officer, said he is still haunted by the ghosts of Ortona. He confessed that he went into an Ortona church for a quick Christmas dinner, sang "Silent Night" with the Seaforths, then knifed and killed a German paratrooper as he returned to his tank.[65] Fifty years after the event, a German stretcher-bearer whom I interviewed for a CBC documentary wept as he recalled the dead and broken bodies. He said he had never been able to celebrate Christmas again: "It's as though I am dead on those days."[66]

Matt had his own grim experience on Christmas day. With CBC sound engineer Art Holmes, he took the recording van to a field hospital behind the lines where an accordionist was playing carols for the wounded. He strung the microphone cable from the van into a ward for "life cases" – those who might or might not live. He recorded several carols and interviewed an English nurse who said, "It's been grand looking after the Canadian soldiers." The ward then began to empty, and Matt was about to roll up the cable and leave when a wounded man appeared to come out of a coma. He said to the accordionist, "Corporal, I've been dreaming of home. Would you play something for me? Play 'I'm Dreaming of a White Christmas'." Matt immediately whispered into the microphone to sound engineer Holmes outside, "Art, start cutting [recording] at once."[67] The corporal sat on the edge of the bed and played and sang. Matt let the sound come full up in the last thirty seconds of his broadcast of the event, adding no words except for his sign-off. He wrote Jean next day about what he felt he couldn't tell his listeners: the soldier died shortly after the carol. "All the horror that had been hardening and callousing in my soul in the last six weeks seemed to dissolve in pity and I stood in the shadows as weak as a child."[68]

The violence in Ortona reached a peak in the next two days. On paths to the town, mule trains were seen carrying both shells and white wooden crosses. Matt described a place "appalling . . . in its mud, its dead, its ruin, its blight and desolation."[69] He wrote of the sickening stench of bodies and human parts. He reported on the killing of twenty-three Loyal Eddies, blown up in a booby-trapped building, and a revenge attack that killed more than forty Germans in similar fashion. He also described how the Canadians developed the ingenious technique of "mouse-holing" – blasting holes from one house to the next to advance without facing the firestorm in the streets.

On December 28, Matt drove again from San Vito to Ortona. It was strangely quiet apart from the chattering of a few machine guns and an occasional enemy shell. A few minutes later, he was the only reporter in the Loyal Eddies' command post when the radio buzzed with an incoming message. A signals officer took off his headphones and turned to the colonel with words that were widely quoted from Matt's report: "Sir, the Jerries are gone or else they're all dead."[70]

There was a note of awestruck pride in one of Matt's last broadcasts from the ruined town. "Call them out," he told his audience. "Dunkirk, Tobruk, Alamein, the delaying action in Burma, the last stand at Sollum . . . Call them out, and then add Moro River. . . . The attacking Canadians beat two of the finest German divisions that ever marched."[71] His pride in Canadian courage and resourcefulness was justified. But neither Matt nor any of the other war correspondents asked if the victory was worth the sacrifice. The battle killed or wounded 2,400 Canadians, and left hundreds of others scarred by shell shock. Rifle companies were stripped of half their strength, the 1st Division forced out of major operations for months. Victory at Ortona did not open the road to Rome, which was liberated only five months later. It merely pushed the German defence line a few kilometres to the north. Francis de Guingand, Montgomery's chief of staff in Italy, later wrote of the Moro campaign, "We began to think about Passchendaele. Had we gone on too long? Were the troops being driven too hard? I feel very definitely that a mistake was made in pressing the . . . offensive as far as it was."[72]

After five months on or near the front, Matt was exhausted. Not even in Libya and Egypt had he faced as long a period of working intensely in dismal conditions. For much of December, he shared a muddy, unheated stone hut in San Vito with Marcel Ouimet of Radio-Canada, a conducting officer, and sound engineer. The work load was demanding. CBC asked him to send daily cable updates for its announcers to read because of delays in getting his broadcasts to air. He was also filing often for Allied, the British newspaper chain owned by Lord Kemsley, and writing two long articles a month for the *Star Weekly*. The feedback was enthusiastic. CBC general manager Ernie Bushnell cabled that "your front-line reporting and recordings are unapproached by any other network,"[73] while chief news editor Dan McArthur described his summary of the Ortona battle as a "masterpiece of radio presentation."[74] There were telegrams of congratulations too from the BBC, which aired many of his broadcasts. The *Star* cabled: "How we miss you now,"[75] despite having its own veteran correspondent, Greg Clark, in the Canadian press camp.

The CBC told Matt he could return to London and take as long as he wanted to recuperate. He drove back to Vasto, over the gullies and roads he had crossed so many times under fire. In Naples, he was welcomed by Colonel Richard "Dick" Malone, the army PR chief, who received daily updates about public reaction to the war coverage. "I suppose you know," Malone told him, "that you are now famous."[76] In Algiers two days later, Georges Vanier, Canada's ambassador to the Free French mission there, gave him star treatment. He sent his limousine to meet him at the airport and invited him to a dinner party that night at the Villa Simian, his luxurious residence. Later, Matt told Jean how strange it felt to be sitting down with men and women in evening dress for a six-course dinner after living off army "compo" rations for six months in the sodden front lines.[77]

Matt spent five days in Algiers, sleeping at first in stretches of sixteen hours and "still feeling a heavy weight on my eyelids and chest." He wrote Jean that his hands were shaky and that he may "have barely escaped a breakdown in health."[78] It is difficult to judge whether he was suffering from excessive physical fatigue or stress disorder – or a mixture of both. In another letter, Matt said he hoped that "soon I shall be able to sleep without sweating dreams of the things I saw beyond the Moro river."[79]

14

D-DAY

"I have looked into the bright eyes of danger and been enchanted."
– MATTHEW HALTON in a letter to Jean, September 24, 1944

WHEN MATT RETURNED TO LONDON, the city was more than ever the centre of his world. By early spring 1944, more than three hundred war correspondents were in town waiting for the Allied invasion of France. It was like an old boys' reunion. In bars and nightclubs, Matt came across colleagues he hadn't seen since Spain, Finland, or Libya. His dearest friend, Sean Fielding, was now a colonel at the War Office. His younger brother, Seth Halton, who had worked at the *Star*, was with Canadian Army Public Relations. His University of Alberta friend Eric Gibbs was the deputy head of army PR. His older circle of London friends, including author and publisher Rache Dickson and German refugees Hans and Elsa Wolfsohn, welcomed him back.

It was party time in London, and Matt, now fully recovered, enjoyed it to the full. He took three weeks off to enjoy a constant round of lunches, dinners, and pub crawls with friends. Despite wartime austerity, he lived extravagantly, frequenting the most expensive restaurants: the Café Royal, the Ivy, La Coquille, and Simpson's. Bert Powley, the editor in charge of the CBC Overseas Unit, recalled that "Matt lived magnificently while I went and had my modest dinner at the BBC canteen."[1] Even with a big income from CBC, the *Star Weekly*, Allied newspapers, and the BBC, Matt still on occasion ran out of money while never failing to send generous cheques to Jean and his parents in Pincher Creek.

Matt resumed his puzzling relationship with Maureen Church, the attractive and ardently left-wing librarian at the Ministry of Information. He was still taking her to dinners and parties with friends, mentioning his sorties with her in letters to Jean without admitting that he was having an affair. His younger brother, Seth, who was often with them, seemed far more worried by the attachment than Matt himself. "This thing has gone too far," Seth wrote in his diary. "There will be heartbreak one way, tragedy if it goes the other."[2] He was apparently referring to fears Church was pregnant. In another diary entry, Seth wrote that he asked Matt to send him several cheques "in case they are needed in the problem Sean Fielding is helping to solve! God, I hope there is no problem!"[3] Two days later, he wrote that Matt, who was away on D-Day preparations, no longer need worry. Fielding had told him all was well.[4]

Matt's enjoyment of London life in no way slowed a career that was still taking off. His reports from Italy had established his reputation with the BBC and he was now frequently asked to contribute to *War Report* and *Radio Newsreel*. He was also writing regularly for Lord Kemsley's Allied newspaper chain, which consisted of three London newspapers and dozens of provincial ones. Allied offered him a permanent job when the war was over and agreed to pay him generously for daily pieces when the D-Day campaign began. At a meeting of the British Newspaper Proprietors' Association, he was listed as one of the six best war correspondents.[5] In the United States, one of his broadcasts from Italy won the top award at the American Radio Institute for the best use of actuality sound and commentary.[6]

Waiting for D-Day was a suspenseful time. The war correspondents became pawns in plans to deceive the Germans about when and where the invasion would take place. In early April, Matt and other correspondents were ordered to pack their bags and report to PR headquarters. But instead of starting out on the greatest military operation in history, as they expected, they were taken by train to Scotland, where they were held incommunicado for a week. Allied Intelligence hoped that German spies would notice their disappearance and not be tipped off about the timing of D-Day when the correspondents vanished before the real event. Finally, on May 30, the war correspondents were summoned to an estate near

London. Matt was one of the privileged few chosen as an "assault journalist" to land on the first day of the invasion. Hundreds of other war correspondents were excluded from the D-Day landings, and some were furious. In a celebrated exchange, one journalist complained about being unable to cover what he called "the biggest story since the Crucifixion." "Yes," replied a senior intelligence officer, "but they managed very well with four correspondents."[7]

The seven Canadian reporters assigned to the assault were sequestered on the south coast for four days prior to D-Day. From the Isle of Wight, they got their first view of part of the vast invasion fleet numbering more than six thousand vessels. Matt was teamed for the Channel crossing with Charles Lynch, a twenty-four-year-old Canadian working for Reuters news agency. "We were a strange pair," Lynch later wrote, "the most experienced Canadian war correspondent and the greenest."[8] On the night of June 5, they joined hundreds of troops from the 3rd Canadian Infantry Division on a requisitioned Irish ferry. There was a piano on the ship that Lynch began playing. He later described how fearful young soldiers clustered around, joining in repeated choruses of the popular Maurice Chevalier song "Louise" ("Can it be true, someone like you could love me, Louise") before the ferocious cannonade began over the Normandy beaches.[9]

By morning church steeples and timbered Norman homes along the coast were in view. Matt and Lynch crowded into an infantry landing craft with troops from the Royal Winnipeg Rifles for the final stretch to the beach at Graye-sur-Mer. The first assault wave on D-Day a few hours earlier had already cleared a path through the mines but there was still shellfire and the chilling sight of dead Canadians lying on the beach or floating in the water. Matt's first broadcast on the landings was solemn but celebratory. He talked of "the few immortal hours" as Canadian soldiers took part in "the most dramatic event of all time."[10]

> I have been through many battles, but I was never as excited as when my time came to go ashore for this was France and the beginning of the end. The rough, swirling tide carried our assault craft over the obstacles and we jumped into more water than we expected – six feet of it – so I had to swim

a yard or two with my pack and waterproof typewriter before I could wade
to shore. Then the struggle across the soft sand, five minutes that will
always be vivid in my mind. . . . We went on down the lane and we saw a
French woman putting a rose on the face of a dead Canadian. . . .[11]

D-Day had all the epic qualities that appealed to Matt's version of history. But there were also moments of farce and humour that didn't fit the heroic narrative. Once past the beach, Matt, Lynch, and their conducting officer were welcomed by an old farmer and his wife who were curiously unconcerned by the gunfire around them. The visitors were plied with Calvados, the raw Normandy apple-jack; given strawberries and cream; and bizarrely shown the farmer's photos and medals from his own earlier military service. Invited to sleep that night in the farmhouse, Lynch later wrote that "Matt and I were the only two men in the entire Allied armies to wind up June 6 in featherbeds."[12]

D-Day was a triumph for Canadian media but not for Matt and Lynch. The first long report from Normandy was written by CP's Ross Munro and was a world scoop. The first film and photos of the invasion were taken by a Canadian army cameraman and photographer and were seen in newsreels and on front pages all over Britain and North America within forty hours. Matt had to wait two days and return to England to make his first broadcast since no recording facilities were yet available in the beachhead. In the interim, he wrote a two-thousand-word account of the landing to be shipped to London and read by another CBC journalist. The report got to England but was lost in the government's censorship bureaucracy. "The hair-brained bastards!" he wrote to Jean. "You risk your life covering the greatest story in history . . . and then it is lost in the Ministry of Information!"[13]

Lynch was equally unlucky. He had hoped to send his first dispatch to Reuters by carrier pigeon. Army PR had brought baskets of pigeons to the nearby village of Courseulles, assuming that they would be a reliable way of getting messages to England before regular communications were established. Lynch followed instructions and placed his copy in a small capsule that was attached to a pigeon. To his distress, the bird took off in the direction of the German lines instead of its home loft in Southampton.

Lynch tried again with other pigeons, which also flew toward the enemy, their sense of direction apparently skewed because it was their mating season. Finally, he shook his fist at the departing birds with a shout that became part of journalistic legend: "Traitors! Damned traitors!"[14] Seventeen-year-old Micheline Trannoy, a resident of the village, watched in astonishment. Fifty years later she told me she remembered *"ces dingues de Canadiens avec leurs pigeons voyageurs"* ("those crazy Canadians with their homing pigeons").[15]

By any measure, the D-Day landings were a brilliant success. But they failed in one key objective – to drive the Germans quickly from Caen, the biggest and most strategically important city in Lower Normandy. It took more than a month of vicious fighting before the city was captured by British and Canadian troops. German counterattacks began the next day, pitting the 3rd Canadian Division against its nemesis in the battle for Normandy, the 12th SS Panzer Division, largely made up of young zealots from the Hitler Youth movement.

No place in the beachhead was safe as the Canadian war correspondents were about to discover. On June 13, Matt and four others were working or relaxing in a manor-house near Courseulles that had been requisitioned as a press centre. Suddenly, German shells started crashing down – twenty over the next one and a half hours with three direct hits. The correspondents jumped to the courtyard from their second-floor rooms and ran to slit trenches as smoke and flames poured from the building. An army cameraman filmed Matt and a PR officer salvaging equipment. A military report on the shelling recommended the officer for a bravery award and cited Matt for being "extremely cool . . . under very dangerous conditions."[16]

After the attack, the war correspondents were moved to a hotel in nearby Bayeux, arriving just in time to witness the emotional welcome given General de Gaulle. The Free French leader had landed at Graye-sur-Mer and now walked down the main street like a Pied Piper leading thousands of cheering citizens behind him. "It was like a scene from a film," Matt broadcast that evening, "the tall, handsome general and the people following, and France soon to be free."[17] In the main square thousands cheered De Gaulle's first address on liberated French soil. For Matt, it was intensely moving. He had been a fervent admirer of de Gaulle since 1940, regarding him as the personification of a France unsullied by collaboration with the Nazis. He was critical of Roosevelt and, to a lesser extent, Churchill for their reluctance to accept de Gaulle as France's legitimate leader and recognize his provisional French government. Now, in one symbolic hour in Bayeux, he saw the General vindicated and French honour restored. "I wish the whole world could have heard the citizens of Bayeux singing *'Aux armes, citoyens, formez vos bataillons,'*[8] the battle cry of the French national anthem.*

In the last weeks of June, the Normandy campaign turned into a war of attrition. There were costly little battles in a countryside where it was difficult for war correspondents to see much of the action.

It wasn't until the first week of July that Matt was able to witness the fury of a major battle in France. The 3rd Division was ordered to attack the town of Carpiquet and its airport as a prelude to expelling the Germans from nearby Caen. Matt and his Radio-Canada colleague, Marcel Ouimet, moved up to the front the night before the battle. Their recording equipment was set up in a stone barn in an observation post overlooking the airport. Eighteen metres in front of them, a line of machine-gunners sat in their trenches. The correspondents were given an unusually detailed briefing, learning far more about the planned assault than most of the soldiers involved. At precisely 5 a.m. on July 4, there would be a huge artillery barrage, supported by squadrons of fighter bombers and the Royal Navy battleship *Rodney* firing its heavy guns from sixteen kilometres away. Then the infantry would attack. The Royal Winnipeg Rifles, the Régiment de la Chaudière, the North Shore Regiment, and the Queen's Own Rifles were to storm across open fields to dislodge the now hated 12th SS Panzer Division from the airport and town. The observation post where Matt was set up was on the flank of the planned assault. It gave him what he called "an orchestra seat" for the battle.[19]

---

* As de Gaulle drove back to the beach that evening to return to England, he passed lines of advancing Canadian soldiers. His aide, Maurice Schumann, said he murmured sadly: "They're going up to the front. How many will come back?"[20] Matt would have felt deeply betrayed had he lived to hear de Gaulle's *"Vive le Québec libre!"* and would likely have pointed out that the General landed on a beach liberated by Canadians.

His CBC broadcast the next day was one of his most theatrical and gripping. It mixed ad lib passages from the battlefield with continuity recorded a few hours later. Shortly after dawn, Matt picked up the microphone:

(Ad Lib) It's two minutes to five. Two minutes to five in Normandy and the sun hasn't risen yet, over us or over the Germans 800 yards away. It will rise on a fearful scene because at 5 o'clock precisely the Canadians are going to attack, and they'll attack with the support of the most enormous concentration of fire ever put down on a small objective. . . .

I am in a stone barn with a company of Western Canadian machine-gunners who are going to be in battle soon, drawing fire to aid the main attack. . . .

At 5 o'clock – and it's now about ten seconds to five – one, two, three, four, five, six, seven, eight, nine, ten. . . Here she goes! (actuality artillery barrage).

(Recorded later) . . . Then a few minutes after the barrage started, the objective below us was covered by a dense cloud of smoke and cordite fumes. In the following recording, you will hear German and Canadian machine guns and German shells that fell on us, and my attempt to describe something of what I saw. And above all, the incessant, earth-shaking and atrocious pounding of the hundreds of guns. Fortunately for you, the sounds as recorded on disc are quiet and tame compared to what they are when we hear them. Even bursting shells that shook us and blasted us sound pretty tame on a disc. Listen to this and then imagine it at least ten times as loud. . . . (actuality)

(Ad lib) And now twenty-five minutes have passed . . . twenty-five minutes of the most . . . I think the most ferocious barrage I have ever seen. All we can see is smoke and the terrible bursts of flame as one of the huge naval shells falls on the enemy position. Occasionally, an enemy shell falls near us, and you can hear as I speak – you can hear the chattering, the hard stuttering of the machine-guns.

(Recorded later) . . . When the smoke cleared away, there were the Canadians – I can't name the regiments [because of censorship] – advancing like automats. Not running. Walking, steady as robots. Some

of our Bren-carriers were hit and went up in vomits of flames.
Occasionally a tank was hit and burst into flame. But still they bore
down on Carpiquet – like fate – firing as they came. . . . Not one man
wavered unless he was wounded or killed. . . .

This is the morning we waited for. A morning in France. A morning
in which the fair fields of Normandy are torn and rent and split apart. . . .

But the Canadians are on Carpiquet, and another hard cruel step
has been taken toward the liberation and the peace. (30 seconds shellfire)
This is Matthew Halton of the CBC *speaking from France.*[21]

The observation post from which Matt and Ouimet watched the battle
came under intense fire several times. One of their drivers was killed by a
mortar bomb; two soldiers close by were wounded.[22] Matt left the battlefield at midday, learning later that the attack was only a partial success.
The Canadians occupied the village of Carpiquet but failed to capture
much of the airfield. Ouimet later wrote to his wife that he had spent the
three worst hours of his life at Carpiquet, fearing at times that he would
not survive. *"Je haïs la guerre"* (I hate war), he told her.[23]

The contrast with the tone of Matt's letter home, written on the same
day, is startling. He told Jean that he felt an "evil exhilaration" on the
front,[24] almost suggesting that he had crossed some line between the thrill
of battle and a perverse attraction to it. "At one moment I'm appalled," he
continued in the letter, "and wonder why we don't all go mad. The next
moment there's a roaring glory and I want to be advancing across those
wheat fields full of poppies with the assault troops."[25] Matt continued to be
drawn to front lines for the rest of the war. Part of the attraction was a
macho pride in overcoming fear, part of it the heightened sense of being
alive when threatened by death. "I have looked into the bright eyes of
danger and have been enchanted," he wrote on a later occasion.[26]

Another inspiration was Canada's front-line soldiers. Like most of the
war correspondents, Matt often found them to be astonishingly brave
against better trained and better equipped German troops. After a speaking tour of Canada later in the year, he told *The Maple Leaf* that "I am not
a rabidly patriotic Canadian. I did not get up and say 'the Canadians are

the best in the world', but I did say, 'if there are better soldiers in the world than the Canadians, I'd like to meet them.'"[27] It is hard not to believe that Matt was pandering to some degree to the home audience, especially after his frequent praise of the dynamism and courage of Wehrmacht soldiers. Yet, in his letters as well as his reports, he was clearly awed by the way 3rd Division troops, most of them untested before Normandy, were facing the horrors of modern warfare. He told Jean that the front-line battalions made him proud to be a Canadian and that, after more than a decade away from home, he now felt reconnected to his country.

A constant echo in Matt's wartime journalism was the notion that nobility can spring out of what he called "the ordure of war." Asked by the BBC to broadcast on his experiences as a war correspondent, he used Tolstoy's *War and Peace* as a theme. He quoted Prince Andrei Bolkonsky on the eve of the battle of Borodino describing war as "the most horrible thing in life" because of its brutality and ugliness. That view was contrasted with the feelings of the Prince's friend, Pierre, who talked of the gallantry that emerges from war and the courage of front-line soldiers "steady and calm all the time to the end."[28] Matt recalled cases of bravery and sacrifice he encountered among British and Canadian troops but was less inclined to glamorize war. Apart from its evil effects, he said, war burdens soldiers with another reality:

> The dreariness is one of the worst things about it. The drudgery and the dirt. The boredom, the wasting of time. Most soldiers, when they look back on their campaigns, won't think of splitting shells and whipping machine-guns. They will think of waiting in convoys in the rain or dust: waiting for an order, waiting for a road-block to be cleared. One of my most lasting memories of war, for example, will not be the day we were surrounded at Sidi Omar and watched from four hundred yards as the guns smashed the German tanks. It will be the memory of soldiers sitting in a truck . . . watching for letters from home; doing dreary things – trying to make tea in a sandstorm, trying to keep dry under a truck during a night of beating rain. Thousands of men have had nearly five years of this. Fine young men with life passing them by as they lie in mud or wait at the road-block.[29]

In Normandy, such hardships rarely worried the Canadian war correspondents. The press camp moved to a derelict chateau just south of Carpiquet. It offered efficient media communications, chefs to prepare meals, "batmen" to drive and do chores for the correspondents, and even a bar to satisfy the reporters' hard-drinking habits. It was the envy of British and American correspondents, a score of whom chose to make it their base.

The war correspondents were a colourful, highly competitive group. Some were inclined to boast about their achievements. Lionel Shapiro of the *Montreal Gazette*, later the author of the bestselling novel *The Sixth of June*, had a habit of rising from his typewriter in the press room and proclaiming that he had just written the finest story of his career. Matt and his former *Star* colleague Greg Clark were hardly more modest. When Matt kept repeating the story of his countdown broadcast at Carpiquet, his friend Ralph Allen said, "You know, Matt, it's in your interest never to tell that story again." "Why not?" Matt asked. "Well," said Allen, "every time you tell it you expose yourself to even greater risks – and one of these days you are going to get killed."[30]

Matt's pairing on D-Day with Charlie Lynch, the young Reuters correspondent, gave rise to a lasting friendship. Like the bonding with Sean Fielding in the desert, it grew partly out of shared danger. Lynch would often join Matt on visits to the front; on several occasions they were pinned down together under fire. In later years, they would both laugh at a letter Matt wrote to Jean describing Lynch as "a grand youngster, who thinks I'm terrific. He's a big fat boy who never heard a shot fired before this and yet has no nerves at all and is always up in the front lines – more than me."[31] Lynch was skeptical of left-wingers, proudly un-intellectual, and almost half Matt's age – not attributes likely to endear him to the older man. Yet he was impressed by Matt's fame, his passionate approach to life, and odd habits, such as spouting poetry on drives to the front. Over the next eighteen months, he also participated in what he claimed was a "roistering, womanizing" side to Matt's life.[32] "He may have liked the reaction he had on me," Lynch said. "It was 'tell me more . . . or lead me astray.' Matt would say, 'Let's go and fuck 'em all.' You'd fall in behind to see what this was all about."[33] Matt, in turn, enjoyed the adulation. He was also flattered to become a kind of moving encyclopedia of war, politics, and geography for a young man who confessed he had no idea where Normandy was until the invasion.

Like other war correspondents, Lynch was occasionally asked to do a war commentary for the CBC. To Matt's embarrassment, he devoted one broadcast to a glowing portrait of his mentor. He touched on Matt's pride in being an Albertan from Pincher Creek; his ten-year crusade against the Nazis; his deep love of France; and his "bravery" in going to battle which "I actually think he enjoys."[34] His one hint of criticism was that Matt's broadcasts sometimes seemed "flowery" when he was shown his scripts. "But then," Lynch added, "when the finished broadcast came through you would realize his artistry, and his knack for catching in words this thing called war."[35]

Matt's reporting thrived on the human drama of war, and on July 10 he found a spectacular example. A day earlier, British and Canadian troops finally began the liberation of Caen – or what was left of it. Just prior to the attack, Allied Bomber Command sent 450 heavy aircraft over the town. They levelled large stretches of the medieval centre that had already been devastated by earlier raids. Streets were now turned into impassable mounds of rubble. Huge clouds of smoke and flame spewed from the ruins – a sight that even Allied soldiers found "frightening" as they watched from the outskirts of the city.[36] They were more distressed the next day when they discovered the bodies of many hundreds of dead and wounded civilians.

Matt and Radio-Canada's Ouimet followed Canadian troops into Caen early the next morning, witnessing some of the most stirring scenes of the Normandy campaign. Soldiers were clearing mines, and French Red Cross workers were searching for wounded as the two correspondents clambered through the ruins. Matt's broadcast took his audience into a day of high drama:

> We came suddenly on to a little square, Place de la Lycée Malherbe. There, to our astonishment, we saw a great church and school that weren't damaged at all. The church was the famous Abbaye-aux-Hommes, a thousand years old. . . . Not one bomb or shell touched this church.

If you could go there and see the rest of Caen, you would say this was a miracle. I went into the church and saw a tapestry of our times that I will never forget. . . . There were two thousand people in there, mostly women and children. They lived and slept for several weeks there. Babies have been born there at the foot of the Sanctuary, and wounded people have been tended above the tomb of William the Conqueror after being brought in from the shambles outside. . . .

Every day in that great lovely church there were scenes that might have come out of Victor Hugo. Throughout all the shelling and bombing during those apocalyptic weeks, the mass was celebrated in the church three times a day. Three times a day those two thousand people, as they knelt, heard the music of the Kyrie Eleison coming from the organ. There was no electricity to supply power to the organ, so three times a day, amid the fury, the children in the church worked the bellows with their hands and feet. Outside, the world crashing and burning but the church never once hit by a bomb or shell. . . .

My colleague and I were almost the first men in British uniform these people had seen, though they'd known that British and Canadian soldiers had got into town yesterday. . . . As we moved slowly down the great nave, hundreds gathered around us to shake our hands. . . . When these people saw our shoulder patches, they cried "Long Live Canada!" We replied, "Long Live France!"[37]

Later that morning, a flag-raising ceremony on the square provided an emotional crescendo to the broadcast. Men and women of the local Resistance movement paraded by as occasional German shells screamed overhead and gunfire still echoed from outlying districts. Many in the crowd wept as they began singing the national anthem. It was recorded and introduced by Matt and heard that night in homes across Canada: "In this recording you can hear the broken and tortured voices of these unbroken people singing the 'Marseillaise' amid the shambles of Caen, amid the gun-fire and amid their dead. (Actuality Sound)."[38]

Later, Matt pointedly wrote in a *Star Weekly* article that "we liberated – and obliterated – Caen."[39] Almost since D-Day, he was troubled by what he felt was excessive Allied bombing in Normandy that was blamed for the deaths of more than half the twenty thousand French civilians killed in the campaign.[40] In a CBC report, he described it as tragic and commented that "if we have to do all this all the way to the Rhine, there's nothing left of France."[41] His letters home about the issue were angrier. Matt singled out the Americans as "murderously indiscriminate. If a couple of stray shots come from a nearby village, they send a couple of hundred heavy bombers over and obliterate it into ashes. Yesterday, on the American front, I saw small towns like Carentan and Valognes reduced to dust and rubble, and hundreds of civilians killed. . . . It's just too ghastly."[42]

Even after capturing most of Caen, the Allies were still hemmed in along their narrow bridgehead on the coast. Six weeks of battles lay ahead. In the small villages and on the high ground south of Caen, Canadians would suffer some of the heaviest losses of the war, often just to gain or lose a kilometre or less. Slowly the Germans were being worn down but they were fighting so efficiently that the outcome of the Battle of Normandy remained uncertain. Cases of battle exhaustion soared on both the Anglo-Canadian and American sectors of the bridgehead. The U.S. Army ordered more chaplains brought in to comfort the troops and set up a brothel for comfort of a different sort.[43]

The campaign was a frustrating one to cover. Matt once said that about 40 per cent of what a correspondent sees in war cannot be described because of censorship, and another 20 percent because the details are too horrible.[44] In France, correspondents were governed by strict rules laid down by SHAEF (Supreme Headquarters Allied Expeditionary Force). Those who violated the rules could lose their accreditation and be expelled from the war zone. No mention of operational details was permitted, including the names of combat units, troop deployments, and casualty figures. Also banned were "Reports likely to injure the morale of Allied forces" or damage the war effort on the home front.[45] Criticism of senior officers was discouraged and temporary blackouts often imposed on news of battle defeats.[46] Matt's radio reports, which were transmitted through London, were subject to an additional level of censorship at the BBC. One of his broadcasts was never aired because he described the courage of a German soldier who kept throwing grenades after he had lost his right arm. Vigorously protested by the CBC, the blocking of the broadcast became a minor *cause célèbre*. The BBC finally agreed it wouldn't happen again.[47]

The correspondents grumbled about censorship but most accepted it as a necessary part of the war effort. "You believed the cause was right," said Ross Munro. "Hitler had to be put down or your world wasn't going to exist."[48] That belief made it easier for most of the correspondents to indulge in a certain amount of cheerleading and playing down of bad news. Usually they self-censored, not wanting to waste time later losing arguments with the censors. In contrast to his broadcasts, Matt's notebooks contain observations that would never have passed the authorities. One entry describes a battle south of Caen as a "folly" and a "massacre," an apparent reference to the disastrous Canadian attacks on Verrières Ridge. He notes that some colonels refused orders to attack and quotes a dispatch rider shouting to officers: "When are you going to give us a rest instead of fucking us around."[49]

Ironically, Matt was under some criticism at home for painting too grim a picture of the war, not for airbrushing its uglier aspects. On his almost daily visits to forward battalions, he described the fighting with words like "terribly severe" and "very savage." The impact was sometimes enhanced by "sound-ups" of roaring bombardments. In one report, Matt said that "it got so that I dreaded each morning because of the things I knew I'd see and hear when I got to the front. Eight or nine weeks of savagery, of villages utterly destroyed, wounded women and children, and missing friends at every regiment, and dead men and a filthy smell, and the awful thing called fear."[50] Some wives back home said his reports were almost too much to bear.[51]

Complaints that Matt was undermining morale came from both senior CBC bureaucrats (probably under pressure from Ottawa) and some listeners. His reports certainly ignored news service guidelines, which stated that broadcasts should "not unnecessarily alarm, or depress listeners" and should strive for "more cheerful or encouraging war news."[52] Fortunately Matt had a strong defender in Dan McArthur, the CBC's chief news editor in Toronto. Stalwart in resisting pressures from senior management, McArthur argued that Canadians should know the real circumstances in which their men were fighting. He later endeared himself to the correspondents by denouncing CBC bureaucracy as "that fungus growth that now covers the whole of the CBC like a green mildew."[53] Nevertheless Matt remained bitter about the accusations that he was damaging Canadian morale. In a later article in *The Maple Leaf,* the army newspaper, he addressed his critics: "Too grim, eh? You want fine heroic stories without any mud or blood or losses on our side. You don't want to be disturbed as you sit beside your radio. . . . Well, that's too bad. And then I'd tell them about the Black Watch . . . ." Your fathers and mothers and sisters and wives didn't want any high-powered pablum. Comfort, if possible. But above all they wanted the truth."[54] His response didn't mention that censorship often made truth-telling impossible.

Like many journalists, Matt was over-sensitive to criticism. Despite some complaints about his "grimness," his audience mail from Canada was overwhelmingly positive. Typically, a Canadian Legion official in Valleyfield, Quebec, wrote of "our deep appreciation of the magnificent job that you are doing."[55] A Maritime listener wrote that Halton could retire at once and feel that he had done more than any one man could be expected to do.[56] Many letters were touchingly concerned about his well-being. A woman who signed herself "Grandmother Betty Ann" said, "When this awful war is over and the dear ones come home – do, dear Matthew Halton, give up this war work. It will get you sooner or later. . . . God bless you, dear boy."[57]

In early August, Matt took a short break from the depressing stalemate on the Anglo-Canadian front. He drove south to American armoured divisions that had punched though German defences and deep into Brittany. It was exhilarating, Matt wrote, to be speeding down long stretches of undefended roads and through towns that had been liberated without being blown apart. In places there were hundreds of destroyed

---

* Three hundred and fifteen members of an assault force of 325 from the Royal Highland Regiment of Canada (the Black Watch) were either killed, wounded, or captured attacking Verrières Ridge on July 25, 1944. It was the costliest battle for Canada since the disastrous Dieppe raid in 1942.[58]

German vehicles – the first evidence of the coming rout of the Nazi army in France. Long American convoys were rolling forward as truckloads of German prisoners passed in the other direction. "History was alive before your eyes. . . . You could begin to think of peace,"[59] he broadcast.

Matt had arranged to meet Charlie Lynch and several other friends at Mont St. Michel, the medieval monastery and village perched magnificently on a tidal island off the Normandy coast. Matt was fond of saying "There's a time for work and a time to live" and this occasion was definitely a time to live. He joined Lynch and a group of American correspondents that included Ernest Hemingway, CBS's Charles Collingwood, and the noted war photographer Robert Capa. A gargantuan lunch followed at the famous local restaurant, La Mère Poularde. Paté, omelettes, roast veal, and various desserts were consumed and swilled down with champagne and vintage wines.

It was late in the afternoon, at the brandy and Calvados stage, that a sharp quarrel broke out between Matt and Hemingway, the two ex-*Toronto Star* reporters. Matt told the author of his great admiration for his novels. He then added that the only fault he could find in them were the descriptions of sexual desire between men and women. As Hemingway began to fume, Matt tried, and failed, to mollify him by saying it wasn't that those passages were bad, only that they didn't match the high standard of the rest of his writing. According to Lynch's account of the exchange, Hemingway then banged his fist on the restaurant's heavy oak table and shouted, "Any fucker who fucking well says I can't write about fucking is a fucking liar. And you, Halton, are full of shit!"[60] Hemingway, flushed with alcohol, then stormed out and drove off in a captured German staff car. Matt and Lynch spent a second day relaxing at Mont St. Michel.

Matt could afford to disappear occasionally. As the pre-eminent correspondent at CBC, he enjoyed the same privileged treatment as he had at the *Toronto Star*. It rankled Marcel Ouimet, his Radio-Canada colleague, that Matt was paid almost twice as much as he was and given priority for key media "pool" positions. Ouimet was a gifted bilingual broadcaster whose complaints were largely justified. Yet the CBC continued to favour Matt, who was gaining ever wider recognition. His account of the entry into Caen drew demands for transcripts from all over Canada. The

Montreal Star reprinted the script, saying it "has not been excelled in any broadcast from any war front to Canada since the war began."[61] The Allied newspaper chain in England put some of his dispatches on its front pages. The BBC was also using more of his broadcasts and translating many of them into foreign languages for its overseas service. Internal memos in the corporation's archives reveal some debate over Matt's broadcasts during the Desert War. A few editors felt they were a refreshing change from BBC style while others argued they were too emotional and too editorial. That debate now appeared to have been decided in Matt's favour. A memo on one of his broadcasts from Brittany states: "This spell-binding piece from Matthew Halton has just come in. I . . . draw it urgently to your notice for its maturity and accuracy in painting some of the pictures we have so long lacked."[62]

Matt's broadcasts were also singled out by Desmond Shawe-Taylor, a noted critic for the London *Sunday Times*. In a comparison of British, American, and Canadian correspondents regularly heard on BBC's *War Report*, Shawe-Taylor offered some flattering comment: "Matthew Halton . . . has recently broadcast some remarkable despatches. He uses no tricks, just reads a script; but what a good script it is! He catches aspects of war which other correspondents neglect: its splendours and miseries are equally present to his imagination. . . . Even the best of radio reporters show a tendency to mechanical efficiency; Mr. Halton remains obstinately and even naively human. In a profession dedicated to the hardboiled, casual and slick he exemplifies the importance of being earnest."[63]

By mid-August, the gloom was lifting from the Anglo-Canadian front. The Germans had finally been pushed off the high ground south of Caen. Canadian tanks and armoured troop carriers had advanced to within five kilometres of Falaise. American troops were moving up in a pincer movement to help trap retreating Nazi soldiers while to the southeast other U.S. forces raced toward the Seine and Paris.

For the first time, Matt was able to drive safely down most of the road between Caen and Falaise: thirty-two kilometres that took almost two months to secure. A huge sign along the way, "To Canada Via Berlin," reflected a new optimism among the troops that they might soon be home. Matt's own elation at the German retreat was marred by sadness at the high cost of victory. In a broadcast on August 15, he talked of regiments who had their grim initiation along the same road. Canadians, he said, should not forget the names of the blasted villages where their regiments had been bled and wasted: May-sur-Orne, Fontenay le Marmion, Hubert Folie, Rocquancourt, Tilly-la-Campagne.

> *Along that road you can see almost everything that is meant by the word "War."* . . . *The destruction of life, the destruction of smiling fields and towns, the destruction of culture and treasures of the past. The monstrous bomb craters, the shambles at every crossroads, the million shell-holes. The crosses of the dead and the dead still being collected from the slit trenches and the wheatfields. The trees, everywhere torn and shredded. The houses and villages and churches, everywhere destroyed. The twisted and burnt-out vehicles and tanks and guns. The road to Falaise.*[64]

It took another week for the final destruction of Hitler's army of Normandy. Matt was not there to see the last two days of the offensive. He was rushing to be present for one of the most dramatic stories of the war: the liberation of Paris, *his* Paris.

FOUR DAYS IN PARIS

"Was this reality – or Hollywood?"
> – MATTHEW HALTON, CBC report, August 27, 1944

NOTHING IN MATT'S LIFE MATCHED THE HIGH DRAMA he lived during the liberation of Paris in August 1944. In four tumultuous days, his craving for adventure and excitement was satisfied beyond expectations. He later described them as his most unforgettable days of the war. Not only was he "hand-in-hand with history" – to use a favourite phrase of his – but he would experience danger, personal glory, and a passionate romance. All in a city he loved, in a country he idealized.

By mid-August, the survival of Paris itself was at stake. As American and Free French forces closed in, a garrison of twenty thousand German troops was ordered to turn the city into a battleground. Plans were made for bridges and famous public buildings to be blown up. Paris, Hitler decreed, must not be allowed to fall to the Allies except as "a field of ruins."[1] He threatened to shatter the city with V-I flying bombs,[2] and no one doubted that his threats were real. Only weeks earlier, large parts of Warsaw were reduced to rubble after an uprising by Polish rebels. On August 19, a similar rebellion was unleashed by Resistance fighters in Paris. Municipalities and police stations were taken over, streets barricaded, and citizens called to arms. "Paris is worth 200,000 dead," declared Henri Rol-Tanguy, the Communist Resistance leader for the Paris region.[3] General Dwight

Eisenhower, the Allied commander, had no real choice. To prevent a blood-bath, he agreed to send French and American forces into the city.

On August 24, Matt and five Canadian colleagues joined some eighty correspondents crowded into a small hotel in Rambouillet. Paris was only fifty kilometres away but German patrols and snipers made the road there too dangerous to pass. Hemingway had been the first to arrive at the hotel and quickly became the target of other correspondents. The novelist was in full guerilla warrior mode. With a .45 pistol strapped to his side, he had enlisted a small group of Resistance fighters, had stashed grenades and machine guns in his room, and was obviously determined to do more than just write about the liberation of Paris. Other correspondents objected strongly to "General Hemingway" breaching the ban on correspondents bearing arms. They argued (quite correctly) that he was endangering the non-combatant status of other correspondents as well as himself. Blows were exchanged with one American reporter, and charges laid against Hemingway with the military authorities. At a judicial investigation months later, the novelist was absolved thanks to his reputation and the intervention of senior U.S. officers.[4]

Early on August 25, it was learned that a few members of General Philippe Leclerc's 2nd Armoured Brigade had slipped into Paris the preceding night. Almost immediately Matt, Ouimet, and their conducting officer, Captain Jack Golding, chalked the word "Canada" in bold letters on their jeep and set off for the capital. As they approached the city, they fell in behind a convoy of Leclerc's tanks and armoured vehicles. Matt described driving down one of the lovely poplar-lined roads of the Île-de-France region, raising his field glasses from time to time, straining for the first sight of the city. "Suddenly we could see the Eiffel Tower and there before us was the most beautiful city in the world. And it had gone mad."[5]

The delirium began soon after the convoy arrived at the Porte d'Italie on the southern edge of the city. It seemed as if everyone in Paris was in the streets, carried away by an enormous surge of joy. Matt's group was swamped by the crowd: men, women, and children pushed forward to thank and embrace the first men in Allied uniform they had seen in four years. Some brought flowers and wine; others burst into an impromptu chorus of the "Marseillaise." Church bells pealed wildly across the city. In his broadcast that day, Matt said the crowd was so dense that at times the jeep couldn't move: "I don't know how we got along those streets. We were among the first vehicles. . . . We drove for miles, saluting with both hands and shouting *Vive la France* till we lost our voices. Every time we stopped for a second, hundreds of girls pressed round the jeep to kiss us, and to inundate us with flowers."[6]

As they drove along the Boulevard Saint-Germain toward the Seine, the crowds thinned. Instead of cheering there was now the sound of tank and machine-gun fire. At a roadblock, police told them they couldn't go further because of fighting with German troops. Matt was impatient to get across the river to the Right Bank where Army PR hoped to set up a press centre at the Scribe, a hotel owned by Canadian National Railways. Both Matt and Ouimet claimed credit for the next move: finding a telephone and getting through to the Resistance, popularly known as the Maquis, to ask for help. Army PR chief Dick Malone, in the same small convoy, said Matt made the call and was promised an escort to get them safely over the river.[7]

From here on, a series of events and encounters happen that Matt described as "sheer Hollywood"[8] although even by Hollywood standards they seem almost absurdly melodramatic. An hour or so after the phone call to the Maquis, a big Citroën rolled up to where the Canadians were waiting. Inside were two young *résistants* and standing on the running board was an attractive blonde wearing a white silk shirt and carrying a submachine gun on her shoulder. Her name was Christiane de Sandfort. She approached Matt, kissed him, and burst into tears, saying he was the first Allied officer in uniform she had seen. Matt described the sequel in a broadcast later that day: "They took me in their car and we drove through the wildly cheering crowds with our arms round each other. We crossed the river to the Île de la Cité, the cradle of Paris history . . . and past Notre Dame, and then up the Avenue of the Opéra to the Scribe Hotel. Here the crowds were just beginning to come into the streets, mad with happiness. My friends were shouting '*Il est Canadien!*' . . . And I knew what it was to feel like a king."[9]

At the Scribe, the CNR hotel's manager, Louis Regamey, told them the hotel had been requisitioned for the Gestapo at the outset of the Occupation and had been vacated only the previous day. He showed them the last registration card, signed by "Joachim Hugo Klapper, Obersturmbannführer," in June 1940. Unknown to the Canadian public, the Gestapo had paid rent for four years to the CNR (and indirectly to its owner, the Canadian government) in a discreetly roundabout way.[10] The Allies would now be paying the bill. Under Klapper's signature, Col. Malone scribbled "Reserved for the Canadian Army." The Scribe became the press centre not just for Canada but for all the Allied countries.

Of more immediate interest to the correspondents were the cases of champagne and cognac that Regamey ordered to be brought up from the hotel cellar. Long hidden from the Gestapo, they were opened and bottle after bottle drunk to celebrate the liberation. Soon there was more news to cheer. American troops were rolling in to support Leclerc's Free French forces. General Dietrich von Choltitz, the German governor of Paris, surrendered without obeying Berlin's order to raze the city, and De Gaulle arrived in triumph, pronouncing his famous lines from the Hotel de Ville: "*Paris! Paris outragé! Paris brisé! Paris martyrisé! Mais Paris libéré . . . avec l'appui et le concours de la France tout entière . . . de la vraie France, de la France éternelle*" (Paris! Paris outraged! Paris shattered! Paris martyred! But Paris liberated . . . with the support and concurrence of the whole of France . . . the true France, eternal France).[11]

By early evening, several other Canadian correspondents had arrived and a signals officer had set up a portable wireless transmitter on the hotel roof. That's where Matt – probably intoxicated as much by the champagne as the story – delivered what became known as his "king-for-a-day" broadcast recounting his entry into Paris. Malone later claimed that it was "a world scoop, the first broadcast out of liberated Paris."[12] But Matt may well have been beaten by CBS's Larry LeSueur, who used the Maquis' clandestine radio system to report on the liberation.[13]

A crowd that Matt estimated to number ten thousand had now gathered outside the Scribe, stretching to the great opera house half a block away. Ouimet was persuaded to appear on his fifth-floor balcony to say a few words. Then it was Matt's turn. He was led by his Maquis friends into the street and lifted to the top of a military vehicle so that more of the crowd could see him. His conducting officer, Captain Golding, described the scene as both slightly comic because Matt had been drinking and immensely moving because of what he had to say.[14] The crowd was hushed as Matt began speaking. "My French is bad but it will be good now," he said, "because I speak with my heart."[15] He talked of what it meant for him to be in Paris at one of the brightest moments in its history. Paris, he said, is more than the most beautiful city in the world. It is a symbol of democracy and freedom. Then Matt explained that his only sadness was that the Canadians who landed in Normandy were not there to share the glory. He named regiments decimated on the road between Caen and Falaise. "They liberated Paris too," he said, by their courage and sacrifice.[16] According to Golding, the crowd exploded in cheers at the end of the speech.[17] "The Parisians understood," Matt wrote later. "And when the Maquis asked for the bronze maple leaf in my cap for their archives, because I was the first Canadian they saw, I gave it to them and explained that it should represent the men on the Falaise road."[18]

Occasional sniper fire could still be heard as dusk turned to darkness on the city's first night of freedom. The carnival atmosphere of the day gave way to more intimate encounters. In astonishing numbers, Parisiennes who earlier rewarded soldiers with kisses and flowers showed their gratitude in other ways. The popular American correspondent Ernie Pyle described it crudely: "Any GI who doesn't get laid tonight is a sissy."[19] A French Red Cross official, Suzanne Torrès, put it more elegantly: *"Bien des Parisiennes ont été trop charitables pour laisser nos garçons passer, dans leur capitale, une première nuit solitaire"* (Many Parisiennes were too kind to let our boys spend their first night alone in their capital).[20] Roman Catholic church authorities in Paris were so worried by the phenomenon that they distributed pamphlets the next day cautioning young women "not to throw away your innocence in the gaiety of the Liberation. Think of your future family."[21] The caution was a night too late.

Matt too enjoyed a relationship that night but one of a longer and more romantic kind. After his speech, he returned to the Scribe with Christiane de Sandfort, the blond Maquis fighter who earlier had guided the CBC group across the city. The *Montreal Star*'s Gerald Clark, one of the later arrivals at the hotel, had a vivid memory of seeing Matt in the lobby "with a bottle in one hand and a girl in the other."[22] Christiane had been an actress before the war and active in the Resistance under the Occupation. She spoke fluent if heavily accented English and was involved in organizing escape routes for Allied airmen shot down over France. She appears to have fallen quickly and rapturously in love with Matt. "I hardly recognize myself," she wrote to him a few weeks later. "Is it possible that I (so bashful) should get so readily whirled away. . . . "[23] On that first night, they talked into the late hours in the Scribe bar. They seemed destined to become lovers even before Matt discovered that Christiane loved English poetry and could recite verse after verse of Shelley in French.

If Liberation Day was dramatic, its sequel on August 26 was no less so. Overnight, French radio announced repeatedly that General de Gaulle would parade down the Champs-Élysées and from there to Notre Dame. More than a million people lined the route when Matt, Christiane, and Col. Dick Malone set out to watch the parade. They stood in the Place de la Concorde, where so much French history had happened and was happening again. Leading the parade on foot came the tall, erect figure of de Gaulle, the self-described "instrument of France's destiny."[24] A thunderous, tearful acclamation was given the man whose political stagecraft was somehow absolving the French of the sin of collaboration. As he turned into the square, shots rang out. Thousands of people hit the ground or took cover behind Leclerc's armoured vehicles. Many panicked but De Gaulle strolled calmly to a waiting staff car and drove off to Notre Dame Cathedral.

It was then that Matt's little group seemed to enter the world of a B-movie. According to Malone's account,[25] he, Matt, and Christiane dashed into the Ministère de la Marine, a stately eighteenth-century building on the Place de la Concorde. They hoped to find shelter from the gunfire in the square. What they didn't know was that the shooting came from the same building and the nearby Hotel Crillon. Snipers – either diehard German soldiers or members of the French Milice, a pro-Nazi paramilitary unit – were on the rooftops. The three visitors were halfway up an ornate marble staircase when shots ricocheted down the stairwell and bullets from outside shattered windows near them. "We lay flat on the stairs," Matt wrote, "and tried to crawl back down to some French sailors who were shooting at the enemy. As we wriggled slowly down on our stomachs, expecting to be hit any minute, I was struck by the utter fantasy of the thing. We had come through all this, to watch Paris in one of the more tremendous and joyous days in all her history – and now we were caught in a battle . . . and I was sliding on my stomach with my friend Christiane down a staircase in the famous French Ministry of the Marine. Was this reality – or Hollywood?"[26]

One dramatic moment faded into another. In an alcove on the stairway, Christiane and the two Canadians took shelter behind a marble statue. Suddenly, a man in civilian clothes came down the steps. Malone took out his pistol and pointed it. "Shoot him!" Matt urged. But Malone didn't press the trigger. He explained later that "to simply fire directly at a man in this way seemed impossible."[27] They waited on the stairs for another half-hour until the shooting died down.

All three of them were shaken by the experience. To calm their nerves, they decided to return for a drink at the Scribe, only to witness another unsettling incident. They were drinking double cognacs at the bar when a young member of the Maquis came in, spoke briefly to Christiane, took her pistol from her handbag, and left as quickly as he came. Several minutes later shots were heard from the street. The young man reappeared and put the weapon back in the handbag. "It is nothing," said Christiane, "he saw a German disguised in civilian clothes . . . and my friend did not have a gun with him so he came in to borrow mine . . . that is all."[28]

The incident was typical of the vast settling of accounts underway across France. It was aptly named *"l'épuration sauvage"* (the savage purge) – a revival of an old French tradition of Jacobin justice. Some German soldiers were lynched or shot when they surrendered or were captured. But the wider targets of revenge were French men and women who had collaborated with the Nazis. At least nine thousand were executed by Resistance or vigilante groups, most without even a token trial. Later, when lawful trials began, almost a hundred thousand people were given sentences that ranged from five years to the death penalty.[29]

Matt wrote and broadcast about the ugly side of the Liberation as well as its glory. Several times in Paris he came across crowds hounding women whose heads were shaved. These were the women whose crime was *collaboration horizontale* – sleeping with Germans for love or money. Often they were paraded half-naked through the streets with swastikas painted on their breasts and foreheads. In Brittany earlier in the month, Matt had seen a girl having her head shaved. Somewhat naïvely, he protested that "revenge solves no problems," and was politely told to mind his own business.[30] Not even Jean-Paul Sartre, the French author/philosopher, had much effect when he condemned the practice as "medieval sadism."[31] More widely quoted was the famous actress Léonie Bathiat, better known as Arletty, who was briefly imprisoned for having an affair with a senior Luftwaffe officer. She commented defiantly that *"mon coeur est français mais mon cul est international"* (my heart is French but my ass is international).[32]

Matt spent two more days in Paris, writing about a city still celebrating amid continued violence. Because of his adventure at the Ministry of the Marine, he didn't witness the single most melodramatic incident of the Liberation: the gunfire at Notre Dame while de Gaulle attended a thanksgiving service. He did broadcast a description of the shooting given him by the American journalist Helen Kirkpatrick, who recounted how the congregation sang the "Te Deum" even as shots echoed through the cathedral.[33] Matt also reported the deadly bombing that occurred overnight. Heeding Hitler's order to destroy Paris, the Luftwaffe sent in 150 aircraft that dropped incendiary bombs on a southeast district. There were eleven hundred casualties and six hundred buildings damaged or destroyed.[34] Yet on the same day another victory parade rolled down the Champs-Elysées, prompting Matt to note the astonishing ability of Parisians to accommodate triumph and tragedy.[35]

Matt's broadcasts on the Liberation were colourful and personalized, conveying the sense of exaltation across the city. They also reflected an enthusiasm that bordered at times on the self-indulgent. In one broadcast Matt included a sound clip of Christiane, describing her as "lovely, sweet, intelligent and brave" and telling his listeners that "I'd like you to hear the voice of a woman of France." Christiane is then heard in a soft voice saying: "I do not speak English well but I want to say Vive le Canada! And I want to say that, after all our four years under the Germans, imagine that moment when I first saw liberators, and the first one I saw was your Matt Halton, now my friend for all my life."[36] Out of touch with Toronto, Matt received no immediate feedback about his Paris broadcasts. He learned only later that the CBC was delighted with his work.

On his fourth and last day in Paris, Matt delivered a strangely personal broadcast, as if speaking intimately to a friend. For some reason he apologized to his audience for not doing a better job of reporting on the Liberation. He was probably exhausted after drinking heavily, eating little, and celebrating with Christiane for a good part of the time. He was also at the emotional peak of his wartime experience. He explained on air that the Liberation in many ways was more important to him than the coming occupation of Berlin. He said it represented the triumph of the cause he had taken up against Nazi Germany more than ten years earlier, and the cause for which he had seen *résistants* in Paris and soldiers in Normandy die.[37] Like most analysts at the time (including General Montgomery), he said he believed the war might be over by Christmas.

Despite the pleasures of liberated Paris, Matt felt a strong pull to rejoin the Canadian regiments. On August 29, he returned to the front – and to the soldiers to whom he felt so connected. There is no record of how he felt about breaking away so suddenly from Christiane. But, for her at least, it was painful. She became something of a joke at the Canadian press centre in Paris where she would show up regularly to ask for news of Matt. In her letters to him, she talks of "living in a daze" and her confidence that their relationship was "already stronger than time, distance, and even war."[38] She implored him to come back soon and said she was consumed every day by thoughts of their time together.[39] One letter took on an almost maternal tinge: "I hope that you still receive good news from your family, and that you are keeping fit, and without too many drinks, eh!"[40] She thanked Matt for the letters and food parcels he sent and always signed off with "my very best kisses."

After the battle of the Falaise Gap, Canadian forces advanced rapidly toward Belgium. Their first priority was to recapture the Channel ports and drive the Germans from the "rocket coast" – the flying-bomb sites from where Hitler's V-Is were hammering England.

Matt drove back to the front along the road to Caen that held such grim memories. Wreckage littered the fields, ruined buildings jutted against the sky, and the stench of death still hung over some places. Particularly poignant for Matt were the signs put up by the provost corps only a few weeks earlier: "You can relax now and drive slowly," to indicate stretches of the road that were no longer sighted by German guns. *"You can relax now and drive slowly,"* Matt reflected. "Many relaxed beside the road. There are scores of white wooden crosses . . . [of] the men who fought without stopping since D-Day."[41]

For a while, the return to the front was easy. Canadian armoured columns were unopposed when they entered Rouen, the Norman capital. Then Dieppe, site of the disastrous Canadian raid in 1942, was taken without a shot being fired. Matt entered the town with regiments that fought in the raid and were now given the privilege of liberating it. He noted that only three hundred survivors of the Dieppe attack were there; most of the five thousand Canadians who took part in the raid had been killed, wounded, or taken prisoner.[42] Friendly crowds greeted the troops with cheers and flowers – a reception that was becoming routine in the liberated towns of France and Belgium. In Brussels, ten thousand people crowded onto the Place de Brouckère, dancing and singing with Allied soldiers. In his report that day, Matt mentioned that a band started playing "We're Going to Hang out the Washing on the Siegfried Line." At the outset of the war, it was a popular song about breaching the German defence line along the Reich's western border. At the time, Matt remarked, the song seemed a bad joke as Nazi troops rolled over Europe. But now "the long nightmare is almost over, we're hanging the washing on the Siegfried Line."[43] No one then was predicting that the nightmare would last another eight months.

On September 17, 1944, Matt and Marcel Ouimet became the first Canadian correspondents to cross into wartime Germany. A day earlier, troops of the U.S. First Army had breached the Siegfried Line near Aachen. Matt's group, including its invaluable sound engineer, Art Holmes, rode in the only jeep in a column of American heavy armour that advanced across the Belgian border. They passed through four largely deserted villages. A few civilians looked sullenly at the ground but one young German inexplicably sprang to attention when he saw the cbc jeep.[44] He may have thought the two correspondents were the commanding officers in the convoy.

For Matt, the visit was both exciting and depressing. It was six years since he was last in Germany, in a convoy of Nazi troops crossing into Czechoslovakia to occupy the Sudetenland. Now he had come full circle, entering Germany in another convoy that signalled the coming end of Hitler's Reich. In a report on the visit, he spoke of his relief on prior assignments when his train crossed the border from nearby Aachen into Belgium, and he recalled a pitiable scene of refugees being dragged off the train at the station there. He later wrote to Jean that there was nothing celebratory about his return to Germany. "I was too preoccupied with my thoughts of all that had happened, and of how I had given the best part of myself in those years to a losing cause."[45]

Two weeks later Matt was reminded of how his early warnings about the evils of the Hitler regime were disbelieved by many in Canada. He had visited and written about the Dachau concentration camp in 1933 and been accused of exaggerating its horrors. So when he was taken in a group of war correspondents to the concentration camp at Breendonk, just north of Brussels, he was shocked but not surprised at what he saw. The correspondents were shown bloodstained rooms where Jews and political prisoners had been tortured and killed. A Belgian Resistance guide explained the obscene details of the camp administration: how prisoners had to take off their clothes, ticket them, and put them on shelves, before they were strung up on the gallows. Matt wrote that Breedonk was a place of filthy memories but also one where there were signs of human courage. On the walls of cells, prisoners had carved defiant messages: "Speed the Victory," "Long Live England," "God give me strength," and "Death to the Flemish Traitors."[46] The guide told him that the chief torturer at the camp was a member of the Belgian SS. Matt ended his report by noting that "there are mad dogs in every country. The difference in Germany is that the mad dogs are in control."[47]

By late September, the Canadian press camp had moved to Boesinghe, a Belgian village once a battleground in World War One. Allied hopes of an early end to the war were shattered by the defeat of the British-led airborne assault on Arnhem in Holland. In a long, morose letter to Jean, Matt admitted to weariness with the war.

> *I am tired of going to battles. . . . I am tired in my mind. I am tired with having to associate with clodhoppers, officers who cannot form one coherent sentence in their own language, and to whom any other language is gibberish. . . . I am tired of bad manners – I am glad that I was brought up in a poor family, and therefore learned manners. I am tired of grossness, and of men who go to Lille each night to couple with whores. I am tired of sawdust sausages and bully beef stew. I am tired of wading through mud to filthy latrines, and of the rush to evacuate before I vomit. . . . I'm tired of my smelly sleeping bag, tired of my dirty clothes.*
>
> *And often, I am tired of myself, hopelessly tired of myself because I am seldom as good as I should be, seldom as disinterested as I should be, seldom as generous.*[48]

Matt's bleak mood was fed by visits to favourite regiments that he had landed with on D-Day: the Regina Rifles, Winnipeg Rifles, Chaudières, and North Shores from New Brunswick. In some units, few of the men he knew in Normandy were still there. "It's appalling," he told Jean, "all new faces, reinforcements."[49] He was haunted, he said, by a poem entitled "Lullabye for the Children of Europe":

> *Dors pour la sombre farandole*
> *Des bataillons morts et maudits.*
> *Tu peux dormir: la terre est folle*
> *C'est ta mère qui te le dit.*

(Sleep for the dark farandole
Of the dead and damned battalions.
You can sleep: the world is mad
Your mother tells you so.)*[50]

Yet the excitement of looking into what he sometimes called "the bright eyes of danger" hadn't disappeared. Matt was back at the Canadian front for the attack on Calais, where German artillery had pounded Britain's south-east coast for years. He was at forward command posts twice, watching infantry advance and the new Churchill tanks send terrifying bursts of flame into German strong points.[51] Calais fell after six days of fighting. Along the Kentish coast, parish churches offered thanksgiving to the Canadians for ending the scourge of German shelling.[52] Nastier battles lay ahead. The priority was clearing the Germans off both banks of the Scheldt Estuary so that the Allies could land vital supplies in the Belgian port of Antwerp. Matt reported on several of the initial battles for the Scheldt and broadcast from the port when its northern suburbs were still in German hands. For the next month Canadians would fight and win one of their grimmest battles of the war across the dikes and flooded fields of western Holland.

For that month, Matt's voice from the front was noticeably silent. Under heavy pressure from Ottawa and CBC management, he reluctantly agreed to return to Canada to spearhead another Victory Loan campaign.

When Matt flew home, he was at the pinnacle of his fame. He found it both flattering and troubling to discover the extent to which he had become a national celebrity. Since the Italian campaign, his voice had brought the war into the living rooms of Canadians. As his growing fan mail indicated, many thought of him as a trusted friend, almost a member of the family. Some – to his embarrassment – regarded him as a hero. In a speech to the Empire Club in Toronto, Matt acknowledged that "we war

---

* The origins of the poem are obscure. It appears to have been written by Louis Cauchois, a member of the French Resistance, and is included in *The Blood of the Poets*, an anthology of poetry about the Resistance published in Bucharest in 1946.

correspondents are over-glamourized people. We get credit very often . . .
for what someone else does."[53] It was a constant theme of his that the real
credit should go to the anonymous soldiers on the front lines.

Over the next three weeks, Matt was involved in an exhausting schedule arranged by the Seventh Victory Bond campaign. He would make two
dozen speeches in eleven cities, as well as doing interviews, CBC broadcasts, and other events to raise funds for the war effort. The victory bond
campaigns, held every six months or so, were the occasion of an outpour-
ing of patriotism. Every gimmick and every available star were used. At
one rally in 1942, the then eight-year-old Dionne quintuplets rode into
Toronto's Maple Leaf Gardens on white tricycles to sing "There'll Always
Be an England."[54] This time the child movie star Shirley Temple appeared
on Parliament Hill with Prime Minister Mackenzie King to launch the
campaign. But Matt was almost as big a draw. His speeches were publi-
cized weeks in advance, his name splashed over posters and ads with the
words "I Saw Our Boys in Action."

His fundraising events were held in theatres, civic auditoriums, and
hotels, with the exception of a mass rally on the steps of Toronto's old city
hall. In Montreal, he shared the platform with General Rod Keller, former
commander of the 3rd Division. In Vancouver, three thousand people
packed the Orpheum Theatre, where his speech was preceded by an
eighty-piece massed band and the singing of "Land of Hope and Glory."[55]
At airports and train stations across Canada, he was sometimes met by the
local mayor. Lieutenant governors and premiers attended his events and,
in Winnipeg, he was honoured by a dinner at Government House.[56] Foster
Hewitt invited him to his booth for an interview during an intermission
in *Hockey Night in Canada*. Yousuf Karsh, already famous for his portraits
of Churchill and other celebrities, asked to photograph him in Ottawa.
Whisky magnate Samuel Bronfman turned up at a reception for him in
Montreal and told him, "I like your stuff." There was laughter when Matt
replied: "I like yours too."[57]

From October to November, local reporters were waiting for Matt at
every stop on his cross-country tour. Invariably, they wanted his views on
the conscription crisis that had boiled into the biggest story of the fall.

Heavy casualties in Europe had caused a desperate need for reinforcements but there were no longer volunteers to fill the ranks. As in World War One, the issue of a compulsory draft was causing bitter debate. Old fault lines between Quebec and English Canada were breaking open. At first, Matt chose to avoid taking sides on the issue, telling disappointed reporters that he wouldn't comment. But after three weeks in Canada, he told both the *Vancouver Sun* and *Province* that he supported partial conscription of the so-called Zombies –members of the home defence units.[58] He knew it was the army's position and he knew how urgently the men were needed in Europe. Two weeks later, a reluctant Mackenzie King was persuaded to accept the compulsory draft of sixteen thousand reinforcements for overseas service.

Matt's Victory Bond speeches followed a pattern. He would start by flattering local sensibilities. Regiments in the city or province where he was speaking were singled out for praise – the Seaforths in Vancouver, the Loyal Eddies in Edmonton, and so on across the country. Then, for most of the time, he would recount his own experiences watching Canadian soldiers in combat in Italy and France. A profile of Matt in *Canadian Business* said he "thrilled audiences with glowing accounts of the valour of Canadian troops.... His speeches have the ring of authenticity and utmost sincerity."[59]

His tone was preacherly and patriotic . He recalled how his long months with Dominion troops made him prouder than ever to be Canadian. "I no longer thought, as I used to, that Canada had missed the stream of history. And I'd think . . . if Canada is as good as these men, then she's a very great country. . . . I saw that she was great on the road from Caen to Falaise. If we can be great in battle then we can be great in peace. And if we can't, we break faith not only with the dead . . . but also with our future."[60]

While avoiding any direct mention of the conscription crisis, Matt suggested there was a lesson for Canada in the way the Chaudières and the North Shores advanced together during the battle of Carpiquet. "If English-speaking Canadians and French-speaking Canadians at home could only get along together one third as well as the Chaudières and North Shores got along . . . then we'd have no worries for the peace."[61] He also referred to some of the uglier talk in English Canada about Quebec's opposition to the draft: "No matter what one's opinions about French Canada . . . nobody can say the French Canadians are taking their present attitude because of lack of guts or physical courage on the battlefield."[62]

Before ending his speeches with an appeal to buy bonds, Matt laid out proposals for the post-war world that reflected his idealism. Not only was a new and more effective League of Nations needed but an international peace force must be put in place to enforce a new reign of global order. National sovereignty, he argued, must be reconciled with some form of supra-national government empowered to police the world.[63] His proposals went considerably further than the plans for the United Nations that were already being negotiated in Washington.

At the end of the rallies, the podium would be swarmed by people wanting to meet him and get his autograph. Matt said there were three questions that he was almost always asked: "When will the war end?" to which he would reply that it might last another six months. "What should we send in our parcels?" to which he replied: chocolates, toilet paper, heavy underwear, cigarettes and, above all, letters. And "What should we do with the Germans after the war?" to which he said "Punish them, police them and educate them" but integrate them in the new Europe.[64]

All of Matt's appearances on the tour were sold out. James Ilsley, the minister of finance, wrote Matt to thank him for "the inspiration given to Canadians by your messages," which he said were a major part of the bond campaign's success that year.[65]

But there were also troubling aspects to the tour – the hundreds of letters and phone calls Matt received about men missing in action. Wives, mothers, and fathers wanted information, and sometimes comfort, from the broadcaster they had grown to trust. Some wanted to know where a soldier was buried so they could at least visualize his grave. One man, weeping at the end of the line, asked him whether his sons would come home safely. A mother who hadn't heard from her son for two months asked him if there was any chance he was still alive. Another woman wrote from North Bay that she had listened to one of his Victory Bonds broadcasts mentioning the North Shore regiment at Carpiquet. Her son was killed there but she said, "Your vivid description of the North Shore going into action on the road to Caen, the heroic effort they put forth, how they fought and died, makes me feel very proud indeed to know he was with them."[66] An Ottawa woman whose son, an officer in the Cameron Highlanders, was killed in Normandy thanked Matt for expressing "the wonderful spirit of the Canadians in action."[67] She enclosed the last letter from her son which said: "Mom's prayers are working wonders for me. . . . I hope the world realizes how good they [the Canadians] are. They are not the best trained or disciplined troops but their courage is monumental. . . . One becomes a veteran quickly in this campaign and I feel that the last fifteen days are as many years."[68]

On Remembrance Day, the CBC asked Matt to broadcast his reflections on war. It was a subject that lent itself to his emotional, moralizing approach:

> *Tonight the tides of memory come in. On the evening of September the first, I came with a British tank regiment into the town of Arras in France. We were flushed with victory. . . . The British and Canadian armies were now rushing swiftly through France and whole nations were gulping the fresh air of freedom for the first time in four years. We drove on from Arras and in a few minutes I saw what I was looking for. I saw two graceful white pylons, delicate but majestic, rising against the lowering sky, for now we were at Vimy Ridge, and the twin pylons were monuments to the Canadians who died there in the roaring glorious Easter of 1917.*
>
> *During that great advance last September, we drove in one hour through the entire depth of the frightful area where in the last war a million men of the British Empire and nearly a million and a half Frenchmen died. That bloody wasted bog.*
>
> *Arras, Ypres and Vimy Ridge . . . and now we went through in an hour almost without losing a life.*
>
> *But as I stood at Vimy Ridge . . . my thoughts went back to Normandy, to that road from Caen to Falaise, and if there were ghosts around Vimy Ridge as we swept past that day, I wonder if they were saying something like this – "Listen, what are you going to do after this war? Perhaps you're going to build a memorial twice as high as this one on the road from Caen to Falaise – to commemorate our sons, the dead*

*and damned battalions, the Black Watch and the North Nova Scotias
and the rest."*

Arras, Ypres and Vimy Ridge.

That was the anthem of the doomed youth of one generation.

*Bretteville, Caen, Tilly and Falaise – that's the anthem for the
doomed youth of another.*

"We died. Our sons died. What are you going to do?" . . .

*That's what the ghosts of Vimy Ridge might have said, it seems to
me, as our columns went hurrying toward Germany.*

*War has brought greatness to the Canadian nation. We are only
twelve millions but our name is honored throughout the world. But that
doesn't mean there's anything good about these wars in which we've lost
so much of the flower of our manpower. We have too many ghosts now
– at the foot of Vimy Ridge – but also in Normandy, Italy, Holland – and
too many ruined lives at home, too many broken-hearted women phon-
ing you and saying, "Do you know anything about my husband? He was
last seen leading his troop of tanks near Falaise."*

Too much of all that.

Splendid things come out of war but war is a thing to be ashamed of.

*Tonight, among our memories of Vimy Ridge and the other war, let's
think of what we can do to ensure that this time there won't be a third.*

This time let's not break faith.[69]

Jean accompanied Matt throughout the Canadian tour. She tried unsuccessfully to get him to ease up on the parties with friends and admirers
and the heavy drinking that inevitably followed his speeches. He would
later tell her how sorry he was to have been so often "sodden with liquor
and fatigue."[70] At the end of the tour, however, he made his usual pilgrimage to Pincher Creek and spent a week in Vancouver with Jean, Kathleen,
and me – two children who barely recognized their father. In an article on
his visit requested by *The Maple Leaf*, he recalled pretending to be a bear
and chasing his squealing, delighted children around the garden.
"Sometimes it all seemed unreal,"[71] he wrote. Mundane experiences were
now so unusual for him: "Especially that night at the hockey game in

Toronto when the Maple Leafs were playing the New York Rangers. . . .
Ten thousand people were going nuts; throwing newspapers and harder
things onto the ice; calling the ref a so-and-so every time he penalized our
side, calling him a swell guy when he put a Ranger off the ice. It was juve-
nile, but it was wonderful. Was I dreaming?"[72]

In the same article, Matt also told the troops about his speeches and
what he said to their relatives and sweethearts. "I did a lot talking," he
said. "I hope I spoke for you."[73]

16

TO BERLIN

"The sad thing, when you've spent many years campaigning, is to come back to the front and realize that you've come home."
— MATTHEW HALTON, CBC broadcast, December 1944

IN MID-DECEMBER 1944, Matt arrived in a muddy, cold press camp near Nijmegen in eastern Holland. He spent the night in his old desert sleeping bag, ate an "unspeakable sausage" for breakfast the next morning, then took off for the front. He was back in the same routine he had lived for most of the past four years. He told his driver to take him to his favourite regiments: the Regina Rifles, North Shores, and Chaudières. They drove past flooded fields, burned-out tanks, and other debris of recent battles. Soon they heard the boom of distant artillery – "the deep malison of the guns," as Matt described it.[1] He wrote Jean that his fatigue began to leave him and he felt the same excitement approaching the forward lines as he had in the past. "There was the war again and I was part of it."[2]

In fact, Canadian troops would not be involved in a major offensive for another seven weeks. After winning the long and bloody battle of the Scheldt, they were stood down for a period of relative quiet. But there were still constant patrols, frequent skirmishes, and a few sharp battles. On Christmas Day, Matt was at the front again, exhilarated to be walking through a pine forest to a machine-gun outpost four hundred yards from the Germans. Irresponsibly, a young company commander he knew asked him if he wanted to fire a few rounds at the enemy lines. Equally irresponsibly, Matt accepted. "Unfortunately," he wrote, "they emptied a few rounds back at us."[3]

Overshadowing all other news at the time was the surprise German offensive known as the Battle of the Bulge. On December 16, the Wehrmacht sent twenty divisions rolling through the hills and thick forests of the Belgian Ardennes. Its aim was to recapture Antwerp and drive a wedge between American and British forces. No Canadians were directly involved but Matt moved to the Ardennes with a Radio-Canada colleague, Benoit Lafleur, and sound engineer Lloyd Moore. Unusually for him, he didn't witness much of the fighting, which was turning into one of the bloodiest American engagements of World War Two. His report – after the German assault had already been partially blocked – described the operation as an impressive example of a still resilient German army. But he also predicted its failure and the likelihood of it being the last great German offensive of the war.[4]

New Year's 1945 was spent in Brussels, the self-proclaimed "Paris of the North." The city was now the recreation centre for the whole northwest front, much as Cairo had been for the warriors of the Eighth Army. Tens of thousands of British, Canadian, and American soldiers would come there to spend their "forty-eights," as they called their allotted forty-eight hours of leave. Expensive black market restaurants flourished. Theatrical productions were imported from London; even the famous Sadler's Wells Ballet had a long run. But it was the hundreds of bars and nightclubs ranging from classy to louche that were the main attraction for men in uniform. In a broadcast about the pleasures of the city, Matt may have shocked some of his listeners by describing a visit to a nightclub where thirty hostesses vied for the attention of a hundred or so officers, selling them overpriced champagne and bad cognac. A barefoot dancer, he recounted, did a veil dance, and "for a few hours men are far from war."[5]

While enjoying the city's offerings, Matt's greatest pleasure was reunions with old friends and fellow correspondents. His closest friends, Sean Fielding and Charlie Lynch, were sometimes in Brussels and ready for a night of roistering. On New Year's Eve, he went to a nightclub with his brother Seth, by now editor of *The Maple Leaf*, Lionel Shapiro, and

Gerry Anglin, now working for *Maclean's*. Anglin said they "got high as skunks" and were badly hung over the next morning when they met in the hotel dining room.⁶ As they were eating breakfast, a swarm of Luftwaffe aircraft flew low over the city, strafing streets and flying on to bomb the airport. The surprise attack, the last major German air operation of the war, was launched to support the Ardennes offensive. It destroyed hundreds of Allied aircraft in Holland and Belgium but failed to stave off looming defeat for the Wehrmacht.⁷

There would be few opportunities for R and R in the next four months. War correspondents were preparing to cover one of the biggest offensives of the war. Its aim was to push the Allies over the Rhine and on to final victory over Hitler's Reich. Dozens of reporters were waiting in the main Canadian press camp in a requisitioned monastery near Nijmegen. Half the building was still occupied by monks whose cowled figures cohabited uneasily with the hard-drinking, poker-playing correspondents.⁸

On February 8, 1945, Matt was at the start line of Operation Veritable, part of the great offensive assigned to the First Canadian Army.* Once again, he used the CBC's portable equipment to record the roar of battle and his own excited voice describing what he saw: "At ten o'clock, the assault formations and tanks were plunging forward in a shuddering ghastly world. One has seen this often enough and still it is appalling and wild excitement."⁹ He described some of the startling contrasts on the battlefield. The assault was led by tanks with rotating flails at their front that beat the ground to explode German mines. But right behind this new example of military technology came soldiers piped into battle the ancient way. "Incredible," Matt wrote, "the wild skirling of the bagpipes rising and falling . . . above the cannonade."¹⁰ The Canadian Army, he exulted, was finally fighting on German soil.

The mission was to capture the heavily fortified strip of German land between the Maas River and the western bank of the Rhine. Dwight

---

* At times in northwest Europe, the First Canadian Army included more foreign troops (mainly British and Polish) than Canadians. It was the only army under Canadian command in the last century.

Eisenhower, Allied Supreme Commander, later said, "Probably no assault in this war has been conducted under more appalling conditions of terrain."[11] First, the thick, heavily defended Reichswald forest had to be crossed. Then there was the countryside along the Rhine, which the Germans had flooded to slow down the Allied advance. From a position four kilometres from the river, Matt described a battle he said resembled a naval operation, noting that the Canadians were describing themselves as water rats and calling their unit commanders "first lords of the admiralty."[12]

A week after the offensive was launched, Matt moved to a forward press camp in a half-wrecked house beside the Reichswald. A Canadian artillery position was just three hundred yards away and occasionally German shells from across the Rhine would land nearby. Instead of making a two-hour drive from the press centre at Nijmegen, Matt could now get to the front in fifteen minutes. He told Jean he was taking fewer risks but still had a compulsion to visit the forward battalions "which sometimes means crawling the last 400 yards on your belly."[13] Matt was now a familiar figure to many of the soldiers. They appreciated that a well-known correspondent would share a little of their danger, if only for a few hours or so. He was even told by Army PR that several regiments complained that they hadn't had a visit from him.[14]

Matt's prominence also won him access to stories the army wasn't always happy to have broadcast. In one instance, he was invited to a roll call and pep talk for a western Canadian highland regiment coming out of battle. Its ranks had been shredded by German counterattacks. A pipe major played "Flowers of the Forest," a lament that seemed to fit the grim setting where so many men had been cut down. A company sergeant-major called the roll with many names unanswered, then the commanding officer addressed the survivors. Matt observed that "fighting men," as he liked to call them, "often don't know what the bigger picture is all about. They strain and sweat and die for the hill or farm house or the crossroads . . . and sometimes they wonder why."[15] This time, though, over the roar of artillery, the colonel said, "You know what we have lost. Let me tell you what we have achieved." He explained that the regiment's attack had secured ground vital to another Canadian unit. Then, one by one, he congratulated the rifle companies, the mortar platoon, and the signallers operating their radios under fire.[16]

Matt's generally heroic portrayal of Canadian soldiers in his broadcasts was not always matched in his letters to Jean. He told her about their systematic looting and destruction of German homes and villages as the Canadians advanced further into the Rhineland. Throughout history armies have looted, and the Second World War was no exception. In Germany, however, the Canadians were among the champions. Matt told Jean that "our troops take what they want, all they can carry . . . and what they can't carry they simply destroy for fun – dishes, glassware, pictures, furniture, houses, anything. You know nothing about the wrath of God until you see a German village we have passed through. . . . Germany is really going to be a wreck when this is over."[17] His observations in a broadcast would never have passed the censors, who allowed only a mention of "isolated" cases of looting.[18]

By the last week of February, Canadians were fighting and suffering through one of their bloodiest campaigns of the war. The main battlefield now was in and around the Hochwald, a densely wooded area that was part of the last German defence line before the Rhine. Matt wrote that "Canada will remember the road from Kleve to the Hochwald as she remembers the road from Caen to Falaise."[19] He was wrong. The Rhineland battle is not well-remembered despite being one of the biggest engagements on the Western Front and leaving more than five thousand Canadian casualties. Historian George Stanley compared it to the slogging battles of the First World War: "There was the same rain, the same mud, the same desperate resistance, the same movement by yards rather than by miles, the same exhaustion, the same weariness."[20] Outgunned and outnumbered by almost ten to one, the Germans managed to turn the Hochwald into a killing ground before being forced to retreat.

Matt made no effort to put a favourable spin on the battle. In one broadcast, he noted that Canadians were given some of the toughest assignments of the war: Falaise, the Channel ports, the Scheldt, and "now we've got the Hochwald fighting and it's as hard as anything we've had anywhere."[21] He spoke of a "regiment [that] had a bad time," of another that "had gone to ground," and of still another that "pulled back" under fire.[22] At a battalion command post under heavy mortar attack, he described the anger of a soldier who shouted (expletives probably deleted): "What the hell's happened to [our] artillery? Why don't they stomp the daylights out of those mortars."[23] At a field hospital, Matt saw a soldier trembling and sobbing but with no visible wound. The medical orderly told him the man was a stretcher-bearer who had succumbed to battle exhaustion, and "there were more and more such cases."[24]

Matt continued to be surprised by the ferocity of German resistance. His interviews with German POWs partly explained why the Wehrmacht continued fighting so well after it was clear the war was lost. SS prisoners remained fanatically loyal to Hitler. One of them told Matt, "The war isn't over while there is still one man left."[25] Other POWs said they were no longer fighting for the Nazi cause but were ready to die to defend the Fatherland.[26] Some felt that defeat would mean a Communist Germany – fears that were stoked by Nazi posters carrying the slogan "Victory or Siberia!" One officer reflected the hope that if Germany held on a little longer, divisions between the Soviets and the West might save the country. He told Matt that "Russia and the western allies will be at each other's throats before this year ends,"[27] a judgment that proved only slightly premature.

The courage of German soldiers and their determination to struggle on stood in sharp contrast to civilian attitudes. Goebbels had appealed to men, women, and children to do everything, even use their kitchen knives, to resist the invaders. Army PR took the threat seriously enough to allow correspondents the right to carry a revolver but it proved unnecessary. Driving in his jeep through dozens of German villages, Matt said he never felt in any danger and was never fired at.[28] He described the civilians he encountered as sometimes sullen but always passive. On several occasions he even requisitioned rooms in German homes and enjoyed having a German family cook for him. Correspondents were exempt from the ban on Allied soldiers fraternizing with Germans – a ban often ignored by soldiers who were friendly with children and young women. Canadian troops joked that when they used condoms, there was no direct contact and thus no fraternization with the enemy.[29]

After the German retreat from the Hochwald, Canadian and British troops battled up to the Rhine and linked up with American forces advancing from the south. The vaunted Siegfried Line was smashed and German troops driven to the east side of the river. On March 24, Matt thrilled to the sight of Allied soldiers crossing the Rhine. For him, the river was a symbol of Germany. He often recalled how as a student he had hiked along its banks with ardent young teenagers singing "Die Wacht am Rhein," the patriotic song that called on Germans to defend the Rhine. Now, if not already victims of the war, some of those men were about to become cannon fodder as an invasion army crossed the river for the first time since Napoleon. The offensive was the biggest airborne operation of the war: wave after wave of Allied transport planes and gliders dropping more than sixteen thousand paratroops behind German lines.[30] Matt watched from a church tower on the west bank, then jumped on an armoured assault craft to cross the river. The operation was so successful that Matt predicted the war would be over in weeks. He wrote in his diary that "the great sensation these days is exhilaration, not fear. How often have I dreamed of this! . . . And now here we go rolling through Germany."[31]

As the Allies drove deeper into the Reich, the human wreckage of war provided an ugly backdrop to the fighting. At first, Matt admitted to a certain vengeful satisfaction to see well-fed Germans fleeing their bombed towns and villages just as so many Nazi victims had been forced out of their homes and countries.[32] Far more troubling for him were the freed slaves from prison camps and factories that he saw almost every day. By the end of April, three million displaced persons of almost every European nationality were thronging the roads of liberated Germany. Many were emaciated; some were starving and in rags. "You wonder," Matt wrote, "if you are not back in the pages of an historical novel, back in the middle ages. Millions of men and women have been uprooted by the Germans and enslaved, and now they are moving around Germany in mobs, looting . . . or crying for home. . . . I have seen women on their knees, tears running down their cheeks, as British tanks rolled past and they knew they were free . . . and even now many of them will go back and find their homes destroyed and their families dead or gone."[33] Matt witnessed other scenes of misery. In

Bedburg, Germany's second-largest mental institution had been shelled and hundreds of its patients were wandering aimlessly nearby. Some were shrieking in terror, others dancing and laughing at their new freedom as battle raged around them. "You wondered," Matt wrote, "whether there was order or reason or sense anywhere in the world."[34]

Bewilderment turned to revulsion when he visited concentration and pow camps in northwest Germany. Near the town of Meppen, liberated by the 4th Canadian Armoured Division, there were at least eight such camps. In one of them, Matt found two thousand Russian prisoners, some of them dying. "We came too late to save them," he said in a cbc broadcast. "They're diseased and starved and beaten. They're skin and bones. Quite literally there's no flesh on them. They are just bags of bones with swollen, ghastly heads."[35] He described the apple trees in blossom around the camp and the early morning chorus of birds and said, "It seemed impossible, almost a blasphemy that birds should sing here in this country of unspeakable evil."[36] He asked a German woman standing nearby if she was surprised that the world hated her country. He received what he would find was a common response: "It's not the Germans who do things like this. It's the Nazis."[37] Other Germans ventured the equally standard view that they were ignorant of atrocities being committed. They were shocked when Matt suggested that Hitler should be locked in a concentration camp and face the same horrors.[38]

In one broadcast, he explained that he hated reporting atrocity stories because he had written so many of them since 1933. But he continued to do so to rebut those "smug souls" at home who still accused him and other reporters of exaggerating the Nazis' willingness to exterminate their enemies.[39] He was unable to get to several of the more notorious camps in the western sector – Belsen, Buchenwald, and Nordhausen – but used other sources to describe the heaps of corpses found in all of them. At a smaller concentration camp near Zutphen in Holland, Matt was with Canadian troops when they found the bodies of Dutch resistance fighters lying beside a wall spattered with blood and brains. Some of the men had been tortured before being shot. Matt said he vomited after seeing "things too horrible to describe."[40] Earlier, in Bande in Belgium, British troops showed him the bodies of thirty-four Belgian boys and men murdered by the Germans as reprisals for the killing of three German soldiers. "If you could see the pitiful young bodies," he wrote, "then you'd realize what a gang of homicidal maniacs has been let loose on Europe these last few years."[41]

By mid-April 1945, the Third Reich was falling apart. The Red Army was meeting fierce resistance but closing in on Berlin. On the western front, there were still pockets of bitter fighting, but thousands of German soldiers were surrendering every day. Matt joined Canadian forces freeing large parts of occupied Holland. Joyful scenes of cheering Dutch people in towns such as Apeldoorn mixed with grim evidence of starvation resulting from German blockades and flooding. Near his press camp, Matt was approached by a local artist wanting to exchange two of his oil paintings for food. Matt gave him as many army rations as he could, and the paintings have decorated Halton living rooms ever since.

On April 27, Matt and the CBC/Radio-Canada crew found themselves racing across central Germany to the small town of Torgau on the River Elbe. Soviet and American troops had just linked up there for the first time. Matt had probably framed his story as soon as he arrived and saw clusters of Russian and American soldiers milling around together. He found an interpreter and approached Private Trofim Kudin, unshaven and unkempt in a dirty uniform. Kudin said he had fought all the way from Stalingrad with the 58th Guards Division. Minutes later, the Russian was shaking hands with the 69th Infantry Division's Private Joseph Iannacone from Philadelphia.[42] It was the perfect scene for Matt to reflect on the future relations of the two emerging superpowers.

> *Both had astonished the world. Private Kudin and his people had . . . bled to death the greatest military machine in history. It was Kudin and company who, in Churchill's words, "tore the guts out of the German army." They did the big job. But Private Iannacone and his people had put six armies into western Europe . . . and then with the British and Canadians destroyed whole German army groups in France and Germany. . . .*
>
> *These are the two men I saw shaking hands on the Elbe.*

If these two men cling fast to each other's hands, the nightmare of war is over, in our time at least, and all is well for our children. If they let go, the future is very dark. . . .

Here on the Elbe we were watching not only the end of the German war with all its miseries, massacres and abominations. We were watching, also, the beginning of the future. Russia had marched across the horizon of history and the old order of things was over. The age in history which began when modern Europe rose from the ashes of Rome ended here on the Elbe. For good or ill, a new epoch began in human affairs. And in a few hours there with the two armies we could see both the hope for the future and the dangers.[43]

Already a small incident reflected tensions surfacing between the Allies. American soldiers told Matt of their irritation that while they allowed the Russians to come freely to their side of the Elbe, the Russians would not allow U.S. soldiers to cross in the other direction. Matt himself was denied access to the Russian side until formal ceremonies the next day.[44] Friction over control of a single river crossing foreshadowed the Iron Curtain soon to fall on a divided Europe.

Mutual suspicions were briefly put aside during ceremonies to celebrate the meeting of East and West. American soldiers and correspondents were finally allowed across a hastily constructed pontoon bridge to the Russian side of the river where a huge banner declared: "Long Live the Inviolable Anglo-American-Russian Friendship."[45] Matt and Radio-Canada's Ouimet were among the visitors. They were driven to a nearby chateau along a route lined by Red Army soldiers presenting arms as the convoy passed. At a banquet that began at noon and ended ten hours later, dozens of toasts were made by Soviet and American generals, each in Russian fashion requiring that the vodka glass be emptied in one gulp. Then lesser officers and guests were asked to toast each other as well. Red Army soldiers performed Cossack dances that were barely appreciated as people succumbed to a never-ending supply of vodka, cognac, and champagne.[46]

"Everybody was roaring drunk," Matt confided in a letter to Jean, "and I was as drunk as the rest."[47] He told her that he had fallen off a table twice as he was trying to makes speeches in German and discovered next day that he was badly bruised. In his account, there was a complete blackout in his mind about what happened during three hours of the party. But he was told later that he had joined a Russian colonel in throwing bottles of cognac at a target in the street.[48] Miraculously, a conducting officer managed to get the CBC party into a jeep at a late hour. The driver may have drunk too much himself because he promptly got lost, driving toward Berlin, unaware whether he was in Allied-occupied territory or not. Finally, the group turned back in the right direction, woke up a doubtless frightened German family, and requisitioned rooms in its home in Naumburg.[49]

The following night Matt was in Weimar, birthplace of the liberal German republic that Hitler buried in 1933. It was strangely fitting that it was here that Matt heard Hamburg radio announce the Führer's death. Of course, the announcer lied, saying Hitler had died fighting Bolshevism, not by shooting himself in the mouth in his Berlin bunker. Matt immediately went out with a colleague to get reaction from local Germans. It was after curfew, the streets were empty, so they went to the first house they came to. An older woman and her daughter who hadn't heard the news opened the door. When told about Hitler's death, the daughter "stepped back in horror as if we had uttered a blasphemy, as if we had said God was dead. 'It can't be true,' she said."[50] It was clear that she was one of those convinced Nazis who expected a miracle from Hitler until the very end. Her mother was silent for ten seconds, then began to cry, not for Hitler, she said, but because the war had taken her husband and her son.[51]

Hitler's death brought back many memories. In an article in the *Star Weekly*, Matt recalled sitting in the Sports Palace in Berlin in 1933 and listening to the almost orgiastic applause of the audience as Hitler screamed, "My Germans, follow me!"[52] He thought of the times he had sat close enough to the dictator to wish he had a bomb and the sacrificial courage to throw it. He remembered the Führer seeming almost in a trance as he emerged victorious from the Munich conference after Chamberlain's "unexampled stupidity and disgraceful poltroonery. We had just handed him Bohemia and the mastery of Europe – and as we did it we squealed, 'Peace in our time'. It has taken our best blood and oceans of tears to wash that slogan off the slate."[53] On his old pulpit again, Matt chastised governments for not having done more to stop Hitler and for casting slurs on the integrity of correspondents who wrote about Nazi crimes. One of Hitler's legacies, he concluded, was to show us that technological progress in the twentieth century had not advanced civilization: "We speak loftily of the 'dark ages' between the fall of Rome and the Renaissance. But never has there been an age as dark as this.... If there is another war on this planet, it will be waged with weapons which will not permit civilized life to go on."[54]

When Matt returned to the Canadian front, the war was in its final days. Admiral Karl Dönitz, Hitler's successor, ordered German troops to fight on, however hopeless the cause. Canadians were still being killed and wounded as they pushed toward the naval base of Wilhelmshaven on the North Sea. Matt saw his last fighting of the war with the Chaudières. He was with them when their battalion headquarters at Jemgum came under attack from air-bursting shells. Allied Typhoon aircraft screamed in low overhead but were unable to knock out the German guns. Matt was advised to leave and told he had three minutes between shell bursts to climb in his jeep and get away. As he drove off, one shell exploded only two hundred yards behind him.[55]

On the night of May 4, Matt was sitting at his typewriter at the forward press camp in Almelo on the Dutch side of the German border. He had just finished writing the opening line of his CBC broadcast: "The German war is rushing to its close but rushing is hardly the right word when every moment is too long."[56] At that moment, Bill Gilchrist of Army PR hurried up to him and said, "Matt, for us, the war is over."[57] Field Marshal Montgomery had just announced that all enemy forces in Holland, northwest Germany, and Denmark had surrendered. The ceasefire was to begin at 0800 the next morning. The Chaudières, poised to attack the town of Emden at 2300 that night, were stood down.

Over the next forty-eight hours, Matt broadcast a series of reports that were among the most moving of any he had written about the war. They were quintessentially his style: sentimental, at times melodramatic but given authenticity and power because he had lived so much of what he described. The broadcasts would long be remembered by relatives happy that separations were over and by those grieving over men who would never come home. For decades, they were a staple of CBC Remembrance Day programs. The first recording was made after a visit to the now silent front lines:

The German war is over – five little words that one hardly dares to speak. During long weary years, and during hours that seemed like years, one sometimes wondered if the carnival of death wasn't a nightmare from which one would happily awake. And now that the nightmare is over, one has to wonder if it isn't a pleasant dream from which we will wake to find the usual mad mornings of war and blood.

Young men have grown old in a morning. Gentle men have grown callous at slaughter. . . . And then someone tells you it's over and your first thought is, "No more Canadians will die." . . .

Not again in this war will Canadians huddle against the wet earth of Europe in shuddering dawns and then rise to their feet and move out into the storm of steel. Not again shall we see brave men who can stand no more. No more mounds of earth beside the road. . . . The anger of the guns has died away. . . . The scars on the body of Europe and, worse still, the scars on her soul will take many years to heal but at least the healing can begin. . . .

Today the sun rises as it hasn't risen for nearly six years and soldiers I've talked to don't quite know what to do about it. They shave and have breakfast. They clean their guns. They try to brush the mud off their clothes. They ask if there is any mail. After all, they've lived strange, dangerous lives. It's hard to believe that no shells will come screaming over. It's hard to believe that if they stand up in the open, nobody will shoot at them. Death has walked at their side. It's hard to believe for a day or two that the nightmare is over. . . .

This is Matthew Halton of the CBC speaking from Germany.[58]

In a longer broadcast later, Matt described the atmosphere when troops first learned of the ceasefire:

At one moment the voices on the Canadian Second Corps' radio sets were saying things like this: "Hello, Mike Four, hello Mike Four. This is Seagull speaking . . . There are snipers in the windmill at the crossroads. Over". "But at a quarter past ten," said the intelligence officer at Second Corps, "all the radio sets went mad with something different. 'Hello command, Hello Command. Is it true? Is it true?'"

And the word came back that it was true. No more attacks, no more guns. No more appalling splitting mornings. No more of the monstrous cannonade under which, so often, they'd gone forward with the blood pounding in their veins. And then, in a flash, silence! No more challenges in the dark. No more snipers' bullets in the dawn light. No more burial parties in the drifting smoke. No more jeep ambulances bumping down the tank tracks and the cratered roads. No more shouts of frenzy or pain. No more attacks. An enormous silence hung upon the cool spring night on Friday, May 4th. No more guns! . . .

Somewhere there is the soldier who fired the last shot at the enemy. Somewhere there is the man who pulled the lanyard of the last field gun to be fired. Somewhere there is the last man who took a prisoner. The last to take his carrier across an open field to the support of harassed friends. Somewhere there's the last man to hear the enormous crashing of a bullet in his brain and to buckle to his knees and to fall sideways in death . . . I wonder who he is?

Whoever he is, he did not live to see the triumph we saw yesterday. . . . Canadians have helped to free many countries and shed much of their choicest blood, and raised themselves in the eyes of the world to the status of a great nation.*[59]

The next four days were a hectic rush to report on surrenders in three different places. The first was in a shabby hotel in the partially wrecked

---

* Years later, Georgina Seeley, a front-line nurse, heard Matt's comment about the last Canadian to die in a repeat of the broadcast on CBC. She wrote that she was on duty in a field hospital on May 5 as the war ended. "There were 26 Canadian wounded and when I went off duty at 7 a.m. there were only 19 left. All I could think of was the arrival of those seven dreaded telegrams arriving at those seven sad homes in Canada."[60]

Dutch town of Wageningen. Matt watched General Johannes Blaskowitz, the German commander in occupied Holland, arrive in a battered Volkswagen. Blaskowitz bizarrely gave the Nazi salute to several dozen reporters, then sat down and meekly accepted the demands of Canadian general Charles Foulkes for the surrender of all German troops in occupied Holland.[61] The following day Matt travelled to Supreme Allied Headquarters in Reims for the unconditional surrender of all German forces in Europe. The Soviets complained that the agreement was not fully legitimate and persuaded the Allies to accept a second surrender ceremony in Berlin the following day. It was Matt's great luck to be chosen as one of only eight Western correspondents to cover the event.

May 8 was one of his most memorable days of the war. The reporters left Paris in an aircraft with British air marshal Arthur Tedder, SHAEF's deputy supreme commander; General Carl Spaatz, commander of U.S. Strategic Air Forces; and General de Lattre de Tassigny, commander-in-chief of the French Army. As the plane reached the Elbe, its two American fighter escorts peeled off and two Soviet fighters soared up to replace them. At Berlin's Tempelhof airport, they were greeted by the Allied anthems and a spectacular march past of ten thousand goose-stepping Soviet soldiers.[62] Unlike the low-key surrender at Reims, the ceremony in Berlin was choreographed for maximum drama.

A procession of forty cars took Allied guests and dozens of Russian officers to the Red Army headquarters in the suburb of Karlhorst. They drove through the heart of Berlin across a city that had largely ceased to exist. Years of Allied bombing – more than England suffered in the entire war[63] – and weeks of Soviet shelling had hollowed out or flattened about 40 per cent of the capital. "What we saw," Matt wrote, "is too appalling for gloating. We saw the fourth city of the world in such overwhelming ruin . . . still burning and smoking, with nothing but jagged edges of brick and stone against the lurid sky."[64] So much of Berlin had disappeared that Matt and his colleagues thought it might be impossible to rebuild.

The surrender ceremony took place just before midnight in a former German army canteen. The room was decked with flags and the banners of the Red Army. A band played patriotic music until Marshal Georgy

Zhukov, whom Matt described as one of history's most brilliant generals, entered and sat down with other Allied leaders. Then a side door opened and guards escorted the captured German generals to the table. Field Marshal Wilhelm Keitel sat defiantly in his chair, his fists clenched. Along with his military medals, he was wearing the Order of Blood that Hitler had awarded him – a message, Matt wrote, that "I come here as a Nazi as well as a Prussian."[65] When Zhukov invited him to sign the act of capitulation, Keitel imperiously signalled that they should bring the document to him. Zhukov responded sharply that he should get up and walk to the other end of the table to sign the surrender order. The commander of the once invincible Wehrmacht, later to be hanged for war crimes, obeyed. Tears were running down the cheeks of a German staff officer as Keitel signed the formal end of the Third Reich. Matt reported that the famous Soviet prosecutor Andrei Vishinsky declared that "Germany has now been torn from the pages of history."[66]

After the ceremony, the Soviets hosted a victory celebration that lasted until daybreak. As in Torgau, guests were plied with caviar and vodka, toasts raised to the Allied leaders, and pledges made to lasting friendship between East and West. Zhukov was cheered when he performed the traditional Russkaya folk dance. Even over the loud music and song, guests could hear great blasts of gunfire as drunken Russian soldiers emptied their ammunition all over Berlin.

There was no sleep for the Western reporters that night. At daybreak they were taken on a tour of what was left of the city. Putrefying bodies could still be seen in the rubble. Matt described a few old men and women, "dazed, frightened scarecrows," desperately searching for food and water.[67] Wrecked tanks were still burning, the detritus of thirteen days of ferocious battle. Famous streets were unrecognizable. The Unter den Linden, where he had watched his first, ominous parade of brownshirts and SS twelve years earlier, was lined by the skeletons of once fine buildings. The Adlon Hotel where he used to stay was in ruins. Government and embassy buildings were demolished. The lovely Tiergarten, where he once walked with Jean on crisp fall days, was stripped bare of trees. Only the Brandenburg Gate, pockmarked by artillery fire, stood more or less intact. The correspondents were allowed to walk through the ruins of Hitler's Chancellery but not into the Führerbunker. Their Soviet escorts pointed to blackened spots in the courtyard where they said the bodies of Hitler and Eva Braun, as well as the Goebbels family, were incinerated.[68]

For Matt, there was a sense of fulfilment – of a personal journey completed. He had been in Berlin at the beginning of the Nazi era. Now he was there for its demise. Hitler's "thousand-year Reich" had lasted a mere twelve years: the length of "my own vendetta against the Nazis," Matt wrote.[69] But his satisfaction was overshadowed by the fearful landscape around him. "This did look like the end of the world," he wrote.[70] He was reminded of the destructive potential of modern weapons. He had written speculatively about the atomic age, unaware that it would begin over Hiroshima three months after V-E Day. He ended one Berlin broadcast with these words: "All round us, in a hundred-square-miles of utter and appalling ruin, was the warning that friendship between East and West was no luxury but the bare necessity for the continuing life of civilization."[71]

POST-WAR

"In a sense, Matt won the war but lost the peace."
— PETER KILBURN, University of Alberta classmate

FOR MATT, THE POST-WAR YEARS MARKED a slow descent from the summit of his career. After witnessing the greatest drama of the century, reporting on peacetime issues, however important, was an anticlimax. What could match the thrill of escaping from behind enemy lines in a raging battle in the desert? Or landing on D-Day? Or liberating Paris? Or witnessing the Götterdämmerung of Hitler's empire? Canadians were turning inward, enjoying a wave of post-war prosperity. Listening to Matthew Halton's broadcasts no longer mattered as much. People would no longer flock to rallies to hear him speak. If that was a letdown for him, much more depressing was the absence of the brave new world he had dreamed of. Friends and colleagues remarked on his disillusionment with the emerging world order.[1] Nazi tyranny in Eastern Europe was replaced by Soviet tyranny. The Cold War set in under the shadow of a nuclear arms race. The United Nations showed few signs of being more effective than the League of Nations before it.

Yet on a personal level, Matt had much to celebrate. He was awarded the Order of the British Empire by King George VI for his wartime broadcasting. There were offers to him to run for parliament on both sides of the Atlantic – from the CCF in Canada and the British Liberal Party.*

But Matt accepted another offer he found much more enticing: to become the CBC's chief European correspondent, the same prized position he had held for the *Toronto Star*. Based in London, he was given a mandate to chase important news anywhere in Europe. He was again under contract, enjoying the freedom to write for any media not in direct competition with the CBC. With frequent articles for the *Star Weekly* and *Maclean's*, and regular appearances on the BBC, Matt would be among the wealthiest journalists in London.

His biggest satisfaction was being reunited with the wife he loved, the daughter he adored, and a five-year-old son he barely knew. After returning to Canada for a brief holiday, Matt brought us back to London in August 1945. With the help of an inheritance Jean had received, he bought an imposing Edwardian mansion in Hampstead, one of the city's most sought-after districts. His new home had a grand central hall, twenty-two rooms, a "butler's pantry," and a large wine cellar. On the south side, steps led down to a terraced garden with oaks and weeping willows. The house quickly became a salon for visiting Canadians and Londoners. If good food was rare under the stringent rationing of post-war Britain, there was no lack of good talk among the journalists, politicians, and war veterans who frequented the Hampstead home.

Matt settled comfortably into the city he knew intimately and where he was connected to an ever-widening circle of old and new friends. He saw a lot of Sean Fielding, his conducting officer in the desert and now editor of *The Tatler*, a fortnightly magazine of high society events and gossip. Fielding was one of the founders of the legendary Thursday Club that included Matt and two dozen other members who would meet for a weekly lunch at Wheeler's seafood restaurant in Soho. Their lunches

---

* The British offer came from Sir Archibald Sinclair, leader of the small Liberal Party, prior to the 1945 election. Matt told him, "But don't you realize that I am Labour?" To which Sinclair responded: "But we are all the same – Liberal and Labour – we all stand for the same thing."[2]

defied the austerity of post-war Britain by offering a choice of oysters, lobster, and Dover sole. A great deal of wine and brandy was consumed, leaving members in a mellow state when they adjourned, often in the early evening.

It was the membership of the Duke of Edinburgh and a talented group of mostly writers and actors that gave the Thursday Club its notoriety. Attending the club was one of Prince Philip's few opportunities to escape the stiff formality of court life and relax at a gathering of lively raconteurs.[3] The conversation was described as "generally of a high order" but tending to lapse into the bar-room variety as lunch progressed.[4] Club members included Michael Parker, the Duke's private secretary; actors Peter Ustinov and James Robertson Justice; Matt's BBC friend Wynford Vaughan Thomas; the editor of the *Daily Express*, Arthur Christiansen; the famous harmonica player Larry Adler; author Sir Compton Mackenzie; the Marquis of Milford Haven; and the society photographer Baron Nahum. Members were allowed to bring a guest. In later years, Kim Philby was an invitee before being denounced as a Soviet spy. Another guest was Aristotle Onassis, who broke the club's male-only rule by arriving with Maria Callas.[5] Guests were sometimes suspected of breaking the club's insistence on secrecy and leaking indiscretions to gossip columnists.

On one occasion, Matt invited his old friend Charlie Lynch to the club. Lynch was puzzled to see members with leather medals strung around their neck inscribed with the words "Battle of Wheeler's, 1950." The explanation centred on a particularly rowdy lunch two weeks previously. Members had decided to play a practical joke against the photographer Baron, wagering that he couldn't take a picture of the cuckoo darting out of the clock above the fireplace. To distract him, Prince Philip and two other members had obtained navy "thunder flashes" that simulated noisy explosions. On the hour, seconds before the cuckoo was to spring out, they lit the fake bombs and threw them toward the fireplace. Apparently no one had cleaned the chimney for years because the explosions blackened the room and everyone in it with soot and smoke. Restaurant patrons on floors below were terrified by the noise. Policemen rushed in, and Prince Philip was hastily smuggled out on a fire escape to avoid a royal scandal. He was pressured to withdraw from the club before Elizabeth became Queen. Lynch met him many years later and got a frosty reaction when he mentioned the Thursday Club.[6]

Rumours about wild goings-on at the Thursday Club were a regular staple of Fleet Street tabloids. The historian Max Hastings, whose father was a member, says the weekly lunches were not much more than a forum for good food and conversation "but that they all got drunk was not in doubt."[7] I remember that the only times when there was a hint of tension between Matt and Jean was when he came home mildly sozzled after a club lunch. A rare (and hilarious) photo of a Thursday Club celebration shows one member kneeling on the floor and Prince Philip seemingly in a trance.

Few North American journalists were as well qualified as Matt to explain the transformation of British society and politics after World War Two. In the general election of July 1945, the Labour Party won a landslide victory that drove Churchill and his Conservatives from office. Most Canadians (and many British) were surprised – even shocked – at the rejection of Britain's wartime hero so soon after his great triumph. But not Matt. For years, he had predicted that a socialist government was inevitable in post-war Britain and that the country would never put up with the inequality of the past. In the 1930s, he had been a familiar figure among Labour Party MPs at Westminster, interviewing opposition leaders such as Clement Attlee, Sir Stafford Cripps, and Ernest Bevin as well as dozens of back-benchers. Now Attlee was prime minister, Cripps and Bevin were in the cabinet, and his revered former professor, Harold Laski, was chairman of the Labour Party Conference. Matt had the kind of access in party circles rarely given Canadian media.

He interviewed Attlee twice for the *Star Weekly* and CBC's *Capital Report*. Sitting in the cabinet room at 10 Downing Street, Matt collected his impressions of the shy little man smoking a pipe in front of him. "In appearance he is unimposing. In personality, he is uninspiring," he wrote later.[8] But in Matt's view, he was far from being the leader cruelly described by Churchill as "a sheep in sheep's clothing." Matt found Attlee to be a man of iron resolve and gave him much of the credit for the social revolution that reshaped Britain. In just four years, Labour created a welfare state "from womb to tomb" – free health care for all, improved access to education, and a national insurance plan that made pension and unemployment benefits available to everyone. The railways, Bank of England, and mining industry were nationalized. Despite the struggling economy and drab post-war austerity, Matt reported enthusiastically about a people healthier and better off than ever. He returned to the coal mining towns of the Rhondda Valley in Wales where he had found such wretched poverty and unemployment in the 1930s. Now, he reported, "there is work, and decent pay, and . . . a new spirit."[9] Matt admitted that Labour's embrace of state planning sometimes led to over-regulation that risked stifling the small entrepreneur. But overall his judgment of the Attlee government was highly positive and reflected his own socialist leanings. "What is happening here," he wrote, "is, in my opinion, the most significant and exciting social experiment in the world."[10]

Matt also hailed the Labour government for building the Commonwealth out of a disappearing empire. Recognizing the inevitable, the Attlee government moved quickly to grant independence to Burma, India, and Pakistan and began the process of decolonization elsewhere. On *Capital Report*, Matt recalled his childhood pride looking at an atlas and seeing so much of the world coloured in the red of empire. "It has been such a marvelous story, the British Empire," he now wrote, "but it could not last forever."[11] He praised Labour's policy of "creative abdication" – offering independence to countries while maintaining ties through the Commonwealth and the Crown. Ever the idealist, he predicted that the Commonwealth would be the forum to spread British ideals of freedom and democracy. Matt was impatient with comments in the United States that Britain was now a second-tier power in decline. At heart he remained a devoted Anglophile, convinced that Britain could still play a hugely influential role in the world. "There is still moral greatness here,"[12] he insisted.

At the outset of 1948, the division of Europe into two hostile camps seemed permanent. Soviet satellite states stretched from the Baltic to the Black Sea: Poland, Hungary, Bulgaria, Romania, and the eastern zone of occupied Germany were locked into Stalin's empire. For a short while Matt hoped that Czechoslovakia might be the shining exception. Reporting from

Prague after the war, he found that Jan Masaryk, his old friend from the Czechoslovak embassy in London, was now foreign minister in a National Front government that included communists but was freely elected. Masaryk invited him to dinner in his apartment in the Czernin Palace where he lived and worked. At one point he remarked to Matt that "there won't be a good world until every man in it can say 'to hell with the government' without fear of losing his job – or his life."[13] Eighteen months later, Masaryk was dead. He had jumped or been pushed from his apartment in what was more probably a murder by Soviet agents than a suicide. Two weeks earlier, the Kremlin had organized a *coup d'état* that turned the country overnight into a police state. Hundreds of prominent anti-Communists were arrested; thousands fled. It was the second time in ten years that Matt wrote about his much-admired Czechoslovakia losing her freedom.

The threat of Soviet aggression became a constant theme of Matt's reporting as he travelled across Europe. The brutality of the Soviet coup in Prague ignited new fears of Communist expansion. In April 1948, the CBC sent him to Rome for the Italian election campaign. Europe was again spooked by war anxiety as the U.S. Seventh Fleet steamed up the Adriatic coast in a show of force. Many assumed the United States would intervene if a victory of Italy's governing coalition of Communists and socialists dragged the country into the Soviet orbit. A week before the election, Matt correctly predicted that the anti-Moscow Christian Democrats would win. He later credited the multi-million dollars in U.S. aid under the Marshall Plan for "saving Italy for the western camp."[14] But relief over the election results was quickly overtaken by a new crisis: the Soviet effort to take over a divided Berlin by blockading its road and rail access to the West. Matt lauded the Allied airlift of supplies that enabled the western zones of the city to survive, arguing that Russian expansionism had to be blocked even at the expense of war. "Along the whole vast periphery of the Soviet empire," he wrote, "Russia is pressing and probing, looking for weak points, trying to extend her frontiers and her influence."[15] Success would mean the spread of an "abominable" system of repression.

The strength of Matt's criticism of communism made the scandal that descended on him in mid-July 1948 all the more absurd. It began when

Norman Jaques, the Social Credit MP for the Alberta riding of Wetaskiwin, rose in the House of Commons to denounce Matt as a dangerous Communist. He claimed that Halton and several other CBC employees had "done their level best to wean away the loyalty of the Canadian people."[16] Without naming any sources, Jaques added that acquaintances of Matt "will admit that he is a Communist,"[17] part of a nest of subversives at the CBC. The Alberta MP, a notorious anti-Semite who once read excerpts of the Protocols of the Elders of Zion into the parliamentary record, was known as a maverick. Even so, his attack on the CBC's star correspondent brought headlines at a time when the U.S. House Committee on Un-American Activities had begun blacklisting radio commentators, Hollywood directors, and screenwriters as alleged Moscow agents.

Matt immediately denied the charges when phoned by the Canadian Press's London correspondent. His scathing comments were quoted by CP: "I have this much in common with Communists: I sympathize with the statement once made by Karl Marx: 'If only people could read!' If Mr. Jaques had ever listened to my broadcasts he could not possibly say sincerely he believed me to be a Communist. In my last Sunday talk, for example, I expressed the fear that Moscow's rejection of the Marshall plan was an indication the Russian Communists didn't even want good relations with the west and preferred chaos to world settlement."[18] He added that it was disturbing that a Canadian MP could utter such obvious untruths.

It was an ugly episode but Matt at least had the consolation of seeing newspaper editorialists spring to his defence. The conservative *Ottawa Journal* said Jaques's comments revealed "an intellectual poverty we should despise." It described Matt as "a first class reporter" who might have been a leftist but had every right to express his views without being "tagged a Red."[19] The Victoria *Daily Times* said, "Halton is too well known as a sturdy Canadian, a gifted writer and speaker and a staunch upholder of democratic traditions to suffer from criticism of this nature. Mr. Jaques has merely discredited himself. His technique is repugnant to most Canadians."[20]

Far more wounding to Matt was a scurrilous profile of him that appeared in *New Liberty*, a popular Canadian magazine at the time. It was written by Wallace Reyburn, one of the coterie of former war correspondents who felt that Matt was pretentious and not "one of the boys." Entitled "The Ego and I," the article was a collection of truths, half-truths, and fabricated quotes. Reyburn began by claiming that Matt told an un-named interviewer that he was the only journalist "giving the true picture of what is going on in Europe."[21] Not only was Matt portrayed as a self-promoter, he was also described as pompous and humourless. Reyburn was sarcastic too about his writing style: "His phrases are so threadbare that they have to be neatly turned or the worn parts would show."[22] There were also snide references to Matt's thinning hair and middle-aged stoop, and innuendoes about his drinking.

The profile did concede that its subject was a popular and respected broadcaster but that did nothing to ease Matt's fury over the article. Accustomed to putting politicians and others under critical scrutiny, journalists are often thin-skinned when they themselves are criticized or misquoted. Matt was no exception. It took some time for Jean and friends to calm him down and persuade him not to sue Reyburn. J. Douglas MacFarlane, a former editor of *The Maple Leaf,* said, "Halton was a big target for journalists," some of whom were envious of his celebrity status, talent, and income.[23] While admiring his work, MacFarlane felt that Matt did take himself too seriously.

For a decade after the war, Matt returned frequently to Germany, the country that fascinated and at times repelled him. He was in Nuremberg twice to attend sessions of the international tribunal trying Nazi war criminals. He hoped the trials would set a precedent for a future system of world justice but also expressed concern that they would be seen as "the conqueror's revenge."[24] Accompanied by Jean, he drove through Germany and Austria to report on what he called the black spring of 1946. He was exasperated by the many Germans who told him that they felt no responsibility for Hitler's crimes, but he pitied the victims of the near-famine that plagued millions of them that year. Walking through the gutted ruins of Frankfurt, he noticed a makeshift store with only one jar of oatmeal for sale and another with nothing to offer but a few turnips. Outside, a girl with a cadaverous face and rickety legs was begging from American soldiers. In one of his broadcasts, Matt mentioned a Winnipeg woman who accused him of being too sympathetic toward the Germans who, she argued, should be treated as harshly as their victims. "We are trying to save Germany for Europe," he responded. "We are trying to see if anything can be done with the twisted and tortured German soul, and we can't do anything with it if they are starving."[25]

Matt also reported on the millions of uprooted and stateless refugees – "part of the measureless upheaval of our times."[26] During the last years of the war, he had written about Jews and slave labourers freed from Nazi camps and factories. Hundreds of thousands were still on the roads out of Germany. But now he was also describing a different kind of refugee, those moving *into* Germany. These were the Volksdeutsche, ethnic Germans expelled from almost every country in east and central Europe. Some had collaborated with the Nazis and were a target of vengeful populations. Driving between Vienna and Salzburg, Matt and Jean stopped in front of a broken-down truck packed with desperate ethnic Germans from Yugoslavia. They said they had lived in Yugoslavia for eight generations but were now being ruthlessly purged. "Hitlerism has made the name of [every] German a curse," Matt wrote.[27] He estimated that about three million Volksdeutsche were affected. In fact, over the next few years, fourteen million ethnic Germans were driven out of east Europe, at least half a million dying on the way.[28] It was ethnic cleansing on a vast scale that received little or no attention in the Western press.

Apart from the Cold War, no other issue preoccupied Matt more than re-arming Germany. He was a reluctant convert to the need for it. He had seen enough of German militarism at its worst and was slow to realize that it had been largely scorched out by the war. By 1950, though, he was writing about an astonishing turnaround: the United States was leading the push for West Germany to remilitarize while many Germans were strongly opposed. For the next two years, Matt wrote scores of articles and broadcasts about the hotly debated European Defence Community (EDC), a plan that would allow a new German army to be formed under multinational EDC command. Again with some reluctance, he supported the proposal: "If the Germans are to march, better that they march at our side."[29] The EDC project was eventually vetoed by the French National Assembly but German rearmament went ahead within the newly created NATO alliance.

In London, Matt was increasingly sought after by the BBC and increasingly well-known to British audiences. He reached fifteen million listeners when he began appearing as a guest panelist on *Twenty Questions*, the radio quiz show that was the BBC's most popular program. He was also a frequent commentator on news programs such as *Topic for Tonight* and *As the World Goes By*. An internal BBC memo credited him for "a number of first-rate jobs" and recommended that he be used more frequently.[30] He was the chosen analyst on stories with a Canadian angle. He was asked to profile both Mackenzie King and External Affairs Minister Lester Pearson, and to interview Pearson on his London visits. When Princess Elizabeth and the Duke of Edinburgh departed for a Canadian tour in 1951, he was at dockside in Liverpool to co-host a live special with the BBC's star broadcaster, Richard Dimbleby. Longer and more exciting assignments followed, often co-productions with the CBC. He spent three weeks in France for a documentary on the country's post-war recovery and political paralysis. His love for exotic travel was fed by a month in Ceylon, Malaya, Hong Kong, India, and Pakistan for a broadcast that preceded the King's annual Christmas Day message to the Commonwealth.

The BBC's greatest compliment to Matt came in June 1954. The public broadcaster had begun preparing an ambitious two-hour special on the still controversial issue of whether Germany should be rearmed. Interviews were recorded with West German chancellor Konrad Adenauer, Foreign Secretary Anthony Eden, French Socialist leader François Mitterand, and dozens of other prominent political and military leaders. The BBC then cast around for a respected figure to review the arguments on both sides of the issue. It chose Matt because of his reputation and expertise on Germany. His summary of the rival arguments was rigorously impartial, masking his own reluctant support for German rearmament within the Western alliance.[31]

Even the best journalism can suffer in hindsight. In Matt's case, there was a slowness to recognize Britain's inevitable decline as a great power, and an exaggeration of the threat of reborn German nationalism. On balance, though, his work was as shrewd in predicting the trend lines of post-war Europe as it had been in forecasting pre-war developments. In 1948, two years before the creation of a common European market for coal and steel – the first major step toward a united Europe – Matt wrote about the need for a customs union and common currency. "Europe cannot tick smoothly," he wrote, "while there are sixteen different systems of tariffs and currencies, and national controls of a hundred different kinds. . . . For the trader today, Europe is a heartbreaking maze of restrictions. . . . To get on her feet and find her strength, Europe must become a federation in which men and money and goods and ideas can circulate freely. . . . There is no doubt that if Europe could create such a system . . . there would be a new flowering of the old and tortured continent."[32]

Matt was also farsighted in predicting that only General de Gaulle could rescue France from her floundering politics. After retiring in 1946, de Gaulle watched as a succession of governments – twenty in just ten years – were weakened by instability at home and wars in France's collapsing empire. Matt had met him during his London exile and again in a group of journalists in 1948. He profiled him for CBC and his print outlets, offering a fine description of him as "lofty, laconic and austere . . . the antithesis of the average Frenchman."[33] He was worried by de Gaulle's authoritarian bent but convinced that he would return to power, govern democratically, and "remove the cancer of government impotence and national indiscipline."[34] Ten years after those words were written, de Gaulle had returned to power and was carrying out the renaissance of French power and prestige that Matt had predicted. To credit him, *Maclean's* published a sketch of Halton gazing at a crystal ball with de Gaulle's face on it.[35]

No special credit is deserved for writing in early 1948, as Matt did, that Jews and Arabs would soon be at war over Palestine. As the United Nations prepared to partition the territory into an Arab and a Jewish state, a violent outcome seemed almost inevitable. But his reports on the future of the newly created Israel and its relations with Arabs pointed the way to much longer-term conflict. Matt's personal sympathies were with the Jewish cause. He had fought anti-Semitism for years and felt the enormity of the Holocaust gave the Jews a right to a national home in Israel. He was also impressed by the resolutely socialist nature of the new state and its achievements in greening the desert. However, he concluded that partition would not succeed because the Arabs rejected it and the Israelis would not be satisfied with half the land. They would want "eventually to get the whole of Palestine . . . by immigration and peaceful penetration."[36] He sympathized with the Palestinian Arabs' sense of injustice about seeing their land carved up and more than 600,000 forced to flee their homes. Looking ahead, he saw no prospect of Israeli-Palestinian peace: "I fear another tragedy is soon to be added to the sombre story of our time."[37]

Through successes and disappointments, Matt always had the steadying support of Jean. Few knew the couple as well as Sean Fielding's wife, Shena, who described Jean as "the rock upon which Matt rested his head, always dependable and always there for him."[38] In later years, my sister, Kathleen, and I marvelled that we had never heard our parents' voices raised in anger against each other. Dorothy Dew, a longtime friend who at times had stayed in our Hampstead home, said, "There was always a lovely feeling with them – not sweet and cloying. . . . You never once went into that house and felt an atmosphere of marital strain."[39] On his foreign assignments, Matt continued to write love letters to Jean and she would still reply that "I love you so very dearly" thirty years after their first meeting. Long after his death, Jean said she had "as perfect a marriage as one ever has; none of them are perfect."[40]

Matt's occasional affairs were one of the imperfections. Jean was aware of his wartime liaisons and possibly of a few fleeting dalliances while travelling afterwards. Close friends agreed that Matt's attraction to women "didn't bother her terribly much"[41] and apparently had no damaging effect on the marriage. It wasn't because Jean was passive or self-effacing. On the rare occasions when there were disagreements between them, Jean's view usually prevailed. For example, Matt – disdainful as ever about organized religion – didn't want his children to be baptized or confirmed. Jean persuaded him otherwise by arguing that religion should be part of our education.

Jean was not always successful in one important role: reining in her husband's extravagant spending. Despite his large income from radio, magazines, and newspapers, Matt was "always living on the edge of the available dough,"[42] as his friend Charlie Lynch accurately stated. He still had a taste for the best restaurants, vintage wines, and costly vacations with his family in Europe. The upkeep of the Hampstead house included an au pair girl and gardener, and my sister and I attended expensive private schools. Another drain on the budget was Matt's financial help for his family. From 1933 he sent a monthly cheque of $50 (worth about $950 in today's dollars) to his mother and father in Pincher Creek. He also helped pay university fees for his younger brothers, Seth and David, and made interest-free loans to help Jim, his older brother. Jean said Matt was both "terribly extravagant and terribly generous" – a lethal combination that sometimes left them struggling to pay bills and taxes.[43]

At the half-century mark, Matt reflected on a Britain beginning to shed its post-war blues. He noted a new self-confidence and signs of a return to relative prosperity. Food rationing continued but the shops were better stocked than they had been in ten years. The country was preparing for the Festival of Britain, a six-month celebration of British creativity in arts, sciences, and manufacturing. Matt declared that "if you can come here this year you will see Britain at her best . . . proud of her past and unafraid of the future; a country that our civilization could not well do without."[44] A Christmas Day broadcast by Matt was tinged with optimism, his script recalling his evocative essays of the 1930s:

> *There'll be damp and fog, and children shouting. There'll be roaring logs in the fireplace to ward off the winter, and the demons outside: the demons of all things undone, that one might have done, and all the mistakes and wrongs that can never be cancelled. Then, as now, there'll be the memories of other Christmases; the best and the worst. For example – your first Christmas away from the old home – that's the worst. And you try to fill in details of the first Christmas of which you have any memory – but all you can remember is being alone in a snowy silence, and hearing the water gurgling under the ice on the creek as you put on your new skates. And always, as long as there's Christmas – this year or*

in 2000 A.D. – there'll be hope, irrational if you like, of a new turning point in human affairs. . . .

Christmas, 1950; a half-way mark . . . I've heard more than one person remark that perhaps this century will be the last in one way – turbulent and bloody in the first half – but then unexpectedly peaceful and prosperous in the second half. The first half certainly has been bad enough – as if a monster chained for a long time in the cellar of the human soul had broken loose. It was to have been the century of the common man. But it produced more suffering and horror than any other period in history. . . . Yet, through all that, the spirit lived and was as strong as ever. I've seen it shining and alive in a battle on Christmas Day, when you might have expected only blasphemy. . . . [45]

In the early 1950s, the CBC in general and Matt in particular were again targeted for alleged left-wing bias. The tides of McCarthyism were spilling over the border, and the word "socialist" was becoming as pejorative as the word "Marxist" for many Canadians. This time, the attacks came from Progressive Conservative MPS as well as Social Crediters. Matt was singled out for his sympathy for social democratic movements in Europe, for his qualms about re-arming Germany, and for his support for Britain's withdrawal from India. [46] Donald Fleming, the Tory broadcasting critic, hounded the CBC to give Matt less time on *Capital Report,* the prestigious Sunday review of the week's events. The *Globe and Mail* and *Montreal Gazette* carried stories about charges that his coverage of the 1950 British election was slanted in favour of the Labour government. There was some truth to the allegations. Matt looked at the facts and interpreted and judged them. He was impressed by Labour's record in establishing a welfare state and mixed economy. He wrote favourably of the party's success in eliminating the wretched poverty of the 1930s. In his view, the Conservatives' acceptance of most of Labour's reforms was a mark of socialism's great achievement.

Matt's own socialism evolved in parallel with the Labour party's move from radicalism to a milder, left-of-centre politics. Apart from being resolutely anti-Communist, he now recognized that improved social benefits depended largely on wealth creation in the private sector. He also acknowledged that "controls, form-filling and bureaucracy" could hurt industry.[47] His politics were in line with the social democracy spreading across western Europe. But that didn't spare him from being reined in by worried CBC bureaucrats. His contributions to the daily *News Roundup* continued but his eight-minute analytical broadcasts for *Capital Report* were now limited to no more than one every three weeks. The same restrictions were clamped on his friend Don Minifie, now the CBC's Washington correspondent, and Douglas Lachance, its gifted reporter in Paris.

Matt resented the new rules and missed the freedom he once enjoyed at the *Toronto Star* to write what he wanted. In some frustration, he turned to his friend Percy Cudlipp, editor of Britain's left-wing *Daily Herald*, who offered him a weekly column. He wrote under a pseudonym (first "Gadfly" then "Vigilant") in order to avoid stirring up his critics in Canada. In the fifty or so columns published in the next eighteen months, Matt let rip some of his passionate feelings about British politics. His first sallies were written in October 1951 just before the general election that returned Winston Churchill's Conservatives to power. In one column, he cited a new study by the esteemed British sociologist Seebohm Rowntree that stated that only one in thirty-six Britons lived in extreme poverty after five years of Labour government compared to one in three in 1935. "Anyone who reads it and then votes Tory," he wrote, "is lacking in either brains or heart."[48] In another polemic, Matt took aim at Conservatives for accusing Labour of "levelling down" the British people: "This is the meanest and tawdriest thing they say. . . . What has happened in Britain in the last few years is the most phenomenal levelling up in our history. . . . The near abolition of soul-killing poverty – and it is levelling down! Food subsidies, free milk and health services that have produced the finest generation of children on earth – and the Tories call it levelling down!"[49] More occasionally, Matt would excoriate the extreme left as well. He devoted one column to "thoughtless" criticism of the United States: "On the day anti-Americanism triumphs in our counsels, the road will be laid wide open for Stalin's technique of aggression and the raw cold wind from the Steppes will blow through all our hearts. That day must not come."[50]

Matt got a closer view of Soviet aggression while reporting from Berlin in September 1953. He described sitting in a open-air café on the Kurfürstendamm in West Berlin, now a showcase of the Wirtschaftswunder, the economic miracle that lifted the West German economy from rubble to prosperity. He watched well-dressed Germans eating pastries and walking past elegant new shops and restaurants. Then, at the Potsdamer Platz, he walked into the drab Soviet sector, past a row of stone-faced Volkspolizei, the paramilitary police. Three months earlier, Soviet troops had crushed a mass uprising in East Germany – the first violent rebellion among Moscow's satellites. Dozens were killed, more than a thousand injured, and another five thousand thrown into the regime's already crowded prisons. Matt managed to interview a dissident Protestant pastor who predicted, thirty-six years prematurely, that the uprising signalled the end of Moscow's European empire.[51] The need for "man-in-the-street" quotes from East Berlin led him into a chilling if slightly comic encounter. He approached a man reading a newspaper and engaged him in conversation. When Matt suggested the Communists were largely responsible for starting the Cold War, the man suddenly said, *"Ausweis!"* (identity card). He was a plainclothes policeman who threatened to detain Matt as a foreign agent if he criticized the East German government.[52] Others he approached closed up like clams.

Matt had already witnessed other evidence of fragmentation in the Soviet bloc. The BBC sent him to Yugoslavia to produce an hour-long documentary after the country's dramatic break with Stalin's Russia. For three weeks he travelled through the six Yugoslav republics, interviewing farmers, factory workers, government ministers, and intellectuals. Milovan Djilas, then a senior official, was already denouncing Stalinism for creating a corrupt and privileged new class. He told Matt the Kremlin had produced "a robot civilization" that had largely destroyed real socialism.[53] But the highlight of Matt's program was a rare interview with Marshal Josip Broz Tito, Yugoslavia's formidable leader and wartime hero. Tito spoke of his hopes of developing a liberalized version of Communism: one that would allow profit-sharing with workers in industry, greater freedom, and more autonomy for the republics. Countries should be free, he argued, to follow independent roads to socialism. With bold words about a country that was threatening to invade Yugoslavia, Tito described Soviet communism as "a Byzantine perversion of socialism."[54] Matt concluded that Tito was "the most important heretic since Martin Luther"[55] – a man whose heresy, if it succeeded, would undermine Soviet imperialism.

By the early 1950s, Matt was so much part of the London scene that it was hard to imagine him returning to Canada. Apart from belonging to the Thursday Club, he was a member of the more sedate Savage Club, where artists, authors, and musicians met for lunch in an elegant Georgian building overlooking the Mall. Norman Depoe, then producer of CBC's *News Roundup*, said Matt was unusually well-connected. Depoe, who later became a broadcast star himself, recounted going to a garden party at the Halton home in Hampstead. "It was sort of overwhelming,"[56] he recalled, to be introduced to guests such as the BBC's Richard Dimbleby, Labour MP Tony Wedgwood Benn, Canadian high commissioner Norman Robertson, CBS correspondent Howard K. Smith, and many others. Matt was "the perfect host," Dimbleby said, "witty, informed, interested in others, of deep sympathy but determined views."[57]

For his BBC and British friends, Matt was also Mr. Canada in London. Always the patriotic Canadian, he never lost his pride in his roots in Pincher Creek. Charlie Lynch teased him that his Canadian persona was a bit hypocritical and that he had become not so much Anglicized as thoroughly "Europeanized."[58] Lynch thought that "he had created a Pincher Creek in his mind that he liked to dwell on and maybe impress people . . . like Hemingway who romanticized Idaho while enjoying the finer things of life in more agreeable places."[59] But my sister and I had no doubt that his patriotism – renewed by Canada's formidable war achievement – was deeply felt. We were made constantly aware of being Canadian and of our father's love for the foothills country of southern Alberta. Kathleen wrote later that "what was an imaginative projection of his childhood became a part of ours. When we actually went to Pincher Creek it was like coming home."[60]

Matt returned to Canada every three or four years for family vacations and lecture tours. In 1952, he welcomed a joint proposal from the CBC and

BBC to spend an extra three months in Canada producing two hour-long documentaries. The topics were hardly exciting: oil production in Alberta and the development of iron ore in Quebec and Labrador. But Matt's sense of curiosity and wonder – his "gee-whiz" enthusiasm – turned them into compelling stories. He described the huge enterprise of six thousand men building roads, airstrips, and a railway across the forbidding terrain of scrub and muskeg in northern Quebec. He went down a mine tunnel to record a commentary and mixed technical details with his impressions of the desolate beauty of the area: "the never-ending lakes and the infinite bush, the black waters . . . the silence, the distance . . ."[61] And in Alberta, six years after oil first gushed from Leduc No. 1, Matt wrote of the boom that was transforming his native province. He interviewed Premier Ernest Manning, lunched with oil millionaires at Calgary's Petroleum Club, and visited oil and gas fields from northern Alberta to the Pincher Creek area. The documentary was prescient in emphasizing the "fabulous" potential of the Athabaska oil sands. It took another fifteen years before the oil sands were in production but already Matt was predicting they would have a profound impact on Canada's economic future.[62] The programs received good reviews on both sides of the Atlantic. Governor General Vincent Massey telegraphed congratulations.

Toward the end of his visit, the CBC asked Matt to record his impressions of Canada and how it had changed. On an earlier visit in 1948, he had talked of how the country's vigour, wealth, and self-confidence stood in contrast to the depressed state of old Europe. He spoke of a country stamped by its climate and magnificent landscape but still undefined. To some of his listeners, he probably sounded condescending when he said, "The Canadian personality is not yet as interesting as its background but it will be some day."[63] His impressions hadn't greatly changed when he broadcast on the same theme after his latest visit. He talked of Canada's extraordinary good fortune and success in playing a role in the world out of all proportion to the size of its population. But he had some tough observations as well: "I've felt some complacency or smugness in the air, too . . . as if some virtue accrued to us personally because our country is so rich. It is almost as if people were thinking: 'We're wonderful guys –we've got oil!' Or nickel or uranium or iron ore. Would we still be great if, like the British, we were fifty million on a small island with nothing left but our hands and our skills?"[64]

Matt was reluctant to accept that Britain's power and prestige in the world was slowly eroding. The Queen's Coronation in 1953 was another occasion for him to celebrate British virtues. The monarchist in him was still alive. He wrote of a people "who like to think they may have before them another Elizabethan age of enterprise, daring and greatness."[65] His coverage of the Coronation, on radio and in print, used extravagant language to describe the "intricate ballet of opulent splendor and historic symbolism."[66] For Matt though, an even greater symbol of British greatness was the aging and infirm prime minister, Winston Churchill, who was rumoured to be about to resign.

When the *Star Weekly* asked him to write an obituary to have ready when Churchill died, Matt proved that he still had a magic touch with words:

> It had to come, but it is black and stunning all the same. One could have wished that the dark would never fall, because the world is a poorer place without him. It is no solace that it had to come. Winston Churchill is dead.
>
> He enriched the world with the gold coin of his genius. He enriched, and in some degree ennobled the lives of all of us who lived in his time; and he has enriched the lives of the unborn millions who will read of him down the centuries to come. Quite simply, and quite truly, he was one of the greatest men that ever lived. And now he has gone from us. He who rallied freedom when the sky was falling has gone into the halls of immortal fame. . . .
>
> This giant who was matched by fate against a giant hour . . . this many-sided lover of the great gift of life – Walter Savage Landor's words might have been written for him: he "warmed both hands before the fire of life." But he enriched mankind and perhaps saved freedom. And now he has gone – to be an inspiration and a challenge down the years to all who can respond to the good, the true and the brave.
>
> Who will ever forget those days and Churchill's leadership when Britain stood alone and liked it? Who will forget his speeches in

parliament and on the radio when he snarled defiance at the Nazis and filled Britain with laughing courage? When he spoke it was as if the long hard road had been lit up with a sudden glory. In his speeches alone – let alone his actions – he left memorials which will live as long as English is spoken. He would stand there in the characteristic pose, his jaw thrust out – the very incarnation of embattled Britain – saying words which electrified the nation and the world and were worth armies to the cause. Because of him, when the air attacks began there was courage in all hearts and victory on all lips. . . .

In those days Churchill not only reflected the tenacity and the fighting qualities of the British people: he brought them forth. Every speech was as good as a battle won. Defiant, eloquent, hopeful, slyly humorous, slashingly contemptuous, moving and noble, shirking nothing – "Come then to the task, to the battle and the toil" – his words challenged us with all the power of great leadership and with the trumpet call of great English, and moved us all to dedicated resolve.

Fate had given us the man to match the hour.[67]

It was no small irony that the obituary, one of the finest examples of his writing, was never published. Matt died almost a decade before Churchill.

DECLINE

"I felt I was watching a tragedy."

– MURIEL KELLY, family friend

NINETEEN FIFTY-SIX WAS THE KIND OF YEAR in which news people thrive. Dramatic events unfolded that would shape the rest of the century. The twentieth party congress in the Soviet Union marked the end of Stalinism. Khruschev came to London to declare a new era of peaceful relations between East and West. But there was no "peaceful co-existence" for Hungary where 2,700 freedom fighters were killed as Soviet troops crushed a national revolution. Then there was the Suez Crisis: Egypt's nationalization of the canal, which led to a disastrous invasion of the country by British, French, and Israeli forces. The crisis was largely resolved by the brilliant diplomacy of Lester Pearson – marking the zenith of Canada's influence in the post-war world. But there would be no analysis from Matt of many of the seismic shifts in world affairs that year, only a long, unexplained silence.

In his final months of reporting, nothing much on the surface appeared to have changed. He was still a conscientious worker, churning out news and interpretative broadcasts for the CBC, and writing frequently for print media. He travelled to the Gold Coast (now Ghana) to produce an acclaimed documentary for the BBC on what was about to become the first independent black dominion in the Commonwealth. He was in Geneva to watch President Eisenhower meet with the Soviet leaders and ease fears of a nuclear holocaust.

He reported from Berlin and Paris again on Germany's rearmament and integration in the NATO alliance. He even did an occasional broadcast about the oddities of British life such as the fact that the London *Times* published its "Personal" column on the front page with entries like this: "Lady Sylvia Gutts-Whytyng wishes to thank all of those who have congratulated her on the recent birth of six kittens and on the success of her memoirs."[1] He wrote about his Thursday Club's annual cricket match, played in the improbably named Essex village of Tolleshunt D'Darcy. There, the boy from Pincher Creek clowned for his friends by going to the wicket and holding his bat over his shoulder, baseball-style.[2] His professional and social life seemed on a familiar, satisfying track.

Yet his mind had moved into darker places. Matt wrote his brother Seth about his "awful dejection of the past few years" and how he wanted "another chance to do better with a life I had nearly messed up."[3] The remarks are mysterious and may reflect the romantic's tendency to over-dramatize. For my sister and me, there was no indication he was prone to depression. He was the same father who was always ready to help with our homework, take us for brisk walks on Hampstead Heath, and reward us for good marks by taking us to expensive restaurants. At the same time, Matt wrote to Lynch and Fielding, his two dearest friends, about his nostalgia for their great times together in the war and about his sense of being on a downward slope in life. He regretted not writing a second book after publishers had besieged him for a sequel to his bestselling *Ten Years to Alamein*. There were other worries: he owed the bank 700 pounds (equivalent to about $10,000 today),[4] and he was being pestered by the CBC over his large expense accounts.[5]

His producers in Toronto were worried too. Frank Peers, supervisor of the CBC's Talks and Public Affairs Department and a great admirer, said Matt felt he was losing the high profile he once had in Canada. "We were aware during his last years that he seemed to be unhappy," said Peers, "and we were afraid that he was becoming a drunk."[6] Another admirer, program organizer Marjorie McEnaney, was convinced Matt was having some kind of mid-life crisis.[7] The truth may have been more prosaic – that Matt's health was failing because of the wear and tear of the war and decades of heavy smoking and drinking. Friends and CBC staff who saw most of him in London said he was never an alcoholic. But they agreed that he drank too much for an increasingly thin body to sustain. His producer for the Canadian documentaries said Matt always carried a big bottle of vitamin B tablets that he claimed were a perfect cure for a hangover.[8] At home, it was often my duty to pour his pre-dinner drinks, usually no more than a gin and tonic or two, or a rum and lemon. I saw him "tight" on occasion but never drunk.

Television may have been another reason for Matt's growing malaise. By 1955 TV reached half the homes in Canada and CBC began pushing its foreign correspondents to produce more reports for its television newscasts. After more than a decade in radio, Matt felt uncomfortable with the new medium and its many technical demands. Michael Maclear, then a young producer for *Newsmagazine*, described filming Matt's analysis of the Bulganin/Khruschev visit to London. It took several hours under the harsh glare of camera lights before there was an acceptable take. The film kept jamming and there were sound recording problems as often happened in the early days of television. "By the end of the session," Maclear recalled, "I sensed that he wanted none of this new-fangled medium."[9] There were other factors: his physical appearance was less than impressive on camera, and his earnest, literate voice somehow didn't come across as effectively on TV as on radio. He delivered several dozen reports for television news that were solid in content but hardly memorable.

In May, Matt returned to Canada for what would be his last trip home. Encouraged by the CBC, he had agreed to do a cross-country lecture tour addressing fifteen Canadian Club audiences and half a dozen other groups. He was also to receive an honorary doctorate from his alma mater, the University of Alberta. Jean accompanied him, providing invaluable support through an exhausting schedule. There would usually be a breakfast meeting with officials, then a lunch speech, then an afternoon tea with the local chapter of the IODE, the organization whose generous scholarship had funded his London studies. Often, there would also be a dinner speech followed almost inevitably by a party in his honour put on by friends and old comrades from the regiments. "He didn't have the stamina anymore," said Hugh Morrison, his old U of A friend. At a dinner at the King Edward Hotel in Toronto, Morrison found that Matt looked "drained. . . . He was a changed man. Something had happened to him physically."[10] Like several others who met him on the tour, Morrison had a curious foreboding that he would never see Matt again.

The lecture tour was well attended and extensively reported in the press. Matt's theme was "The New Challenge from Russia." In a somewhat alarmist tone, he warned that the West was in danger of losing the battle of peaceful competition with the Soviet Union. Of particular concern to him was the fact that Russia was producing far more scientists and engineers than the United States and Britain. Eighteen months before the launch of *Sputnik*, the world's first orbiting spacecraft, Matt quoted Soviet officials predicting that the U.S.S.R. would soon be first into space. A year before the Russians launched the first intercontinental ballistic missile (ICBM), he predicted they were leading the Americans in ICBM development.[11] His assessment of Soviet technological progress was on the mark. Much less so was his observation that Russia could become "the world's mightiest industrial nation."[12]

More than 4,200 people watched Matt get his doctoral degree – so many that the U of A's Spring Convocation ceremonies had to be held in the Edmonton Gardens hockey arena. In a stirring introduction that quoted Matt's own mantra, F.M. Salter, chair of the university's English department, described Matt as an "indispensable" interpreter of world affairs who "has maintained out of soul-scarring experience that 'idealism is the only realism.'"[13] Standing in his doctoral gown before a large cluster of microphones, Matt recalled his halcyon days as a student when he felt he knew the answers to so many of the world's problems. Now, three decades later, he confessed he was far less sure of the answers. He promised the graduates he would not offer them advice, then did just that. He told them not to worry about security but to enjoy "the lovely adventure of life."[14] Too many Canadians, he said, were caught up in a disturbing growth of materialism, excited only by money, real estate, and resource booms. "If you said that, because of our wealth, the intellectual elite were growing in numbers, or that the spirit of disinterested public service, or of enlightened self-interest was developing . . . it would be more exciting, more important, and would provide more comforting evidence that we can meet the challenges ahead."[15]

In full preacherly flight now, Matt urged the students to think in terms of one world. "One world means the brotherhood of man. And I think of the implications in the phrase, 'one brotherhood of man': the intermarriage of the races; the sharing of everything. Why should 15 million Canadians have all this, in a small world, when 400 million Indians have a spoonful of millet."[16]

Many of the parents in the audience probably felt that Matt's message was naïvely idealistic. Some may even have shuddered at the thought of their sons and daughters intermarrying and sharing their wealth with other races. But Arthur Kroeger, an Alberta farmer's son who received his B.A. that day, said he was deeply inspired by the speech.[17] He went on to become one of Canada's greatest public servants.

By midsummer, Jean was convinced that Matt's health was failing. She tried unsuccessfully to persuade him to have a checkup at the Mayo Clinic where her brother-in-law was a surgeon. But Matt insisted that he was fine and would prefer to spend time with his mother and father in Pincher Creek. Local officials there insisted on their native son honouring the community with yet another speech. Otherwise, Matt's time was taken up with the usual rituals: walks along the creek; fishing expeditions and drinking with his brothers, Seth, David, and Jim; and a drive with his mother to Waterton Lakes to gaze at mountains he had climbed as a boy.

His mother, whom he cherished, worried about his gaunt face and loss of weight. She later recounted that the "dear one wasn't eating enough here to keep a bird alive."[18] She would long have a sorrowful memory of Matt's departure from the old Halton house on Charlotte Street. "If I could only forget how he held me tight and sobbed, then came back from the door and sobbed again, and said 'Mother, I'll never be so long again. I'll come back next year.'"[19]

On his return to London, Matt was quickly caught up in what became the biggest story of the year: the Suez Crisis. On July 26, Egypt's president,

Gamel Abdel Nasser, announced he was nationalizing the Suez Canal. British warships and paratroopers were soon heading to the eastern Mediterranean, and plans were laid for an attack to establish international control of the strategically vital waterway. The operation would involve British, French, and Israeli troops.

For the first three weeks of August, Matt chronicled the failing diplomatic efforts to reach a settlement with Nasser. An eight-minute analysis for CBC's *Capital Report* was as incisive as ever. He described British rights over the canal as "slender and arguable" and said "military action now would be illegal, unnecessary, and catastrophic."[20] He accurately predicted that most of the world would line up against Britain and that the use of force would stir up East-West tensions and inflame nationalism in Asia and Africa. "If Britain cannot handle the crisis successfully," he said, "she will be on her way down . . . in power and prestige."[21] And that was exactly what happened.

As tensions mounted, a twenty-four-nation conference was hastily convened in London. A proposal was agreed on for a new international agency to administer the canal. On August 23, the conference ended with Matt predicting there was little chance of Egypt accepting the proposal. Apart from the likelihood of Anglo-French military action, he warned that the crisis could drag Russia and the West into confrontation. The broadcast concluded with these words: "The feeling here tonight is that we face a very dangerous hour."[22] And then came the sign-off that Canadians had heard on countless occasions for more than a decade: "This is Matthew Halton of the CBC speaking from London." Neither Matt nor his audience knew that it would be his last broadcast.

Jean had finally succeeded in overcoming Matt's stubborn resistance to having a hospital checkup. The test results were alarming. Matt was diagnosed with a gastric ulcer that had developed into a large tumour partially blocking the entrance to his stomach. Abdominal surgery was urgently required and in the first week of September Matt went into London's St. Thomas Hospital. The operation removed part of his stomach and left him very ill for a week. He had congested lungs for several days and, apparently delirious at one point, tore off his IV tubes by mistake when there was no nurse around to replace them. Later that week, he wrote to his mother, "All is well with me, I shall soon be a new man,"[23] but neither statement proved true.

After three weeks in hospital, Matt returned home, expecting to convalesce for six weeks then return to work. From this stage on, his condition becomes something of a mystery, subject only to conjecture from friends and family. The only certainty is that Matt was a changed person. On weekends, I would return home from my boarding school in Canterbury, and my sister from Oxford University. We found our father unusually subdued as if some light had dimmed within him. Bernard Trotter, manager of the CBC's London office, came to visit and was struck by the change, saying "He was not himself."[24] Ominously his memory was now slipping. At lunch one day in early November, Muriel Kelly, a family friend, mentioned that British and French troops had invaded Port Said and taken control of the Suez Canal. She recalled her shock when Matt suddenly said, "I'm sorry but I can't remember what it is all about." Kelly said she felt that she "was witnessing a great tragedy."[25] A mind that could once recite hundreds of poems, pull dates and names from centuries of history, was now at times crashing.

On November 28, there was a cheerful gathering in the sitting room of our Hampstead home. A visiting Canadian friend was there as well as Kelly and her husband, a doctor. Matt sat in a chair with a rug over his knees, frail physically but his face animated. "He had a whisky," Kelly recalled, "and we all laughed about it and he talked and listened and was like his old self again."[26]

That night he had a stroke and was rushed back to hospital, where he drifted in and out of a coma for five days. He was unable to speak but recognized Jean occasionally and clasped her hand. Early on December 3, Matt died, at the age of fifty-two. The cause of death was described as a blood clot in the brain. But Dr. Kelly, who had watched him deteriorate over the previous months, was convinced that dementia was a factor as well, in Matt's case a condition known medically as "early onset dementia."[27] His surgeon at St. Thomas's wrote Jean that, if he had lived, "he would never be the great and famous person that he was, the true 'him', and it was merciful that he was spared any realization of this."[28]

If Matt feared his reputation was fading in his final years, he would have been astonished by the reaction to his death. As soon as the news reached Canada, CBC announcer Earl Cameron went on the air with a short bulletin: "A voice that has been familiar for many years on overseas broadcasts to Canada will be heard no more."[29] Later, the gravelly voiced Bill McNeil, another well-known announcer, opened *News Roundup* with an eloquent tribute:

"Ladies and gentlemen, a great Canadian died today. A man who hasn't actually lived in Canada except for a year here and there since 1932. Yet this man's voice and his pen are as well known here as if he'd been your next door neighbor. The man is Matthew Halton, born in Pincher Creek, Alberta, 52 years ago. . . . A great reporter, a Canadian first and always."[30] Matt's voice was then heard from his last broadcast on Suez as solemn music played in the background. An hour-long biography was aired a week later and included tributes from a dozen colleagues.

On the day after his death, almost every Canadian newspaper carried obituaries and editorials. Matt's old employer, the *Toronto Star*, saluted the correspondent "whose typewriter and voice brought the world closer to Canada."[31] The *Lethbridge Herald* said Matt wrote "with a lucid, forceful style that not infrequently packed a flash of the genius of great reporting."[32] Several newspapers noted that his voice and writing had reached into more Canadian homes than any other Canadian journalist. The *Ottawa Citizen* praised "his sympathy for the underdog, his passion for freedom, and his capacity for enthusiasm."[33] The Regina *Leader-Post* described him as a man of "deep convictions and earnest disposition" who showed bitterness on occasion but never cynicism.[34] The only hint of criticism came from Gordon Sinclair, his crusty former colleague at the *Star*. In his radio and TV column that week, Sinclair said Matt worried too much about politics "over which he had no control and little influence."[35]

Reaction in the United States and Britain testified to a reputation that shone far beyond Canada. At a meeting of the National Union of Journalists in London, regular business was interrupted as fellow reporters paid tribute.[36] The BBC described him as "one of the first and most insistent voices to awaken North America to the evils of Nazism." It said "his vivid style, his urgent, sincere voice, made him a compelling broadcaster."[37] A producer in the BBC's Talks Department said, "We all vastly admired him both as a man and a superlative professional in his chosen sphere."[38] An obituary in the *Manchester Guardian* said, "The death of Matthew Halton removes a link between this country and Canada that will not easily be replaced."[39] *The Times* of London described Matt as "a sympathetic reporter of life and public affairs in Britain" who "felt a duty, amounting almost to a mission, to interpret Britain to his countrymen."[40] The *New York Times* recorded the highlights of his career in its obit column.

Perhaps a stronger measure of Matt's impact on people was the reaction of family, friends, and listeners. Well over a thousand letters of condolence were received – hundreds by Jean in London, hundreds at CBC offices, and hundreds more at his parents' home in Pincher Creek. His brothers Seth, David, and Jimmy and his sister Annie gathered to comfort their mother, Mary Alice, who for a week was "engulfed in despair" over Matt's death.[41] His brother David commented that Matt took the affairs of the world as a personal affront so at least he would be spared seeing Britain's humiliating retreat from Suez that signalled the end of its role as a great imperial power.[42]

In London, the letters sent to Jean were a testament to both the breadth and depth of Matt's many friendships. His wartime soulmate, Charlie Lynch, was sitting in the New York office of Reuters when he heard Matt was dead. He told me he bowed his head and wept for long minutes before cabling Jean that "I loved him too and mourn with you."[43] His other closest friend, Sean Fielding, was also devastated. According to Fielding's wife, he "was never again quite the same."[44] Condolences came from his old professors, wartime comrades, Fleet Street friends, CBC colleagues, and many others. Veterans Matt had known wrote about their admiration for a man who joined them so often at the sharp edge. George Hardy, his Classics professor at the U of A, wrote of his former student's brilliance, idealism, and crusading zeal against stupidity and injustice.[45] Andrew Cowan, a former manager of CBC's London office, wrote about the delight he took in Matt's company: "his bubbling laughter, his lucid exposition, his moral wrath, his lyric descriptions and exciting reminiscences."[46] Joan Lorraine, an office assistant, broke down in tears when she learned Matt had died.

She wrote that his desk was deliberately left as it was for almost two months. His last script was in his drawer, the studio and recording time marked on the top, and a few last-minute alterations pencilled in.[47]

But it was the sense of personal loss among his listeners and readers that might have touched Matt the most. Many of them said that they had been puzzled by his long silence, especially in moments of high drama in Suez and Hungary. One fan wrote that "it was impossible to listen to his low, somewhat melancholy voice drawing vivid, sympathetic or perceptive pictures so that you almost felt you were there, without developing an affection for this man. . . . You can realize his gift when you consider that people like us [who] have never seen him, knew nothing of him personally, and yet feel as though bereft of a personal friend."[48] Another listener from Vancouver told Jean that "his voice was a comfort and his mind a guiding light. . . . It is safe to say there never was a Canadian commentator of such stature."[49] Mrs. Irene Sidam, whose son fought in the Moro River campaign, wrote that "we have CBC commentator Matthew Halton to thank for keeping us informed at this time. . . . His voice seemed a direct link with ourselves and our boys on the battlefields."[50]

The funeral was held at Golders Green Crematorium in Hampstead three days after he died. High Commissioner Norman Robertson represented the Canadian government; Charles Jennings flew from Canada for the CBC; Jack Golding, the PRO who was with him in liberated Paris, led a uniformed delegation from the Canadian armed forces. There were executives, producers, and correspondents from the BBC; at least half a dozen former war correspondents; diplomats, reporters, Eighth Army veterans, and many others. The bakery millionaire Garfield Weston, who later told Jean and her children he was confident they would carry "the same brave spirit Matt exemplified so magnificently,"[51] sat close to Matt's long-time socialist friend, Graham Spry.

Jean, mindful of Matt's dislike of religious ritual, insisted on a short, simple service. The lesson was read from the Revelation of Saint John the Divine, perhaps chosen for a verse about God's order to "Write: for these words are true and faithful." A small choir sang from the balcony. Then Sean Fielding, whom Matt liked to call his guardian angel in the desert war, delivered the eulogy. He spoke almost inaudibly, at times literally shaking with emotion.

We are here to say good bye to our friend Matthew.

I am not sure whether he would have approved. But for once he cannot say that we are coming laboriously to our point, and then demonstrate in his own lovely, lucid way that we are muddle-headed and wrong.

And that is our sorrow.

A very remarkable man has been part of our lives, and now he has gone – leaving us both richer and poorer. Richer for having known him. Poorer for having lost him. We are cast down with sorrow – and this is something Matthew understood. He knew about pain, and sorrow, and grief.

But he also knew about love and had the mystical quality of inspiring it in others. So I think he would be cross with me if we grieved too long. There are some other things about which he would be cross.

He would be cross with me if I said he was a good husband and father.

But he was.

He would be cross with me if I said he was a great reporter.

But he was.

He would be cross if I said he was a true, loyal and loving friend.

But he was.

He would be cross with me if I said he was a good soldier.

But he was.

He would be cross with me if I talked too long. So I shall not do so. I will finish now, and ask him to overlook my unsure voice and shaking hands. I loved him very much.

As the last prayer was voiced, Matt's closed oak casket slid through the door and out of sight. At that moment Jean's whole body shook violently. For my sister and me, sitting on either side of her, it was both shocking and deeply endearing. Until then, Jean had kept her emotions in tight check, and now the façade of strength had broken down, her loss laid bare.

There was never the slightest doubt that Matt's ashes would go home to Pincher Creek. On a crisp winter day he was buried in the family plot in a cemetery in view of the foothills he roamed as a boy. A dozen family members attended the ceremony, as well as a reporter from the *Pincher Creek Echo*. The reporter was probably unaware that forty years earlier a precocious twelve-year-old boy had burst into print in the *Echo* with his description of "the restful brook along the shimmering aspens."

POSTSCRIPT

"Matthew Halton, in a way, was our Ed Murrow."

– KNOWLTON NASH, former CBC anchor,
in the History Channel documentary *Dispatches from the Front*

OF ALL THE HONOURS MATT RECEIVED, none would have pleased him more than the one bestowed on the day after his funeral. On December 7, the Pincher Creek School Board voted to have its new school named after him. A year later, the Matthew Halton High School was formally opened. Ultra-modern for the time, its twenty-one classrooms, library, and auditorium reflected a prospering community far different from the pioneer village where he was born. Words from the concluding paragraph of *Ten Years to Alamein* are inscribed on a bronze plaque over the school's main entrance: "Idealism is the only realism."

Students in social studies at Matthew Halton High are almost the only students in Canada who are taught about Matt's career. In journalism schools, the correspondent once known as "Canada's Ed Murrow" rarely gets more than a passing mention. The reporter whom author Pierre Berton described as "Canada's greatest foreign correspondent"[1] has become a largely unknown figure for almost all but a dwindling number of the wartime generation.

With regard to war coverage, Berton's claim that Matt was the greatest Canadian foreign correspondent is arguable. Ross Munro of the Canadian Press was unmatched for the sheer volume of his battlefield reporting, not to mention his scoops in getting out the first stories from the Dieppe,

Sicily, and Normandy landings. But partly because of the immediacy of radio, and partly because of the vividness of Matt's war reporting, no other Canadian correspondent had the same impact at home or as large a profile internationally. As the war ended, Byng Whittaker, then a noted BBC editor and commentator, had described him as "one of the finest news broadcasters to be heard anywhere."[2] And more than three decades later, Dick Malone, the former army PR chief and later editor-in-chief of the *Globe and Mail*, reflected on the vitality and emotion of Matt's war reporting. Of his tendency to the sentimental, Malone said, "Today it might sound corny . . . but it didn't then"[3] – not when emotions were running so high in a nation at war. The citation on Matt's admission to the News Hall of Fame spoke of his "sensitive, colorful and compassionate style. . . . He took his listeners beyond the traditional boundaries of the news media."[4]

Nor is there any doubt of Matt's importance in helping to establish the CBC as a strong national institution whose preeminence in Canadian broadcasting lasted for several decades. His wartime broadcasts, along with those of Peter Stursberg and the French network's Marcel Ouimet, gave a new legitimacy to radio news. They fostered a national pride in the war effort that contributed to the self-confident Canada emerging from the conflict. A new vision was born of a country that could play a role in world affairs disproportionate to the size of its population.

Debate over whether the World War Two correspondents were propagandists for the Allied cause didn't begin until long after Matt's death. Ironically, it was his close friend, Charlie Lynch, who helped launch the debate. In *The First Casualty*, a revisionist history of war reporting, Lynch was quoted as saying, "We were a propaganda arm of our governments. At the start, the censors enforced that, but by the end of the war we were our own censors. We were cheerleaders."[5] In some respects, the charge was demonstrably true – and Matt was no exception. Like other war correspondents, he felt he was part of a crusade against one of history's most evil regimes. Accepting censorship and easing up on critical scrutiny of some military actions were considered an acceptable price to pay to help win what would later be described as "the last good war." Journalistic ethics in covering the conflict were simply not an issue at the time. Nor, in Matt's case, did he face any criticism for becoming a salesman of Victory Bonds at patriotic rallies on the home front.

The only direct attack on Matt's war reporting came more than thirty years after his death. A CBC docudrama, *The Valour and the Horror*, judged by war historians and the CBC's own ombudsman to be flawed and inaccurate in parts,[6] took issue with his description of "superb" Canadian soldiers storming the beaches on D-Day. More seriously, the program accused him of lying – falsely attributing to Matt a quote that, in fact, came from a Canadian soldier about German troops surrendering in Normandy.[7] Undoubtedly, his broadcasts, like the dispatches of other war correspondents, tended to glorify Allied victories and minimize defeats. Yet recent studies are sharply divided over whether the correspondents were more propagandists than reporters.[*] My own detailed study of Matt's broadcasts in Italy and northwest Europe found that, despite delays and omissions, they gave listeners a generally accurate picture of the war that conforms with later histories.

While his battle dispatches brought him fame, Matt's most significant achievement as a journalist was his reporting on Nazi Germany for the *Toronto Star*. The thirty-part German Series he wrote in 1933 was one of the most comprehensive and outspoken early accounts of Nazi tyranny. The Pulitzer Prize–winning American reporter Leland Stowe praised Matt for his "marked moral courage in recognizing the menace of totalitarian dictatorship and reporting it without a moment's hesitation."[8] Matt was also lauded for his clairvoyance in predicting Hitler's next moves throughout the 1930s. University of Toronto professor Harold Troper noted "the prescience of his warnings of the catastrophic consequences posed the world by Nazi militarism and racism."[9] Equally farsighted was Matt's conviction that a Second World War could be avoided if the Allies were prepared to use force against Nazi Germany at the time of the

---

* In *The Fog of War*, Mark Bourrie concludes that despite censorship "these reporters did give the Canadian public a very vivid and accurate account of the war." A contrary view by Timothy John Balzer in *The Information Front* claims that censorship turned the media watchdog into "a blind and partly deaf animal."[10]

Munich crisis or earlier. At the Nuremberg trials, field marshals Erich von Manstein and Wilhelm Keitel testified that the German army could never have won a war on two fronts in 1938 against the combined French, British, and Czech forces (not to mention the Red Army).[11]

Matt's style of writing is out of fashion now. Where today the emphasis is on cool, detached reporting, he was passionately involved in the news he considered important. Quick to wield a sword against what he felt was injustice or stupidity, Matt was often heavily editorial. He looked at the facts then made judgments about who was right or wrong on controversial subjects. It was only in the post-war period, under the constraints of CBC policy, that his reporting became more conventional and less editorial. Before then, he was rarely neutral, subscribing to the mantra of his *New York Times* colleague Herbert Matthews that "a newspaperman should work with his heart as well as his mind."[12]

Matt's death left a void in Jean's life. She had devoted her life to the man whom, in the words of a friend, had "placed her just a little above the angels."[13] She had calmed his anxieties, put up with his weaknesses, and always been his steadfast supporter. For a while after his death, she wrote that she was living in "an awful nightmare. . . . I still cannot believe Matt has really gone but I think he is just away on another assignment abroad."[14] The sight of his portable typewriter on his desk and his worn old briefcase told her otherwise. Never as sentimental as Matt, Jean nevertheless kept two mementoes in her purse for the forty-five years that remained of her life. One was the University of Alberta dance card where she had scrawled *Je t'aime* over his name. The other was a crumpled piece of paper on which Matt had copied a poem by Christina Rossetti that he sent her before landing with Canadian troops in Italy. Its last two lines read,

> *Better by far you should forget and smile*
> *Than that you should remember and be sad.*

In fact, Jean had little time to dwell on her sadness. With his usual carelessness about money, Matt left her with little to pay for hospital costs, income taxes, and outstanding bills. Because he was on contract rather than staff at the CBC, he wasn't eligible for a pension. His old friend Charles Jennings, now a corporation executive, had to fight to squeeze out a special grant from the Board of Directors of two thousand dollars. Jean found it a "pitifully small" recognition of someone who had done so much to enhance the CBC's reputation.[15] She began taking in lodgers at the Hampstead home and was soon engaged as the social secretary at Canada House, where she worked for six high commissioners from George Drew to Paul Martin Sr. She retired to Canada in 1978 and died twenty-three years later at the age of ninety-four.

My sister and I followed Matt into journalism. Both of us had observed at close hand our father's intense enthusiasm for his work and seen our home enlivened so often by scintillating characters from the press and politics. After finishing at Oxford, Kathleen worked successively for *Newsweek*, the *London Sunday Times*, and the *Observer* before writing several novels and a biography of her husband, the drama critic Kenneth Tynan.

I worked briefly for the *Calgary Herald* and *Ottawa Citizen* in an era when you still typed your stories on old Underwoods and finished the day at the nearest tavern. After a stint with the Canadian edition of *Time* magazine, I joined the CBC and spent most of the next forty years as a foreign correspondent, privileged to have that "front seat at the peep show of life" once celebrated by Matt's boyhood hero, Sir Philip Gibbs.

On June 6, 1994, I was in Normandy for a CBC fiftieth anniversary special on the D-Day landings. It was a damp day, the sun only occasionally breaking through an overcast sky. At low tide, I took a long walk across the beach near Courseulles where my father had come ashore on that most dramatic of days. Canadian veterans, alone or in small groups, were wandering along the sand. Some would pause to stare out at the grey-green Channel as if transfixed by memories. At one moment I found myself remembering a line from *Ten Years to Alamein* where Matt described a moment of high danger during an attack. "I realized intensely," he wrote, "the truth of the saying that some men live twice as long as others in the same span of years."[16] Suddenly, there were tears in my eyes, not so much of sorrow over a journey cut absurdly short but more in marvel at my father's extraordinary life.

AUTHOR'S NOTE

EVERYTHING IN THIS BIOGRAPHY is sourced to Matt's print and broad-cast journalism; his diaries, notebooks and letters; interviews with his contemporaries; and his own stories and observations that so often enliv-ened the family dinner table. I have tried scrupulously to avoid embellish-ing the book with imaginative detail, or to attribute thoughts or feelings to Matt for which there is no evidence.

Two great national institutions helped make this book possible. The Canada Council provided me with a generous grant and Library and Archives Canada (LAC) – the institutional memory of our country – was unfailingly helpful with my research.

A biography of Matthew Halton was first discussed shortly after his death. Publishers approached his two friends, Rache Lovat Dickson and Sean Fielding, but were unsuccessful in persuading them to write a memoir. Forty years later the Alberta author Kenneth Dyba took up the challenge, conducting more than ninety interviews with Matt's friends and colleagues before having to move on to other projects. Ken's inter-views were of immense value in shaping my own biography, and my thanks to him are boundless.

For years, a trove of research material was stored at the publisher Lester & Orpen Dennys, where it was meticulously sorted by Susan Burns, now my publisher's wife.

When the material was later supplemented by more letters, transcripts, and interviews and turned over to LAC, Kara Quann did an excellent job re-cataloguing the Halton archive under the able supervision of Senior Archivist Rob Fisher.

I am indebted to friends who read all or parts of the manuscript. The improvements suggested by Alan Grossman, Andrew Cohen, Charlotte Gray, Tim Cook, Paul Gaffney, Jonathan Lovat Dickson, and Rodney Moore were invaluable.

In Pincher Creek, Harvey Wuth, curator of the Kootenai Brown Pioneer Village, shared his encyclopedic knowledge of local history to my great benefit.

Layla Mashkoor did valuable work unearthing Matt's writings from a variety of media.

At the *Toronto Star*, Astrid Lange, Carol Elder, and MaryJo Lavelle gave generously of their time in tracking down photos and articles in the *Star Weekly*. I am also most grateful to Allison Lennox and Brent Michaluk at the CBC for digging out information from the corporation's archives.

Doug Pepper, my publisher at McClelland & Stewart, showed admirable patience as deadlines were stretched because of the daunting volume of research material. Apart from being a pleasure to work with, my editor, Jenny Bradshaw, provided a skilful guiding hand in trimming verbiage and sharpening the focus of the book. I am also grateful to others at M&S and Random House of Canada for their help in producing the book, notably its eagle-eyed copy editor Wendy Thomas, designer Leah Springate, production coordinator Valentina Capuani, and publicist Shona Cook.

In the course of researching and writing *Dispatches from the Front*, I have benefited from the help of scores of other people, including (in alphabetical order):

Gene Allen, Christine Anderson, Timothy John Balzer, Ted Barris, Aimé-Jules Bizimana, Cindy Boucher, Bob and Mary-Jo Burles, Nicole Chauvelle, Tamar Chute, the Hon. Joe Clark, Beth Entz, Sylvia Faoro, John Fielding, Roderick Gibbs, Barbara Gillespie, Edmund Griffiths, Naomi Griffiths, Paul Egert, Bessie Halton, Don Halton, Steve Harris, Sarah Jennings, Joan Jewell, Ruth Kereliuk, Susan Langlois, Michael Maclear, Richard MacFarlane, Jean MacNaughton, Barbara Mahoney, Jean Matheson, Richard Menkis, Birga Meyer, Gillian Wadsworth Minifie, Hugh Whitney Morrison, Jeff Noakes, Jack Ondrack, Helen Piddington, Daniel Priollet, B.J. Scott, Ellen Shoeck, Bill Silver, Peter

Smith, Zilla Soriano, Lib Spry, Peter Stursberg, Gwyn "Jocko" Thomas, Joe Thomas, Craig Thompson, Harold Troper, Bernard Trotter, Joe Turner, Lord George Weidenfeld.

Finally, I owe heartfelt gratitude to my wife, Zoya, for putting up with my long preoccupation with researching and writing this biography.

ILLUSTRATION CREDITS

All photographs are courtesy of the author, with the exception of the following. Page numbers refer to the photographic inserts.

Photo Section #1:

Page i: (middle) Courtesy of the Kootenai Brown Pioneer Village Archives. Accession # 998.102.57.

Page iii: (top left) Print Collector/Hulton Archive/Getty Images; (top right) National Geographic/Getty Images; (bottom left) City of Toronto Archives, Fonds 1244, Item 10093.

Page v: Courtesy of the *Toronto Star.*

Page vi: (bottom) Unknown/ Library and Archives Canada/ 3612992.

Page vii: (bottom) Courtesy of the *Toronto Star.*

Photo Section #2:

Page i: Courtesy of the *Toronto Star.*

Page ii: (top) Credit: Ashley and Crippen Studio/ Library and Archives Canada/ 3612981; (middle) Courtesy of the CBC.

Page iii: (top) Michael M. Dean / Canada. Dept. of National Defence / Library and Archives Canada / PA-141705; (bottom) Library and Archives Canada.

Page iv: (bottom) Hulton Archive/Getty Images

Page v: (bottom) Unknown/ Library and Archives Canada/ 3612980.

Page vi: (top) Courtesy of John Fielding.

Page vii: (top) Courtesy of the British Broadcasting Corporation; (bottom) Canadian Broadcasting Corporation / Library and Archives Canada.

Page viii: (bottom) Courtesy of the University of Alberta.

NOTES

Preface

1. Zilla Soriano, "The Theatre of War: The Shock-and-Shell Chronicles of Matthew Halton." *Ryerson Review of Journalism*, Spring 1988.
2. Charles Lynch, interview with the author. June 4, 1994.
3. Ross Harkness, *J.E. Atkinson of the Star.* Toronto: University of Toronto Press, 1963, p. 299.

Chapter 1: Shithouse Halton's Son

1. Freda Bundy, "In the Foothills of the Rockies," Archives of Kootenai Brown Pioneer Village, Pincher Creek. The "Alberta" referred to by the Marquis of Lorne was the name of the southern district of what was then the North West Territory. The province as a whole only became known as Alberta when it entered Confederation in 1905.
2. Ellen Schoeck, *I Was There: A Century of Alumni Stories About the University of Alberta, 1906–2006.* Edmonton: University of Alberta Press, 2006, p. 3.
3. Matthew Halton, letter to Jean Halton, n.d. Matt's older brother, James Halton, said both his parents worked at various times as child labourers.
4. *Prairie Grass to Mountain Pass: History of the Pioneers of Pincher Creek and District.* Pincher Creek Historical Society, 1974, pp. 49–55.
5. Isobel Hoover, letter to Kenneth Dyba, July 22, 1980. Library and Archives Canada (LAC).
6. Kenneth Dyba and Joe Thomas, interview with James Halton. Jan. 27, 1979. LAC.
7. Diana Wilson, ed., *Triumph and Tragedy in the Crowsnest Pass.* Surrey, B.C.: Heritage House Publishing Company, 2005, pp. 143–45.
8. Bundy, "In the Foothills of the Rockies." Archives of Kootenai Brown Pioneer Village, Pincher Creek.
9. Reprinted in the *Pincher Creek Echo*, May 12, 2006.
10. Anna H. Edwards, "Halton Hi-Lites." Matthew Halton High School, Spring Bulletin. Reprinted from *Pincher Creek Echo*, n.d.
11. Kenneth Dyba and Joe Thomas, interview with James Halton. Jan. 27, 1979. LAC.
12. Sir Philip Gibbs, *Adventures in Journalism.* New York: Harper and Bros, 1923, p. 2.
13. Matthew Halton, *Lethbridge Herald.* "Matt Halton Had 'Nose for News' as *Herald's* Pincher Correspondent." Fortieth Anniversary Issue, Dec. 11, 1947.
14. Wilfrid Eggleston, *Lethbridge Herald*, July 12, 1954.

15. Ibid.

16. Ibid.

17. Jean Burns, interview with the author. Aug. 13, 2006.

18. Matthew Halton, letter to Jean Campbell. Nov. 27, 1930. LAC.

19. Ibid.

20. Sam Halton, letter to Mary Alice Halton. Jan. 25, 1917. LAC.

21. Ibid.

22. Sam Halton, letter to Mary Alice Halton. June 17, 1917. LAC.

23. Matthew Halton, speech to IODE meeting, St. Paul's Church, Toronto, Nov. 11, 1940. LAC.

Chapter 2: Starting Out

1. Matthew Halton, letter to parents. Mar. 13, 1924. LAC.

2. Matthew Halton, letter to parents. Apr. 7, 1923. LAC.

3. Matthew Halton, letter to parents. Apr. 24, 1923. LAC.

4. Mary-Jo Burles, interview with the author. Aug. 12, 2006.

5. Report of Inspector of Schools. Heath Creek, Sept. 10, 1923. LAC.

6. Mary-Jo Burles, interview with the author. Aug. 12, 2006.

7. Schoeck, I Was There, p. 49.

8. Ibid., p. 55.

9. Rache Lovat Dickson, The Ante-Room. Toronto: Macmillan Company of Canada Ltd., 1959, p. 230.

10. Matthew Halton, The Dream. Student essay, London, 1930. LAC.

11. Hugh Whitney Morrison, interview with the author. June 23, 2006.

12. "Varsity's Most Unusual Character." The Gateway, Nov. 19, 1925.

13. Kenneth Dyba, interview with Walter Herbert. June 2, 1980. LAC.

14. Jean Halton, interview with the author. June 15, 2001.

15. Ibid.

16. Barbara Gillespie, interview with the author. Dec. 15, 2013.

17. Matthew Halton, letter to parents. n.d. LAC.

18. Kenneth Dyba, interview with Norman Thorardson. July 15, 1980. LAC.

19. Ibid.

20. Matthew Halton, letter to Jean Campbell, n.d. LAC.

21. Jean Campbell, letter to Matthew Halton, Aug. 8, 1926, n.d. LAC.

22. Matthew Halton, letter to Jean Campbell. Dec. 22, 1926. LAC.

23. Matthew Halton, Convocation Address, Edmonton, May 17, 1956.

24. George Hardy, A Tribute to Matthew Halton. CBC, Dec. 10, 1956.

25. Matthew Halton, editorial. The Gateway, March 22, 1929.

26. Matthew Halton, "What Is Religion?" The Gateway, Jan. 17, 1929.

27. Ibid.

28. J. Cormack, letter to the editor. The Gateway, Jan. 31, 1929.

29. Ibid.

30. Felp Priestley (using pseudonym "The Sow's Ear"), "Prophet and Loss." *The Gateway*, Feb. 21, 1929.

31. Matthew Halton, "Quaecumque Vera Again." *The Gateway*, Jan. 31, 1929.

32. Kenneth Dyba, interview with Felp Priestley. Aug. 20, 1979. LAC.

33. Matthew Halton, "Religious Discussion." *The Gateway*, Feb. 28, 1929.

34. Hugh Whitney Morrison, interview with the author. June 23, 2006.

35. Hugh Whitney Morrison, "Alberta Wins Trophy." *The Gateway*, Nov. 12, 1928.

36. Hugh Whitney Morrison, interview with the author, June 23, 2006.

37. Matthew Halton, letter to parents. April 10, 1928. LAC.

38. Matthew Halton, letter to Jean Campbell. June 25, 1928. LAC.

39. Matthew Halton, letter to Jean Campbell. n.d. LAC.

40. Matthew Halton, letter to parents. Aug. 30, 1928. LAC.

Chapter 3: To Europe

1. Matthew Halton, "Southern Alberta Student's Impressions in England." *Lethbridge Herald*, Oct. 31, 1929.

2. Matthew Halton, letter to Jean Campbell. Written aboard SS *Melita*, Sept. 30, 1929. LAC.

3. Matthew Halton, "Southern Alberta Student's Impressions in England." *Lethbridge Herald*, Oct. 31, 1929.

4. Kenneth Dyba, interview with Kathleen Gordon. Sept. 14, 1979. LAC.

5. Ibid.

6. Matthew Halton, "London and the Theatre," *Lethbridge Herald*, Mar. 7, 1931.

7. Kenneth Dyba, interview with Kathleen Gordon. Sept. 14, 1979. LAC.

8. Matthew Halton, letter to parents, Dec. 2, 1929. LAC.

9. Matthew Halton, "London's Historic River." *Lethbridge Herald*, April 12, 1930.

10. Ibid.

11. Matthew Halton, letter to Jean Campbell. Nov. 11, 1929. LAC.

12. Ibid.

13. Matthew Halton, letter to Jean Campbell. n.d. LAC.

14. Christopher Sykes, *Nancy: The Life of Lady Astor*. London: Collins, 1972.

15. Matthew Halton, letter to parents. Aug. 17, 1930. LAC.

16. Ibid.

17. Matthew Halton, "The Angel of Cliveden." *Lethbridge Herald*, Nov. 15, 1930.

18. Matthew Halton, letter to parents. n.d. LAC.

19. Ibid.

20. Matthew Halton, letter to parents. Dec. 29, 1929. LAC.

21. Matthew Halton, letter to parents. Jan. 2, 1930. LAC.

22. Matthew Halton, "On a Distant Prospect." *Lethbridge Herald*, Apr. 14, 1931.

23. Matthew Halton, "Southern Alberta Student's Impressions in England." *Lethbridge Herald*, Oct. 31, 1929.

24. Matthew Halton, "Britain's Younger Politicians." *Lethbridge Herald*, July 11, 1930.

25. Ibid.

26. Matthew Halton, "Europe: Union or Reaction." *Lethbridge Herald*, June 5, 1932.

27. Matthew Halton, "Southern Alberta Student's Impressions in England." *Lethbridge Herald*, Oct. 31, 1929.

28. Ibid.

29. Matthew Halton, "Peculiarly Un-British." *Lethbridge Herald*, May 2, 1931.

30. Matthew Halton, *Canada in Perspective. Essay – Part III*. King's College, n.d. LAC.

31. Matthew Halton, "Foreheads Villainous Low." *Lethbridge Herald*, May 2, 1931.

32. Ralph Miliband, "Harold Laski's Socialism." *The Socialist Register*, 1995, pp. 239–33. And Spartacus.schoolnet.co. I am also indebted to Arthur A. Ekirch's essay "Harold J. Laski: The Liberal Manqué or Lost Libertarian" in *The Journal of Libertarian Studies*, Vol. IV (2), Spring 1980.

33. Ibid.

34. Kenneth Dyba, interview with Jean Campbell. Sept. 8, 1979. LAC.

35. Matthew Halton, letter to Jean Campbell, Dec. 8, 1929.

36. Matthew Halton, letter to Jean Campbell. n.d. LAC.

37. Matthew Halton, letter to Jean Campbell. n.d. LAC.

38. Kenneth Dyba, interview with Jean Campbell. Sept. 25, 1979. LAC.

39. Matthew Halton, letter to Jean Campbell. n.d. LAC.

40. Ibid.

41. Matthew Halton, letter to Jean Campbell. n.d. LAC.

42. Matthew Halton, letter to Jean Campbell. June 8, 1931. LAC.

43. Matthew Halton, letter to parents. n.d. LAC.

44. Matthew Halton, "On the Way to Ypres." *Lethbridge Herald,* Nov. 8, 1930.

45. Ibid.

46. Matthew Halton, letter to parents. Aug. 28, 1930. LAC.

47. Ibid.

48. Matthew Halton, "Home Thoughts from Alsace." *Lethbridge Herald*, Nov. 13, 1930.

49. Matthew Halton, "Storm over Germany." *Lethbridge Herald*, Dec. 13, 1930.

50. Matthew Halton, "A Rhemish Miscellany." *Lethbridge Herald*, Nov. 26, 1930.

51. Matthew Halton, *Two Works of Art*. Essay. n.d. LAC.

52. Matthew Halton, "A Glance at the French." *Lethbridge Herald*, Jan. 27, 1931.

53. Matthew Halton, letter to Seth Halton. Nov. 29, 1930. LAC.

Chapter 4: A Star Rising

1. For details about Toronto, I have drawn mainly on Charis Cotter's excellent *Toronto Between the Wars* (Toronto: Firefly Books Ltd., 2004) and Mark Harrison's "Toronto: The Good, the Bad, and (Sometimes) the Ugly" (*Toronto Star Centennial Magazine*, n.d.).

2. In comparison, the *Toronto Star* today publishes just three editions.

3. Gwyn "Jocko" Thomas, interview with the author. June 13, 2006.

4. Kenneth Dyba, interview with Wilf Sanders. July 23, 1979. LAC.

5. Gwyn "Jocko" Thomas, interview with the author. June 13, 2006.

6. Kenneth Dyba, interview with Gordon Sinclair. Feb. 16, 1979. LAC.

7. Ibid.

8. Matthew Halton, letter to Jean Campbell. n.d. LAC.

9. Scott Young, *Gordon Sinclair: A Life and Then Some*. Toronto: Macmillan of Canada, 1987, p. 82.

10. Ross Harkness, *J.E. Atkinson of the Star*. Toronto: University of Toronto Press, 1963, p. 162.

11. Ibid., p. 289.

12. Pierre Berton, "The Greatest Three-Cent Show on Earth." *Maclean's*, Mar. 15, 1932.

13. Harkness, *J.E. Atkinson of the Star*, p. 276.

14. Jack Brehl, "The Titan of The Star's Newsroom." *Toronto Star*, May 18, 1992.

15. Gwyn "Jocko" Thomas, interview with the author. June 13, 2006.

16. Harkness, *J.E. Atkinson of the Star*, pp. 244–47, and J.H. Cranston, *Ink on My Fingers*. Toronto: The Ryerson Press, 1953, p. 151.

17. Gwyn "Jocko" Thomas, interview with the author. June 13, 2006.

18. John Herd Thompson and Allen Seager, *Canada 1922–1939: Decades of Discord*. Toronto: McClelland & Stewart Ltd., 1985, p. 229.

19. Kenneth Dyba, interview with Gordon Sinclair. Feb. 16, 1979. LAC.

20. Kenneth Dyba, interview with William Shields. April. 5, 1980. LAC.

21. Matthew Halton, letter to Jean Campbell. May 1932. LAC.

22. Ibid.

23. Matthew Halton, "Viscountess de Sibour near Death in China When Plane Crashes." *Toronto Star*, Apr. 29, 1932.

24. Matthew Halton, letter to Jean Campbell. May 1932.

25. Ibid.

26. Ibid.

27. Matthew Halton, "The Great Microphone Mystery." *Toronto Star Weekly*, June 18, 1932.

28. Matthew Halton, "Carla Jenssen: British Spy Extraordinary." *Toronto Star Weekly*, June 4, 1932.

29. Matthew Halton, letter to Jean Campbell. New York, May 1932.

30. Matthew Halton, "The Dance Is Nearly Over Says Alice in Wonderland." *Toronto Star*, May 4, 1932.

31. Ibid.

32. Thompson and Seager, *Canada 1922–1939*, p. 202.

33. Kenneth Dyba, interview with Bob Hill. Aug. 1979. LAC.

34. "Imperial Conference." *Time Magazine*, July 25, 1932.

35. Matthew Halton, "Duty on Lollipop Is Cut but Humbug Tariff a Snag." *Toronto Star*, July 26, 1932, and "Alice Finds More Wonders to Puzzle Her in Ottawa." *Toronto Star*, July 25, 1932.

36. Kenneth Dyba, interview with Wilfred Eggleston, June 1, 1980. LAC.

37. Ibid.

38. Harkness, *J.E. Atkinson of the Star*, p. 185.

39. Kenneth Dyba, interview with Robert Turnbull. Dec. 6, 1979. LAC.

40. Matthew Halton, "If We Can't Eat Gold What Is the Good of it All?" *Toronto Star*, Aug. 9, 1932.

41. Matthew Halton, letter to Jean Campbell. Aug. 1932. LAC.

42. Ibid.

43. Kenneth Dyba, interview with Wilfred Eggleston. June 1, 1980. LAC.

44. Kenneth Dyba, interview with Robert Turnbull. Dec. 6, 1979. LAC.

45. Matthew Halton, letter to Jean Campbell. Sept. 1, 1932. LAC.

46. *Toronto Star*, "Wedding Announcements." Sept. 15, 1932.

47. Jean Campbell, interview with the author. July 12, 1999.

48. Matthew Halton, "Can't Renege Says Hoover on Our U.S. Principles." *Toronto Star*, Nov. 1, 1932.

49. Matthew Halton, letter to his parents. n.d. LAC.

50. Matthew Halton, "U.S. Tariff Ruined World, Roosevelt Tells the Star." *Toronto Star*, Nov. 5, 1932.

51. Matthew Halton, letter to his parents. n.d. LAC.

52. Ibid.

Chapter 5: Return to Europe

1. Hugh Morrison, interview with the author. June 23, 2006.

2. Kenneth Dyba, interview with Kathleen Gordon, Sept. 14, 1979. LAC.

3. Matthew Halton, "Royal Bonds Tied Strongly When Britain Obtains Oil." *Toronto Star*, July 11, 1933.

4. Matthew Halton, "Russia Is in Earnest in Offer to Canada, Won't Fail in Payment." *Toronto Star*, Jan. 11, 1933.

5. Matthew Halton, "Bennett Sphinx-like if Russia Mentioned." *Toronto Star*, Jan. 12, 1933.

6. Matthew Halton, "Speculation Is More Heinous than Murder in the New Russia." *Toronto Star*, Feb. 9, 1933.

7. Matthew Halton, "Spend Day in Russian Home to Learn Ways of People." *Toronto Star*, Jan. 21, 1933.

8. Matthew Halton, "Russia Faces Crisis, Many Near Starvation." *Toronto Star*, July 31, 1933.

9. Matthew Halton, "Asked Only to 'Be Fair' When Given Russian Visa." *Toronto Star*, Feb. 6, 1933.

10. Matthew Halton, "Value of Rouble Varies from Nothing to Infinity." *Toronto Star*, Feb. 15, 1933.

11. Ibid.

12. Matthew Halton, "Moscow Exultant, Marks Success of Big Experiment." *Toronto Star*, Feb. 8, 1933.

13. Matthew Halton, "Lenin's Widow Not Content with Progress of Soviet Russia." *Toronto Star*, Feb. 14, 1933.

14. Ibid.

15. Matthew Halton, "Nazis Put a Price on Einstein's Head." *Toronto Star*, Sept. 12, 1933.

16. Ibid.

17. Matthew Halton, "Science Sends World Back to Middle Ages." *Toronto Star*, Nov. 15, 1934.

18. Matthew Halton, "'Almost Done' Says Scientist of Flight 20 Miles into the Air." *Toronto Star*, Jan. 26, 1934.

19. Matthew Halton, "Mussolini Gifted Madman Says Swiss Psychologist." *Toronto Star*, Oct. 18, 1935.

20. Ibid.
21. Matthew Halton, "England Captivated by Her Charm." *Star Weekly*, Nov. 7, 1936.
22. Matthew Halton, "Gielgud Is London's Idol." *Toronto Star*, May 11, 1938.
23. Ibid.
24. Matthew Halton, "Wait for Good One, Sock It: Babe Ruth's Home Run Plan." *Toronto Star*, Feb. 12, 1935.
25. Matthew Halton, "Don't Let Fear Knock Knees, Lady Lion-Tamer's Motto." *Toronto Star*, Feb. 26, 1935.
26. Matthew Halton, "Motorcycle Is Hobby of Lawrence of Arabia." *Toronto Star*, Apr. 19, 1933.
27. Matthew Halton, "'Just Wonderful' Says New Governor's Lady." *Toronto Star*, Apr. 13, 1935.
28. Matthew Halton, "Trotsky Brands Moscow Trial Major Fraud." *Toronto Star*, Aug. 22, 1936.
29. Matthew Halton, "2,000 People in Indian Jails for Years Without Trial." *Toronto Star*, Feb. 19, 1936.
30. Matthew Halton, "Lloyd George Blazing New Trail." *Toronto Star*, Mar. 11, 1935.
31. Ibid.
32. Matthew Halton, "'War Not Inevitable' Says Lloyd George." *Toronto Star*, Aug. 4, 1939.
33. Matthew Halton, "Was Once a Criminal to Want Prohibition." *Toronto Star*, Oct. 3, 1935.
34. Matthew Halton, "'No Mean City' Focuses Eyes on Slums of Glasgow." *Toronto Star*, Jan. 7, 1936.
35. Matthew Halton, "Cut Relief to Jobless March." *Toronto Star*, Feb. 22, 1934.
36. Matthew Halton, "Hell's Half Acre." *Star Weekly*, June 8, 1933.
37. Matthew Halton, "Valiant Men of Rhondda Chase Spectre of Despair." *Toronto Star*, May 9, 1934.
38. Matthew Halton, "Tyranny of the Old School Tie." *Star Weekly*, Oct. 3, 1937.
39. Matthew Halton, "Ho! For Helion Bumpstead." *Star Weekly*, June 17, 1933.
40. Matthew Halton, "No Despair in France." *Toronto Star*, June 1936.
41. Matthew Halton, "See Only France, Britain Holding Torch of Culture." *Toronto Star*, July 10, 1933.
42. William Shirer, *The Collapse of the Third Republic*. New York: Simon & Schuster, 1969, p. 219.
43. "War Torn Paris Relived Days of Bastille's Fall." *Toronto Star*, Feb. 13, 1934.
44. Matthew Halton, "Even Pacifists Go Militant as War Clouds Threaten." *Toronto Star*, Dec. 6, 1934.
45. Matthew Halton, "Japs Don't Want War But Won't Surrender Jehol Area." *Toronto Star*, Mar. 17, 1933.
46. Matthew Halton, "Even Pacifists Go Militant as War Clouds Threaten." *Toronto Star*, Dec. 6, 1934.
47. Matthew Halton, "Italians Shout 'Glory' Leaving for Africa." *Toronto Star*, Sept. 26, 1935.
48. Matthew Halton, "Canada's Stand on African War Called Timid." *Toronto Star*, Sept. 4, 1935.
49. Pierre Berton, *Marching as to War*. Toronto: Anchor Canada, 2002, p. 314.
50. Matthew Halton, "Charge Efforts to Use Mr. King as Leader in Weakening League." *Toronto Star*, May 25, 1937.
51. Carlton McNaught, *Canada Gets the News*. Toronto: The Ryerson Press, 1940, p. 143.

52. Matthew Halton, "'Deeply Touched,' Says Exile Looking for Cheaper Home." *Toronto Star*, Dec. 11, 1933.

53. Kenneth Dyba, interview with Gordon Sinclair. Feb. 16, 1979. LAC.

54. Matthew Halton, "Canada Home of Best Food and Ugliest Buildings." *Toronto Star*, Sept. 16, 1935.

55. Ibid.

56. Ibid.

Chapter 6 : "The German Series": Sounding the Alarm

1. Details of the parade are taken from several of Matt's *Toronto Star* articles, notably "Prussian Mothers Scream Battle Cry as Nazis March," Mar. 6, 1933, and "Nazis Send a Girl to Lunatic Asylum," Oct. 20, 1933.

2. Matthew Halton, "Prussian Mothers Scream Battle Cry as Nazis March," *Toronto Star*, Mar. 6, 1933.

3. Ibid.

4. Matthew Halton, *Ten Years to Alamein*. Toronto: S.J. Reginald Saunders and Company Ltd., 1944, p. 21.

5. Matthew Halton, "German Children Taught Pre-War Hate Sentiment." *Toronto Star*, Mar. 27, 1933.

6. Walter Winchell, Column for *Toronto Star*. New York, Mar. 29, 1933.

7. Harkness, *J.E. Atkinson of the Star*, p. 300.

8. Halton, *Ten Years to Alamein*, p. 24.

9. Matthew Halton, "Jews Flee to London Still Bearing Scars of Nazi Atrocities." *Toronto Star*, Apr. 10, 1933.

10. Matthew Halton, "'Jews Are Not Blameless for Scourge' Says Rabbi." *Toronto Star*, April, 29, 1933.

11. Matthew Halton, "Jews Just 'Pariah Dogs' in Germany, Rabbi Finds." *Toronto Star*, Aug. 31, 1933.

12. Barbara S. Mahoney, *Dispatches and Dictators*. Oregon: Oregon State University Press, 2002, p. 133.

13. Louis Lochner, *Always the Unexpected*. New York: The Macmillan Company, 1956, p. 252.

14. Morris Heald, *Transatlantic Vistas: American Journalists in Europe 1910–1940*. Ohio: Kent State University Press, 1988, p. 169.

15. Howard K. Smith, *Last Train from Berlin*. New York: Alfred A. Knopf, 1942, pp. 49–51.

16. Robert Dell, "General Instruction for German Propaganda Relative to North and South America." *Germany Unmasked*. London: Martin Hopkinson Ltd., 1934.

17. Matthew Halton, "German Exiles Live in Terror of Nazi Police." *Toronto Star*, Apr. 6, 1935.

18. Ernst "Putzi" Hanfstaengl, *Hitler: The Missing Years*. London: Eyre & Spottiswoode, London, 1957, pp. 276, 294.

19. Matthew Halton, "'German Citizenry War Mad' Says Halton." *Toronto Star*, Oct. 16, 1933.

20. Walter Lippmann, *New York Herald Tribune*. May 19, 1933.

21. Matthew Halton, "Germany Is Aligned Blindly, Fanatically Under Hitler's Lead." *Toronto Star*, Oct. 19, 1933.

22. Matthew Halton, "Magic Words Hitler Uses Tell Wrongs." *Toronto Star*, Sept. 16, 1933.

23. Matthew Halton, "In Fear of Assassins Hitler Always Uses Plane in His Travels." *Toronto Star*, Nov. 7, 1933.

24. Matthew Halton, "Opponents of Nazis Who State Opinions Thrown into Prison." *Toronto Star*, Oct. 21, 1933.

25. Matthew Halton, "Hitler Revives Duel to Inoculate Youth with 'Blood and Iron.'" *Toronto Star*, Oct. 31, 1933.

26. Ibid.

27. Matthew Halton, "Man Must Destroy or Perish, Germany Teaches Her Children." *Toronto Star*, Nov. 4, 1933.

28. "Banse's Book Was Official." Editorial. *Toronto Star*, Nov. 13, 1933.

29. "Banse's Book Prohibited." Editorial. *Globe*, Nov. 11, 1933.

30. Matthew Halton, "Beaten by Employees Jew Remained Silent Fearing Worse Abuse." *Toronto Star*, Oct. 27, 1933.

31. Matthew Halton, "Journalists Convinced Reichstag Was Fired By Nazi Emissaries." *Toronto Star*, Nov. 9, 1933.

32. Matthew Halton, "Beaten by Employees Jew Remained Silent Fearing Worse Abuse." *Toronto Star*, Oct. 27, 1933.

33. Matthew Halton, "'Hitler Is Paving Way for Red Revolution' Is German's Warning." *Toronto Star*, Nov. 18, 1933.

34. Matthew Halton, "Big Families Needed to Provide Warriors German Women Told." *Toronto Star*, Nov. 6, 1933.

35. Matthew Halton, "'God Bless Our Battle' Every German Is Compelled to Pray." *Toronto Star*, Nov. 2, 1933.

36. Matthew Halton, "Big Families Needed to Provide Warriors German Women Told." *Toronto Star*, Nov. 6, 1933.

37. Matthew Halton, "'We'll Smash France' Chant Nazi Troops." *Toronto Star*, Nov. 1, 1933.

38. Ibid.

39. Halton, *Ten Years to Alamein*, p. 28.

40. Ibid., p. 29.

41. Lagerordnung (Disciplinary and Penal Code), Dachau Concentration Camp, October 1, 1933. Articles 8–16.

42. Matthew Halton, "Big Families Needed to Provide Warriors German Women Told." *Toronto Star*, Nov. 6, 1933.

43. Matthew Halton, "'Hitler Is Paving Way for Red Revolution' Is German's Warning." *Toronto Star*, Nov. 18, 1933.

44. Ibid.

45. "Halton Revelations Editorially Lauded." Reprinted in the *Toronto Star*, Nov. 28, 1933.

46. Thompson and Seager, *Canada 1922–1939*, p. 322.

47. *Mail and Empire*. Editorial. Toronto, Jan. 11, 1934.

48. *Montreal Gazette*. Editorial. Montreal, Aug. 18, 1933.

49. Erland Echlin, *Globe*, July 31, 1933.

50. Erland Echlin, "Opera Is Thronged Despite Upheaval in German Reich." *Globe*, Aug. 24, 1933.

51. Erland Echlin, *Globe*, Aug. 1, 1933.

52. Graeme S. Mount, *Canada's Enemies: Spies and Spying in the Peaceable Kingdom*. Toronto: Dundurn Press Ltd., 1993, p. 57.

53. Ibid., p. 57.

54. Erland Echlin, "Chancellor Argues Aim Is Peace." *Globe and Mail*, Aug. 19, 1933.

55. Kenneth Dyba, interview with Bob Hill. Aug. 1979. LAC.

56. Rev. C.H. Phillips, Letters to the Editor, *Lethbridge Herald*. Oct. 20, 1933.

Chapter 7: Royal Interludes

1. Matthew Halton, "Lansbury Declares that Monarchy Is not the Worst Anachronism." *Toronto Star*, Dec. 7, 1934.

2. Ibid.

3. Matthew Halton, "Nazi Plot to Kill Marina Charged by English Paper." *Toronto Star*, Nov. 17, 1934.

4. Matthew Halton, "Lansbury Declares that Monarchy Is not the Worst Anachronism." *Toronto Star*, Dec. 7, 1934.

5. Matthew Halton, "Empire May Soon Know if New King Plans to Marry." *Toronto Star*, Jan. 22, 1936.

6. Matthew Halton, "Hatred of Sham Honesty Purpose Ennobled George." *Toronto Star*, Jan. 21, 1936.

7. Matthew Halton, "London Warm in Denial King Drops His Aitches." *Toronto Star*, Dec. 28, 1935.

8. Ibid.

9. Matthew Halton, "Edward VIII, White-Faced, Tense Drops Earth upon Father's Bier as It Vanishes from Human View." *Toronto Star*, Jan. 28, 1936.

10. Matthew Halton, "Jews Swallowing Germany Excuse for Prosecution Talk with Prince." *Toronto Star*, May 19, 1933.

11. Quoted in "King Eager to Make Britain 'Land for All'." *Toronto Star*, Feb. 1, 1936.

12. Matthew Halton, "Impatience against Injustice Determination to Do His Duty Characteristic of New King." *Toronto Star*, Jan. 25, 1936.

13. Matthew Halton, "Empire May Soon Know if New King Plans to Marry." *Toronto Star*, Jan. 22, 1936.

14. Frances Donaldson, *Edward VIII*. London: Weidenfeld & Nicolson, 1974, p. 116.

15. Philip Williamson, *Stanley Baldwin: Conservative Leadership and National Values*. Cambridge: Cambridge University Press, 1999, p. 326.

16. Susan Williams, *The People's King: The True Story of the Abdication*. London: Penguin Books Ltd., 2003, p. 134.

17. R.H. Hubbard, *Rideau Hall*. Montreal and London: McGill-Queen's University Press, 1977, p. 187.

18. Matthew Halton, "London Tense as Epic Drama Nears Climax." *Toronto Star*, Dec. 8, 1936.

19. Williams, *The People's King*, pp. 177, 198–99.

20. Matthew Halton, "Edward Weeps, Bidding His Brother Farewell." *Toronto Star*, Dec. 11, 1933. (Matt never appears to have mentioned Edward VIII's support for closer ties with Nazi Germany.)

21. Ibid.

22. Matthew Halton, "Moving Good-By Ends Eight Days of Royal Drama." *Toronto Star*, Dec. 12, 1936.

23. Matthew Halton, "Predicts Peace Must Die or Be Reborn This Year." *Toronto Star*, Apr. 24, 1937.

24. Matthew Halton, "Little Princess." *Star Weekly*, Feb. 20, 1937.

25. Matthew Halton, "Coronation's Court of Claims." *Star Weekly*.

26. Matthew Halton, "Long Live the King." *Star Weekly*, May 1937.

27. Matthew Halton, "Little Princess." *Star Weekly*, Feb. 20, 1937.

28. Ibid.

29. Matthew Halton, "Thousands Serenade King in Pitiless Rain at 6 A.M." *Toronto Star*, May 11, 1937.

30. Matthew Halton, "Memories of Magnificence Still Haunt Westminster." *Toronto Star*, May 13, 1937.

31. Matthew Halton, "Most Gorgeous Spectacle Ever Known to Man." *Toronto Star*, May 12, 1937.

32. Matthew Halton, "Beautiful Lady Nunburnholme Attends Queen." *Toronto Star*, May 1, 1939.

33. Matthew Halton, "Their Majesties Must Take Lifeboat Drills during Ocean Voyage." *Toronto Star*, May 5, 1939.

34. Matthew Halton, letter to his parents. Feb. 14, 1939.

35. Matthew Halton, "Big Event in Our Lives Say King and Queen of Canadian Tour." *Toronto Star*, May 6, 1939.

36. Ibid.

37. Ibid.

38. Ibid.

39. Ibid.

40. Matthew Halton, "Princess Would Love to Canoe on Rivers Here." *Toronto Star*, May 3, 1939.

41. Rodney Moore, former assistant press sec., Buckingham Palace. Interview with author, June 1, 2009.

42. J.E. Atkinson, telegram to Matthew Halton. May 8, 1939. LAC.

43. Matthew Halton, "Guns Roar, Bands Play, King Sails under Flags of 65 Lands He Rules." *Toronto Star*, May 6, 1939.

44. Thompson and Seager, *Canada 1922–1939*, p. 327.

45. Ibid, p. 328.

Chapter 8: Twilight of Peace

1. *Foreign Correspondent*, directed by Alfred Hitchcock. Walter Wanger Productions. 1940.

2. Matthew Halton, "'Hitler's Fate Is Sealed', Says Writer He Attacked." *Toronto Star*, June 24, 1939.

3. Leland Stowe, letter to Kenneth Dyba. Dec. 3, 1978. LAC.

4. Matthew Halton, "Prison Awaits Anti-Nazis When Saar Again German." *Toronto Star*, Jan. 14, 1935.

5. Matthew Halton, "10,000 Anti-Nazis in Saar Changed Vote Last Minute." *Toronto Star*, Jan. 29, 1935.

6. Matthew Halton, "Hitler Cries 'Peace' But Rattles Sabre as Saar Is Reclaimed." *Toronto Star*, Mar. 15, 1935.

7. Matthew Halton, "Hundreds Flee into Exile Saar Plebiscite Sequel." *Toronto Star*, Jan. 15, 1936.

8. Matthew Halton, "'Hold on Till Spring' Germans Tell Italy in Every Car of Iron." *Toronto Star*, Mar. 6, 1936.

9. Matthew Halton, "Nazi Orators Take Rest until Olympics Are Over." *Toronto Star*, Aug. 5, 1936.

10. David Clay Large, *Nazi Games: The Olympics of 1936*. New York: W.W. Norton and Company, 2007, p. 182.

11. Matthew Halton, "German Protestant Pastor Prays for Jews, Gets Jail." *Toronto Star*, Feb. 28, 1936.

12. Elmer Dulmage, "We Should Have Boycotted the Hitler Olympics." *Vancouver Province*, Jan. 29, 1980.

13. Matthew Halton, "German Protestant Pastor Prays for Jews, Gets Jail." *Toronto Star*, Feb. 28, 1936.

14. James Pitsula, "Strange Salute," *The Beaver*, vol. 84 (4). Aug./Sept. 2004, pp. 14–19.

15. Werner Haag, Letter to Direktor, RDV, Berlin. Bundesarchiv, Ausland-Korrespondenz. R8077/218. June 10, 1936.

16. Matthew Halton, "Delirious Thousands Cheer Reichsführer as Olympiad Opens." *Toronto Star*, Aug. 1936.

17. Ibid.

18. Pitsula, "Strange Salute," pp. 14–19.

19. Matthew Halton, "Hitler Daily More Popular Black Guardsmen Assert." *Toronto Star*, Aug. 25, 1936.

20. Elmer Dulmage, "We Should Have Boycotted the Hitler Olympics." *Vancouver Province*, Jan. 29, 1980.

21. Matthew Halton, "Canada Beats Brazil Cagers in First Game." *Toronto Star*, Aug. 7, 1936.

22. Matthew Halton, "Loaring of Canada Wins Second Place in 400-Metre Race." *Toronto Star*, Aug. 4, 1936.

23. Matthew Halton, "'Man No Longer a Man' Behind Olympic Façade." *Toronto Star*, Aug. 24, 1936.

24. Large, *Nazi Games: The Olympics of 1936*, p. 142.

25. Pitsula, "Strange Salute," pp. 14–19.

26. Elmer Dulmage, "We Should Have Boycotted the Hitler Olympics." *Vancouver Province*, Jan. 29, 1980.

27. Matthew Halton, letter to his parents. Nov. 28, 1937.

28. Matthew Halton, "Gracie Gets $10 a Minute, Says She Gives Most Away." *Toronto Star*, May 23, 1935.

29. Ibid.

30. Matthew Halton, "Canadian Inspires Briton." *Star Weekly*, June 11, 1938, and "Big Dough in Bread." *Maclean's*, Aug. 15, 1948. Also letters to family.
31. Ibid.
32. Matthew Halton, "Grey Owl Seeing London Has Trapped Animal Feeling." *Toronto Star*, Feb. 13, 1936.
33. Ibid.
34. Matthew Halton, "Grey Owl Sought Friends in Belaney's Native Town." *Toronto Star*, Apr. 19, 1938.
35. Matthew Halton, "Grey Owl's Boyhood Full of Indian Lore Say English Aunts." *Toronto Star*, Apr. 20, 1938.
36. Matthew Halton, "English Neglect Seen as Fatal to Scotland." *Toronto Star*, Feb. 6, 1936.
37. Matthew Halton, "Extremism Delays Union in Erin, Cosgrave Says." *Toronto Star*, May 8, 1936.
38. Ibid.
39. For the background of the Spanish conflict, I have relied on Hugh Thomas, *The Spanish Civil War*. London: Eyre and Spottiswoode Ltd., 1961.
40. Caroline Moorehead, *Gellhorn: A Twentieth Century Life*. New York: Henry Holt and Company, 2003, p. 108.
41. Ibid., p. 110.
42. Ibid., p. 111.
43. Harkness, *J.E. Atkinson of The Star*, p. 303.
44. Matthew Halton, "Spaniards Won't Fight in Good Old Summer." *Toronto Star*, June 16, 1936.
45. Matthew Halton, "City Parks Strewn with Dead as Battle Still Rages Bitterly." *Toronto Star*, Nov. 9, 1936.
46. Matthew Halton, "British, French and U.S. Warships at Barcelona." *Toronto Star*, Dec. 1, 1936.
47. Michael Petrou, *Renegades: Canadians in the Spanish Civil War*. Vancouver: UBC Press, 2008, p. 149.
48. Thomas, *The Spanish Civil War*, p. 188.
49. Matthew Halton, "Tribunal in Barcelona Like Shot From Film of French Revolution." *Toronto Star*, Dec. 28, 1936.
50. Halton, *Ten Years to Alamein*, p. 65.
51. Ibid., p. 65.
52. Ibid., p. 66.
53. Matthew Halton, "British, French and U.S. Warships at Barcelona." *Toronto Star*, Dec. 1, 1936.
54. Matthew Halton, "On the Spanish Front." *Star Weekly*, Jan. 9, 1937.
55. Ibid.
56. Matthew Halton, "Tears for Spanish Eyes." *Star Weekly*, Aug. 6, 1938.
57. A fuller account of Krehm's involvement in Spain is provided in Petrou, *Renegades: Canadians in the Spanish Civil War*, pp. 148–57.
58. Matthew Halton, "Freed from Spanish Jails Canadian Sees Madrid Win." *Toronto Star*, Oct. 8, 1937.

59. My main sources for background on the Mackenzie-Papineau Battalion are Michael Petrou's *Renegades*, cited above, and Mark Zuehlke, *The Gallant Cause: Canadians in the Spanish Civil War*. Mississauga: John Wiley & Sons Canada Ltd., 1996.

60. Halton, *Ten Years to Alamein*, pp. 51–52.

61. Ibid., pp. 51–53. Also Mark Zuehlke's *The Gallant Cause*, pp. 273–74.

62. Matthew Halton, "Toronto Commander Tells of Heroic Feats of Canucks in Spain." *Toronto Star*, Jan. 27, 1939.

63. Halton, *Ten Years to Alamein*. p. 54.

64. Ibid., p. 59.

65. A.A. Macleod, receipt for £200 contribution from Garfield Weston. LAC.

66. Eric Downton, *Wars Without End*. Toronto: Stoddart Publishing Co. Ltd., 1987, p. 31.

Chapter 9: To the Abyss

1. Matthew Halton, "'Hold on Till Spring' Germans Tell Italy in Every Car of Iron." *Toronto Star*, Mar. 6, 1936.

2. Matthew Halton, "The Mediterranean Is Seen Becoming Fascist Lake." *Toronto Star*, Sept. 16, 1936.

3. Halton, *Ten Years to Alamein*, p. 45.

4. Thompson, and Seager, *Canada 1922–1939*, pp. 313–14.

5. Blair Neatby, *William Lyon Mackenzie King 1932–1939: The Prism of Unity*. Toronto: University of Toronto Press, 1976, p. 177.

6. Matthew Halton, "Interesting, Valuable Says Canada's Premier of Talks with Hitler." *Toronto Star*, June 29, 1937.

7. Ibid.

8. William Lyon Mackenzie King, *Diary*. June 29, 1937. LAC.

9. Ibid.

10. Ibid.

11. Ibid.

12. Matthew Halton, "'Too Small For War,' Says Hitler, Calls It Suicide." *Toronto Star*, July 2, 1937.

13. Richard Cockett, *Twilight of Truth: Chamberlain, Appeasement and the Manipulation of the Press*. London: Weidenfeld and Nicolson, 1989, p. 120.

14. Franklin Reid Gannon, *The British Press and Germany 1936–1939*. Oxford: Clarendon Press, 1971, p. 147.

15. Ibid., p. 206.

16. Matthew Halton, "Critics of Living in England Say Canada Much Worse." *Toronto Star*, Jan. 31, 1938.

17. Cockett, *Twilight of Truth*.

18. Ibid., p. 41.

19. Pierre Berton, *The Great Depression: 1929–1939*. Toronto: McClelland & Stewart Inc., 1990, p. 417.

20. Matthew Halton, letter to parents. Nov. 28, 1937. LAC.

21. Norman Rose, *The Cliveden Set*. London: Jonathan Cape, 2000, p. 4.

22. Sykes, *Nancy*, p. 403.

23. Matthew Halton, "That Cliveden Set: Do the Astors and Their Friends Rule Britain's Parliament with a Pro-Fascist Fist." *Toronto Star*, May 28, 1938.

24. Claud Cockburn, *I Claud: The Autobiography of Claud Cockburn*. London: Penguin Books, 1967, p. 180.

25. Matthew Halton, "That Cliveden Set: Do the Astors and Their Friends Rule Britain's Parliament with a Pro-Fascist Fist." *Toronto Star*, May 28, 1938.

26. Sykes, *Nancy*, p. 407.

27. Matthew Halton, "All Say They Just Hate Him But Aberhart Seen Winner." *Toronto Star*, Sept. 1, 1938.

28. Berton, *The Great Depression*, p. 212, and *Aberhart*, CBC Radio Documentary, Jan. 10, 1962.

29. Matthew Halton, "Blames Premier Aberhart as Woolly-minded Drifter." *Toronto Star*, Aug. 4, 1937.

30. Matthew Halton, letter to his parents. Oct. 18, 1938. LAC.

31. Matthew Halton, "Many Hate Aberhart But Fear CCF Rule Would Prove Worse." *Toronto Star*, Sept. 3, 1938.

32. Matthew Halton, "'Am Doing God's Work' Is Aberhart's Reason for Remaining on Job." *Toronto Star*, Sept. 2, 1938.

33. Matthew Halton, "Promises Without Reason Are Binding on Aberhart." *Toronto Star*, Sept. 7, 1938.

34. Ibid.

35. For the narrative of events leading to the Munich crisis, I have depended on many sources, notably Ian Kershaw, *Hitler 1936–1945: Nemesis*. New York: W.W. Norton & Company, 2000; William Shirer, *The Nightmare Years 1930–1940*. Boston: Little, Brown and Company, 1984; and Halton, *Ten Years to Alamein*.

36. Matthew Halton, "Czechoslovakia Immune From Europe's War Fever." *Toronto Star*, July 23, 1936.

37. Matthew Halton, "Sees Death of Democracy if Czechoslovakia Fails." *Toronto Star*, Apr. 27, 1938.

38. Matthew Halton, "Will Die to Last Man Ere Yielding Sudeten, Czechs Tell Halton." *Toronto Star*, Sept. 16, 1938.

39. Vincent Sheean, *Not Peace But a Sword*. New York: Doubleday, Doran & Company, Inc., 1939, p. 218.

40. "Sudetens Atop 'Volcano' Halton Tells the World." Report on Halton's CBS broadcast. *Toronto Star*, Sept. 19, 1938.

41. Matthew Halton, transcript of CBS interview with William Shirer. Sept. 22, 1938. LAC.

42. Ibid.

43. Ibid.

44. Matthew Halton, "As I Saw Him – 'Hitler of Godesberg Munich Step By Step.'" *Toronto Star*, Oct. 22, 1938.

45. Ibid.

46. Ibid.

47. Matthew Halton, "German Boys March Sadly Away to War But Nazis Stay Home." *Toronto Star*, Sept. 27, 1938.

48. Ibid.

49. Neville Chamberlain, BBC broadcast. Sept. 27, 1938.

50. Matthew Halton, "I Saw a Nation Die." *Star Weekly*, Nov. 5, 1938.

51. Halton, *Ten Years to Alamein*, p. 79.

52. NBC broadcast. Library of Congress, Recorded Sound Reference Center, Washington, D.C., Oct. 1, 1938.

53. Ibid.

54. Ibid.

55. "Halton Broadcasts Official Peace News as Pact Being Signed." *Toronto Star*, Sept. 30, 1938.

56. J.E. Atkinson, cable to Matthew Halton. Oct. 30, 1938. LAC.

57. Matthew Halton, "I Saw a Nation Die." *Star Weekly*, Nov. 5, 1938.

58. Gannon, *The British Press and Germany 1936–1939*, p. 7.

59. Ibid., p. 45.

60. Shirer, *The Nightmare Years 1930–1940*, p. 364.

61. Gannon, *The British Press and Germany 1936–1939*, p. 225.

62. Berton, *The Great Depression*, p. 468.

63. Roy Jenkins, *Churchill: A Biography*. New York: Farrar, Straus and Giroux, 2001, p. 527.

64. Halton, *Ten Years to Alamein*, p. 78.

65. Matthew Halton, "Handful of Soldiers Bedecked in Flowers Liquidate Versailles." *Toronto Star*, Oct. 3, 1938.

66. Matthew Halton, "I Saw Czechoslovakia Swallow Its Gall Cup to Save Civilization." *Toronto Star*, Oct. 5, 1938.

67. Matthew Halton, "200,000 Hitler Troops Seen by Halton Along Maginot." *Toronto Star*, Oct. 11, 1938.

68. Kershaw, *Hitler 1936–1945*, p. 123.

69. Matthew Halton, "See This New Year Darkest for Jews." *Toronto Star*, Sept. 17, 1936.

70. Matthew Halton, "The 20th Century Huguenots." *Toronto Star*, Jan. 11, 1936.

71. Matthew Halton, "Dream of Peddler Creates Great City." *Toronto Star*, Sept. 22, 1934.

72. Matthew Halton, "See This New Year Darkest for Jews." *Toronto Star*, Sept. 17, 1936.

73. Matthew Halton, "Canadian Shakes Up Bones of Two Ex-Kings." *Toronto Star*, Dec. 15, 1938.

74. Ibid.

75. Matthew Halton, "'France Is Very Ill' as Strike Ordered." *Toronto Star*, Nov. 25, 1938.

76. Matthew Halton, "Leon Blum Hope of France Surrounded by Enemies." *Toronto Star*, June 4, 1936.

77. Matthew Halton, "United France to Oppose Fascism, Asserts Herriot." *Toronto Star*, Nov. 12, 1937.

78. Matthew Halton, "From Madame Gamelin's Album." *Star Weekly*, Dec. 9, 1939.

79. Matthew Halton, "Jitters Chased Britain Prepares to Enjoy Easter." *Toronto Star*, Apr. 6, 1939.

80. Manuscript of Matthew Halton's memoir, *Ten Years to Alamein*. n.d.

81. Matthew Halton, "Modiste to Her Majesty." *Star Weekly*, Apr. 25, 1939.

Chapter 10: To War

1. Wikipedia. "SS *Athenia*." Wikipedia.org/wiki/SS_Athenia.

2. Matthew Halton, "I Thought of Babies Who Died When Our Lifeboat Was Cut Up." *Toronto Star*, Sept. 6, 1939.

3. Jess Bigelow, letter to Kenneth Dyba. Jan. 29, 1979. LAC.

4. Matthew Halton, "London Musters Full Resources Against Nazism." *Toronto Star*, Sept. 9, 1939.

5. Matthew Halton, "Children of the Storm." *Star Weekly*, Nov. 18, 1939.

6. Matthew Halton, "Britain Has Edge on Nazis by Knowing Weather First." *Toronto Star*, Dec. 13, 1939.

7. Matthew Halton, "Neville Chamberlain Seen as Successor to Baldwin." *Toronto Star*, Jan. 10, 1936.

8. Matthew Halton, "'Spilt Milk to Be Mopped' John Bull's View of War." *Toronto Star*, Oct. 2, 1939.

9. Matthew Halton, "Britain's Man of the Hour." *Star Weekly*, Dec. 2, 1939.

10. Mackenzie King. Diary, June 10, 1939. LAC.

11. Matthew Halton, "Britain's Man of the Hour." *Star Weekly*, Dec. 2, 1939.

12. Matthew Halton, "War's Most Thrilling Event, London Paper Calls Canuck Arrival." *Toronto Star*, Dec. 20, 1939.

13. Roy Jenkins, *Churchill: A Biography*. New York: Farrar, Straus & Giroux, 2001, p. 567.

14. I have relied on these sources for details of the Winter War: William R. Trotter, *A Frozen Hell: The Russo-Finnish Winter War of 1239–40*. Chapel Hill: Algonquin Books, 1991; Max Hastings, *All Hell Let Loose: The World at War 1939–1945*. London: Harper Press, 2011; John Keegan, *The Second World War*. New York: Penguin Books USA Inc., 1990; and Leland Stowe, *No Other Road to Freedom*. New York: Alfred A. Knopf, 1941.

15. Matthew Halton, "Sweden Feverishly Builds Its Maginot Within Sounds of War." *Toronto Star*, Feb. 5, 1940.

16. Halton, *Ten Years to Alamein*, p. 106.

17. Matthew Halton, field notebook. Finland, n.d.

18. Matthew Halton, "'Finland First,' Communist Kills 200 Russ, Then Dies." *Toronto Star*, Feb. 8, 1940.

19. Matthew Halton, "Cat-Eye Finns Fire in Dark." *Toronto Star*, Feb. 14, 1940.

20. Matthew Halton, "Russian Prisoners Gasp as Butter and Meat Given Them by Finns." *Toronto Star*, Mar. 8, 1940.

21. Matthew Halton, "Halton Gallops Along with Finland's Ghosts on Arctic Battlefield." *Toronto Star*, Jan. 18, 1940.

22. Matthew Halton, "I Rode with a Finnish Ghost Patrol." *Star Weekly*, Mar. 2, 1940.

23. Ibid.

24. Matthew Halton, "Encircled by Russians, Halton Nearly Taken." *Toronto Star*, Jan. 24, 1940.

25. Matthew Halton, "'Hold Forever' With 150,000 Recruits, Finns Tell Halton." *Toronto Star*, Feb. 15, 1940.

26. Matthew Halton, "Halton in Front Line of Finns Gets Taste 'Personal Shelling'." *Toronto Star*, Mar. 5, 1940.

27. Ibid.

28. Matthew Halton, "'Do We Hate Russians? No! We Hate Russia' Say Finns." *Toronto Star*, Feb. 27, 1940.

29. Matthew Halton, "Men Die as They Eat." *Toronto Star*, Jan. 11, 1940.

30. Matthew Halton, field notebook. Finland, n.d.

31. Trotter, *A Frozen Hell*, p. 264.

32. Winston Churchill, *The Second World War: The Gathering Storm*, Vol. 1. London: Cassell and Co. Ltd., 1949, pp. 325–26.

33. Matthew Halton, "Every C.A.S.F. Man Has 2 Pairs Boots 3 Uniform Changes." *Toronto Star*, n.d.

34. J.L. Granatstein and Desmond Morton, *A Nation Forged in Fire: Canadians and the Second World War 1939–1945*. Toronto: Lester & Orpen Dennys, 1989, p. 16.

35. Matthew Halton, "'No More Passchendaeles' Canadian Army Heads Vow." *Toronto Star*, April 29, 1940.

36. Matthew Halton, "German Military Training Begins at Age of 8 Years." *Toronto Star*, July 26, 1936.

37. Matthew Halton, "Old Land Is Steeled for Sternest Ordeal Sees Victory Certain." *Toronto Star*, May 11, 1940.

38. Ibid.

39. Jenkins, *Churchill*, p. 588.

40. Ibid., p. 599.

41. Hastings, *All Hell Let Loose*, pp. 90–91.

42. Matthew Halton, "Stood on White Cliffs of Dover and I Saw Blood Red Sky of War." *Toronto Star*, May 25, 1940.

43. Halton, *Ten Years to Alamein*, p. 135.

44. Ibid., p. 135.

45. Ibid., pp. 137–39.

46. Ibid., p. 140.

47. Ibid., pp. 139–40.

48. Harkness, *J.E. Atkinson of The Star*, p. 312.

49. Halton, *Ten Years to Alamein*, pp. 143–44.

50. Matthew Halton, "Return to Homeland." *Toronto Star*, July 13, 1940.

Chapter 11: A Short Time in Exile

1. Halton, *Ten Years to Alamein*, p. 144.

2. Kenneth Dyba, interview with Gerald Anglin. May 22, 1979. LAC.

3. Matthew Halton, "'Nothing We Shouldn't Give Britain' U.S. Senator Cries." *Toronto Star*, Sept. 27, 1940.

4. Halton, *Ten Years to Alamein*, p. 143.

5. Doris Kearns Goodwin, *No Ordinary Time: Franklin and Eleanor Roosevelt: The Home Front in World War II*. New York: Simon & Schuster, 1994, p. 187.

6. Granatstein and Morton, *A Nation Forged in Fire*, p. 33.

7. Matthew Halton, "Joint Defense Rolls on 'Just Like Ol' Man River'." *Toronto Star*, Sept. 12, 1940.

8. Matthew Halton, "Britain the Citadel." CBC Broadcast, July 14, 1940. Reprinted in *Toronto Star*, July 15, 1940.

9. Frank R. Elliott, letters column. *Toronto Star*, July 16, 1940.

10. Matthew Halton, "The Old Bells of London Town Are Crying Urgently to the New World for Speed." CBC Broadcast, Sept. 22, 1940.

11. *Ottawa Journal* editorial, "Halton Speech Is Reminder of I.O.D.E. Win." Reprinted in *Toronto Star*, Sept. 26, 1940.

12. Matthew Halton, "Third Term for Roosevelt Seen as Wilkie Weakens." *Toronto Star*, Sept. 19, 1940.

13. Matthew Halton, "The War Reviewed." *Toronto Star*, Oct. 12, 1940.

14. Matthew Halton, "'They'll Be Pleased, Won't They' Empire, Canada Will Be Pleased F.D.R., Eyes Shining, Tells Halton." *Toronto Star*, Nov. 6, 1940.

15. Matthew Halton, "Woman of the White House." *Star Weekly*, Jan. 18, 1941.

16. Ibid.

17. Ibid.

18. Ibid.

19. Matthew Halton, "I.O.D.E. Fills St. Paul's to Hear Halton Address." *Toronto Star*, Nov. 10, 1940.

Chapter 12: The Desert War

1. Matthew Halton, letter to Jean Halton. Feb. 13, 1941. LAC.

2. C.P. Stacey, *Six Years of War*. Vol. 1. Ottawa: Department of National Defence, 1955, pp. 193–94.

3. Matthew Halton, letter to Jean Halton. Mar. 7, 1941. LAC.

4. Matthew Halton, letter to Jean Halton. Feb. 13, 1941. LAC.

5. Ibid.

6. Matthew Halton, "Indomitable Coventry Survives Gethsemane on Good Friday Morn." *Toronto Star*, Apr. 12, 1941.

7. War Office. *Regulations for Press Correspondents*. Oct. 1939. LAC.

8. Matthew Halton, "Dockland's Dwellers Dare Hitler Do Worst Won't Flee His Bombs." *Toronto Star*, Feb. 13, 1941.

9. Ibid.

10. Matthew Halton, "Bomb Deals Out Death as Dance Band Plays 'Oh Johnny' in London." *Toronto Star*, Mar. 10, 1941.

11. James M. Minifie, *Expatriate*. Toronto: The Macmillan Company of Canada Ltd., 1976, p. 145.

12. Matthew Halton, letter to Jean Halton. Apr. 19 1941. LAC.

13. Matthew Halton letter to Jean Halton. Mar. 21 1941. LAC.

14. Matthew Halton, letter to Jean Halton. Mar. 30 1941. LAC.

15. Howard K. Smith, *Events Leading up to My Death: The Life of a Twentieth Century Reporter*. New York: St. Martin's Press, 1996, p. 100.

16. Charles Ritchie, *The Siren Years*. Toronto: McClelland & Stewart Ltd., 1974, p. XII.

17. George Weidenfeld, interview with the author. Nov. 6, 2006.

18. George Weidenfeld, *Remembering My Good Friends: An Autobiography*. New York: Harper Collins Publishers, 1995, p. III.

19. Matthew Halton, letter to Jean Halton. Mar. 30, 1941. LAC.

20. Kenneth Dyba, interview with Helen Silverthorne. July 28, 1978. LAC.

21. Jean Halton, interview with the author. July 12, 1999.

22. Eric Thompson, "Canadian Warcos in World War II: Professionalism, Patriotism and Propaganda." *Mosaic* 23, Summer 1990, pp. 55–72.

23. Matthew Halton, "Halton in Thick of Battle Before Damascus." *Toronto Star*, June 17, 1941.

24. Halton, *Ten Years to Alamein*, p. 154.

25. Matthew Halton, "'Brave but Foolish' Free French Rescued by British Artillery." *Toronto Star*, July 5, 1941.

26. Matthew Halton, "Hot Sands, Hot Metal Five Months of Fire But Tobruk Is Held." *Toronto Star*, Aug. 23, 1941.

27. Matthew Halton, "Desert Driving Injures More than Enemy Fire." *Toronto Star*, July 29, 1941.

28. Sean Fielding, *They Sought Out Rommel: A Diary of the Libyan Campaign*. London: Whitefriars Press Limited, 1942 (Issued by the War Office for the Ministry of Information), p. 17.

29. Matthew Halton, "I Saw Our Guns Stop Rommel." *Star Weekly*, Nov. 24, 1941.

30. Matthew Halton, "Exciting Cairo Is Crossroads of Victory's World." *Toronto Star*, Aug. 5, 1941.

31. Matthew Halton, "Losing Blood, Still Canadian Roars into Curtain of Foe Fire." *Toronto Star*, Aug. 2, 1942.

32. John Bierman and Colin Smith, *The Battle of Alamein*. New York: Viking Penguin, 2002, p. 2.

33. Ibid., p. 114.

34. Jonathan Dimbleby, *Richard Dimbleby: A Biography*. London: Hodder and Stoughton, 1975, p. 104.

35. Matthew Halton, letter to Jean Halton. July 12, 1941. LAC.

36. Matthew Halton, letter to Jean Halton. Feb. 27, 1942. LAC.

37. Matthew Halton, letter to Jean Halton. Undated, 1942. LAC.

38. Halton, *Ten Years to Alamein*, p. 167.

39. Ibid., p. 178.

40. Matthew Halton, "The Men of Tobruk Faithful unto Death." *Toronto Star*, Sept. 5, 1941. (Reprint of CBC/BBC broadcast).

41. Halton, *Ten Years to Alamein*, p. 173.

42. Ibid., p. 189.

43. Alan Moorehead, *A Late Education: Episodes in a Life*. London: Penguin Books, 1976, p. 131.

44. Matthew Halton, letter to Jean Halton. Feb. 27, 1942. LAC.

45. Ibid.

46. Matthew Halton, letter to Jean Halton. Apr. 15, 1942. LAC.

47. Halton, *Ten Years to Alamein*, pp. 280–81.

48. Fielding, *They Sought Out Rommel*, p. 44.

49. Matthew Halton, "Nazi Ghost Divisions Daren't Face British Axis Loses 200 Tanks." *Toronto Star*, Nov. 24, 1941.

50. Tom Pocock, *Alan Moorehead*. London: The Bodley Head, 1990, p. 109.

51. Matthew Halton, "I Saw Our Guns Stop Rommel." *Star Weekly*, n.d.

52. Gregory Clark, "Halton Story on Page One Relieves Fear of Capture." *Toronto Star*, Nov. 28, 1941.

53. Matthew Halton, "Weary British Pursue Nazis." *PM*. Dec. 28, 1941.

54. Matthew Halton, letter to Jean Halton. Dec. 27, 1941. LAC.

55. Matthew Halton, "Jack-O-Lantern Dinner Held in Bengazi Ruins Then Back to Battle." *Toronto Star*, Dec. 29, 1941.

56. Matthew Halton, "Khyber Pass Stands to Arms." *Star Weekly*, n.d.

57. Matthew Halton, "Up Tradition-Soaked Gun-Bristling Khyber Halton Sees Frontier." *Toronto Star*, Oct. 15, 1941.

58. Ernest G. Paine, "India Looks to Canada as Pattern for Future." *Toronto Star*, Apr. 25, 1942.

59. Halton, *Ten Years to Alamein*, p. 241.

60. Matthew Halton, "Gandhi Is Saintly Humbug Assert Scion of Moguls." *Toronto Star*, Mar. 6, 1933.

61. Halton, *Ten Years to Alamein*, p. 246.

62. Matthew Halton, letter to Hugh Morrison. Feb. 13, 1942. LAC.

63. Ibid.

64. Matthew Halton, letter to Jean Halton. June 15, 1942. LAC.

65. Ibid.

66. Matthew Halton, letter to Hugh Morrison. Feb. 13, 1942. LAC.

67. Matthew Halton, "Withdrawal in Libya was 'Brilliant Feat' Halton Tells Canada." *Toronto Star*, July 6, 1942. Transcript of CBC/BBC broadcast.

68. Matthew Halton, "Death May Be on the Horizon but Let's Go Swimming." *Toronto Star*, June 25, 1942.

69. Halton, *Ten Years to Alamein*, p. 266.

70. Matthew Halton, "Death May Be on the Horizon but Let's Go Swimming." *Toronto Star*, June 25, 1942.

71. Ashley Edwards, letter to Matthew Halton. Apr. 11, 1944. LAC.

72. Bierman and Smith, *The Battle of Alamein*, pp. 198–99.

73. Matthew Halton, "Withdrawal in Libya was 'Brilliant Feat' Halton Tells Canada." *Toronto Star*, July 6, 1942. Transcript of CBC/BBC broadcast.

74. Matthew Halton, letter to Jean Halton. June 27, 1942. LAC.

75. Matthew Halton, letter to Jean Halton. July 24, 1942. LAC.

76. Matthew Halton, "'Got a Spare Cigar?' Soldier Asks Premier Gets One Treasures It." *Toronto Star*, Aug. 19, 1942.

77. Bierman and Smith, *The Battle of Alamein*, p. 232.

78. Matthew Halton, letter to Jean Halton. July 24, 1942. LAC.

79. Matthew Halton, "'In Cairo Soon,' Woman Wrote to German Lad but He's Dead in the Desert." *Toronto Star*, Sept. 8, 1942.

80. Winston Churchill, *The Second World War: Volume IV The Hinge of Fate*. London: Cassell & Co. Ltd., 1951, p. 541.

81. Matthew Halton, cable to Jean Halton. Sept. 13, 1942. LAC.

82. Matthew Halton, letter to Jean Halton. Aug. 23, 1942. LAC.

83. Matthew Halton, CBC broadcast. Oct. 4, 1942. CBC Archives.

Chapter 13: The Road to Ortona

1. Halton, *Ten Years to Alamein*, p. 43.

2. Ibid.

3. Ibid., p. 319.

4. Ibid.

5. *Times Literary Supplement*. July 1944.

6. "Lessons of the Desert Heroes." London *Star*, June 23, 1944.

7. "Years of Folly and Retreat." *Globe and Mail*, Oct. 28, 1944.

8. M.J. Herrernan, "Road into War." *Montreal Gazette*, Oct. 28, 1944.

9. Bernard Montgomery, letter to Matthew Halton. Feb. 7, 1947. NAC.

10. Program for "Matthew Halton and Dramatic Appeal." Bond Shell Show Rally, Vancouver, May 11, 1943.

11. Matthew Halton, "Victory Loan Campaign Appeal." CBC Archives, Nov. 2, 1942.

12. Knowlton Nash, *The Microphone Wars: A History of Triumph and Betrayal at the CBC*. Toronto: McClelland & Stewart, 1994, p. 178. (Paperback edition.)

13. Matthew Halton, letter to Jean Halton. n.d. LAC.

14. Harkness, *J.E. Atkinson of the Star*, p. 313.

15. Kenneth Dyba, interview with Bryan Vaughan. Oct. 23, 1979.

16. Harkness, *J.E. Atkinson of the Star*, p. 313.

17. Kenneth Edey, letter to Kenneth Dyba. Aug. 26, 1980.

18. Matthew Halton, "I Saw Good Men Die." *Star Weekly*, Sept. 18, 1943.

19. Ralph Allen, *Ordeal by Fire: Canada, 1910–1945*. Toronto: Doubleday Canada Ltd., 1961, p. 430.

20. David J. Bercuson, *Maple Leaf Against the Axis: Canada's Second World War*. Toronto: Stoddart Publishers, 1995, p. 163.

21. Matthew Halton, letter to Jean Halton. Aug. 26, 1943. LAC.

22. Wallace Reyburn, letter to Kenneth Dyba. Apr. 14, 1979.

23. Matthew Halton, letter to Jean Halton. Aug. 12, 1943. LAC.

24. Matthew Halton, letter to Jean Halton. Sept. 2, 1943. LAC.

25. A.E. Powley, *Broadcast From the Front*. Toronto: A.M. Hakkert Ltd., 1975, p. 53.

26. Matthew Halton, letter to Jean Halton. Sept. 29, 1943.

27. Matthew Halton, "See Naples and Cry." *Star Weekly*, Nov. 20, 1943.

28. Daniel G. Dancocks, *The D-Day Dodgers: The Canadians in Italy, 1943–1945*. Toronto: McClelland & Stewart Inc., 1991, p. 139.

29. Chris Vokes and John Maclean, *My Story*. Ottawa: Gallery Books, 1985, p. 123.

30. Matthew Halton, CBC Report. Nov. 17, 1943. CBC Archives.

31. Allen, *Ordeal by Fire*, p. 441.

32. Paul Johnson, letter to his wife. Oct. 29, 1943. LAC.

33. Kenneth Dyba and Joe Thomas, interview with Bill Gilchrist. June 30, 1980.

34. Art Holmes, interview. *Between Ourselves*. Nov. 11, 1978. CBC Archives.

35. Matthew Halton, CBC Report. Oct. 23, 1943. CBC Archives.

36. Paul Johnson, letter to his wife. Oct. 29, 1943. LAC.

37. Matthew Halton, CBC Report. Oct. 19, 1943. CBC Archives.

38. Matthew Halton, CBC Report. Nov. 19, 1943. CBC Archives.

39. George Powell, *I Never Made Love in a Canoe*. Victoria, B.C.: Trafford Publishing, 2005, p. 125.

40. Matthew Halton, letter to Seth Halton. Nov. 26, 1943. NAC.

41. Jock Carroll, *The Life and Times of Greg Clark*. Toronto: Doubleday Canada Ltd., 1981, p. 232.

42. Ken Pagniez, transcript of interview with Doug Amaron. CBC, n.d. LAC.

43. Kenneth Dyba, interview with Wallace Reyburn. Sept. 6, 1979. LAC.

44. Kenneth Dyba, interview with Lloyd Moore. May 31, 1980. LAC.

45. Matthew Halton, CBC Report. Dec. 1, 1943. CBC Archives.

46. Zuehlke, *Ortona*, p. 121.

47. Matthew Halton, CBC Report. Dec. 8, 1943. CBC Archives.

48. Ibid.

49. Ibid.

50. Matthew Halton, CBC Report. Dec. 10, 1943. CBC Archives.

51. Matthew Halton, letter to Jean Halton. Dec. 20, 1943. LAC.

52. Matthew Halton, CBC Report. Dec. 11, 1943. CBC Archives.

53. Ibid.

54. Nash, *The Microphone Wars*, p. 207.

55. Zuehlke, *Ortona*, p. 119.

56. Helen Piddington, letter to the author. Dec. 8, 2011. Also referenced in Piddington's *Rumble Seat*. Madeira Park, B.C.: Harbour Publishing Co. Ltd., 2010, p. 258–59.

57. Aileen Rebecca Oder, *Hello Soldier*. Winnipeg: North Star Press, 1975, pp. 15–16.

58. Ibid., pp. 11–12.

59. Ibid., p. 39.

60. Matthew Halton, CBC Report. Dec. 28, 1943. CBC Archives.

61. Dancocks, *The D-Day Dodgers*, p. 187.

62. Ibid., p. 187.

63. Halton, CBC Report. Dec. 28, 1943.

64. Matthew Halton, letter to Jean Halton. Dec. 26, 1943. LAC.

65. Edmund Griffiths, personal interview. June 23, 2012.

66. CBC TV. *Return to Ortona: A Battlefield Redemption*. Documentary. First aired Feb. 1, 1999.

67. Matthew Halton, CBC Report. Dec. 25, 1943. CBC Archives.

68. Matthew Halton, letter to Jean Halton. Dec. 26, 1943. LAC.

69. Matthew Halton, CBC Report. Jan. 3, 1944. CBC Archives.

70. Matthew Halton, CBC Report. Jan. 4, 1944. CBC Archives.

71. Matthew Halton, CBC Report. Jan. 4, 1944. CBC Archives.

72. Allen, *Ordeal by Fire*, p. 444.

73. Matthew Halton, letter to Jean Halton. Jan. 1, 1944. LAC.

74. Dan McArthur, cable to Matthew Halton. Feb. 7, 1944. LAC.

75. Matthew Halton, letter to parents. Jan. 7, 1944. LAC.

76. Matthew Halton, letter to Jean Halton. Jan. 21, 1944. LAC.

77. Matthew Halton, letter to Jean Halton. Jan. 14, 1944. LAC.

78. Matthew Halton, letter to Jean Halton. Jan. 23, 1944. LAC.

79. Matthew Halton, letter to Jean Halton. Jan. 21, 1944. LAC.

Chapter 14: D-Day

1. Kenneth Dyba, interview with A.E. (Bert) Powley. Oct. 27, 1978. LAC.

2. Seth Halton, personal diary. Apr. 9, 1944. (In possession of daughter, Christine Anderson.)

3. Ibid. May 31, 1944.

4. Ibid. June 2, 1944.

5. Cecil Brooks (Matt's agent), quoted in letter from Matthew Halton to Jean Halton. May 28, 1944. LAC.

6. Dan McArthur, cable to Matthew Halton. Apr. 9, 1944. LAC.

7. Pocock, *Alan Moorehead*, p. 183.

8. Charles Lynch, CBC Report. Aug. 7, 1944. CBC Archives.

9. David Halton, interview with Charles Lynch. June 4, 1994.

10. Matthew Halton, CBC Report. June 6, 1944. CBC Archives.

11. Ibid.

12. Charles Lynch, *You Can't Print That*. Edmonton: Hurtig Publishers, 1983, pp. 55–56.

13. Matthew Halton, letter to Jean Halton. June 15, 1944. LAC.

14. Lynch, *You Can't Print That*, pp. 56–57.

15. Micheline Trannoy, interview with the author. July 4, 1994.

16. Capt. J.C. Wilson, *Report on Shelling of Billets*. June 15, 1944. LAC.

17. Matthew Halton, CBC Report. June 15, 1944. CBC Archives.

18. Ibid.

19. Matthew Halton, "I Saw a Terrible Splendor." *Star Weekly*, July 29, 1944.

20. Henri Amouroux, *Joies et Douleurs du Peuple Libéré. La Grand Histoire des Francais sous l'Occupation*. Paris: Éditions Robert Laffont, S.A. 1988, p. 552.

21. Matthew Halton, CBC Report. July 4, 1944. CBC Archives.

22. Aimé-Jules Bizimana, *De Marcel Ouimet à René Lévesque: Les Correspondants de Guerre Canadiens-Français durant la Deuxième Guerre Mondiale*. Montreal: VLB Éditeur, 2007, p. 184.

23. Ibid., p. 185.

24. Matthew Halton, letter to Jean Halton. July 8, 1944. LAC.

25. Ibid.

26. Matthew Halton, letter to Jean Halton. Sept. 24, 1944. LAC.

27. Matthew Halton, *The Maple Leaf*. Dec. 23, 1944.

28. Matthew Halton, BBC Postscript. Aug. 6, 1944. Reprinted in *The Listener*. London, Aug. 19, 1944.

29. Ibid.

30. George Powell, *Compact Record of the Life and Times of the Canadian War Correspondents Association*. Booklet, 1994.

31. Matthew Halton, letter to Jean Halton. July 1, 1944. LAC.

32. Kenneth Dyba, interview with Charles Lynch. May 30, 1980. LAC.

33. Ibid.

34. Charles Lynch, CBC Report. Aug. 7, 1944. CBC Archives.

35. Ibid.

36. Antony Beevor, *D-Day: The Battle for Normandy*. New York: The Penguin Group, 2009, p. 267.

37. Matthew Halton, CBC Report. July 10, 1944. CBC Archives.

38. Ibid.

39. Matthew Halton, "Caen: A Terrible Warning." *Star Weekly*, Aug. 12, 1944.

40. Beevor, *D-Day*, p. 519.

41. Matthew Halton, CBC Report. June 22, 1944. CBC Archives.

42. Matthew Halton, letter to Jean Halton. June 22, 1944. LAC.

43. Olivier Wieviorka, *Normandy*. London: The Belknap Press of Harvard University, 2008, p. 256.

44. Matthew Halton, *Victory Bond Appeal*. CBC. Nov. 2, 1942.

45. Timothy John Balzer, *The Information Front: The Canadian Army and News Management during the Second World War*. Vancouver: UBC Press, 2011, p. 185.

46. Mark Bourrie, *The Fog of War: Censorship of Canada's Media in World War II*. Toronto: Key Porter Books, 2011, p. 185.

47. Kenneth Dyba, interview with A.E. (Bert) Powley. Oct. 27, 1978. LAC.

48. Kenneth Dyba, interview with Ross Munro. Mar. 22, 1980. LAC.

49. Matthew Halton, fragments of his personal notebook. July 28, 1944.

50. Matthew Halton, CBC Report. Aug. 9, 1944. CBC Archives.

51. Kenneth Dyba, interview with Doug and Fran Harkness. July 3, 1980.

52. Nash, *The Microphone Wars*, p. 183.

53. Ibid., p. 202.

54. Matthew Halton, *The Maple Leaf*. Dec. 23, 1944.

55. J. Atkins, letter to Matthew Halton. Sept. 14, 1944. LAC.

56. Dan MacArthur, letter to Matthew Halton. Aug. 28, 1944. LAC.

57. "Grandmother Betty Ann," letter to Matthew Halton. Undated, 1944. LAC.

58. Bercuson, *Maple Leaf Against the Axis*, p. 34.

59. Matthew Halton, CBC Report. Aug. 9, 1944. CBC Archives.

60. Lynch, *You Can't Print That*, pp. 70–72, and Halton family oral history.

61. Matthew Halton, *Montreal Star*, July 17, 1944.

62. Vincent Alford, "Memo to Miss Benzie." BBC Archives. Aug. 10, 1944.

63. Desmond Shawe-Taylor, *Sunday Times*. London, Aug. 20, 1944.

64. Matthew Halton, CBC Report. Aug. 15, 1944. CBC Archives.

Chapter 15 : Four Days in Paris

1. Keegan, *The Second World War*, p. 411.

2. Alistair Horne, *Seven Ages of Paris*. New York: Vintage Books, 2004, p. 370.

3. Ibid, p. 370.

4. Jeffrey Meyers, *Hemingway: A Biography*. New York: Harper and Row, 1985, pp. 405–7.

5. Matthew Halton, "It was a Moment of History." *Star Weekly*, Sept. 23, 1944.

6. Matthew Halton, CBC Report. Aug. 26, 1944. CBC Archives.

7. Richard S. Malone, *A World in Flames 1944–1945*. Toronto: Collins, 1984, p. 69.

8. Matthew Halton, "It was a Moment of History." *Star Weekly*, Sept. 23, 1944.

9. Matthew Halton, CBC Report. Aug. 26, 1944. CBC Archives.

10. Gerald Clark, *No Mud on the Back Seat*. Montreal: Robert Davies Publishing, 1995, p. 79.

11. Horne, *Seven Ages of Paris*, p. 372.

12. Richard S. Malone, interviewed on CBC Radio, *Between Ourselves*. Nov. 11, 1978. CBC Archives.

13. Andy Rooney, *My War*. New York: Times Books, 1995, p. 203–4.

14. Jack Golding, letter to Jean Halton. Jan. 13, 1957. LAC.

15. Matthew Halton, CBC Report. Aug. 29, 1944. CBC Archives.

16. Ibid.

17. Jack Golding, letter to Jean Halton. Jan. 13, 1957. LAC.

18. Matthew Halton, "It Was a Moment of History." *Star Weekly*, Sept. 23, 1944.

19. Rooney, *My War*, p. 208.

20. Amouroux, *Joies et Douleurs du Peuple Libéré*, p. 727.

21. Horne, *Seven Ages of Paris*, p. 727.

22. Kenneth Dyba, interview with Gerald Clark. March 7, 1980.

23. Christiane de Sandfort, letter to Matthew Halton. Sept. 12, 1944. LAC.

24. Charles de Gaulle, *Mémoires de Guerre. Vol 2. L'Unite 1942–1944*. Paris: Librairie Plon, 1956, p. 379.

25. Richard S. Malone, *Missing from the Record*. Toronto: Collins, 1946, pp. 185–87.

26. Matthew Halton, CBC Report. Aug. 27, 1944. CBC Archives.

27. Malone, *Missing from the Record*, pp. 186–87.

28. Ibid., pp. 187–88.

29. Horne, *Seven Ages of Paris*, p. 377.

30. Matthew Halton, CBC Report. Aug. 9, 1944. CBC Archives.

31. Amouroux, *Joies et Douleurs du Peuple Libéré*, p. 533.

32. Geoffrey Nowell Smith, *The Oxford History of World Cinema*. Oxford University Press, 1996, p. 347.

33. Matthew Halton, CBC Report. Aug. 27, 1944. CBC Archives.

34. Larry Collins and Dominique Lapierre, *Is Paris Burning?* New York: Simon and Schuster, 1965, p. 340.

35. Matthew Halton, CBC Report. Aug. 27, 1944. CBC Archives.

36. Ibid.

37. Matthew Halton, CBC Report. Aug. 29, 1944. CBC Archives.

38. Christiane de Sandfort, letter to Matthew Halton. Sept. 2, 1944. LAC.

39. Christiane de Sandfort, letter to Matthew Halton. Sept. 22, 1944. LAC.

40. Christiane de Sandfort, letter to Matthew Halton. Sept. 12, 1944. LAC.

41. Matthew Halton, CBC Report. Aug. 29, 1944. CBC Archives.

42. Matthew Halton, CBC Report. Sept. 2, 1944. CBC Archives.

43. Matthew Halton, CBC Report. Sept. 6, 1944. CBC Archives.

44. Bizimana, *De Marcel Ouimet à René Lévesque*, p. 224.

45. Matthew Halton, letter to Jean Halton. Sept. 21, 1944. LAC.

46. Matthew Halton, CBC Report. Sept. 30, 1944. CBC Archives.

47. Ibid.

48. Matthew Halton, letter to Jean Halton. Sept. 24, 1944. LAC.

49. Ibid.

50. Ibid.

51. Matthew Halton, CBC Report. Sept. 25, 1944. CBC Archives.

52. Ross Munro, *Gauntlet to Overlord*. Toronto: Macmillan Company of Canada, 1945, p. 222.

53. Matthew Halton, speech to the Empire Club. Toronto, Nov. 28, 1944. Also broadcast on CBC. CBC Archives.

54. Jeffrey A. Keshen, *Saints, Sinners, and Soldiers: Canada's Second World War*. Vancouver: UBC Press, 2004, p. 34.

55. *Vancouver News-Herald* (clipping). Nov. 1944.

56. *Winnipeg Free Press*. "Lt.-Governor's Dinner Honors Matthew Halton." Oct. 29, 1944.

57. Jean Halton, interview with the author. July 12, 1999.

58. Matthew Halton, interview in the *Vancouver Province*. Nov. 6, 1944.

59. Norman Bakes, *Canadian Business*. Dec. 1944.

60. These were standard lines in Matt's Victory Bond speeches, repeated in a CBC broadcast. Oct. 22, 1944. CBC Archives.

61. Ibid.

62. Ibid.

63. Matthew Halton, speech to the Empire Club. Toronto, Nov. 28, 1944.

64. Matthew Halton, *The Maple Leaf*, Dec. 23, 1944.

65. James Ilsley (Minister of Finance), letter to Matthew Halton. Nov. 16, 1944. LAC.

66. Alex Chalmers, letter to Matthew Halton. Oct. 24, 1944. LAC.

67. Norah O'Neill, letter to Matthew Halton. Oct. 22, 1944. LAC.

68. Ibid.

69. Matthew Halton, CBC Commentary. Nov. 11, 1944. CBC Archives.

70. Matthew Halton, letter to Jean. n.d.

71. Matthew Halton, "People in Canada Eager for News from Overseas." *The Maple Leaf*, Dec. 23, 1944.

72. Ibid.

73. Ibid.

Chapter 16: To Berlin

1. Matthew Halton, CBC Report. Dec. 1944. CBC Archives.

2. Matthew Halton, letter to Jean Halton. Dec. 20, 1944. LAC.

3. Matthew Halton, letter to Jean Halton. Dec. 26, 1944. LAC.

4. Matthew Halton, CBC Report. Dec. 31, 1944. CBC Archives.

5. Matthew Halton, CBC Report. Feb. 4, 1945. CBC Archives.

6. Kenneth Dyba, interview with Gerry Anglin. May 22, 1979. LAC.

7. Malone, *Missing from the Record*, p. 172.

8. Matthew Halton, letter to Jean Halton. Feb. 16, 1945. LAC.

9. Matthew Halton, CBC Report. Feb. 9, 1945. CBC Archives. LAC.

10. Ibid.

11. George F.G. Stanley, *Canada's Soldiers*. Toronto: The Macmillan Company of Canada Ltd., 1960, p. 378.

12. Matthew Halton, "Through Mud, Flood and Fire." *Star Weekly*, Mar. 3, 1945.

13. Matthew Halton, letter to Jean Halton. Mar. 10, 1945. LAC.

14. Ibid.

15. Matthew Halton, CBC Report. Feb. 25, 1945. CBC Archives.

16. Ibid.

17. Matthew Halton, letter to Jean Halton. Mar. 1, 1945. LAC.

18. Balzer, *The Information Front*, p. 118.

19. Matthew Halton, personal diary. Feb. 21, 1945. Quoted in *Star Weekly*, Mar. 24, 1945.

20. Stanley, *Canada's Soldiers*, p. 378.

21. Matthew Halton, CBC Report. Mar. 3, 1945. CBC Archives.

22. Matthew Halton, CBC Report. Mar. 7, 1945. CBC Archives.

23. Matthew Halton, CBC Report. Mar. 3, 1945. CBC Archives.

24. Matthew Halton, CBC Report. Mar. 5, 1945. CBC Archives.

25. Matthew Halton, "The 'Hot Rake' in the Reich." *Star Weekly*, Apr. 28, 1945.

26. Matthew Halton, CBC Report. Jan. 5, 1944. CBC Archives.

27. Ibid.

28. Matthew Halton, "Major Assault across Rhine." *Star Weekly*, Apr. 21, 1945.

29. Matthew Halton, letter to Jean Halton. Mar. 27, 1945. LAC.

30. Matthew Halton, "Major Assault across Rhine." *Star Weekly*, Apr. 21, 1945.

31. Mathew Halton, personal diary. Apr. 10, 1945. Quoted in "A Trail of Slime and Crime." *Star Weekly*, May 5, 1945.

32. Matthew Halton, CBC Report. Mar. 7, 1945. CBC Archives.

33. Matthew Halton, "A Trail of Slime and Crime." *Star Weekly*, May 5, 1945.

34. Matthew Halton, personal diary. Feb. 23, 1945. Quoted in "The Flowers of the Forest." *Star Weekly*, Mar. 2, 1945. Also Malone, *Missing from the Record*, p. 183.

35. Matthew Halton, CBC Report. Apr. 23, 1945. CBC Archives.

36. Ibid.

37. Ibid.

38. Ibid.

39. Matthew Halton, diary, Apr. 17, 1945. Quoted in "At the Deathbed of Germany." *Star Weekly*, May 12, 1945.

40. Matthew Halton, CBC Report. Apr. 7, 1945. CBC Archives.

41. Matthew Halton, CBC Report. Jan. 13, 1945. CBC Archives.

42. Matthew Halton, "A Handclasp for the Future." *Star Weekly*, May 19, 1945.

43. Ibid.

44. Ibid.

45. Matthew Halton, CBC Report. May 1, 1945. CBC Archives.

46. Bizimana, *De Marcel Ouimet à René Lévesque*, p. 268.

47. Matthew Halton, letter to Jean Halton. May 3, 1945. LAC.

48. Ibid.

49. Matthew Halton, "This Legacy of Evil." *Star Weekly*, May 26, 1945.

50. Ibid.

51. Ibid.

52. Ibid.

53. Ibid.

54. Ibid.

55. Matthew Halton, CBC Report. Apr. 26, 1945. CBC Archives.

56. Matthew Halton, CBC Report. May 5, 1945. CBC Archives.

57. Ibid.

58. Ibid.

59. Matthew Halton, CBC Report. May 6, 1945. CBC Archives.

60. Georgina Seeley, letter to author. June 26, 1995. LAC.

61. Matthew Halton, CBC Report. May 6, 1945. CBC Archives.

62. Matthew Halton, CBC Report, May 9, 1945. CBC Archives.

63. David Clay Large, *Berlin*. New York: Basic Books, 2000.

64. Matthew Halton, CBC Report. May 9, 1945. CBC Archives.

65. Ibid.

66. Ibid.

67. Matthew Halton, "At the Grave of Hitlerism." *Star Weekly*, June 2, 1945.

68. Smith, *Events Leading up to My Death*.

69. Matthew Halton, "At the Grave of Hitlerism." *Star Weekly*, June 2, 1945.

70. Matthew Halton, "Correspondents Recall Their Best Stories." CBC *Times*, Mar. 11–17, 1956.

71. Matthew Halton, CBC Report. May 9, 1945. CBC Archives.

Chapter 17: Post-War

1. Kenneth Dyba, interview with Frank Peers. July 21, 1979. LAC.

2. A.E. (Bert) Powley, interview with Kenneth Dyba. Oct. 27, 1978. LAC.

3. Tim Heald, *The Duke: A Portrait of Prince Philip*. London: Hodder & Stoughton, 1991, pp. 107–8.

4. Larry Adler, "A Memoir of the Thursday Club." *London Review*. Winter edition, 1984, p. 42.

5. Ibid.

6. Charles Lynch, *A Funny Way to Run a Country*. Edmonton: Hurtig Publishers, 1986, pp. 193–94.

7. Max Hastings, *Did You Really Shoot the Television?: A Family Fable*. New York: HarperCollins, 2011.

8. Matthew Halton, *Capital Report,* CBC. Feb. 18, 1949. CBC Archives.

9. Matthew Halton, "Why There's a Crisis in Coal." *Star Weekly,* Aug. 30, 1947.

10. Matthew Halton, "This Astonishing Achievement." *Star Weekly,* Mar. 5, 1949.

11. Matthew Halton, *Capital Report,* CBC. Feb. 22, 1952. CBC Archives.

12. Matthew Halton, "Britain Is Not Dead Yet." *Star Weekly,* May 17, 1947.

13. Matthew Halton, "Inquest on Czechoslovakia." *Star Weekly,* May 8, 1948.

14. Matthew Halton, "Victory for the Vatican." *Maclean's,* June 1, 1948.

15. Matthew Halton, "Peace or War." *Star Weekly,* May 22, 1948.

16. Canadian Press, "CBC Commentator, Matt Halton, Called Communist by Alta. M.P." *Calgary Albertan,* July 14, 1947.

17. Ibid.

18. Ibid.

19. Editorial, "About This Vile Business of Name-calling." *Ottawa Journal,* July 15, 1947.

20. Editorial, "Loose Talk." Victoria *Daily Times,* July 15, 1947.

21. Wallace Reyburn, "The Ego and I." *New Liberty,* Dec. 1948.

22. Ibid.

23. Kenneth Dyba, interview with J. Douglas MacFarlane. Apr. 23, 1979. LAC.

24. Matthew Halton, "Thou Shalt Not Kill." *Maclean's,* Nov. 15, 1946.

25. Matthew Halton, CBC Report. April 13, 1946. CBC Archives.

26. Matthew Halton, "Europe's Unwanted Millions." *Star Weekly,* July 6, 1946.

27. Ibid.

28. Hastings, *All Hell Let Loose,* pp. 653–54.

29. Matthew Halton, "Rebirth of Germany's Army." *Star Weekly,* Oct. 31, 1953.

30. BBC internal memo, S.W. Bonarjee to Mr. Green, March 8, 1951. BBC Archives.

31. Matthew Halton, "Should Germany Be Rearmed? An International Inquiry." BBC Home Service, June 18, 1954.

32. Matthew Halton, "A Chance for Europe." *Star Weekly,* April 24, 1948.

33. Matthew Halton, "De Gaulle Is Ready for Cue to Adopt His Favorite Role as the Rescuer of France." *Star Weekly,* Mar. 29, 1952.

34. Matthew Halton, "Like Napoleon, De Gaulle Sees Himself as a Man Picked by Destiny." *Star Weekly,* Oct. 30, 1948.

35. *Maclean's,* "Man of France." Jan. 15, 1948.

36. Matthew Halton, "Tragedy in the Promised Land." *Star Weekly,* March 6, 1948.

37. Ibid.

38. Kenneth Dyba, interview with Shena Fielding. Sept. 17, 1979. LAC.

39. Kenneth Dyba, interview with Dorothy Dew. May 8, 1979. LAC.

40. Kenneth Dyba, interview with Jean Halton. Sept. 8, 1979. LAC.

41. Kenneth Dyba, interview with Charles Lynch, May 30, 1980. LAC.

42. Ibid.

43. Kenneth Dyba, interview with Jean Halton. Sept. 8, 1979. LAC.

44. Matthew Halton, "Festival of Britain to Tell the Story of British Accomplishment." *Star Weekly,* Apr. 28, 1951.

45. Matthew Halton, "Christmas Day Talk." CBC. Dec. 25, 1949. CBC Archives.

46. Frank Peers, interview with Kenneth Dyba. July 21, 1979. LAC.

47. Matthew Halton, "How Socialism Is Working Out." *Star Weekly*, July 10, 1948.

48. Matthew Halton ("Gadfly"), "York Gives the Lie to Tory Talk." *Daily Herald*, n.d. NAC. (Some of the *Herald* clippings in the archives are not dated.)

49. Matthew Halton ("Gadfly"), "Don't Be Fooled Tomorrow." *Daily Herald*, Oct. 24, 1951. LAC.

50. Matthew Halton ("Vigilant"), "Mischief Makers in Our Midst." *Daily Herald*. n.d. LAC.

51. Matthew Halton, "One Day in Berlin." *Star Weekly*, Sept. 26, 1953.

52. Matthew Halton, "Berlin – Where East Meets West." *Star Weekly*. n.d. 1953.

53. Matthew Halton, *Window on Yugoslavia*. BBC, Nov. 28, 1950.

54. Ibid.

55. Ibid.

56. Kenneth Dyba, interview with Norman Depoe. Nov. 7, 1979. LAC.

57. Richard Dimbleby, *A Tribute to Matthew Halton*. CBC, Dec. 10, 1956. CBC Archives.

58. Kenneth Dyba, interview with Charles Lynch. May 30, 1980. LAC.

59. Ibid.

60. Kathleen Tynan (Halton), letter to Matthew Halton High School. Feb. 22, 1960.

61. Matthew Halton, *Iron from the North*. CBC, Sept. 24, 1952. CBC Archives.

62. Matthew Halton, *Canada Strikes Oil*. CBC, Nov. 16, 1952. CBC Archives.

63. Matthew Halton, *The Canadian Personality*. CBC, Sept. 18, 1948, CBC Archives.

64. Matthew Halton, *Our Special Speaker*. CBC, Sept. 31, 1952. CBC Archives.

65. Matthew Halton, "Halton Reports on the Coronation." *Star Weekly,* June 20, 1953.

66. Ibid.

67. Matthew Halton, "Churchill – Hail and Farewell." *Star Weekly*, unpublished. LAC.

Chapter 18: Decline

1. Matthew Halton, *Assignment Abroad*. CBC. Jan. 24, 1955. CBC Archives.

2. Matthew Halton, CBC Report. June 18, 1948. CBC Archives.

3. Matthew Halton, letter to Seth Halton. Sept. 17, 1956. LAC.

4. Matthew Halton, letter to his mother. Feb. 19, 1956. LAC.

5. W.H. Hogg, CBC Chief News Editor, letter to Matt. Aug. 12, 1955. LAC.

6. Kenneth Dyba, interview with Frank Peers, July 21, 1979. LAC.

7. Ibid.

8. Kenneth Dyba, interview with Norman McBain, Nov. 25, 1979. LAC.

9. Michael Maclear, interview with the author, June 27, 2006.

10. Hugh Whitney Morrison, interview with Kenneth Dyba, Apr. 24, 1979. LAC.

11. Matthew Halton, "The New Soviet Challenge." *Edmonton Journal*, May 17, 1956. LAC.

12. Ibid.

13. F.M. Salter, introducing Matt at U of A Spring convocation, May 7, 1956. Reprinted in *The New Trail,* May 1956.

14. Matthew Halton, Convocation Address, U of A, May 17, 1956.

15. Ibid.

16. Ibid.

17. Arthur Kroeger, interview with the author, Feb. 6, 2006.

18. Mary Alice Halton, letter to Jean, Oct. 20, 1957. LAC.

19. Mary Alice Halton, letter to Jean, Jan. 10, 1957. LAC.

20. Matthew Halton, CBC *Capital Report*. Aug. 5, 1956. CBC Archives.

21. Ibid.

22. Matthew Halton, CBC *News Roundup*. Aug. 23, 1956. CBC Archives.

23. Matthew Halton, letter to his mother. n.d. Sept. 1956. LAC.

24. Kenneth Dyba, interview with Bernard Trotter, June 4, 1980. LAC.

25. Kenneth Dyba, interview with Muriel Kelly. n.d. May, 1980. LAC.

26. Ibid.

27. Muriel Kelly, interview with the author, Nov. 15, 2005.

28. Dr. John Richardson, letter to Jean Halton. Dec. 6, 1956. LAC.

29. Earl Cameron, CBC News Bulletin. Dec. 3, 1956. CBC Archives.

30. Bill McNeil, *News Roundup*. Dec. 3, 1956. CBC Archives.

31. *Toronto Star*. Dec. 3, 1956. LAC.

32. Editorial, *Lethbridge Herald*. Dec. 4, 1956.

33. Editorial, *Ottawa Citizen*. Dec. 4, 1956.

34. Editorial, *Regina Leader-Post*. Dec. 4, 1946.

35. Gordon Sinclair, *Toronto Star*. Dec. 4, 1956. LAC.

36. Patrick Morley, Sec. National Union of Journalists, letter to Jean. Dec. 14, 1956. LAC.

37. BBC *Radio Times*, "A Canadian Who Loved Britain." Dec. 14, 1956.

38. Stephen Banarjee, letter to Jean. Dec. 4, 1956. LAC.

39. *Manchester Guardian*, "Matthew Halton." Dec. 6, 1956.

40. *The Times* (London). Obituary. Dec. 5, 1956.

41. Annie Halton (Moser), letter to Jean Halton. Dec. 10, 1956. LAC.

42. Jean MacNaughton, letter to Jean Halton. n.d. Dec. 1956. LAC.

43. Charles Lynch, interview with the author, June 5, 1994.

44. Kenneth Dyba, interview with Shena Fielding, Sept. 17, 1979.

45. George Hardy, letter to Jean Halton. Dec. 10, 1956. LAC.

46. Andrew Cowan, letter to Jean. Dec. 3, 1956. LAC.

47. Joan Lorraine, "A Tribute." CBC *Staff Magazine*. Jan. 22, 1957.

48. Mrs. John Riley, letter to Jean Halton, Dec. 4, 1956. LAC.

49. Jaqueline Wasserman, letter to Jean Halton, Dec. 7, 1956. LAC.

50. Irene Sidam, letter to Jean. Dec. 1956.

51. Garfield Weston, letter to Jean Halton, Dec. 27, 1956.

Postscript

1. Pierre Berton, "The Greatest Three-Cent Show on Earth." *Maclean's*, March 15, 1952.

2. Byng Whittaker, speech to the Empire Club, Feb. 8, 1945.

3. Kenneth Dyba, interview with Richard Malone. Dec. 7, 1978.

4. Citation on Matthew Halton's admission to the News Hall of Fame, April 24, 1982.

5. Phillip Knightley, *The First Casualty: The War Correspondent as Hero, Propagandist, and Myth Maker from the Crimea to Vietnam.* London: André Deutsch Ltd., 1975, p. 333.

6. David J. Bercuson and S.F. Wise, *The Valour and the Horror Revisited.* Montreal: McGill-Queen's University Press, 1994, and Jack Granatstein, *Who Killed Canadian History?* Toronto: Harper Collins Publishers Ltd., pp. 116–20.

7. *The Valour and the Horror,* Part 3: "In Desperate Battle: Normandy 1944." CBC docudrama, 1992.

8. Leland Stowe , letter to Kenneth Dyba. Dec. 3, 1978.

9. Harold Troper, letter to the author. Dec. 7, 2012.

10. Bourrie, *The Fog of War,* p. 189.

11. William Shirer, *The Rise and Fall of the Third Reich.* New York: Simon and Schuster, 1960, pp. 423–24.

12. Herbert Matthews, *A World in Revolution.* New York: Scribners, 1971, p. 6.

13. Willis Ambrose, letter to Jean Halton. Dec. 4, 1956. LAC.

14. Jean Halton, letter to Seth Halton. Feb. 10, 1957. LAC.

15. Ibid.

16. Halton, *Ten Years to Alamein,* p. 15.

SELECT BIBLIOGRAPHY

Abella, Irving, and Harold Troper, *None Is Too Many: Canada and the Jews of Europe, 1933–1948.* Toronto: Key Porter Books Ltd., 1983.

Allen, Ralph. *Ordeal by Fire: Canada 1910–1945.* Toronto: Doubleday Canada Ltd., Toronto, 1961.

Amouroux, Henri. *Joies et Douleurs du Peuple Liberé: La Grand Histoire des Français sous l'Occupation.* Paris: Éditions Robert Laffont, S.A., 1988.

Balzer, Timothy John. *The Information Front: The Canadian Army and News Management during the Second World War.* Vancouver: UBC Press, 2011.

Beevor, Antony. *D-Day: The Battle for Normandy.* New York: The Penguin Group, 2009.

Bercuson, David J. *Maple Leaf Against the Axis: Canada's Second World War.* Toronto: Stoddart, 1995.

Bercuson, David J., and S.F. Wise, *The Valour and the Horror Revisited.* Montreal: McGill-Queen's University Press, 1994

Berton, Pierre. *The Great Depression 1929–1939.* Toronto: McClelland & Stewart Inc., 1990.

——. "The Greatest Three-Cent Show on Earth, Part 1." *Maclean's,* Mar. 15, 1952.

——. *Marching as to War.* Toronto: Anchor Canada, 2002.

Bierman, John, and Colin Smith. *The Battle of Alamein.* New York: Viking Penguin, 2002.

Bizimana, Aimé-Jules. *De Marcel Ouimet à René-Lévesque: Les Correspondants de Guerre Canadien-Français durant la Deuxième Guerre Mondiale.* Montreal: vlb Éditeur, 2007.

Bourrie, Mark. *Fog of War: Censorship of Canada's Media in World War Two.* Toronto: Key Porter Books Ltd., 2011.

Carroll, Jock. *The Life and Times of Greg Clark.* Toronto: Doubleday Canada Limited, 1981.

Churchill, Winston. *The Second World War: The Gathering Storm,* Vol. 1. London: Cassell and Co. Ltd., 1949

Clark, Gerald. *No Mud on the Back Seat: Memoirs of a Reporter.* Montreal: Robert Davies Publishing, 1995.

Cockburn, Claud. *I Claud: The Autobiography of Claud Cockburn.* London: Penguin Books, 1967.

Cockett, Richard. *Twilight of Truth: Chamberlain, Appeasement and the Manipulation of the Press.* London: Weidenfeld and Nicolson, 1989.

Copp, Terry. *Fields of Fire: The Canadians in Normandy.* Toronto: University of Toronto Press, 2003.

Cotter, Charis. *Toronto Between the Wars: Life in the City 1919–1939.* Toronto: Firefly Books Ltd., 2004.

Cranston, J.H. *Ink on My Fingers*. Toronto: The Ryerson Press, 1953.

Dancocks, Daniel G. *The D-Day Dodgers: The Canadians in Italy, 1943–1945*. Toronto: McClelland & Stewart Inc., 1991.

De Gaulle, Charles. *Mémoires de Guerre. L'Unité 1942–1944*, Vol 2. Paris: Librairie Plon, 1956.

Dell, Robert. *Germany Unmasked*. London: Martin Hopkinson Ltd., 1934.

Dimbleby, Jonathan. *Richard Dimbleby: A Biography*. London: Hodder & Stoughton, 1975.

Donaldson, Frances. *Edward VIII*. London: Weidenfeld & Nicolson, 1974.

Downton, Eric. *Wars Without End*. Toronto: Stoddart Publishing Co. Ltd., 1987.

Edwards, Bob. *Edward R. Murrow and the Birth of Broadcast Journalism*. Hoboken, N.J.: John Wiley & Sons Inc., 2004.

Fielding, Captain Sean. *They Sought out Rommel: A Diary of the Libyan Campaign (Nov 16–Dec 31, 1941)*. London: Whitefriars Press Limited, 1942. Issued by the War Office for the Ministry of Information.

Gannon, Franklin Reid. *The British Press and Germany 1936–1939*. Oxford: Clarendon Press, 1971.

Gibbs, Sir Philip Hamilton. *Adventures in Journalism*. New York: Harper and Bros., 1923.

Goodwin, Doris Kearns. *No Ordinary Time: Franklin and Eleanor Roosevelt: The Home Front in World War II*. New York: Simon & Schuster, 1994.

Granatstein, J.L., and Desmond Morton. *A Nation Forged in Fire: Canadians and the Second World War, 1939–1945*. Toronto: Lester & Orpen Dennys, 1989.

——. *Who Killed Canadian History?* Toronto: Harper Collins Publishers Ltd.,

Hanfstaengl, Ernst "Putzi." *Hitler: The Missing Years*. London: Eyre & Spottiswoode, 1957.

Harkness, Ross. *J.E. Atkinson of the Star*. Toronto: University of Toronto Press, 1963.

Harrison, Mark. "Toronto: The Good, the Bad and (Sometimes) the Ugly." *Toronto Star Centennial Magazine*.

Hastings, Max. *All Hell Let Loose: The World at War 1939–1945*. London: Harper Press, 2011.

——. *Did You Really Shoot the Television?: A Family Fable*. New York: HarperCollins, 2011.

Heald, Morris. *Transatlantic Vistas: American Journalists in Europe 1910–1940*. Kent, Ohio: Kent State University Press, 1988.

Heald, Tim. *A Portrait of Prince Phillip*. London: Hodder & Stoughton, 1991.

Horne, Alistair. *Seven Ages of Paris*. New York: Vintage Books, 2004.

Hubbard, R.H. *Rideau Hall*. Montreal and London: McGill-Queen's University Press, 1977.

Jenkins, Roy. *Churchill: A Biography*. New York: Farrar, Straus and Giroux, 2001.

Keegan, John. *The Second World War*. New York: Penguin Books USA Inc., 1990.

Kershaw, Ian. *Hitler 1889–1936: Hubris*. New York: Penguin Books, 1998.

Keshen, Jeffrey A. *Saints, Sinners and Soldiers: Canada's Second World War*. Vancouver: University of British Columbia Press, 2004.

Knightley, Phillip. *The First Casualty: The War Correspondent as Hero, Propagandist, and Myth Maker from the Crimea to Vietnam*. London: Andre Deutsch, 1975.

Large, David Clay. *Berlin*. New York: Basic Books, 2000.

——. *Nazi Games: The Olympics of 1936*. New York: W.W. Norton & Company Inc., 2007.

Lipstadt, Deborah E. *Beyond Belief: The American Press and the Coming of the Holocaust 1933–1945*. New York: The Free Press, 1986.

Lochner, Louis. *Always the Unexpected*. New York: The Macmillan Company, 1956.

Lovat Dickson, Rache. *The Ante-Room*. Toronto: Macmillan Company of Canada Ltd., 1959.

Lynch, Charles. *You Can't Print That*. Edmonton: Hurtig Publishers, 1983.

Mahoney, Barbara S. *Dispatches and Dictators: Ralph Barnes for the Herald Tribune*. Corvallis: Oregon State University Press, 2002.

Malone, Richard. *Missing From the Record*. Toronto: Collins, 1946.

——. *A World in Flames 1944–1945*. Toronto: Collins, 1984.

Matthews, Herbert. *A World in Revolution*. New York: Scribner's, 1971.

McNaught, Carlton. *Canada Gets the News*. Toronto: The Ryerson Press, 1940.

Meyers, Jeffrey. *Hemingway: A Biography*. New York: Harper and Row, 1985.

Minifie, James M. *Expatriate*. Toronto: The Macmillan Company of Canada Ltd., 1976.

Moorehead, Alan. *A Late Education: Episodes in a Life*. New York: Penguin Books, 1976.

Moorehead, Caroline. *Gellhorn: A Twentieth Century Life*. New York: Henry Holt and Co., 2003.

Mount, Graeme S. *Canada's Enemies: Spies and Spying in the Peaceable Kingdom*. Toronto: Dundurn Press Ltd., 1993.

Munro, Ross. *Gauntlet to Overlord*. Toronto: Macmillan Company of Canada, 1945.

Nash, Knowlton. *The Microphone Wars: A History of Triumph and Betrayal at the CBC*. Toronto: McClelland & Stewart, 1994. (Page references from paperback edition, 1995.)

Neatby, Blair H. *William Lyon Mackenzie King 1932–1939: The Prism of Unity*. Toronto: University of Toronto Press, 1976.

Oder, Aileen Rebecca. *Hello Soldier*. Winnipeg: North Star Press, 1975.

Paassen, Pierre Van. *To Number Our Days*. New York: Charles Scribner's Sons, 1964.

Peers, Frank W. *The Politics of Canadian Broadcasting*. Toronto: University of Toronto Press, 1969.

Petrou, Michael. *Renegades: Canadians in the Spanish Civil War*. Vancouver: UBC Press, 2008,

Piddington, Helen. *Rumble Seat*. Madeira Park, B.C.: Harbour Publishing Co. Ltd., 2010.

Pincher Creek Historical Society. *Prairie Grass to Mountain Pass*. History of the Pioneers of Pincher Creek and District. Calgary, 1974.

Pitsula, James M. "Strange Salute." *The Beaver*, Aug./ Sept. 2004, Vol. 84, Issue 4.

Pocock, Tom. *Alan Moorehead*. London: The Bodley Head, 1990.

Powell, George. *"Compact Record" of the Life and Times of Canadian War Correspondents Association*. Booklet, 1994.

——. *I Never Made Love in a Canoe*. Victoria, B.C.: Trafford Publishing, 2005.

Powley, A.E. *Broadcast from the Front*. Toronto: A.M. Hakkert Ltd., 1975.

Reyburn, Wallace "The Ego and I." *New Liberty*, Dec. 1948.

——. *Some of It Was Fun*. Toronto: Thomas Nelson and Sons Ltd., 1949.

Ritchie, Charles. *The Siren Years*. Toronto: McClelland & Stewart Ltd., 1974.

Rooney, Andy. *My War*. New York: Times Books, 1995.

Rose, Norman. *The Cliveden Set*. London: Jonathan Cape, 2000.

Schoeck, Ellen. *I Was There: A Century of Alumni Stories About the University of Alberta, 1906–2006*. Edmonton: The University of Alberta Press, 2006.

Sheean, Vincent. *Not Peace but a Sword*. New York: Doubleday, Doran & Company, Inc., 1939.

Shirer, William L. *The Nightmare Years 1930–1940*. Boston: Little Brown and Company, 1984.

——. *Berlin Diary: The Journal of a Foreign Correspondent 1934–1941*. New York: BBS Publishing Co., 1995.

Smith, Howard K. *Events Leadings up to My Death: The Life of a Twentieth Century Reporter*. New York: St. Martin's Press, 1996.

——. *Last Train from Berlin*. New York: Alfred A. Knopf, 1942.

Stacey, C.P. *Six Years of War*. Vol. 1. Ottawa: Department of National Defence, 1955.

Stanley, George F.S. *Canada's Soldiers*. Toronto: The Macmillan Company of Canada Ltd., 1960.

Stowe, Leland. *Nazi Means War*. New York: McGraw-Hill Book Company Inc., 1934.

——. *No Other Road to Freedom*. New York: Alfred A. Knopf Inc., 1941.

Stursberg, Peter. *The Sound of War*. Toronto: University of Toronto Press, 1993.

Sykes, Christopher. *Nancy: The Life of Lady Astor*. London: Collins, 1972.

Thomas, Hugh. *The Spanish Civil War*. London: Eyre and Spottiswoode Ltd., 1961.

Thompson, Eric. "Canadian Warcos in World War II: Professionalism, Patriotism and Propaganda." *Mosaic* 23, Summer 1990.

Thompson, John Herd, and Allen Seager. *Canada 1922–1939 Decades of Discord*. Toronto: McClelland & Stewart Limited, 1985.

Trotter, William R. *A Frozen Hell: The Russo-Finnish Winter War of 1939–40*. Chapel Hill: Algonquin Books, 1991.

Troyer, Warner. *The Sound and the Fury: An Anecdotal History of Canadian Broadcasting*. Toronto: John Wiley and Sons Canada Ltd., 1980.

Vokes, Chris (Major General), and John Maclean. *My Story*. Ottawa: Gallery Books, 1985.

Weidenfeld, George. *Remembering My Good Friends: An Autobiography*. New York: HarperCollins Publishers, 1995.

Wieviorka, Olivier. *Normandy*. London: The Belknap Press of Harvard University, 2008.

Williams, Susan. *The People's King: The True Story of the Abdication*. London: Penguin Books Ltd., 2003.

Williamson, Phillip. *Stanley Baldwin: Conservative Leadership and National Values*. Cambridge: Cambridge University Press, 1999.

Wilson, Diana, ed. *Triumph and Tragedy in the Crowsnest Pass*. Surrey, B.C.: Heritage House Publishing Co. Ltd., 2005.

Young, Scott. *Gordon Sinclair: A Life . . . and then Some*. Toronto: Macmillan of Canada, 1987.

Zuehlke, Mark. *Ortona: Canada's Epic World War II Battle*. Toronto: Stoddart Publishing Company Ltd., 1999.

INDEX